THE FISHY
SMITHS

A BIOGRAPHY OF
JLB & MARGARET SMITH

MIKE BRUTON
HONORARY RESEARCH ASSOCIATE
SOUTH AFRICAN INSTITUTE FOR AQUATIC BIODIVERSITY
GRAHAMSTOWN

Published by Penguin Books
(an imprint of Penguin Random House South Africa (Pty) Ltd)
The Estuaries No. 4, Oxbow Crescent (off Century Avenue), Century City, 7441 South Africa
PO Box 1144, Cape Town, 8000 South Africa
www.penguinrandomhouse.co.za

Penguin
Random House
South Africa

First published in 2018
1 3 5 7 9 10 8 6 4 2

PUBLISHER: Pippa Parker
EDITOR: Helen de Villiers
DESIGNER: Ryan Africa
COVER DESIGN: Janice Evans
TYPESETTER: Deirdré Geldenhuys
CARTOGRAPHER: Liezel Bohdanowicz
PROOFREADER AND INDEXER: Emsie du Plessis

solutions
Printed by **novus print**, a Novus Holdings company

MIX
Paper from
responsible sources
FSC
www.fsc.org   FSC® C022948

Penguin Random House is committed to a sustainable future for our business, our readers
and our planet. This book is made from Forest Stewardship Council ® certified paper.

ISBN 978-1-77584-646-8 (print)
ISBN 978-1-77584-647-5 (ePub)

FRONT COVER, CLOCKWISE FROM TOP: Margaret and JLB Smith with Marlin at Rhodes University in the
early 1960s; Margaret and JLB Smith admiring colour plates of parrotfishes for the first *Ichthyological
Bulletin of Rhodes University* in 1956; Margaret and JLB Smith illustrating and examining fishes on the
1951 expedition to Mozambique; JLB and Margaret Smith collecting specimens on the 1951 expedition.
TITLE PAGE: Margaret and JLB Smith in Grahamstown in the 1950s.

The secret of life is to have a task,
something you devote your entire life to,
something you bring everything to
every minute of the day for the rest of your life.
And the most important thing is,
it must be something you cannot possibly do.

– Henry Moore, sculptor

Dedicated to the memory of JLB and Margaret Smith,
and the students they spawned.

CONTENTS

Acknowledgements

T HE WRITING of this ambitious book would not have been possible without the support of a wide range of people. Firstly, I am very grateful to William Smith, son of JLB and Margaret Smith, and his wife, Jenny, for their patient and unwavering support of this endeavour. They not only provided valuable information, photographs, videos, radio interviews and rare archival material but also checked facts and provided strong support for the publication of the book. Ian Sholto-Douglas, son of Margaret Smith's elder sister, Flora Sholto-Douglas, his wife, Ishbel, and their daughter, Catherine Braans, also provided valuable insights on the Smith and Sholto-Douglas families, as did Donald Brierley Smith, stepson of Bob Smith, on Bob's family.

Information on JLB Smith's first wife, Henriette Cecile Pienaar, and her family, has been obtained from the archives of the Albany Cultural History Museum and the National Archives in Cape Town courtesy of Fleur Way-Jones, the 'Murray Family Register 1794–1977' compiled by Caroline Murray (1978), and the 'Murray Family Register' by Teo Louw (2012). I also obtained valuable information from interviews with members of the Pienaar family, especially Rénee Muller (née Rénee Pienaar de Klerk), eldest daughter of Henriette's sister, Helene Pienaar, and therefore Henriette's niece. Rénee knew Henriette Pienaar well as she lived with her, or was closely associated with her, for over 30 years. I also interviewed Rénee's husband, John Anton Muller, and her younger sister, Andree-Jeanne Tötemeyer, and their cousin, Renette Schröder, all of whom confirmed the information that Rénee had shared with me. I am very grateful to them for their kind assistance.

Many friends, acquaintances and colleagues of JLB and Margaret Smith from around the world responded positively to my questionnaire survey about their life and work. I am especially grateful to Shirley Bell, Nancy Tietz, Tesza Musto, Martin Davies, Allan Heydorn, John Wallace, Mary-Louise and Mike Penrith, Rudy van der Elst, George and Margo Branch and Hans Fricke for their comprehensive responses. Valuable information was also received from Lynnath Beckley, Keith and Rosemary Hunt, Mike Cluver, 'Ticky' Forbes, Kathleen Heugh, Jenny Day, Trevor Harrison, Jean-Pierre de Kock, Colin Buxton, Malcolm Smale, Rik Nulens, Christine Flegler-Balon, Arnand Read, Brian and Sue Allanson, John Minshull, Butch Hulley, Nikki Kohly, the Hewson family, Peter Spargo, Hamish Robertson, Anton Bok, Roy Lubke, Heather Tracey, John Gardener, Nick James and Alistair and Brenda Weir.

The Managing Director of the South African Institute for Aquatic Biodiversity (SAIAB), Angus Paterson, was a tower of strength throughout this project and allowed me to have unlimited access to the Institute's resources. The way in which he embraced the project as if I was 'part of the Institute's DNA' was very gratifying. Angus also kindly agreed to write the Foreword, and gave permission for me to use valuable photographs and documents from the Institute's library and archives. The Senior Librarian at SAIAB, Sally Schramm, and the Librarian, Maditaba Meltaf, were extremely helpful throughout the project and went out of their way to help it succeed; it would not have been possible without their assistance. Past and present staff of SAIAB provided valuable information and insights, including Jean Pote, Wouter Holleman, Ofer Gon, Robin Stobbs, Glenn Merron, Alan Whitfield, Paul Skelton, Eric Anderson and Penny Haworth.

I am grateful to Cornelius Thomas, Director, and Kylie van Zyl, Rhodes University Archivist, at the Cory Library for Humanities Research at Rhodes University, for their unstinting support, as well as to Rob Gess and Helen Barber of the Albany Museum. I thank Geraldine Morcom, Director of the East London Museum, and the museum board for permission to use images from their archives.

I am grateful to Michael Davies-Coleman, Mike Brown, Johann Maree, Trevor Letcher, Kelvin Rivett, John and Lizzie Rennie, David Roux and Daneel Ferreira for information on the careers of JLB Smith and Doug Rivett in chem-istry, and to Nancy Tietz, Geraldine Morcom and Jeff Swanson for information on Marjorie Courtenay-Latimer. Paul Maylam kindly provided information on the history of Rhodes University and Sandy Shell, biographer of George Cory, offered valuable guidance on historical writing as well as useful infor-mation on Cory. I also thank Bronwyn Bruton, Karlien Breedt, Tony Bruton,

Paul Murray, Anita Grant, Brian Ingpen, Jane Zimmerman, Irene McCulloch, Willie 'Bomber' Burger, Jan-Hendrik Hofmeyr, Graeme Murray, Claerwen Howie and Ken Gillings for further valuable information.

I am deeply grateful to Pippa Parker, Publisher at Struik Nature, for agreeing to publish this biography and for guiding me through the publication process. The arduous task of editing the manuscript was carried out by Managing Editor, Helen de Villiers, whose meticulous attention to detail improved the manuscript immeasurably; once again, it was a pleasure working with her. I also thank Janice Evans for designing the book's cover, and Ryan Africa and Deirdré Geldenhuys for the page design and typesetting, respectively; and Belinda van der Merwe for her energetic marketing.

Finally, I thank my wife, Carolynn, for once again assisting me in a myriad ways and for creating space for me to write this tome. I am also grateful to Ryan, Tracey, Craig and Anja Bruton for their wholehearted support of my writing career.

Picture credits

Foreword

As the first director of the JLB Smith Institute of Ichthyology (now the South African Institute for Aquatic Biodiversity – SAIAB) who never met either of the Smiths, I find the timing of the writing of *The Fishy Smiths – A Biography of JLB & Margaret Smith* by Professor Mike Bruton to be entirely opportune. JLB passed away the year I was born and Margaret just before I got to Rhodes University as an undergraduate.

As happens with life's natural succession there has been a changing of the guard at SAIAB and many of those who knew the Smiths are now retired or have passed on. The new generation of researchers and students cannot help but be aware of the legacy of the Institute and the enormous contribution that the Smiths made to ichthyology in southern Africa, forever etched into the Institution's DNA. However, as with any great historical story, time does have a way of massaging the past to a point where folklore and fact are sometimes intertwined and, with JLB having been quite an unconventional figure, there is no shortage of 'JLB stories'. Both JLB and Margaret were rigorous scientists and I have no doubt would have wanted the telling of their lives and the broader story of ichthyology to be related as accurately as possible. This biography provides an honest treatment of the Smiths as real people, and their human flaws and phenomenal capabilities are dealt with in equal measure.

The story of the Smiths is often told through the lens of the discovery of the coelacanth in 1938 and the subsequent hunt for a second specimen. *Old Fourlegs* gives a gripping account of this adventure, but the Smiths' contribution to ichthyology was far broader and their lives so much more than the 14-year search period that spanned the disruptive years of the Second World War.

While the coelacanth saga certainly provided the impetus for JLB's and subsequently Margaret's careers, in my mind their broader contribution to the field of ichthyology, and the formation of the JLB Smith Institute, eclipse the coelacanth discovery. This biography clearly outlines how a chemistry professor and his wife (and former student), through sheer determination, and at times against great odds, defined ichthyology in southern Africa in the 20th century and left a legacy that will extend well into the 21st. The Smiths' direct scientific legacy is SAIAB, which is now a National Research Facility of the National Research Foundation, and the Department of Ichthyology & Fisheries Science at Rhodes University, both of which are internationally rec-ognised centres of learning in ichthyology. These two institutions currently have a postgraduate school of over 90 students, 20 research staff, a fleet of vessels, specialised laboratories, offices in Port Elizabeth and Durban and, of course, the National Fish Collection. Graduates of these institutions are found in ichthyological research and fisheries management posts throughout the world and, to a person, are very proud alumni of the Smith legacy. Not bad for a boy from Graaff-Reinet and a young girl from Indwe – both small towns in the rural Eastern Cape!

The *Fishy Smiths* biography clearly documents how the legacy the Smiths left to science was not the result of a single fortuitous discovery in 1938, but rather a result of decades of selfless, driven research. This was always under-pinned by JLB's obsessive work ethic and prodigious intellect; and by Margaret's initial devotion to JLB and his research, and then her emergence as a leader in her own right.

The book clearly unpacks the personalities of both JLB and Margaret and the forces that shaped them through their lives. The struggles, challenges and controversies in their lives, in childhood and as adults, both professional and private, are all examined, with the chapter on JLB's first marriage to Henriette Cecile Pienaar, and their children, being covered in detail for the first time.

Professor Bruton is undoubtedly the best person to have tackled a biography of this iconic couple: through his personal knowledge of the Smiths, his lifelong, deep connection with the Institute and his first-rate scientific and archival research capabilities, he has ensured an honest, gripping and seamless read. JLB's *Old Fourlegs* was a publishing sell-out; the *Fishy Smiths* is worthy of carrying on this tradition.

The biography stands as a testament to two amazing people and will enable researchers and students at both SAIAB and Rhodes University, and interested people worldwide, to fully understand the personalities behind the genesis of ichthyology in Grahamstown and southern Africa.

DR ANGUS PATERSON

MANAGING DIRECTOR, SOUTH AFRICAN INSTITUTE FOR AQUATIC BIODIVERSITY

MAY 2018

Dr Angus Paterson, Managing Director of the South African Institute for Aquatic Biodiversity, with a coelacanth on the 75th anniversary of the first capture.

Preface

J AMES LEONARD Brierley ('JLB') Smith and Margaret Mary Smith (née Macdonald) were a remarkable pair of South African scientists who forged a working relationship that changed the course of ichthyology in South Africa. During their inspirational and eventful lives they overcame many obstacles and created opportunities for many others who followed in their footsteps. Although they are best known locally and internationally for their research on the coelacanth, they contributed in many other ways to the scientific study of fishes (ichthyology), as well as to many other fields, yet neither of them has had a comprehensive biography written about them.

JLB Smith (who was variously known as 'Len', 'Leonard', 'LB Smith', 'JLB Smith', 'Doc', 'the Professor' and 'JLB' during his lifetime) was best known for his work on fishes, although he was employed for a longer period as a chemistry researcher and teacher than as an ichthyologist. He was a chemistry academic for 24 years (1922–1946) and an ichthyologist for 22 years (1946–1968), but there was a considerable overlap between his two careers, and his most famous contribution to ichthyology (the description of the first coelacanth) took place during his tenure as a Senior Lecturer in Chemistry (1939). He was an active amateur ichthyologist from 1931 to 1939 but reverted mainly to chemistry during the Second World War. After initially aspiring to become a medical doctor, Margaret Smith sacrificed her career ambitions to partner and work with JLB Smith as an ichthyologist, fish illustrator and general factotum for 30 years from their marriage in 1938 until his death in 1968.

As a budding young ichthyologist at Rhodes University I knew them both: JLB Smith briefly from January 1966 until his death in January 1968, and Margaret for 21 years, from January 1966 to her death in September 1987.

I vividly recall an experience in 1966 during my first year at Rhodes University. After several unsuccessful attempts to breach the phalanx of JLB's women protectors, I reached the 'Holy of Holies', where I asked the Great Man a few inane questions, and he politely answered. After 20 minutes I took my leave, but during our conversation he hadn't once lifted his head from the microscope under which he was examining a fish. On another occasion he showed the second coelacanth specimen to a group of students. I reached out my hand to touch a scale and received a sharp rap over the knuckles with a ruler.

Later we became more friendly and I even went on a few country walks with him. I remember him, then aged 69 years, as a stern man who led a very spartan lifestyle with all trivialities trimmed away so that he could focus his energy on fishes. Many years later, after completing my PhD in ichthyology and studying at the Natural History Museum in London, I joined the staff of the then JLB Smith Institute of Ichthyology as Senior Lecturer in Ichthyology. Margaret, by now widowed, was the Director at the time and we worked closely together to develop the teaching of ichthyology in South Africa, I later succeeded her as Director of the Institute, which subsequently was renamed the South African Institute for Aquatic Biodiversity, SAIAB. From discussions with Margaret, as well as with Jean Pote, who had served as personal assistant to JLB (and subsequently to Margaret, this author and others), I learned about the Smiths' extraordinary and inspirational lives.

JLB Smith and, to a lesser extent, Margaret wrote extensively in the popular literature about their work, especially in *Grocott's Daily Mail*, *The Eastern Province Herald* and in various outdoor and angling magazines, such as *Field & Tide*. JLB also wrote three popular books on his fish research and fish-collecting expeditions. The first, *Old Fourlegs – The Story of the Coelacanth*, his epic chronicle of the discovery of the first and second coelacanths, became one of the most popular books of science non-fiction in the world at the time; the other two (*Our Fishes* and *High Tide*) were published shortly after his death.

Numerous short articles have been written about JLB and Margaret Smith, notably by Shirley Bell, Humphry Greenwood, Robin Stobbs, Peter Jackson and by me. In 1951 a Durban-based writer and photographer, Peter Barnett, accompanied the Smiths on a fish-collecting expedition to northern Mozambique and chronicled his experiences in an absorbing book, *Sea Safari with Professor Smith* (1953). Barnett provided valuable insight into the psyche of JLB Smith on this arduous trip, including his obsession with detail and his phenomenal work ethic, as well as the strongly supportive role played by his wife, Margaret. Shirley Bell also wrote an entrancing book, *Old Man Coelacanth* (1969), effectively a version of *Old Fourlegs* for a younger audience, which provides further insight into his character. In 1969 Margaret published *J.L.B. Smith. His Life, Work, Bibliography and List of New Species*, which provides a useful outline of his main accomplishments.

I published a brief review of *The Life and Work of Margaret M. Smith* in 1982, and co-edited *The Biology of* Latimeria chalumnae *and Evolution of Coelacanths* (1991), together with John A Musick and Eugene K Balon, which reviews the Smiths' work and brings coelacanth research up-to-date. In my autobiography, *When I was a Fish – Tales of an Ichthyologist* (2015), I describe my working relationship with JLB and Margaret and the role they played in the discovery of the first and second coelacanths. This theme is explored further in my two most recent books, *The Annotated Old Fourlegs – The* Updated *Story of the Coelacanth* (2017) and, for younger readers, *The Amazing Coelacanth* (2018).

On 23rd January 1968, 16 days after JLB Smith had died, Margaret wrote to Shirley Bell, whom they regarded as their 'literary daughter': 'I have had a number of people badger me to write his biography. This I do not think I can do, it must be left to some outsider. I feel I should write up my autobiography in other words my life with him. Now I am not a writer, I find it difficult to get down to any writing and in one way have to be forced to do it. My suggestion to you is this, that I should write this in a series of articles to *Animals* [the natural history magazine that Shirley edited] on the condition that I retain the copyright and later on can weld it into a book. How do you react to this suggestion?'

In a follow-up letter to Shirley Bell dated 1st February 1968, Margaret wrote, 'About his biography: you know you do not have to get my permission or anyone else's for that matter. As far as I know people just decide to write a biography. His only brother whom I have never met and with whom he really had nothing in common ... lives at Uvongo Beach ... The name is Cyril Smith. Now about the production of the book: I think your suggestions are sound ... I think it a good idea to approach Bulpin.' (TV Bulpin was a popular and prolific non-fiction author of the time.) Unfortunately, nothing came of these plans.

In 1979 Margaret Smith reviewed the impact of their work in a paper entitled 'The influence of the coelacanth on African ichthyology', and several review articles appeared on or shortly after the 50th anniversary of the discovery of the first coelacanth, all of which chronicled the Smiths' involvements with the coelacanth.

This book, ambitiously called a biography, is an attempt to pull disparate pieces of information together and to create a chronicle of JLB and Margaret Smith's extraordinary lives. It made sense to write a joint biography as their lives and careers were intimately intertwined, at home and at work, from the date of their marriage in 1938 until his death 30 years later. Even after 1968 Margaret's main preoccupation was to preserve and build on JLB Smith's legacy, which she did very effectively, as these pages will show.

In addition to reviewing the existing literature, I have interviewed many people who knew the Smiths, with whom they worked or who were in some way players in their life story, and also conducted a questionnaire survey via email with those I could not interview. I received a very positive response to this survey. I also spent many hours in the library and archives of the South African Institute for Aquatic Biodiversity, as well as in the archives of the JLB Smith Institute of Ichthyology, which are held in the Rhodes University Archive housed in the Cory Library for Humanities Research at Rhodes University in Grahamstown. Information was also retrieved from the National Archives in Cape Town and the archives of the Albany Museum, East London Museum, Stellenbosch University and other sources, and from private people.

These researches revealed many previously unknown, or poorly known, facets of their lives, such as JLB Smith's student years in Stellenbosch and Cambridge, his clashes with the Head of Chemistry, Sir George Cory, when he first arrived at Rhodes, his first marriage to Henriette Pienaar from a prestigious Afrikaans family, the impact of his teaching and research in organic chemistry, his failure to secure the Chair of Chemistry, and the remarkable fish-collecting expeditions that the Smiths mounted to East Africa. I also record the extraordinary metamorphosis that Margaret underwent after JLB Smith died in January 1968.

Their story also embraces the lives of many people with whom they worked, in particular George Cory, Marjorie Courtenay-Latimer, Eric Hunt, an unlikely parade of politicians including the Prime Minister (Dr DF Malan), Rex and Hilda Jubb (the successful freshwater fish research team that the Smiths nurtured), Jean Pote (his devoted secretary), Shirley Bell (writer/journalist who became a close family friend), Rosamund Marian ('Nancy') Tietz (Director of the East London Museum from 1987 to 1997), Phil Heemstra, who took over JLB Smith's mantle as the leading marine fish taxonomist in southern Africa, and many others. JLB and Margaret's remarkable son, William, also receives extensive mention, as he is definitely a 'chip off the old block' and followed an amazing career of his own.

Not being an historian, I may not have done justice to the Smiths' endeavours and achievements. But as an ichthyologist and informal science educator, I hope that I have, at least, captured something of the essence of their lives and times. And as I am one of the few living people who knew both the Smiths as well as many of the other players in their lives, I do feel qualified to write this biography – they are 'living people' to me, not just historical figures.

Storytelling is a sensory union of ideas and images, a process of re-creating the past in terms of the present. I have tried to bring the past to life through thoughts, illustrations and word pictures, while using a scientific, 'evidence-based' approach by supporting my conclusions or interpretations with concrete examples or first-hand opinions. My 27 years in the ichthyology establishment in Grahamstown in various capacities, including as Director, and years of extensive research, combined with an unquenchable thirst for knowledge about the coelacanth, which I have felt since I was a child, have made it possible for me to sketch this intimate portrait of two great South African lives.

MIKE BRUTON
2018

Southern Africa

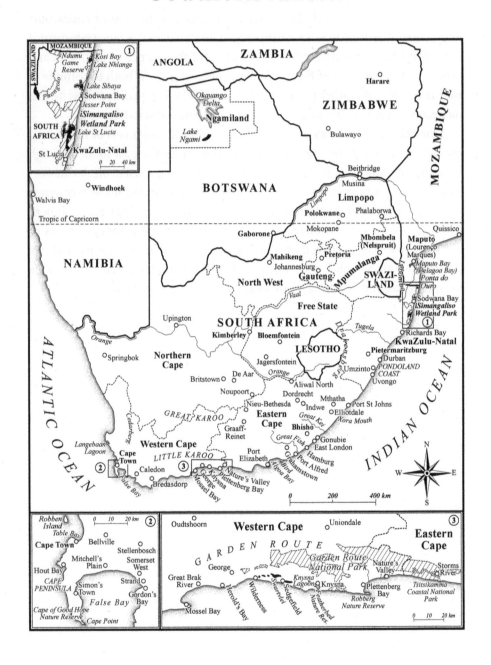

East coast of Africa

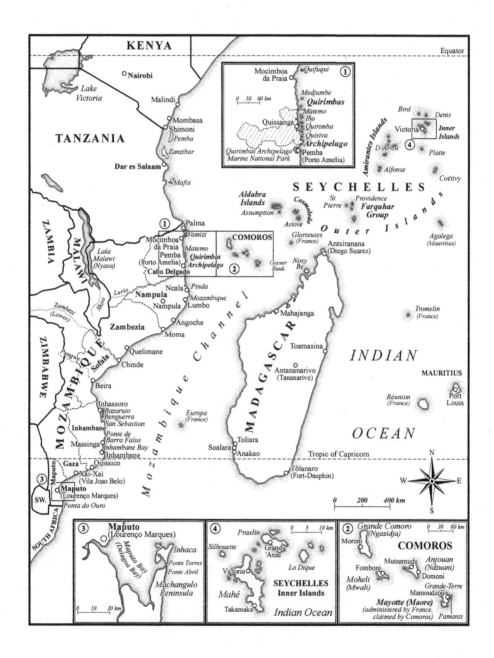

KENYA

Equator

Nairobi

Lake
Victoria

Malindi

Mombasa
Shimoni
Pemba

TANZANIA

Zanzibar

Dar es Salaam

Mafia

Mocímboa
da Praia — Quifuqui

Medjumbe
Quirimbas
Matemo
Ibo
Quirimba
Quisiva
Archipelago
Pemba
(Porto Amelia)

Quissanga

Quirimbas Archipelago
Marine National Park

0 30 60 km

Bird   Denis

Victoria   Inner
            Islands

Amirantes Islands

D'Arros   Platte

Alfonse

Coëtivy

Aldabra
Islands
Assumption

Cosmoledo

St   Providence
Pierre   Farquhar
          Group

SEYCHELLES

Outer Islands

Astove

Agalega
(Mauritius)

Palma

Vamizi

Mocímboa
da Praia
Pemba
(Porto Amelia)
Cabo Delgado

COMOROS

Matemo
Quirimbas
Archipelago

Glorieuses
(France)

Geyser
Bank

Nosy
Be

Antsiranana
(Diego Suarez)

ZAMBIA

MALAWI

Lake
Malawi
(Nyasa)

Lurio

Ncala

Pinda

Tromelin
(France)

Zambezi
(Lower)

Shire

Nampula

Nampula

Mozambique
Lumbo

Mahajanga

Zambezia

Angoche

Moma

Toamasina

INDIAN

ZIMBABWE

Pungwe

Sofala

Quelimane

Chinde

Antananarivo
(Tananarive)

MAURITIUS

MADAGASCAR

Réunion
(France)

Port
Louis

Beira

Inhassoro
Bazaruto
Benguerra
San Sebastian
Ponte de
Barra Falsa
Inhambane Bay
Inhambane

Europa
(France)

MOZAMBIQUE

Inhambane

Massinga

OCEAN

Mozambique Channel

Toliara

Soalara Anakao

Tropic of Capricorn

Gaza

Quissico

Xai-Xai
(Vila Joao Belo)

Maputo

Maputo
(Lourenço Marques)

SW.

Ponta do Ouro

Tôlanaro
(Fort-Dauphin)

N

W   E

S

0   200   400 km

SOUTH AFRICA

③ Maputo
    (Lourenço Marques)

Maputo
Bay
(Delagoa Bay)

Inhaca

Ponte Torres
Ponte Abril

Machangulo
Peninsula

Victoria

0   10   20 km

④ Praslin

Silhouette

Grand
'Anse

La Digue

Mahé

SEYCHELLES
Inner Islands

Takamaka   Indian Ocean

0   5   10 km

② Grande Comoro
    (Ngazidja)

Moroni

Fomboni

Moheli
(Mwali)

Mutsamudu   Anjouan
             (Ndzuani)

Domoni

Grande-Terre

Mamoudzou

Mayotte (Maore)
(administered by France,
claimed by Comoros)   Pamanzi

COMOROS

0   30   60 km

CHAPTER 1

JLB Smith's childhood

Karoo to Bishops

JAMES LEONARD Brierley Smith was born on 26th September 1897 in Graaff-Reinet, Cape Province (now Eastern Cape). His father, Joseph Smith, descended from seafaring folk, was a peripatetic postmaster; his mother, Emily Ann Beck, was a beautiful but bad-tempered woman who had a poor relationship with her son. Emily was convinced that she had married beneath herself and took out her bitterness on her hus-band and family. She showed little interest in her elder son or, later, in his children, even though she went on to become a librarian in Knysna, where the Smiths had a holiday cot-tage. By all accounts Smith had an unhappy and unsettled childhood (Ian and Ishbel Sholto-Douglas, pers. comm., 2016). When he won his first bursary, he bought himself some new shirts but his mother confiscated them on the grounds that his father had never been able to wear new shirts (W Smith, pers. comm., 2017). According to the *Dictionary of South African Biography* (Anon, 1968–1987), JLB's parents 'had little in common with their elder son as they were quite unable to understand his sensitivity, his enquiring mind, and his craving for knowledge, education and culture', although this assessment does seem to be unfair to his father.

JLB Smith in Graaff-Reinet, aged 3 or 4 years, wearing a sailor suit that he apparently hated.

1

According to Professor Dr Andree-Jeanne Tötemeyer (pers. comm., 2017), youngest sister of Smith's first wife's niece, who knew JLB's mother, she was a domineering and violent woman ('a real virago') who beat Len mercilessly as a child. He developed a lifelong aversion to the female singing voice as his mother was in the habit of beating her children and then singing loudly to cover their cries (J Smith, pers. comm., 2017).

Joseph Smith was himself a keen angler but, as he spent most of his life inland, he could only pursue his hobby on occasional visits to Knysna and more frequently after the family had settled in Stellenbosch in 1912, and later in Somerset West, when he was probably in his 40s and JLB was in his late teens. JLB Smith had a 'slightly younger' brother, Cyril, with whom he spent his early childhood. Nothing is known of him except that he lived as an adult in Uvongo, KwaZulu-Natal, until at least February 1968, had little or no contact with JLB, and never met either of JLB's wives. JLB also had a sister, Gladys, of whom very little is known except that she broke off their relationship at a very early age; the only record of any contact with her is in January 1968 when Margaret Smith, JLB's second wife, wrote to inform her of his death.

Eastford House in Knysna where JLB Smith spent childhood holidays in the early 1900s, and developed a love for fishing. Note the Cape cart, in which the family travelled to and from George.

Thus, having endured a difficult childhood, JLB Smith left his unhappy home as early as he could, breaking off all relations with his mother, brother and sister (Weinberg, 1999; Maylam, 2017; J Smith, pers. comm., 2017). He does not mention his blood relatives at all in his voluminous popular writings later in life.

In *Old Fourlegs – The Story of the Coelacanth* (1956), Smith briefly describes his early life:

JLB Smith at the age of 8 years with his father and mother.

'My life has throughout been a series of contrasts and changes, many due to the peculiar circumstances of South Africa. Of English parents, I was born in 1897 in the inland Karoo town of Graaff Reinet. In the midst of the stress and bitterness of the Boer War my early years were spent in an atmosphere of deification of all that was British, and hatred and scorn for the "Boers", and indeed of anything South African as distinct from British, including the country itself.

'It has always been my uncomfortable instinct not to accept uncritically the opinions of others, and while this has ultimately been an asset in my scientific career, it did not always create the most cordial relations at home or at school.

'My early education was at several small Karoo village mixed schools, and later at the abruptly different atmosphere of "Bishops", modelled on an English Public School. The next violent contrast was the Victoria College at Stellenbosch, predominantly Afrikaans and reputedly steeped in Nationalism and Politics, but I encountered a peaceful tolerance towards my firm political views. There I gave my heart to Chemistry.

'When the Great War came, in company with thousands of others of like age, on the 7th August 1914, I was called up from school and put into khaki and barracks in Wynberg, then into the tender care of a Regular British regiment for training. The enforced close company of this strange unnatural substratum of society was a bewildering experience. ... After about a month some of us were returned to school as too young for campaign, and I went on to University life at Stellenbosch. As I was set on taking part in the war, I arranged at once to go to England to join the Royal Flying Corps after my "Intermediate" Examination at the end of the year (1915). However, General Smuts, at that time almost a god to me, appealed to everyone to enlist for German East Africa first, so instead of learning to soar through the skies, I became an earth-bound, foot-slogging infantry-man instead. Thousands of half-trained men of all ages were jammed into a transport at Durban, and fed mainly on bread, tinned rabbit, and tea. While most others gambled I counted heads and life-boats and was appalled at the quotient, but we got safely to Mombasa, and thence to the badly mismanaged campaign that followed.

'After sundry misadventures, including contracting malaria, dysentery, and the acute rheumatic enlargement of several major joints, I spent some months in military hospitals, first in Kenya, where I nearly died, then was shipped, helpless, back to the Union, and to hospital at Wynberg. Eventually I returned, virtually a physical wreck, to University life at Stellenbosch ... Then came another abrupt change from Afrikaner Stellenbosch to Cambridge in England, where I carried out research in chemistry ... Despite my undiluted English blood and early upbringing, I found myself resentful of criticism of South Africa, especially of comments on Smuts I heard in quite high circles. I became conscious for the first time of being a "South African", and those from my own country I met over there were no longer "English" or "Afrikaans", but my own people. The childhood-fostered gap between "Briton" and "Boer" in my mind just closed up' (Smith, 1956).

JLB Smith was educated at schools in Noupoort, De Aar, Aliwal North (all inland towns) and finally in Cape Town, as his parents relocated around the Cape Province of South Africa to their eventual home in Somerset West. Although it was a cultural shock moving from unsophisticated rural schools to a traditional 'English' private school, he was fortunate to complete his schooling at the prestigious Diocesan College ('Bishops') in Cape Town between 1912 and 1914. This school, named after its founder, Bishop of Cape Town, the Right Reverend Robert Gray, states in its founding prospectus published in the late 1820s, 'That a college be founded in Cape Town, for the promotion of sound Learning and religious Education in Southern Africa ... especially for the dif- fusion of such knowledge in the higher branches of Literature and Science' (Gardener, 1997).

The mission includes 'creating a climate characterised by high expectations, respect for excellence in all areas, tolerance, mutual respect and caring concern for human kind and the natural world around us' (Gardener, 1997). Smith identi- fied with these lofty goals and benefited greatly from his formal tuition as well as his interactions with the other scholars at Bishops. His education had reached a new level after assorted mediocre experiences in rural schools, and his self- esteem and confidence began to assert themselves for the first time.

JLB Smith entered Bishops in the first term of 1912 in Junior Sixth Form A, and won the Mathematics Prize in that year. The first headmaster, Henry Master White, was 'One of that happy band of mid-nineteenth-century scientists who, before the grim days of specialisation, took all nature to their province … he loved to wander around his domain, botanizing, geologizing and zoologizing. His boys went with him. They could not have found a surer way of mastering science' (McIntyre, 1950). The young Len Smith (or 'LB Smith', as he was called then), whose curiosity would probably have been suppressed in the rural schools that he had attended thus far, must have thrived in this environment.

The period 1912 to 1914 was difficult at Bishops. The school was in financial trouble and the number and quality of students had declined, although the staff were still first class. Uncertainty had surrounded the declaration of the Union of South Africa in 1910, and war clouds were looming in Europe. The withdrawal of government funds, and the possible need for the school to amalgamate with its great rival, the South African College School (SACS), had created an air of despondency. However, in an editorial in the June 1905 *Diocesan School Magazine* it is reported that, 'Our chemical laboratory is already as well equipped as could possibly be desired' and it was also noted that 'On Saturday evening, May 27th, Mr. Brackenbury Bayly very kindly came and lectured to the School Boarders on Radium. The lecture was illustrated by lantern slides and by a piece of radium which was passed all round and reverently handled and inspected.'

During JLB Smith's time at Bishops the Headmaster was Canon Owen Jenkins, a capable cleric; but Smith's main teacher was Professor RND ('Barty') Sutton, the Vice-Principal, who influenced him to develop an interest in chemistry (McIntyre, 1950), a discipline that had been taught at the college since 1869 when it became a compulsory subject in the Cape Board examinations (Gardener, 1997).

Bishops also had a museum, started in 1887 by the Debating Society, which was developed over the next two decades by a series of passionate curators (McIntyre, 1950; Gardener, 1997). Its collection included an eclectic array of items, from a box of copper ore and minerals and stones to fossil ferns, plant seeds, seashells from

RND 'Barty' Sutton, JLB Smith's first chemistry teacher.

Madagascar, insects, the sword of a swordfish, stuffed snakes and iguanas, the skeleton of a 'sea-pig', and ethnographic artefacts. By June 1888 it was reported that the museum 'was beginning to attain very respectable dimensions'.

The museum soon outgrew the space available to it, a situation that was exacerbated in 1910 when an appeal was made for the donation of items 'to remind Bishops boys of the honourable history of their school' (Gardener, 1997). As a result, cultural archival items soon took precedence in the museum and, in 1910, the natural history specimens 'were removed to a garret to make room for the College washing' (McIntyre, 1950). JLB Smith discovered this 'treasure trove' in the garret and, according to McIntyre (1950), 'It fired his imagination and spurred him to inquiry'. He also apparently volunteered to assist in the restoration of the specimens, many of which were by then somewhat damaged and decomposed. Today Bishops has an excellent archive and museum of cultural artefacts relating to the proud history of the school but the few remaining natural history specimens have been dispersed for display in subject classrooms and laboratories.

Brooke Wing, Diocesan College, where JLB Smith's chemistry classes were held, ca 1914.

So JLB Smith entered a school in transition, an institution with fine traditions but an uncertain future, and he made the best of the opportunity. But he was not the only famous scientist to emerge from Bishops: other important scientists and technologists who were graduates of Diocesan College include James Greathead (1844–1896, at Bishops from 1859 to 1860), inventor of the 'Greathead Shield' that was used to drill the tunnels for the first London Underground trains (Bruton, 2010, 2017) and Alexander Logie du Toit (1878–1948, at Bishops from 1889 to 1896), the geologist who helped propagate the theory of continental drift and the formation of Gondwanaland (Gardener, 1997). In 1953 the research of JLB Smith and Alex du Toit was selected to represent Bishops at the South African Schools Science Festival at Rhodes University (letter from JLB Smith dated 4th July 1953, Rhodes University Archive).

Alexander Logie du Toit.

There is little mention of JLB Smith's extramural involvements at Bishops in school magazines between 1912 and 1914. He was not a high achiever in sports and apparently did not make his mark in the Debating Society, except by contributing to the museum, which this society had started. It seems that he focused mainly on his academic studies at Bishops.

We do know that Smith had a serious bicycle accident when he was about 17 years old, speeding down a dusty farm road at high speed and colliding with a gate 'that wasn't there before'. He catapulted over the handlebars and landed heavily on his back, knocking himself out in the process. Many years later his medical doctors concluded that this accident might have been the cause of the kidney and other internal organ problems that he experienced for the rest of his life. It was only after he died that it was found that he had only one functional kidney, which must have contributed to his health issues. Furthermore, the doctors realised that his radical diets and vigorous exercise regimes might not have been beneficial for someone with only one kidney (J Smith, pers. comm., 2017).

Having passed his Junior Certificate (second class) at the end of 1912 and his Senior Certificate (second class) in 1913, he matriculated (first class) at the end of 1914, winning the Gorham Prize and the History Prize.

In JLB's matriculation year the First World War broke out and, under the mobilisation order issued by the South African Defence Force on 8th August 1914, he was briefly drafted to the Cape Town Highlanders' Regiment and then, as Quartermaster Sergeant, to the Standerton Commando (Diocesan College newsletters, March 1914, March 1915). He served with the citizen force only from early August until September 1914 when, along with most school boys, he was discharged.

Cover of *The Diocesan College Magazine*, 1914.

A fellow draftee from Bishops recorded a typical day's routine in the citizen force in 1914 in his diary: '6 a.m. Reveille. 7 a.m. Roll call parade. 8 a.m. Breakfast (dry bread and slop water tea). 9 a.m. to 12.30 p.m. Drill order. [Lunch]. 2 to 4.30 p.m. Drill order. 5 p.m. Tea (same as breakfast). 10 p.m. Lights out. 10.1 to 11 p.m. Fight with insects. It is getting jolly monotonous.' (*The Hindoo*, Diocesan School Magazine, September 1914, p. 10).

JLB's life up to this point – his dysfunctional home circumstances and fragmented schooling – reflects what many survive on their path to adulthood. And his performance at school, while showing promise, perhaps did not immediately set him apart as the remarkable figure he was to become. But the difficulties of his early years must surely have helped to build the steely determination and fire that characterised his later career.

CHAPTER 2

Young whippersnapper
Studies and pranks in Stellenbosch

I N 1915, after his matriculation examination, Smith was refused re-enlistment on account of his youth, and so he enrolled at Victoria College in Stellenbosch, a college of the University of the Cape of Good Hope. Victoria College would become Stellenbosch University on 2nd April 1918. At the end of that year he passed first in the Union of South Africa in the Intermediate Examination of the University of the Cape of Good Hope and was awarded several bursaries and exhibitions, including the coveted Croll Exhibition.

Although he had already made arrangements to travel abroad to join the Royal Flying Corps, he responded to an appeal to join the campaign in East Africa and instead enrolled in the 12th South African Infantry Battalion as a machine gunner (MM Smith, 1969). This decision was fortuitous (for science) as the survival rate of Royal Flying Corps troops was very low. After only cursory military training he was despatched to German East Africa (today Burundi, Rwanda and mainland Tanzania), where he became embroiled in the gruelling military campaign that was later to be led by General Jan Smuts. Smith loathed the military, hated the British, and blamed Smuts for the military imbroglio that they found themselves in (W Smith, pers. comm., 2017). He did, however, achieve something in the military, an early example of his exceptional organisational ability: he and a small team broke the British record for the fastest time to assemble and then fire a field artillery gun (W Smith, pers. comm., 2017).

The young scientist-turned-soldier contracted various tropical diseases, as did many others; and, after several months in hospital, he was discharged as permanently medically unfit for further service. He retained his sense of humour, though and, according to his friend Ernst Malherbe (1981b), he regaled incredulous ladies who visited him in Wynberg Hospital with tall tales of giant

JLB Smith as a student at Victoria College, Stellenbosch, ca 1918.

mosquitoes, '… worse than the Germans. We had to fight them with our bayonets – they were huge creatures almost like little aeroplanes'. The aftermath of these diseases would, however, affect him for the rest of his life.

Smith returned to Victoria College in the third term of 1916 and resumed his studies. Although he was handicapped by repeated bouts of malaria, he quickly made up for lost time and graduated with a Batchelor of Arts degree in chemistry from the University of the Cape of Good Hope at the end of 1917 (Shell, 2017). Despite going fishing in the weeks before the final examinations (W Smith, pers. comm., 2017), he once again achieved the highest marks for chemistry in the Union of South Africa and won the Bartle Frere Exhibition and the Stellenbosch University Exhibition (MM Smith, 1969).

While at Victoria College, and notwithstanding his physical limitations, Smith engaged actively in sports. At the time he was the best student golfer, although he normally used only one club, and he played rugby and tennis. He was also an avid cyclist; in January 1919, he embarked on a 'cycle tour around the Cape Peninsula' with four friends, including the future Cabinet Minister Eben Dönges (letter from EG Malherbe to Margaret Smith, 12th September 1968). He was keen on camping and mountaineering but his favourite pastime, after bee-keeping, was angling. Fishes became his new passion and he travelled to the coast by train, ox-wagon and bicycle to catch fishes, once cycling from Stellenbosch to Cape Point and back on unpaved, sandy roads. He also had a keen interest in classical literature and was apparently an authority on George Bernard Shaw and William Shakespeare.

In his account of life at Victoria College, Smith (1956) does not mention the mischievous pranks that he perpetrated with three of his student friends, as they were all sworn to secrecy until the last survivor could reveal the truth. The 'Heavenly Quartet', as they were dubbed by a lady friend, Janie Nel, comprised four men who would all achieve fame in their professions: JLB Smith (chemistry and ichthyology), Ernst G Malherbe (Director of the National Bureau for Educational and Social Research and Vice-Chancellor of the University of Natal), Frikkie Meyer (Head of Iscor) and W Kupferburger (a pioneering mining geologist) (Malherbe, 1981a, b). Other fellow students at Victoria College who went on to achieve fame and fortune included Eben

Dönges, Paul Sauer, HJ van Eck, AL Geyer and ET Schumann.

Malherbe outlived the rest and, in his memorable autobiography, *Never a Dull Moment*, as well as in a *Matieland* article, he describes some of their outrageous pranks (Malherbe, 1981a and b). They decided that Stellenbosch was a 'sleepy hollow' and 'needed from time to time a bit of a waking up'; on two separate occasions, they even gave the college an unannounced half-day holiday. One prank involved arranging for all the clocks in the university residences, as well as the clock on the main-building wall in the college quadrangle and the clock on the Dutch Reformed Church

The 'Heavenly Quartet' in 1917. From left, back: JLB Smith, W Kupferburger; front: Frikkie Meyer, Ernst Malherbe.

tower, to be reset one half-hour fast. This prank required meticulous planning and considerable climbing skill and risk taking. In particular, to move the handles of the clock on the main building, one of the pranksters was suspended by his feet, head downwards, from a window 10 metres above the ground (Malherbe, 1981a, b). This prank caused chaos on the campus and in town as ordinary people did not wear wrist watches in those days but relied on tower clocks; only clerics and high-ranking officials carried pocket watches. Students turned up early for their lectures and, in due course, left, as it seemed the lecturers were all late. People travelling to Cape Town by train missed their 'Cape cart' taxis, and pandemonium ensued. The culprits were never caught, thanks to their compact never to discuss their pranks with anybody (except for Janie Nel, who helped to turn back the clocks in the women's residence, *Harmonie*, and later became Malherbe's wife) (Malherbe, 1981a).

About a year later they perpetrated an even more ambitious prank. After careful planning they managed, between midnight and 5 a.m., to barricade (from the inside) the whole of the main college building where the class-rooms were located. The next morning students and professors wandered around the building, unable to enter, and eventually went home. It took the technical staff until midday to enter the building. 'Despite an official enquiry by the authorities they never even remotely associated any of the four of us with these strange disruptions of the regular lectures in the college' (Malherbe, 1981a, b).

The pranksters also noticed that, in the residential area of town where most of the professors and elite of the town lived, the home owners displayed fancy names on their garden gates. Malherbe explained:

'We decided that it would cause quite [a] stir if, during one night, we could interchange all these names. It took us a couple of weeks to study carefully how each one of these name plates was fixed because on no account did we want to damage them. ... We worked in pairs, Meyer and I worked together while Smith and Kupferburger worked together, each pair having its own allocation of names to interchange. For example, we interchanged *Avond Rust* for *Morgenson. Melrose* we put on the gate of the house where lived a pretty girl called Rose whom we often visited. *Bloemhof,* which was the name of the Girls' High School, we put a mile away on to the fence of a vineyard' (Malherbe, 1971).

The 'Heavenly Quartet' 20 years later, in about 1937.
From left: JLB Smith, Frikkie Meyer, Ernst Malherbe and W Kupferburger.

On another house they put the sign 'Births and Deaths Registration' from the Magistrate's Office next to the Police Station, and they fixed the 'Police Station' sign to the gate of the Girls' High School hostel. The outcome was further pandemonium.

Their most outrageous prank involved placing large enamel chamber pots on the pinnacles of the towers above the prestigious boys' and girls' schools in town. A howling south-easter blew that night, making this a very hazardous undertaking that required all their considerable climbing skills. At the Boys' School, Smith and Malherbe climbed up a long ladder and then hoisted themselves up 'by trusting to the strength of the guttering' (Malherbe, 1971). Near the top of the tower Malherbe climbed onto Smith's shoulders and placed the 'potty' onto the tower pinnacle with a long bamboo pole. The next morning the students brought the school's 'new badge' to the attention of the Headmaster, the formidable Paul Roos (South Africa's first Spring-

Cartoon from *Matieland* magazine (Malherbe, 1981a) showing cadets shooting at the chamberpot on the tower pinnacle at Victoria College, with a furious Paul Roos in the foreground.

bok rugby captain). Roos was furious and ordered the caretaker to take the obscene object down. When this worthy failed to dislodge it, Roos instructed the school cadets to shoot the offending object off the tower. The Girls' School did not have cadets and the chamber pot stayed on top of their tower for several weeks until the south-easter blew it off (Malherbe, 1981a). JLB Smith's participation in these pranks demonstrates that, as a youth, he had a playful and mischievous side to his character, a trait that only his closest friends and relatives knew later in life.

JLB's predilection for pranks was passed on to his son by his second marriage, William, who later said that JLB enjoyed pranks because of the 'precise planning' that was necessary to bring them off (Weinberg, 1999). While studying for his Master of Science degree at Natal University, William, egged on by a group of students, felt that it was unfair that the screening of a film on the birth of a baby was for females only. He planted a stink bomb that cleared the theatre in a very short time, so that no-one could see the movie. When he was hauled up in front of the entire Senate, and the Vice-Chancellor (no less than JLB Smith's student friend, Ernst Malherbe), they demanded to know what chemical he had used: 'The same stuff [phenyl iso-cyanide] that you and my father used at Stellenbosch University as students to break up a political rally' (W Smith, pers. comm., 2017). This riposte probably increased his punishment but, according to William, it was worth it!

By the end of 1918 Smith had completed his MSc degree (with distinction) in chemistry, one of the most brilliant chemistry students in the early history of South Africa (K Breedt, pers. comm., 2017; MM Smith, 1969; Shell, 2017) and one of the first five students to achieve this qualification at Victoria College. Smith was awarded the British Government Research Scholarship and the HB Ebden Scholarship for overseas study. This represented a considerable fraction of the scholarships available to young South Africans at the time.[1]

---

1 Other South Africans who won the Ebden Scholarship include Sir Basil Schonland (1896–1972), famous for his research on lightning, his involvement in the development of radar during the Second World War and for becoming the first President of the Council for Scientific and Industrial Research (CSIR); and Hendrik van Eck (1903–1970), who became Chairman of the Industrial Development Corporation.

CHAPTER 3

Chemistry rules

From student to senior lecturer

A FTER A brief stint as a staff member of Victoria College in Stellenbosch, during which he also ran a paint factory, JLB Smith enrolled at Cambridge University in England on his Ebden Scholarship, becoming a scholar of Selwyn College and Demonstrator in Chemistry (MM Smith, 1969). Here he carried out pioneering research on mustard gases under the direction of Sir William J Pope and, later, on photosynthesising dyestuffs and related compounds, under the direction of the renowned Dr William Hobson Mills. This research later found application in photography (Rivett, 1996). Smith's work was published in a series of scientific papers, and he received the degree of Doctor of Philosophy in 1922.

While at Cambridge University Smith continued to be involved in student pranks. On one occasion he and his cronies noticed a group of municipal workers digging up the road outside their residence to lay a pipe. They told the workers that a group of students dressed up as policemen would approach them soon and demand to know what they were doing. They then went to the local police station and told the officer-on-duty that a group of students dressed up as municipal workers was digging up the road outside their residence. They then sat back and watched the mayhem (W Smith, pers. comm., 2017).

JLB Smith as a student at Cambridge University in 1920.

On another occasion, during a discussion on gravity, Smith dropped a metal bucket full of water several storeys down the middle of a spiral stairway, just to see what would happen. The bucket, a prized possession of the janitor, gouged a 3-centimetre-deep hole in the cement floor but also, spectacularly, was concertina'd down to a fraction of its size. Smith then returned the flattened bucket to the janitor's cupboard. The next day the perplexed janitor approached Smith, told him that he knew he was the perpetrator, and asked him how he had done it! Smith and his friends also investigated the chemistry of flatulence. A volunteer agreed to pass wind, which they lit with a match. The result was spectacular but the unfortunate volunteer couldn't sit down for weeks (W Smith, pers. comm., 2017).

Smith played rugby for Selwyn College and participated in many social activities at Cambridge. He travelled widely in Britain and continental Europe, where he learned to speak German (and some Italian) and made many

JLB Smith trout fishing in the River Dee in England, ca 1921.

JLB Smith and the motorbike on which he went sightseeing and fly fishing while studying at Cambridge University in the early 1920s.

scientific contacts. He also indulged his hobby of fly fishing and bought a motorbike to take him to his favourite fishing haunts. During this time he realised that, despite his 'English upbringing', he was a true South African and proud to be one (Smith, 1956; Bell, 1969). In later years his patriotic zeal would affect many of the decisions he made. As Shirley Bell (1969) later wrote, '… his deep love of South Africa shines through his writing like a warm, glowing light'.

In late 1922 he returned to the Union of South Africa to accept a temporary appointment in the Chemistry Department at Rhodes University College (RUC) in Grahamstown, which was headed at the time by the legendary Sir George Edward Cory (1862–1935). Cory had triumphed over extreme hardship and a difficult upbringing to become first a schoolmaster and then (in 1904) one of the four founding professors of RUC (Shell, 2017). Like Smith, he had a strong interest in a field – in his case, South African history – unrelated to his main academic discipline and would ultimately take early retirement from academia in order to pursue it.

Some of the excitement generated by research being done overseas at this time in the field of chemistry was conveyed to Grahamstown by Cory in a series of public lectures. According to Michael Brown, who became Professor of Physical Chemistry at Rhodes University in 1986, his lectures were always well illustrated by 'clever and brilliant experiments' and he was a popular and fascinating presenter.[1]

Sir George Cory, Professor of Chemistry at Rhodes University College, in 1923.

On his appointment as Head of Chemistry at RUC, Cory worked hard at setting up the department during the day but pursued his historical research after hours. As in Smith's case, his hobby became an all-consuming passion. His field work was carried out on foot and he undertook epic walking tours of the Eastern Cape during the university holidays to do interviews and gather material for this historical research, somewhat reminiscent of JLB's epic East African fish-research expeditions in the 1940s and 1950s.

When Cory's assistant, RA Page, took six months' leave in 1923, JLB Smith was appointed as Page's leave replacement to the post of Lecturer (RUC Council; MS 16,911). Cory initially formed a very positive impression of Smith. 'He was an excellent teacher in all branches, but especially in Organic. We got on very well to start with. I thought he was so good and would be such an acquisition to the College, that I worked hard to keep him on permanently after Page came back. It was a bit of a fight as the College was very disinclined to increase the staff. However, in the

Sir George Cory in field gear, on the cover of Sandra Shell's book, *Protean Paradox*.

---

1 Marguerite Poland (2008) captured Cory's personality beautifully in her vivid history of St Andrew's College. 'Like a small, gleeful wizard he ensconced himself in the Gothic chemical laboratory, which stood on the lawn between Upper and Lower. Spirited, controversial, opinionated and as pugnacious as a terrier, George Cory presided over his bell jars and burners for the next ten years, his mortar board askew, his pince-nez glinting with fire'.

end it was done' (Cory, 1922/23; Shell, 2017). On 11th April 1924, the Senate approved Smith's promotion to Senior Lecturer on Cory's recommendation. Soon Smith had gained a reputation as 'a brilliant if irascible teacher'; he liked students who worked hard but cared little for those who did not. He was considered to be 'extraordinarily gifted' and 'endowed with a photographic memory' (Maylam, 2017). 'His students still remember his quick movements, the measured, almost pedantic way he delivered his lectures, and his habit of not looking directly at whoever was talking, then swinging round suddenly to hold the speaker in a penetrating stare' (Weinberg, 1999).

But Smith was soon at loggerheads with the 'Old Guard', including Cory, who had graduated to chairs in the university college from being teachers, and looked askance at research work. One of the turning points probably came when Smith refused to spend his own time washing up students' lab apparatus at the end of the year, but offered to pay an unskilled person to do his share (MM Smith, 1979). This style was quite unlike that of Cory, who wrote in his unpublished 'Recollections', 'I had to do all the "bottle-washing" and in fact all the cleaning of the place except the actual sweeping. But I liked doing it – and always felt proud of the place when it looked in order' (Cory, 1922/23; Shell, 2017).

After JLB's permanent appointment had been confirmed, his sometimes abrasive and wilful personality started to create tension in the Chemistry Department (Shell, 2017). According to Cory (1922/23), Smith dedicated his time to his six students to the exclusion of all else, had scant regard for the needs of others in the Department, and made arbitrary decisions for the scheduling of his classes (Shell, 2017).

In 'Recollections', from which Sandra Shell drew much of the material for her biography, Cory states:

'He had his laboratory down stairs. He helped himself liberally to all apparatus and materials from above, without any consideration [for] what inconvenience he was causing us. Page got very angry. One day I went down to Smith's place and found it locked up and no students. On enquiries I found that, in the *middle of term* – he had given them *four days' holiday*. Of course I expostulated with him and told him that even I had no authority to do such a thing without the sanction of Senate. It was getting quite impossible to work with him'.

One wonders where they went fishing?

Cory was himself cantankerous and explosive if challenged or crossed, and was not afraid of public confrontations (Shell, 2017). He resigned his professorship in chemistry well ahead of his retirement date – as Smith would later do on account of his own conflicting interests – to pursue his historical research. Cory served on the committee that appointed his own successor and opposed Smith's candidature, later writing:

'On the whole he made things very unpleasant. When I resigned and was on the committee to choose a successor, Smith was a candidate. I opposed it. He was young – about 26. There could be no question about his ability as a teacher but he seemed so irresponsible, that I was not going to take the responsibility of recommending him for the management of the department. He did *not* get the post. He was very wrath and wrote to me a very insulting letter. A Dr Barker was put in – a first class man' (Shell, 2017).

In the Senate minutes dated 1st July 1925 (RUC Senate Special Meeting) it is recorded that, 'Professor Cory spoke in favour of the appointment of a Physical Chemist and warned the meeting against the appointment of Dr Smith on personal grounds'. No-one seems to have noticed that one of Cory's arguments against Smith was his youth, yet Barker was four years younger than Smith. The only two members of the College Senate at the time with doctorates, Selmar Schonland, Head of Botany, and James Duerden, Head of Zoology, both fought bitterly to have Smith appointed to the Chair, but they were overruled, the excuse being that organic chemistry was a static subject of the past, with no future. How wrong they were!

Once Barker, the physical chemist, was appointed, Smith, the organic chemist, was expected to continue his teaching and research in organic chemistry. This setback upset Smith sufficiently to cause him to want to leave RUC. There are letters in the Rhodes University Archive that indicate that he unsuccessfully applied for the post of Chair of Chemistry at both Natal University College in Pietermaritzburg (in 1939) and the University College of the Orange Free State in Bloemfontein

Cartoon by Boonzaier of Sir George Cory in Cape Town in the 1930s.

(in 1941) (Pote, 1997; Rhodes University Archive). Both these applications were made after the discovery of the first coelacanth so it seems that, even then, and somewhat surprisingly, his mind was still set on a career in chemistry. But the winds of change had started to blow and ultimately chemistry's loss would prove to be ichthyology's gain.

When Cory returned from six months' leave in England he commented:

> 'From all accounts he [Barker] does not have too good a time with Smith. Since my time, the place has been vastly improved – more rooms added and no expense spared in additional equipment. What a difference to the time I started, with just one half assistant. Now a full professor at £800, Smith at £600, Dugmore at £400 and four assistants at £250 each or the equivalent in board etc.' (Shell, 2017).

William Francis ('Billy') Barker was, of course, no slouch. When he was appointed to succeed Cory he was only 24 years old and had an excellent academic and research record. He served as Professor and Head of Chemistry at Rhodes University for 36½ years until his retirement in 1961.

Many years later, on 15th May 1968, Margaret Smith, JLB's second wife, wrote to Shirley Bell, a family friend and editor whose magazine, *Animals*, had just been terminated by the publisher:

> 'My experience in life has been that what at the time seems to be a dreadful catastrophe often turns out for the very best … The worst thing that ever happened to my husband was his not getting the Chair of Chemistry. He was in every way best qualified and a magnificent teacher, but local jealousy saw to it that an inferior man was placed over him. This nearly killed him, but it did turn him eventually into the Ichthyologist, and looking back we can see that this almost crushing blow to his pride and everything else was responsible for his becoming a world figure in another discipline. So don't worry too much, just take things as they come and enjoy them while you have them.'

CHAPTER 4

Organic chemistry
Building a career in Grahamstown

ESPITE THIS setback, and his heavy teaching duties, JLB Smith continued to pursue his research interests in mustard gases and photosynthesising dyestuffs, and developed a new interest in the essential oils of indigenous South African plants. In July 1946 the British journal *Nature* reported that the Council of the Royal Society of South Africa had awarded the first Marloth Memorial Medal to JLB Smith and one of his students, DEA (Doug) Rivett, for a paper they had co-authored entitled, 'The essential oil of *Agathosma apiculata* Meyer', which had been published in the *Transactions of the Royal Society of South Africa* (Smith & Rivett, 1946).[1] *Agathosma apiculata* is commonly known as buchu. It has aromatic leaves and a distinctive garlic scent is released when the leaves are crushed. It grows on granite as well as limestone soils in low-altitude coastal areas.

Professor DEA (Doug) Rivett.

In their paper Smith & Rivett (1946) state:

> 'Prominent among the herbal remedies employed by the rural populace of South Africa are the various plants designated broadly as "Buchu". Chiefly these are members of the large family Rutaceae, of which many representatives, chiefly endemic species and many endemic genera, occur in South Africa. One of the characters of this family is that all, or almost all, of the species secrete essential oil, usually concentrated in special glands in the

---

1 After Smith and Rivett's paper, a 72-year gap would ensue before the Marloth Medal was awarded again – in 2018 to Professor Guy Midgley for his outstanding contributions to ecology and ecological policy.

leaf … Much of the reputed medicinal value of these plants is attributed to the essential oil they contain. Generally an infusion of the dried leaves is employed, and this from our observation may contain much or little of the oil according to the manner of its preparation. Since from our determinations it appears that the leaves always lose a considerable portion of the more volatile components of the oil in drying, it may be presumed that those … are not the portion of major clinical importance. It is possible that the pungent odour of the leaves and of the infusions prepared from them have in the case of some plants at least been responsible for inducing in the credulous an exaggerated belief in their curative properties.'

Smith and Rivett straddled the disciplines of organic chemistry, botany and indigenous knowledge in this important publication. Although they were healthily sceptical about the restorative properties of buchu infusions, they were at least aware of traditional uses of the plant. It took several decades more for others to realise the full potential of buchu.[2]

Doug Rivett was one of many organic chemists taught by JLB Smith who went on to achieve international acclaim. He first arrived at Rhodes University College (RUC) as an undergraduate student in 1939 and carried out his MSc research – on the sulphurous constituents of sea buchu – under the supervision of Smith. He completed his doctorate in organic chemistry at Cambridge University under the supervision of Nobel laureate, Lord Todd. After stints at Princeton and at the CSIR back in South Africa, and a mission at a top-secret chemical warfare facility in England, he returned to his *alma mater* in 1962 as a senior lecturer, eventually becoming Professor of Organic Chemistry in 1981. Like Cory before him, he enjoyed presenting 'Chemistry Magic Shows' to the next generation of young scientists.

In an obituary read at Doug's memorial service on 30th January 2010 by Mike Davies-Coleman (pers. comm., 2017), many parallels between the characters of Rivett and Smith become apparent:

---

2 Today it is an essential component of the new-age 'nutraceuticals' industry in South Africa and has been combined with other products arising from indigenous knowledge, such as rooibos tea and bitter ghaap (*Hoodia gordonii*), to create nutritious drinks and medicines. Buchu leaves are chewed to cure stomach complaints, rheumatism and gout, and the leaves are crushed to make 'buchu brandy', a potent drink, and to flavour food, soft drinks, wine and perfume. The San and Khoi-Khoi use buchu as an insect repellent and deodorant, and mix it with sheep fat to make skin moisturisers. Until recently most buchu has been harvested from wild plants but the international demand for the herb has encouraged many farmers in the Cedarberg district to grow it commercially in irrigated fields (Bruton, 2010, 2017a).

'Doug was as straight as an arrow with no airs and graces. He was a doer and not a talker and he always judged people by what they did as opposed to what they said they would do. He did not tolerate fools and abhorred those who wasted time, especially in the laboratory. He had no interest whatsoever in scandal or petty politics. He was, however, a supportive mentor and a wise counsellor to young scientists of all generations and a most loyal and wonderful friend and colleague.'

Rivett's unpublished personal recollections, written in May 2004 (to which the Rivett family gave access thanks to the kind intervention of Mike Davies-Coleman), give an indication of the high standard that Smith set in his chemistry teaching, and provide an insight into the close working relationship that JLB enjoyed with his students, and the kind of research that they jointly carried out:

'But it was Dr JLB Smith, Senior Lecturer in Organic Chemistry, who really inspired me like no other. We did not have any organic chemistry in the first year and it was he who introduced us to this new branch of the subject. "Doc" Smith's lectures were meticulously prepared and delivered. Periodically he would stop and ask the class a question to ensure that we were following what he said. He used a didactic approach to teaching and did not take kindly to too much disturbance. The underlying principles of organic chemistry were then poorly understood and one had to learn a large number of apparently unrelated reactions' (Davies-Coleman, *in litt.*, 2017).

'"Doc" Smith was also in charge of the Chem II quantitative inorganic practicals. He was very particular about how we used the balances. Weights had to be meticulously set in decreasing order on the one pan and during titrations the burette taps had to be turned with the left hand while stirring the flask with the other. There was no talking so the atmosphere in the lab was rather strained but you did learn to concentrate in what you were doing. Amongst the experiments I particularly recall was the determination of the percentage silver in a tickey (3 penny piece) when you had to dissolve your own coin in nitric acid and then titrate the solution with standard sodium chloride solution. This experiment was definitely illegal, but interesting' (Davies-Coleman, pers. comm., 2017).

'During the third term he took us for Qualitative Organic Analysis using a book he had written [Smith, 1940a]. Unknown compounds were determined

23

by a set procedure. Early on in this a sodium fusion was required to deter-mine the presence of nitrogen, sulfur and halogens and he took great pains to show us how to carry out this potentially dangerous experiment efficiently and safely. Our compound was then separated into various groups, e.g. bases by solubility in mineral acid, etc. A final melting point for solids or boiling point for liquids confirmed the structure by consulting the literature.

'I had decided to do my MSc thesis with "Doc" Smith, who wrote to me in the new year asking me to find out all I could about *Agathosma apiculata*, sea-buchu. Has its essential oil been investigated? Where does it grow? I consulted the University Library, and Botany department for books on essential oils and found that the essential oil of this plant had not been studied. ... *Agathosma apiculata* was collected at the Kowie and steam-distilled. ... The buchu oil I was preparing had a strong and unpleasant odour which soon permeated the chemistry building and surrounding areas. I used to change to a boiler-suit at work in an effort to keep the smell off my regular clothes. In later years when I met fellow-students they invariably pulled my leg regarding this smell and I became known as Buchu Rivett!

'One Saturday afternoon in April, much to my surprise, I discovered that my buchu oil contained sulfur so I hurried up to "Doc" Smith's house and told him. He was equally excited and said he wasn't aware of the presence of sulfur in any plants of this family, Rutaceae. Moreover, the oil contained considerable amounts of sulfur which was later shown to vary according to the time of year the plant was collected and distilled, 8.5% in August and 11% in March. ... By the end of the year I had prepared a draft of my thesis which I sent to "Doc". He scrutinised it, made numerous alterations and told me to start again. In my writing he taught me a great deal about organizing one's material and being punctilious in what you say. Anyway, my thesis was received in time for the next April graduation and I got my degree with distinction. When our paper was latter published in the S.A. Royal Society Proceedings it received the Marloth Medal.'

Doug Rivett also authored an article in the *Ichthos* newsletter entitled 'JLB Smith, the chemist, as I knew him', in which he shares his observations on Smith's character:

'When I came to Rhodes in 1939, Doc Smith, as he was generally known, was in his early forties, at the height of his intellectual powers, and Senior

Lecturer in organic chemistry. ... He was a superb lecturer. His lectures were carefully prepared and clearly delivered. On such occasions he wore the customary black gown. But his ideas on the theory of organic chemistry reactions were unorthodox (as I discovered later), although in all fairness it should be remembered that this facet of the subject was still in its rudimentary stages. He made frequent use of problems in his lectures (of which I too am a great believer) and had written a book on the subject, *Numerical and Constitutional Exercises in Organic Chemistry* in collaboration with Professor Rindl of Bloemfontein.

'Naturally he ran the organic chemistry practicals for the second and third years where one was taught the usual techniques of filtration, crystallisation, distillation, etc. used in preparing organic compounds. In addition, we identified unknown compounds using his book *A Simplified System of Organic Identification* (1940). He was also in charge of the quantitative and qualitative inorganic practicals. Over the years he had devised his own scheme for qualitative analysis which was used and improved by successive classes of students. The first edition of his book *A System of Qualitative Inorganic Analysis* appeared in 1941. I find it interesting to read in my copy the alterations my class had to make as it shows how he continually strove to improve shortcomings in the scheme. It should be stressed that the spectroscopic methods of analysis in use today were unknown then and the methods we used are nowadays referred to as "wet chemistry".

'It must be emphasized that while Doc Smith was carrying his full share of teaching duties in the Chemistry Department his ichthyological plate was overflowing! He had identified the first live coelacanth early in 1939 and must have found far too few hours available in his day for all he wanted to do. He used to arrive in the Chemistry Department ... punctually at 9.30 a.m. after several hours work in the morning at home, always dressed in a light grey suit. He wasn't a sociable person, not easily approachable, stern and unsmiling. For him life was a serious business with time to be used to the full.

'But he had a lot of time for his students, especially the better ones. Once a year on a Sunday morning the third years were invited to tea at his house on Rhodes Avenue. I am not aware of any other staff member who did this. He also had the interests of the broader student community at heart and in 1943 became chairman [of] the Students (now Sports) Union even though he was a very busy person.

'I got to know Doc even better during my MSc year where for my thesis he put me on to examining the volatile oil of *Agathosma apiculata*, a pungent shrub growing on the coast at Port Alfred. It was then that I discovered that he suffered from bouts of stomach upset, the result of dysentery originating from the East Africa campaign during World War I, that left him weak and very frustrated.

'Doc was extremely apprehensive of cyanide and very sensitive to its smell. On one occasion, minutes after starting a second year lecture, he suddenly ordered the class to leave the room immediately as he smelt cyanide. This was later traced to an open bottle. It is well known that people vary considerably in their sensitivity to the smell of highly toxic hydrogen cyanide gas. Some cannot smell it at all. Needless to say the class was filled with fear and trepidation! The occasion made a deep impression on at least one member of the class as he recounted the event to me fifty years later!' (Rivett, 1996).

According to Mike Davies-Coleman (pers. comm., 2017), who studied chemistry at Rhodes University under Doug Rivett and later served as Professor of Organic Chemistry and Head of the Chemistry Department:

'JLB Smith was a rigorous analytical organic chemist who demanded non-negotiable accuracy from undergraduate chemists in analytical practicals. A student was only able to go onto the next practical if his (I guess there were very few hers around back then in the thirties and forties at university certainly in chemistry) analytical mastery passed muster with JLB Smith. JLB Smith also demanded complete silence in undergraduate practicals and there was no talking allowed.'

He further comments:

'Chemistry was a robust science back in those days with plenty of bangs and copious clouds of fumes and gases. It was not for the faint hearted. I know because Doug was fearless in the lab and was always keen to do chemistry on the robust scale. He would have got this from his training under JLB Smith.'

As a young staff member of RUC, Smith participated in sport and games (mainly tennis and bridge) and coached the college's 3rd to 5th rugby teams. He was also an active member and eventually Chairman of the RUC Sports Union well into the 1940s (K van Zyl, pers. comm., 2017). About 50 years later, on 21st October 1974, his second wife, Margaret, wrote to John Donald, Secretary of the Sports Union:

> 'I am both touched and delighted to have been elected an Honorary Vice-President of the Rhodes University Sports Union. You are probably unaware of the fact that, when we were first married, my husband, Professor J.L.B. Smith, was Chairman of the Sports Union (called Athletics Union at that time). In this capacity he did the work of the Sports Officer – supervised the staff and, with Joe King, was responsible for the remolding of the Great Field.'

JLB Smith, Chairman of the RUC Sports Union, at a swimming gala in 1943.
Front right: Four-year old William Smith.

One of JLB's contemporaries on the Sports Union committee (a Mr Sutherland) regarded him as 'a bit odd', even 'slightly round the bend', and 'an honest but sickly man' (SATV documentary, 1976). In 1931 an important athletics event took place on the Great Field at RUC. Danie Joubert, a student at Stellenbosch University, equalled the world 100 yards dash record of 9.4 seconds. The official time-keeper was JLB Smith (K van Zyl, pers. comm., 2017)!

Although his passion for fishing was developing into a serious, even an overwhelming interest, 'Doc' Smith was – officially – still fully occupied in the teaching of, and research in, organic chemistry. In spite of his extraordinary capacity for work, something would have to give.

CHAPTER 5

Henriette Pienaar

First marriage, and raising a young family

T HE ONLY hint gleaned by even the closest associates of JLB Smith in Grahamstown that he had had a first marriage was a comment in the 1976 SATV documentary *They called him Doc*. There it is stated that he was depressed in the 1930s following, among other things, the failure of his first marriage. His second wife, Margaret, told colleagues that JLB had enjoyed fishing with 'his son, Bob' – clearly not William, the only child from his marriage to Margaret. The best conclusion one could draw was that Bob was the issue of an earlier marriage. The name Henriette Cecile Pienaar is scarcely recorded in any publications that review the life and work of JLB Smith except, very briefly, in Thomson (1991) and Weinberg (1999). As a result, details about his first wife are revealed here for the first time (see the Acknowledgements, page vii, for the author's sources).

Four Afrikaans families made a significant contribution to the development of education and theology in the early years of the Union of South Africa: the Murrays, Pienaars, Neethlings and Hofmeyrs. It was from this pioneering stock that Henriette Cecile Pienaar was born on 12th November 1897 in Somerset West.

Henriette's maternal grandfather, Dominee Johannes Henoch Neethling, came from a very prominent family. He married Maria Murray, daughter of the original Scottish immigrant Andrew Murray, and was founder, with John Murray and NJ Hofmeyr, of Victoria College, which became Stellenbosch University in 1918. Her paternal grandfather, Barend Theodorus Pienaar, was a highly respected sheep farmer who decided not to join the Great Trek, instead buying and farming the new merino sheep, and becoming very wealthy. On one of his four farms he established the village of Nieu-Bethesda in 1875, now an important cultural destination.

Theo Pienaar, Henriette's eldest brother, Springbok rugby captain in 1921.

Henriette's father, Pieter Johannes ('JP') Pienaar (1860–1952), who was born in Nieu-Bethesda on 1st October 1860, was a prominent Dutch Reformed Church Minister in Somerset West for 45 years (1891–1936). He married Henrietta Christiana Neethling (1864–1955), an actress, author, poet and musician. They had 13 children, nine boys and four girls, of whom Theodorus ('Theo') Barend Pienaar (1888–1960) was the eldest, and Henriette, the sixth child and second daughter. They were known as the 'Rugby Pienaars' because of the size of their family and the fact that seven of her brothers played provincial rugby. Theo, in particular, excelled in the sport and was a member of Boy Morkel's famed 1914 Western Province team, considered by many to be the finest provincial team ever assembled in South Africa. In 1921, at the age of 33 years, he led the first Springbok rugby team to tour Australia and New Zealand.

JLB Smith's father, Joseph Smith, was Postmaster in Stellenbosch and then Somerset West at the time that his son was a scholar at Diocesan College in Cape Town (1912–1914). The Smiths lived across the road (Lourens Street) from the Pienaar parsonage in Somerset West – a huge property that extended to the banks of the Lourens River. The proximity of their homes means that JLB (or 'Len', as he was known at this time) and Henriette would almost certainly have met. They are also likely to have known each other during JLB's student years at Victoria College (1915–1918) and it is likely that they corresponded during his years at Cambridge University (1919–1922). The fact that they had known each other for so long before their marriage explains how their wedding could take place so soon after Smith returned to South Africa from England in late 1922.

In the 1976 SATV documentary it is stated that Smith returned from England 'with his young wife' but there is no evidence of this, and Henriette's family are unaware of her travelling to England at that time. There is also apparently no correspondence between JLB Smith and Henriette in the archives of the SAIAB and Rhodes University Archive in Grahamstown. JLB Smith and Henriette might have chosen to dispose of all the correspondence between them, or Henriette's role in his career might have been purged from the record or ignored. Several correspondents who knew Margaret Smith in her later years commented that she had 'cleansed' the archives in both the Ichthyology Institute in Grahamstown and the South African Museum (now Iziko) in Cape Town in order, in their opinion, to cast JLB Smith in a positive light. Margaret is also known to have disposed of the so-called 'Crackpot files' in the Department of Ichthyology, which included oddball letters from people around the world asking for unrelated advice, disputing the theory of evolution, expressing disrespect for JLB, etc.

Henriette Pienaar (far right, back row) with her sisters and friends, in the 1920s.

At the age of 25, Henriette married JLB Smith on 22nd August 1922 in her father's parsonage in Somerset West. By all accounts, the Pienaars did not approve of her choice of partner as, although they respected JLB's academic achievements, they did not find him to be a likeable character and objected to his somewhat eccentric behaviour. For instance, when he brought Henriette to Somerset West shortly before the birth of their second child, Cecile, he would lie '… half naked, with only a pair of shorts on, on a long table standing beside the tennis court in the gardens of 'De Oude Pastorie' in Lourens Street. At the time he was following a special diet of eating nothing but paw-paws' (A-J Tötemeyer, pers. comm., 2017). He would also walk about the house 'almost naked with only a type of nappy on like Mahatma Ghandi' (A-J Tötemeyer, pers. comm., 2017). After the marriage Henriette was displaced from her family and disappeared with this strange scientist into the relative oblivion (as far as the Pienaars were concerned) of the English university town of Grahamstown.

Henriette was tall and elegant with a fair 'Irish' complexion and long black hair that was always tied back in a natural look, rather than the elaborate, 'permed' hair-dos fashionable at the time. Although she was intelligent, and qualified as a nursery school teacher, she was not academically inclined and would probably have regarded JLB Smith's double life as a lecturer-cum-ichthyologist as an imposition on their family life rather than an exciting challenge. She was not lean and athletic – as JLB and Margaret were in their youth – but tended towards plumpness after their marriage, and had no interest in sports or angling, although she did enjoy casual outdoor activity and relaxing days at the beach.

Henriette's nickname to intimate friends was 'Hatta' but her parents and siblings called her 'Ha-Riette', with a soft 'h'. According to several close family members (see Acknowledgements, page vii), Henriette was a lovable, happy, 'always smiling' personality in her youth, and a soft-hearted, home-loving, family-oriented person as an adult. She was quiet, sincere and generous, and enjoyed homely activities, such as knitting, sewing, reading, drawing, gardening (especially with geraniums), cooking and baking, as well as the company of children.

Henriette was apparently a good mother and would have created a stable home for Smith during their 14-year marriage at an important formative stage in his career as a young academic. In the 1920s their lives would probably have been predictable and comfortable and, dare one say it, happy; although, later in life, JLB Smith would comment 'As far as I am concerned, a happy person is a useless person. It is only people who are discontented and dissatisfied who achieve something' (SATV documentary, 1976).

JLB Smith with his eldest son, Bob, daughter-in-law Gerd and their children.

JLB and Henriette had three children. For the confinements of the first two, Robert and Cecile, JLB took Henriette to her parents in Somerset West so that her mother could take care of her and the Pienaar family midwife could handle the births.

Robert ('Bob') Brierley Smith was born on 20th July 1923 in Somerset West. He later married a Norwegian, Gerd Follesø, a teacher, in 1951. He was deputy principal or principal of schools in Mtunzini, Park Rynie, Howick and Estcourt in KwaZulu-Natal, and a lecturer at the Durban Teachers Training College. Bob and Gerd adopted two children, Donald (1958) and Cathy (1960). Donald became one of JLB's favourite 'gillies' (fishing assistants) and went angling with him at the Knysna Heads from dawn to dusk when Bob and his family spent Christmas holidays there between 1957 and 1967. Bob retired to George in the mid-1970s, where he died in July 2009.

Cecile ('Pats') Brierley Smith was born on 10th January 1925 in Somerset West and was a Wren in the Second World War. She went on to marry Edwin ('Eddy') Thurston, a pilot, in 1924 and they had six children. Cecile, who died in 1996, was devoted to her father and very close to her brother, Bob.

JLB and Henriette's relationship started to deteriorate in the late 1920s and early 1930s when he followed his medical doctor's advice to spend more time out-of-doors and developed his passion for fishing and healthy exercise. According to members of the Pienaar family who were interviewed, there was considerable friction in the Smith household during these years.

Many years later Margaret, JLB's second wife, commented, 'I never did get into sewing much – I think my husband didn't like it because whenever he and his first wife had a disagreement she'd go and sit at her machine and sew furiously!' (Horning, 1979).

Their third child, Shirley Brierley Smith, was born in Grahamstown, 12 years after their marriage and just two years before their divorce. She would later marry Johannes Hugo Viljoen, a veterinarian, although the marriage did not last. They had three children, and chemistry continued to run in the family as Shirley's second son, Murray Viljoen, holds a doctorate in chemistry, just like his grandfather. Shirley died in the Strand on 2nd June 2018 at the age of 84 years.

Shirley Brierley Smith (aged 7 years), JLB Smith's youngest daughter from his first marriage to Henriette Pienaar.

In the 1935 Voters' Roll JLB Smith ('owner') and Henriette Cecile Smith ('occupier') are recorded as living in Gilbert Street, Grahamstown (F Way-Jones, pers. comm., 2017). The reality was, however, that Henriette's personality and aspirations seem to have been diametrically opposite to those of JLB Smith in the mid-1930s, at a time when he was increasingly consumed in the practice of his dual careers, and regularly embarked on rugged fishing trips.

JLB was apparently 'furious' when he heard about Henriette's third pregnancy (with Shirley), which didn't fit into his plans at all (A-J Tötemeyer pers. comm., 2017). They were separated for several months in 1936 before their divorce (National Archives) when Henriette, at JLB Smith's suggestion, visited her family in Somerset West to show them their young daughter, Shirley, aged two – and never returned.

The divorce in 1937 was a disgrace on the Pienaar family and devastating for Henriette. For a while after this, Pats and Bob continued to live in Grahamstown with their father and his new wife Margaret, but Shirley stayed with Henriette and only met the family once, many years later, during a reunion in Knysna.

Henriette relocated to Pretoria for a year, where she lived with her sister Helene, and helped raise her children. She then moved to 10 Union Avenue, Pinelands, in Cape Town, where she bought a house with the divorce settlement she had received from JLB Smith. She rented out rooms in this house, and eventually the whole house, in order to generate income, as she received no steady income after the divorce. At one stage she worked temporarily at the Princess Alice Orthopaedic Hospital in Retreat, Cape Town, which she helped to transform into a happy convalescent home for children of all cultures. She eventually moved to Gordon's Bay where she cared for her ageing parents, who died in the 1950s.

Henriette never remarried, even though she was only 40 at the time of the divorce and lived for another 34 years. The Pienaar family remained bitter towards Smith throughout his life, even after he had achieved world fame, and refused all contact with him. Henriette died at Groote Schuur Hospital in Cape Town on 6th June 1971 at the age of 74 years, 3½ years after JLB Smith had died.

Henriette was JLB Smith's wife for 14 years, bore him three children, and sustained him during his formative years as an ichthyologist, yet he never mentioned her again in his extensive writings.

CHAPTER 6

Buchu to blacktails
Transition to ichthyology

SMITH HAD spent most of his childhood inland in the dry Karoo and developed his love of angling only after his family had travelled by ox-wagon to Knysna in 1903 and he saw 'this silvery thing jump out of the water' (Smith, 1956). Margaret relates, in the 1976 SATV documentary, *They called him Doc*, that after they returned inland, the young JLB was so frustrated that he couldn't go fishing that he once 'fished' for the neighbour's fowls with a hook and line, but was caught and punished! Smith later told friends that the first fish he caught as a small boy was a blacktail, *Diplodus sargus*, in Knysna lagoon; from then on he never lost his passion for angling (W Smith, pers. comm., 2017). In the chapter on 'Seabreams' authored by JLB and Margaret Smith in *Smiths' Sea Fishes* (Smith & Heemstra, 1986), the blacktail is described as 'a voracious and cunning fish that will take almost any bait, but is not easily hooked in clear water or with coarse tackle. About the best fighter of our inshore angling fishes'. Later in life, angling became a form of recreation that helped heal his bruised spirit and tired body.

From the mid-1920s onwards, when he was a chemistry lecturer at Rhodes University College (RUC), and known by his colleagues as 'Len', JLB organised fishing holidays along the coast near Port Alfred, taking selected students by train and then ox-wagon to remote fishing spots, where they camped out. These fishing camps were disciplined and well organised and it was considered a privilege to be invited on them. JLB had also further developed his interest in bee-keeping and made his own bee hives. He was reputed to spend hours watching the

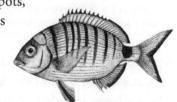

Blacktail, *Diplodus sargus*.

JLB Smith with his catch near Hamburg, Eastern Cape, in the 1920s.

JLB Smith in the 1920s on the ox-wagon in which he went fishing near Hamburg.

bees fly to and fro and observing the dance that they performed when they returned to the hive and communicated to other bees where they had collected their pollen.

Smith became informally involved in the Albany Museum's fish collection from the late 1920s onwards and began methodically to catalogue and classify the collection. By 1937 he had become an authority on Eastern Cape marine and freshwater fishes (Gon, 2002). By 1938, according to Margaret Smith (1969), he had given up all active sports (except walking and angling) and now focused entirely on his research on chemistry and fishes. He was a Trustee of the Albany Museum in Grahamstown from 1930 to 1955, and Chairman from 1946 to 1947, during a very busy time in his life. He also served on the committee of the local government school for boys (now Graeme College) from 1934 to at least 1940.

To improve access to his favourite fishing spots, in 1928 JLB Smith acquired his 'Blue House' fishing cottage adjacent to Knysna Lagoon, a simple abode made of corrugated iron cladding on a timber frame. As one of his many 'real life' chemistry experiments, he painted it with Reckitt's Blue (a laundry detergent with blue fabric brighteners comprising ultramarine and baking soda) to keep the mosquitoes away as it was surrounded on two sides by the tidal mudflats of the Salt River. He designed a replacement Blue House (which still exists) in 1944 but it was completed only in 1950, at a cost of £1,300 (Rhodes University Archive) and is now a guesthouse. The new house included a small laboratory with shelves piled high with bottled specimens and a simple microscope on the lab bench. There were also 'tons of books and lots of weather, water temperature, atmospheric pressure, depths, etc of the Lagoon and fishing logs depicted on several types of maps in the main house as well as the "lab"' (J and W Smith, pers. comm., 2018). JLB spent many happy summer holidays fishing in the Knysna Lagoon and 'Narrows', but spent most of his winter holidays on the coast nearer Grahamstown, at Xora Mouth and elsewhere.

In the 1976 SATV documentary, Margaret Smith commented that JLB was so passionate about angling that, 'If he was in his coffin, and he heard a reel scream, he would sit up!' She also said that angling was one of the few 'normal' things that JLB regularly did, and

Drawing by Liz Tarr of Keppel Barnard.

that, when she could sense that he was under excessive strain, they would escape to Knysna so that he could go fishing and relax. She also recalled an event when they were travelling back to Grahamstown by train from Lourenço Marques (now Maputo) after an exhausting expedition during which they had handled over 30,000 fishes, either caught by them and their helpers or bought in fish markets. A weary JLB remarked to Margaret, 'I would like to go to Knysna and fish'.

While he was still lecturing in chemistry, JLB's childhood enthusiasm for fishing was growing in intensity, even bordering on obsession. But he soon found that he could not identify many of the marine fishes that he caught, as the available literature was inadequate and he was far removed from any practising ichthyologists. Motivated to improve the situation, Smith began to publish scientific papers that revised the classification of local marine and freshwater fishes and brought new distributional records and new species to the attention of the scientific community.

During the 1930s he maintained a prodigious correspondence with Keppel Barnard (1887–1964), the accomplished taxonomist and later Director of the South African Museum (now the Iziko South African Museum) in Cape Town (Gon, 1994), sometimes writing to him on a daily basis (Gon, 2004), requesting literature, illustrations and advice. Without modern amenities such as copying machines, Barnard would hand-write copies of species descriptions, trace drawings, and send them to Smith (Gon, 2002).

In a letter to Barnard dated 20th April 1934 Smith jokingly wrote, 'My papers should really all appear as by "Barnard (with Smith)"', but they never

37

co-authored any publications. In fact, throughout his long ichthyology career, the only person with whom Smith co-authored a scientific paper, book or chapter in a book (or even a popular article) was his second wife, Margaret! This is in contrast to his papers on chemistry, most of which were co-authored with other scientists.

Keppel Barnard published over 200 scientific papers (similar to Smith's prodigious output), including important monographs on marine fishes (in 1925, 1927, 1948), freshwater fishes (1943), and crustaceans and molluscs. He had a reputation for working very fast: '… the man who, it was said, could describe three new species a day and never change a word, the man who drew new types free-hand on scraps of paper and sent them off for publication' (Brown, 1982).

Smith held Barnard in high esteem and once wrote to him that he had '… admiration for your intellect which I rank second to none in your field in the Southern Hemisphere' (Gon, 2004), but the sentiment wasn't always reciprocated, as Mike Brown observes:

> 'I never knew him to say an unkind word about anyone. The closest he ever came to it was in an article in which he wrote about the discovery of the first living Coelacanth by Miss Courtenay-Latimer, remarking that it was then "sent to someone in Grahamstown". He could not stand J.L.B. Smith, but chose to ignore his existence rather than write something disparaging about him. … There was a great deal to be learnt from Keppel Barnard, but I think the most important was scientific humility. Science to him was a constant adventure and he could not understand that there were those to whom research was an ego-boosting experience' (Brown, 1982).

It seems that Barnard approved of 'Smith the avid backroom scientist' in the 1930s but, like many other scientists of the day who preferred to slave away in relative obscurity, he disapproved of the high profile that Smith (with the help of the media) fashioned for himself after the discovery of the first coelacanth.

There is no doubt that Smith did seek publicity for his work, but there was good reason for it – he needed financial and logistical support to achieve his ambitious plans to mount lengthy fish-collecting expeditions up the East African coast and to publish lavishly illustrated books on fishes that would be useful to both scientists and laypeople. Barnard was a prolific writer and highly influential scientist, but he published almost all his work in the *Annals of the*

South African Museum and other scientific journals, and his three 'popular' books were all written in technical language and illustrated in black-and-white.

JLB Smith also had a major fall-out with Dr Cecil von Bonde, Director of the Marine Biological Survey (MBS) in Cape Town from 1928, especially over the poor curation of a valuable marine fish collection made for the MBS using the research vessel *SS Pickle* (Gon, 2002). In a letter dated 1ˢᵗ September 1947, Smith commented, 'When I think of those thousands of valuable specimens that have been lost I could weep, or alternatively cut a few throats. It is one of the greatest scientific crimes I have ever heard of.' Von Bonde's retort was that Smith's work was '… of little value to the Fishing Industry' (Gon, 2002). Many years later, in a letter dated 18ᵗʰ January 1959, Smith labelled his old nemesis, now Director of the Fisheries Development Corporation, as '… an arrogant conservative, a pessimist and a defeatist' in connection with the latter's criticism of plans to build a marine research facility in Durban.

The American ichthyologist Carl Hubbs (1968) described Smith's career at this stage, 'Since 1931, following an initial career in chemistry, he had been publishing short faunal and revisionary papers on marine fishes of South Africa, thereby establishing for himself a modest reputation as a descriptive ichthyologist'. Of his later career, Hubbs (1968) wrote, he 'issued a seemingly unending stream of papers, mostly short and succinct, and generally of high quality'.

During the 1930s and until 1941, all the fish specimens that Smith collected were lodged in the Albany Museum and he did his fish research there (or at home) and published under the museum's name. Then, on the afternoon of Saturday, 6ᵗʰ September 1941, a devastating fire gutted the main building of the Albany Museum and changed the course of ichthyology in Grahamstown. Practically all the exhibited collections, including many fishes and several type specimens (a unique specimen on which the description of a new species of animal – or plant – is based) that had been collected by JLB Smith, were destroyed (Gon, 2002, 2004).

Fortunately, fire fighters isolated the two newer wings of the museum where the wet collections were held and students and town people, supervised by JLB and Margaret Smith, formed a human chain that quickly removed the collections from those buildings that were still threatened by the fire. The fire not only destroyed irreplaceable holdings and displays in the Albany Museum but also caused a major financial crisis during the difficult war years (and the recession that followed) from which the museum took decades to recover (Skelton, pers. comm., 2017).

The fish collections were initially taken from the Albany Museum to RUC for safe-keeping, which immediately raised the issue of the provision of adequate and secure accommodation (and professional curation). The crisis was exacerbated when the Smiths resumed their expeditions after the Second World War and brought considerable amounts of material back to Grahamstown. For instance, their two expeditions in 1946 yielded over 1,000 specimens, including 93 species new to the collection and 17 species new to science (Gon, 2004). Soon they had one of the world's best collections of East African fishes. The critical situation strengthened Smith's case for his appointment as Professor of Ichthyology and for the establishment of a Department of Ichthyology at RUC.

Eventually the freshwater fish collection was returned to the Albany Museum when Rex Jubb moved there from the Department of Ichthyology in 1961, but the marine fish collections, which had mainly been made by JLB Smith, were retained by RUC and are now in the holdings of the South African Institute for Aquatic Biodiversity (SAIAB). The freshwater fish collection has since also been moved from the Albany Museum to the SAIAB.

JLB Smith timidly published his first short ichthyological paper, 'New and little known fishes from the south and east coasts of Africa', in the *Records of the Albany Museum* in 1931. At the time South Africa had no scientists studying marine fishes, as Dr Keppel Barnard (1887–1964) had published most of his marine fish papers by 1927 (although his last papers on freshwater and marine fishes appeared as late as 1943 and 1948), and declared that he was 'sick of fishes' (MM Smith, 1979). Barnard typified the dying breed of polymath scientists of the 19th and early 20th centuries and was quite happy to shift his research focus from fishes to crustaceans and molluscs, which were his real interest. He retired as Director of the South African Museum in March 1956 and died in 1964 (Gon, 2002).

Between 1931 and 1945 Smith published 28 papers on fishes as well as, in 1937, a chapter on fishes in the *Guide to the Vertebrate Fauna of the Eastern Cape*, published by the Albany Museum. JLB illustrated his first scientific paper himself with what he considered to be reasonable sketches but which are, in hindsight, simplistic and inaccurate. Dr HW Parker, a herpetologist working at the British

Museum (Natural History) (now the Natural History Museum) in London, who had been a student with Smith at Cambridge University, wrote to him saying that he was surprised to see a chemist publishing a paper on fishes. He commented that the text was quite good but the illustrations were terrible! For his next fish paper, also published in 1931, Smith spent many hours drawing and redrawing the illustrations, and produced an adequate rendition of a new species of lanternfish, *Myctophum (Nasolychnus) florentii.*

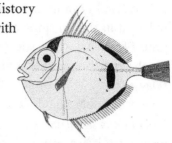

JLB Smith's diagrammatic illustration of a fish in his first publication on the topic.

JLB's publications soon attracted the attention of local and international scientists and he was appointed Honorary Curator of Fishes in the four local Eastern Cape museums in Grahamstown, Port Elizabeth, King William's Town and East London. His parallel lives not only doubled his work load but also led to entanglements with two completely different communities of people: academics and students on the one hand, and laypeople, anglers and commercial fishermen on the other.

Smith continued to illustrate his own papers until 1941 but, from 1943, in a paper entitled, 'Interesting early juvenile stadia of certain well-known South African fishes', published in the *Transactions of the Royal Society of South Africa*, his young wife, Margaret, took over this important role. Little did she know that this humble beginning would lead to a distinguished career in scientific illustration. Even though Smith pursued his studies on fishes part-time, he did receive official recognition for this work as, from 1933 to 1945, the Research Grants Board in Johannesburg allocated £100 per year towards his ichthyological research (Rhodes University Archive). The functions of this Board were taken over by the CSIR in 1946.

When Smith tried to identify the fishes that he caught in the 1920s and 1930s with the few books available to him he met with little success. 'The "keys" were intelligible only to those already so expert as not to need them, so that it was a dreadful job trying to identify unknown fishes' (Smith, 1956). He set out to solve this problem and, combining his knowledge of mathematics and ichthyology – unusual for a taxonomist – he created a numerical system for identifying fishes based on counts of hard spines and soft rays in their fins, combined with scale counts along the lateral line (or lateral series if there is no lateral line) and around the body or caudal peduncle. As fishes show considerable variability in their meristic (countable) traits, this variation has to be reflected in the fin spine and ray and lateral line scale count formulae. He probably used the meristic data on fishes in Keppel Barnard's various monographs on fishes, as well as his own data, to compile these identification keys (Day, 1977).

For example, the dorsal and anal fin spine and ray formula for the elf, *Pomatomus saltatrix*, is D VII–VIII + I, 23–28; A II, 23–27; LL 90–100. This means that it has seven to eight (+ 1) hard spines and 23 to 28 soft rays in the dorsal fin (D), two hard spines and 23 to 27 soft rays in the anal fin (A), and 90 to 100 scales in the lateral line (LL). In case you catch a coelacanth, its formula is: D VIII + 30; A 27–31; LL 76–82 + 15–23. This means that it has eight hard spines and 30 soft rays in the dorsal fin, 27 to 31 soft rays (but no hard spines) in the anal fin, and 76 to 82 scales in the lateral line, with an additional 15 to 23 scales in the lateral line's extension onto the central lobe of the tail fin. The system took Smith over a year to figure out, entirely in his spare time, and he allegedly wrote out more than a million figures to compile it (Smith, 1956); but, once he had perfected it, it worked well and allowed him to identify most common species quickly and accurately. JLB commented later, 'This was a tremendous step forward, and gave me power that normally comes from much longer experience' (Smith, 1995).

Assembling what had become a huge body of scientific discovery, in 1949 Smith produced one of the first comprehensive colour-illustrated tomes on southern African vertebrates: *The Sea Fishes of Southern Africa*. This was published after Austin Roberts' 1940 *The Birds of South Africa*, but before equivalent books on the other vertebrate groups (amphibians, freshwater fishes, reptiles and mammals).

In the various editions of the *Sea Fishes* book a 'Fin Formula Key to Bony Fishes' is given for most species, with the least variable feature (the number of anal fin spines) given in the left-hand column followed by the other traits (dorsal fin spines, anal fin soft rays, and dorsal fin soft rays) in increasing order of variability. For most species, this identification key works very well and can be used by non-specialists, but fishes are such variable creatures that there are inevitably some complications. For instance, the dorsal fin may be split into two or more parts, the last soft ray may be divided at its base into two (but only counts as one), and spines or rays may not be completely developed and easily visible in young fishes. The fin spine and ray and scale count formula nevertheless provides a quantitative way to identify most fishes to the species level, a method that is not applicable to most other vertebrate groups. Some regard Smith's key as a more important contribution to ichthyology than the discovery of the coelacanth.

There was some disdain in academic circles regarding what came to be known as Smith's 'D 'n A formula'. In the 1960s Dr Frank Talbot at the South African Museum in Cape Town, as part of the ongoing repartee between marine biologists in Cape Town and Grahamstown, sent a goldfish to JLB Smith with a note to say that the dorsal and anal fin counts didn't work; JLB was offended by the prank and blew his top (N Tietz, pers. comm., 2017)!

But the key was welcomed by anglers and commercial fishermen and is still widely used today. In the flyleaf text in the 1977 edition of the *Sea Fishes* book it states, '… he effectively reduced 'nature' to numbers and made the identification of any fish – on the basis of its fin count – a simple matter. … His Main Key is regarded by many as his greatest contribution to ichthyology'.

Smith even devised formulae for calculating the weight of a bony fish, or shark, from its length, taking into account the extent to which the fish's body shape diverges from being a double cone. To calculate the weight of a bony fish in pounds, the greatest girth (in inches) is squared, multiplied by the length in inches, and then divided by a figure between 700 and 1,000 (obtained from a table), depending on how much the body tapers. For sharks, the formula is: $8.1 \times L. 2.8 \times 10-5$, with 'L' being the length in inches.

Smith also introduced a numbering system for marine fishes in *The Sea Fishes of Southern Africa*, which was continued in later editions, and is still widely used by scientists and anglers today. The *Smiths' Sea Fishes* number comprises the number of the fish family followed by the species number after a decimal point. Due to taxonomic revisions, the fish numbers in subsequent revisions have changed from those in the original 1949 edition. A conversion table from the old to the new fish numbers is therefore provided in *Smiths' Sea Fishes*. As examples, the new numbers for some selected species are 1.1 (sixgill hagfish), 14.1 (great white shark), 31.1 (sixgill stingray), 35.1 (coelacanth), 178.1 (elf or shad) and 270.4 (trunkfish).

JLB Smith, the expert angler, ca 1930.

JLB Smith was, of course, an expert angler who combined his knowledge of fishes, aquatic habitats and organic chemistry to outwit his prey. When fishing from a boat, he made his own sinkers and traces, and never let his line, hook or bait wallow in the bilges where they could acquire 'foreign tastes'. He was also aware that the pheromones (hormones released into the outside environment) of humans might repel fish if they were detected on the bait, and even postulated that the relative success of women anglers might be because their pheromones contain more fish attractants (Bruton, 2017b)! He kept meticulous notes on what he caught, and where, as well as on the state of the tide and phase of the moon. He was also renowned for his success in predicting what he would catch on a given day. He filled his boat on days when other anglers caught nothing and seemed to be able to land a given prey at will. Smith (1977) also waxed philosophical about angling:

> 'The angler is in many ways a wise and fortunate man for, though it is not generally realised, angling is virtually the only remaining method in any civilised area whereby men in numbers may legitimately satisfy the primitive urge to secure meat by direct action.'

However, as this author stated in his autobiography, *When I was a Fish – Tales of an Ichthyologist*:

> 'It is almost sacrilegious to say so, as JLB Smith is a demi-god in South African ichthyology circles, but he also caught, with rod and line, far more fishes than necessary. Judging by the groaning ropes of fishes that he hooked off the southern and eastern Cape coasts, portrayed in photographs in the Ichthyology archives, he was one of the most insatiable anglers of his day. He could not have eaten all the fishes that he caught, nor did he need so many replicates for his scientific collections.'

Although JLB did catch prodigious numbers of fishes he was also a 'fair' angler who tried to level the playing fields between 'predator' and prey. He used light tackle and small hooks and made optimal use of his knowledge of fish behaviour, habitat preferences, activity patterns and bait preferences. He was also very conscious of the factors that scared fishes away, such as noise in the boat. He rubbed his hands and fishing line in fish guts before casting and insisted on complete silence while fishing. He also released fish that had only been hooked in the mouth (as they could recover) but kept those that had been hooked in the throat or stomach. He quickly despatched those fishes that he kept, and broke off one or two gill arches to allow the fish to bleed, which improved their flavour.

Bob, JLB's son from his first marriage with Henriette Pienaar, had this to say about JLB Smith the angler:

'From 1926 to 1941 I fished with my father, or was with him at Knysna during the Christmas holidays. … From about the age of 35, my father seldom used heavy tackle. We did a lot of sea fishing using river tackle and a drift bait, and caught many fish. A fish of two or three pounds [0.9–1.3 kilograms] took some handling, it was exciting, and it also gave the fish a sporting chance of escape. J.L.B. Smith did enjoy solitude, whether it was from the rocks, the beach or the boat. He was first and foremost an angler, and a very good one. Fishing was an abiding passion with him – he enjoyed catching them, outwitting them and also eating them.

'But he found it frustrating and also infuriating when he collected a specimen which he could not identify from the existing literature; from there it was but a short step to the point when he began collecting specimens and working to do something about the scientific side. He had that sort of enquiring mind. For health reasons, he had to do a lot of walking. In very short order he could identify and name every plant that grew in the veld near Grahamstown; he also became interested in the proteaceae, which also set me going.

'Success at angling depends on so many factors: what bait to use, how to present it, where, when and how different fishes feed, and the variable factors such as barometric pressure, winds, water temperature, tidal flow, etc. My father's knowledge was gained over many years of careful observation and experimentation.

'Experiments with regard to noise were also carried out, mainly because of its effects on still-water fishing. I would submerge at different distances, and he would make noises in the boat, e.g., bang a tin, scrape a rowlock, even hurl an anchor into the water. Sound travels clearly and rapidly, especially that of an outboard motor. Unusual noise does scatter fish, and cause them to become wary. He took careful note of the configuration of sand and mud banks at low tide, and the water movement as the tide rose or fell. Likely places were tried, and those that proved successful were named and cross bearings found. Each fishing spot was used under specific conditions of tide, weather, and so on.

'While he itched to get his line into the water, J.L.B. Smith was never foolhardy. Whenever he arrived at an unknown stretch of beach, he would spend up to half an hour or more, watching the sea. Up in a sand dune, or on a high rock, well out of reach of the water, he would sit and watch, particularly if there was deep water close in. Only when he was satisfied that it was reasonably safe did he cast in.

'Tackle in the early days, i.e. from 1926 to about '35, was a light Indian cane rod, which we made ourselves, a wooden centre-pin reel with a backing of 300 yds of w ½ cord or 6 cord green line, and a 40 yd length of gut line joined very carefully to the green line. The gut had to be wet to be able to cast with it, but the 40 yds went out quite well with just the weight of the bloodworm to take it out. Later he tried the "coffee grinder" fixed spool reel, but found it irksome not to have full, direct control on the reel ... he noticed small, funnel-shaped indentations in the sand-banks exposed at low tide. We dug, and out came the bloodworm – in 1926, an absolute killer of a bait, and in 1993 still one of the best in the lagoon. He reasoned that it was superior when used whole, and quickly solved the problem of how to get it on the trace undamaged. As far as I am aware, it was he who developed a type of spiral "connector" which made it a simple process, and it was extremely efficient. Again for health reasons, he found it very difficult to dig these, so I, my stepmother (Prof Margaret Mary) and step- [half] brother William, all became adept at it.

'From Grahamstown, sea fishing spots which my father liked particularly were Xora mouth (Transkei), Igoda mouth (west of East London), and the Fish River area ... He did take some awful chances, and usually came back soaked from having had to swim out of danger. I can still remember one night when he and another fisherman came back looking shaken. They had gone into a gully from the seaward end, and were working their way towards the shore [spearing soles], when a shark, which had also gone in there for a snack, made a frantic dash for the open sea, and in the process, bowled Dad over like a ninepin ... Duiker Rock, or J.L.B. Smith rock as it is now known, and situated on the Western Head at Knysna, was far and away his dream fishing place. ... Somehow he discovered that the Western Head was private land, and not public property as was generally accepted in Knysna. He took a trip to the Deeds Office in Cape Town, confirmed that it was private, and promptly bought it, an area of 140 ha. He fished from that rock until shortly before his death.'

Smith's passion for angling even extended to using ox-wagons to reach the remotest fishing spots, and his manic work ethic allowed him to combine these different interests without compromising standards.

In the book *Old Fourlegs*, Smith (1956) admits that, to a large extent, he did not conform to the norms of society. He was an academic who was keen on fishing, and a chemist who studied fishes. But he achieved a much higher public profile than most of his academic colleagues and led an anachronistic, self-centred lifestyle, traits that fostered resentment against him in some circles. Also, unlike most academics, he was equally at home in a lecture hall or labora-tory, on a remote beach or on the tossing deck of a fishing trawler.

'I endured the miseries of small trawlers on South Africa's stormy seas, often so seasick as barely able to crawl along the slippery heaving decks to scratch among the slimy rubbish shoved aside. To the crews I was no longer a remote scientist who expected them to do his dirty work while he stayed in a com-fortable museum ashore, and they changed from indifference to interest and sometimes to enthusiasm. I went out with small line-boats and lived with the coastal trek-netters. I walked to remote lighthouses, and to coastal farms and stores (reminiscent of George Cory's epic research hikes), always talking fish, fish, fish. All this took time and effort but paid handsome dividends, and a steady stream of treasures came rolling in' (Smith, 1956).

As John Day (1977) wrote:

'"Doc" Smith became known among anglers and trawler skippers as the man who could not only name queer fish but could tell them what baits to use and where to catch them.'

Notwithstanding his ever-deepening obsession with both fishing and ichthy-ology, he was mainly preoccupied during the Second World War with teaching and researching chemistry as he had very limited opportunities to do field research on fishes. It was during this time that he wrote and published his three textbooks on chemistry, *A Simplified System of Organic Identification* (1940, with an American edition in 1943), *Numerical and Constitutional Exercises in Organic Chemistry* (1941, with a Spanish edition in 1955), and *A System of Qualitative Inorganic Analysis* (1941, with new editions in 1943, 1944 and 1949).

According to Mike Brown, who studied at the University of the Witwatersrand before moving to Rhodes University, JLB's textbooks were still in use at Wits during his first year there in 1956, some 15 years after their original publication.

Throughout JLB Smith's writings one is aware of his analytical approach to life. He is constantly counting, classifying and evaluating events and objects around him (including other people). Peter Jackson (1969), who studied chemistry as an undergraduate at Rhodes University from 1946 to 1948, recalled:

'I and my fellow-students made much use of his two "taxonomic" chemistry textbooks (Smith 1940, 1941), both essentially keys to the identification of unknown substances by progressive tests with known reagents. They show that the bent of his mind, whether in chemistry or ichthyology, always leant towards problems of identification and classification.'

JLB knew he risked running foul of the authorities by attempting to excel in two different fields simultaneously, and by placing too much emphasis on research. As he states in *Old Fourlegs*:

'University staff are normally appointed and paid for teaching, and while research is officially encouraged, anyone who devotes more than normal time to such work runs the risk of being regarded as not giving proper attention to the teaching for which he is paid. It is certainly looked on as peculiar and possibly even as reprehensible to teach in one subject and do research work in another. At the time of the first Coelacanth I was told that it is competent for the head of a University to order a member of the staff to desist from doing research work, even in his spare time, if in the opinion of the head it may be prejudicing the efficiency of this teaching work. All this is fundamentally sound. In general, no man can serve two masters; at least, not for long' (Smith, 1956).

In 1945 and 1946, when the troops returned from the War, the combination of Smith's enormous teaching work load and his private research on fishes became almost unbearable and he realised that he had arrived at a parting of the ways. He was further motivated by his ongoing difficulty working under the authority of other people and knew that he would be most productive in an environment in which he was in charge. He realised, too, that his passport out of relative obscurity in chemistry would lie in developing a leadership role in the discipline of ichthyology. Both fields made use of the scientific method – proposing hypotheses and then trying to refute them using empirical data gathered by experiment and observation – and whatever he turned his hand to would be fuelled by his insatiable curiosity and a ferocious work ethic.

At about this time he was again advised by his medical doctors to spend more time out-of-doors as he was still suffering from the aftereffects of tropical diseases he contracted during the East Africa campaign of the First World War. He embraced this challenge with relish and his scientific interests shifted towards topics that offered ample opportunities to work outdoors – fish and fishing.

By the mid-1940s he was ready to metamorphose from an organic chemist into an ichthyologist, an astonishing transformation, but one that was within his capabilities. He committed to abandoning the well-trodden path of a pure academic, and to planning his own career. The way ahead was sometimes difficult and conflict-ridden, but it eventually gave him great satisfaction. He soon found that many people supported his new career path; their support played an important role in erasing the uncertainties that he still felt about his 'big decision'.

He remained deeply interested in his teaching and research in chemistry and retained this interest into the early 1960s, according to his private correspondence. For instance, in 1960 he corresponded with Drs RA Dyer, DHS Horn and LE Codd at the Department of Agricultural Technical Services about aromatic plants and their essential oils, and commented on a list of the aromatic oils in local plants. There are also many references in his popular writings that represent 'crossovers' between the two disciplines: for instance, detailed but clear explanations of carbon-14 dating, the fossilisation process, the chemistry of fish physiology, the use of explosives, or the chemicals in bait or human skin that may attract or repel fishes.

In *Old Fourlegs* Smith (1956) comments:

'Most men find learning new things increasingly difficult after the age of thirty, and indeed I had experienced that myself in chemistry, trying to keep up with the progressive changes in theory. I started my study of fishes when already past thirty, and it was astonishing to discover that my brain soaked it up like a sponge, and even now it is still the same. I can only suppose it must be a kind of natural affinity.'

CHAPTER 7

Margaret Mary Macdonald
A new lifetime partner

MARGARET MACDONALD's father, William Chisholm Macdonald MD, FRCS (1871–1919), was born in Dunedin, New Zealand. He had recently qualified in Edinburgh as a medical doctor and was *en route* back to Dunedin when his ship docked in Simon's Town in late 1899. The Second South African War (1899–1902) had just started and Macdonald was instructed by the British authorities to break his voyage and proceed to Kimberley to provide medical services there during the siege of the British mining town by the Boers. Cut off from the outside world from October 1899 to February 1900, the town was shelled by the Boers nearly every day (except Sundays), and the casualties eventually comprised 42 dead and over 135 wounded.

While caring for the wounded at Kimberley Hospital, senior surgeon Macdonald met a young nursing sister, Helen Evelyn Zondagh (born 1877), a descendant of the Voortrekker leader, Johannes Jacobus Uys, whose origins in South Africa can be traced back to 1668. Margaret's great-great-grandmother was Sarah Uys who, as a girl of 13, had loaded her father's guns at the Battle of Blood River. Helen was to become William Macdonald's wife and Margaret's mother. She was unusually well-qualified for a woman in those days, having trained as both a teacher and a nurse, and later became mayor of Indwe, the first female mayor in the Cape Colony. She was also active in civic affairs and was the local golf champion. In an interview with Beryl Richards (1987) Margaret said, 'Mother was very like me and understood my ways. I have always taken an interest in public affairs and in working for the community in which I live and in this I follow in her footsteps'. Later, JLB Smith was to develop great respect for his mother-in-law and they had a strong relationship (J Smith, pers. comm., 2017).

William Macdonald and Helen Zondagh were married after the Second South African War ended, and settled in the village of Indwe in 1903 (Richards, 1987). Indwe, 297 kilometres north of East London in the interior of the Eastern Cape, shares the isiXhosa name of the blue crane (*Anthropoides paradiseus*), South Africa's national bird, which occurs there in large numbers.

Although Indwe is relatively insignificant today, it was an important, though rough, coal-mining centre then, and the fourth town in South Africa (after Kimberley, Johannesburg and Cape Town) to receive electricity. The 'Indwe Railway Collieries and Land Company' was formed in Kimberley in 1894, with De Beers playing a major role, and a railway line to the town was completed in March 1896. By 1899 the Indwe coal mine was producing over 100,000 tons of coal a year. Although the coal boom was short-lived, and the colliery closed in 1917 after better quality coal was discovered in the Transvaal, it was in this booming little industrial town, with its beautiful natural surroundings, that the Macdonalds set up a medical practice and raised a family in their home, 'Inverness'. They had three children: Flora (1906), Chisholm (1908) and Margaret Mary (1916).

Margaret's father was active in church and civic affairs and was a popular medical doctor, described in a memoir published shortly after his death as 'a scholarly and deep-thinking physician, but he possessed a human side, so that all could bring their troubles and none were sent away uncomforted' (*The Frontier Guardian*, Dordrecht, 8th May 1919) – traits that Margaret inherited.

Margaret Mary Macdonald (right) as a young child, early 1920s.

Margaret Mary Macdonald (known as 'Mary' as a child) was born on 26th September 1916 in Indwe, on the same day of the year as her future husband, JLB Smith (though 19 years later). (Margaret and JLB's son, William, grew up believing that all parents were born on the same date.) Sadly, William Macdonald died of a cerebral haemorrhage in Indwe on 26th April 1919. Margaret was just 2½ years old and Flora and Chisholm were 13 and 11 respectively, and their mother had to raise the three children alone by teaching and acting as a midwife. 'She opened several nursing homes in Indwe for "catching babies", as the nearest medical facilities were in Dordrecht 43 km away' (I Sholto-Douglas, pers. comm., 2016). Another disaster later struck the family when a candle lit by young Chisholm[1] set fire to the wooden stairs and 'Inverness' was burnt down, with little being saved. Many years later Margaret would give the name 'Inverness' to her home at 37 Oatlands Road, Grahamstown, where she stayed with her elder sister, Flora, from 1972 until their deaths in 1987.

Flora was educated at Collegiate Girls' High School in Port Elizabeth and then the University of Cape Town, where she studied education, and initially took up a teaching post at Indwe Primary School; her salary helped to pay Margaret's university tuition fees (which the family could ill afford) at Rhodes University College (RUC) (I Sholto-Douglas, pers. comm., 2016). In 1933, Flora married Robert Sholto-Douglas, an employee of the Receiver of Revenue, and continued her teaching career (English and Music) at Bryanstown High School and later St Catherine's in the Transvaal (now Gauteng). After Margaret commenced her university studies in Grahamstown in 1934, their mother, Helen Macdonald, moved to Florida in the Transvaal to live with Flora and her husband.

By the time Margaret reached school-going age, Indwe had developed substantially and she attended Indwe High School, where she was Head Girl and Head Scholar as well as chairman of the debating society, captain of netball and tennis, and holder of the tennis shield for girls from 1929 to 1932.[2] Margaret achieved a first-class pass in her matriculation exam, which helped her to gain entrance to RUC in Grahamstown.

Margaret was also an accomplished singer and musician and, at the 1933 Wodehouse Eisteddfod, won eight medals for singing (soprano and mezzo soprano), violin in trio, recitation, and for composing a sonnet, an English essay and a poem. She may have inherited her 'singing genes' from her father as he reportedly had an 'exceptionally fine bass voice' (*The Frontier Guardian*, 8th May 1919).

A slim Margaret Smith at the age of 40 years in the laboratory of the Department of Ichthyology in 1956.

---

1 Chisholm attended Rondebosch Boys High School and then become an attorney in Cape Town, but died tragically in a car accident in 1947, at the age of 39.

2 Margaret's class apparently included some other stellar performers, as 12 of her classmates went on to become cabinet ministers, judges or other luminaries (I Sholto-Douglas, pers. comm., 2016).

At the East London Eisteddfod in 1933 she won the gold medal for singing (girls under 17 years) and before she matriculated in 1933, she was also awarded music certificates for piano and harmony by the University of South Africa.

Margaret said of her early life that she had had a happy and carefree childhood, playing simple games of hide-and-seek with her sister, brother and cousins in the large house and spacious garden, and hiking, 'nature studying' and riding horses in the rural countryside. Music and singing were also an important part of her early upbringing and she remembered many family concerts and musicals. She learned to play the piano, like all well-educated girls of her age, but preferred singing, especially in choirs. Later, while an undergraduate at RUC, she lived in a room just above the Woods' family shop in Grahamstown after she left residence, and Muriel Woods remembers her singing frequently in the evenings (I and I Sholto-Douglas, pers. comm., 2016).

There was also a serious side to her personality, and she had a scholarly bent as a child. She took a keen interest in her parents' discussions on their careers in medicine and civic affairs, and resolved early on to become a medical doctor who could serve her community, in the footsteps of her late father. As her family had to make a considerable financial sacrifice to send her to university, she was doubly motivated to make a success of her studies. At that time one of the few ways in which a woman could study medicine was to obtain a BSc degree at any university and then register for postgraduate studies at a university with a medical faculty. The family chose RUC as it was relatively nearby and had a well-developed student residential system for girls. (Rhodes would only become a stand-alone university, independent of the University of the Cape of Good Hope, in 1951.)

Margaret Macdonald attended RUC from 1934 to 1936, during which time she was an active member of various committees and led a rich social life. In a 1976 SATV documentary she stated that she had heard about JLB Smith on her second day at Rhodes during a tour of the campus when she was told that one of the university's most famous scientists worked in the Chemistry Department – but studied fishes. Whereas others were known as 'Doc this' or 'Doc that', he was simply known throughout the campus as 'Doc'.

She did not meet him during her first year but, in her second year, he taught organic chemistry to the BSc undergraduates and also handled most of their practical work. Margaret remembered the first day that she met him, on 1st April 1935, April Fool's Day. 'Everyone was in class waiting for him to arrive … suddenly the door opened a chink and a couple of little saucers "came in" … they started giving off tear gas and there was a rush for the door.' As Margaret and a friend escaped from their doorside seats ('I had had a funny feeling about that class …') and fled up the corridor, they saw JLB around a corner convulsed with laughter (Richards, 1987).

This incident, however, did not foreshadow an informal atmosphere in the classroom. 'We were terrified of him, he was a real martinet – the beginning of wisdom is the fear of the Lord, and guess who the Lord was!' she said in the 1976 SATV documentary. She did mention, though, that he was courteous to the students and would ask their permission if he wished to speak for even a few minutes over the scheduled lecture time (Richards, 1987). In their third year JLB Smith 'became more human' but 'still kept us on our toes', and showed a gift for considering the needs of his students and addressing their problems. He was an inspiring, though strict, teacher and Margaret benefited greatly from his tuition.

She completed her BSc in 1936, majoring in physics and chemistry (with distinction) and also attended the Grahamstown Training College's School of Music, where she obtained her University Teachers' Licentiate in Music (UTLM; Singing) from the University of South Africa. In 1937 she was appointed as a Senior Demonstrator in the Chemistry Department where her duties included assisting with the practical work that JLB Smith supervised.

Much later, in 1945 and 1946, she would tutor students in chemistry at RUC and, in 1945, taught physics at St Andrew's College. When her son, William, began teaching chemistry to students in 1959 (while still a student himself), she supported him strongly. According to Trevor Letcher (pers. comm., 2017), Professor of Chemistry at Rhodes University from 1981 to 1991, Margaret also championed the hosting of school science festivals at the university.

At the end of 1937 Margaret travelled to Johannesburg, to the home of her elder sister, Flora, with the intention of starting her studies in medicine the following year at the University of the Witwatersrand. 'I was going to be a career woman', she says in the 1976 SATV documentary, 'I had no interest in marriage'. JLB Smith, however, had other ideas. He had seen in his young student and research assistant the kind of spark and grit that attracted him in a partner, and that Henriette had lacked. Even though he realised that they had very different personalities (as had been the case with JLB and Henriette), he decided to propose to Margaret and followed her to Johannesburg, where he first asked her mother and then informed Margaret 'that she was going to marry him'.

This was probably not the ideal way to propose to a headstrong young woman, and Margaret's initial, firm response was, 'Oh no, you aren't', but she eventually relented when he persisted and emphasised how much he needed her ('When JLB spoke, no-one could resist'). According to William Smith and his wife, Jenny, they had a strong mutual attraction from the outset, and Margaret also felt sorry for this 'divorced man with three children to raise, given his position in the academic community and frail health and six months to live!' (J Smith, pers. comm., 2017). It was common currency that JLB had suffered permanent damage as a result of the tropical diseases he had contracted during the First World War and from injuries he sustained in a serious bicycle accident in 1915, and he seems to have used this as further leverage to win Margaret's hand. At the age of 21 years she decided to sacrifice her medical career and agreed to marry him. Although her mother apparently assented to the match, Margaret's sister Flora 'loved saying unkind things about JLB. She never forgave him for marrying Margaret!' (Shirley Bell, pers. comm., 2017). Flora's main issue was that JLB had prevented Margaret from following in her father's footsteps and becoming a medical doctor; she was of the (well-founded) opinion that Margaret would have made a superb MD.

Margaret and JLB Smith shortly after their wedding in 1938.

Their modest wedding, a civil ceremony, took place in a church in Florida, Transvaal (now Gauteng), on 14th April 1938 and is recorded in the Registry of the Presbyterian Church (F Way-Jones, pers. comm., 2017). According to Margaret, she was nervous at the wedding as she was unsure how she would be able to live with this 'great brain', who some claimed had less than five years to live, at the most (SATV documentary, 1976). She said many years later (Horning, 1979): 'I was terrified of him before we married, and stayed a little scared all our 30-odd years together'.

She realised, though, that they complemented one another well, as she was physically strong whereas he was relatively weak. She also realised that he would give her complete freedom to become the tomboy that she had always wanted to be. She commented later (Horning, 1979):

'He had an excellent intellect, and I could never understand why he chose to marry me. For one small thing, he was 40 and I was just 21. I knew I'd have to work at our marriage from the outset, and that's the secret to success.'

And work she did, making herself indispensable.

'There were only two areas where I could [contribute]. And boy did I use them! One was my mathematical ability and the other my robust health … My husband was a very frail man, and I taught myself to row for him and run a boat for him and fish for him. I nearly throttled myself with tackle the first time I tried to cast.'

Soon she was digging up mud prawns, fishing, diving and doing the 'dirty work' on his field trips. Later, during their epic fish-collecting expeditions up the East African coast:

'Margaret did most of the physical work, keeping the camp in order, cooking, preserving the fish, even rowing the boat, yet she still found time for her fish paintings' (Bruton, 1988).

As far as her name was concerned, she later explained that, '"Mary Macdonald" sounded good, but "Mary Smith" was grim', so she adopted the married name of Margaret Smith. In later years, JLB would admonish family members who called her Mary by saying, 'There is no Mary here, her name is "Margaret"' (I Sholto-Douglas, pers. comm., 2016).[3]

At the tender age of 21 years she was catapulted into a ready-made family that included JLB's two teenage children from his marriage to Henriette, Robert

---

3   JLB's lighter side is revealed by his regular use of an expression of surprise to Margaret: 'By Hades, Ma, diddly da and little fishes'.

('Bob') and Cecile ('Pats'), who were only 7 and 8 years younger than she was, respectively, as well as the baby, Shirley (4 years old), for whom JLB and Margaret developed a strong admiration later in life (W Smith, pers. comm., 2017).

JLB insisted that Margaret should be a mother to his children, and she accepted this challenge with relish. She remarked, later in life, that being a step-mother 'was one of the easiest of her motherly duties' but that JLB was so strict that she acted as a buffer, and relates how she once heard one of the children say 'that's the worst of these old fogies – they've forgotten what it's like to be young!' Margaret claimed that, as a result of her successful handling of the stepchildren, she developed an inflated opinion of her ability as a mother. When their first (and only) child, William Macdonald Smith, was born in Grahamstown on 25th June 1939, she changed this opinion: 'William arrived two weeks early and has been in a hurry ever since!' (MM Smith, 1996). After William, there was no thought of having any further children because of JLB's obsessive devotion to his career and especially 'the fish'. JLB wanted her to have at least one child 'to keep her company as he believed that with his precarious health he might die in 1938' (J Smith, pers. comm., 2017).

Margaret quickly settled into married life with JLB Smith in Grahams-town. In private she called him 'Len' (after his middle name, Leonard, as he had been known at school and as an undergraduate) but in public he was 'the Professor'; everyone else called him 'JLB' or 'Doc'. She later commented, 'A wife can be independent or indispensable, not both. I chose to be indispensable'. She supported his work in chemistry and also took a keen interest in his angling and fish-collecting hobby. She was happy to endure the hard-ship of arduous fishing trips to the coast, during which they often camped out overnight, a prospect that would have been unthinkable for Henriette, as would the even more strenuous fish-collecting expeditions of the 1940s and 1950s. It is clear that the changed emphasis in JLB's life in the late 1920s and early 1930s, from a comfortable, home-based existence as a university academic to a peripatetic and passionate angler and fish researcher, eventu-ally caused the breakdown of his first marriage, and ushered in the historic 'Margaret' era.

According to an *Ichthos* article and an unpublished memoir by Glyn Hewson (1999, 2004), son of a next-door-neighbour in Grahamstown, the Smiths lived in a simple house, designed by JLB, on erf 65 in Gilbert Road on a property belonging to Miss A Tidmarsh and Miss M Sleading. Hewson remembers the Smiths from his childhood:

'In this unique community, JLB and Margaret Smith together with William, with their own brilliance and eccentricity, added their own stamp and style. To this 11 year old, JLB was an awesome figure: he seemed to be perpetually in motion, both physically and mentally. Lean, tanned and severe, he and Mrs Smith, no less tanned and strong, only strode: through roads between the students residences to their "Department"; or seemingly ceaselessly across the hills around Grahamstown, through the late light of afternoons, come summer, come winter. I had started doing a lot of cross-country running then and would frequently see them. There was always a smile, always a wave, but never a break in the rhythm and purpose of their striding. They were so together.'

JLB Smith continued his teaching and research in chemistry and avidly pursued his amateur interest in fishes. By then he was the acknowledged authority on the marine and freshwater fishes of the Eastern Cape and, with Margaret's help, handled a voluminous correspondence with anglers and ichthyologists. Little did they know it, but this was the beginning of a remarkable husband-and-wife partnership that was to change the course of ichthyology in Africa. Many years later Peter Jackson wrote:

'I first met Margaret Smith with her husband in 1946, of course, as it was unusual to see one without the other. She was then a solemn young woman who seldom laughed or smiled and rarely spoke unless spoken to. She was so constantly with "the Professor" as she called him and seemed to share his thoughts so much that they appeared almost an inseparable entity' (Jackson, 1996).

With his new-found research assistant, Smith immediately sprang into action and, within a few months of their wedding, mounted an expedition to Mozambique in 1938. During this trip they examined the fish collection in the Museu Alvarez da Castro in Lourenço Marques (now the Natural History Museum, Maputo) and then collected fishes off Beira, Delagoa Bay and Inhaca Island. Smith also described several new species and created a new fish family (Pentapodidae, butterflybreams, since synonymised with the Nemipteridae) based on their collections (Gon, 1996). He soon realised that many of the fishes found off the east coast of South Africa originated from tropical East Africa and that, to understand the classification and distribution of South

African fishes, he needed to have a good knowledge of East African fishes as well. This realisation changed the course of his career.

Margaret described her relationship with JLB Smith to Glynis Horning (1979):

'Playing alternatively Mother and First Mate made for what she describes as a Dr. [Jekyll] and Mr. Hyde situation. "On shore and mixing with people I was The Lady – my husband would hold doors open for me and walk on the outside of the pavement. But at sea he'd duck under the hatch before me without a thought. The Liberationists would have loved him."'

In 1946 the Smiths went on a second expedition to Mozambique and then, shortly after returning to Grahamstown, embarked on an Irvin & Johnson trawler from Port Elizabeth to collect deep-sea fishes. These two expeditions contributed over 1,000 specimens, including 17 species new to science, to the Albany Museum collection, which had now become one of the best collections of East African fishes in the world. The year 1946 also marked the end of JLB's formal research connection to the Albany Museum, but not before he had prepared a draft document motivating to the CSIR for the establishment of a fish research institute at the museum (Gon, 2002). He remained the Honorary Curator of Fishes there until 1967.

In spite of Margaret's active participation in their expeditions, on which she dived and caught many new specimens, her childhood had not prepared her for the aquatic existence that she would pursue as an adult:

'I grew up in the small town of Indwe, that lies near the foot of the Stormberg range just before it merges into the Drakensberg. There were no swimming baths or dams near the town, and the only river was either a raging flood or a dry donga. Although I could ride anything with four legs by the time I was ten, had been brought up "tough" by my older brother, had superb health and a fine physique, my only knowledge of water was that from a tap' (MM Smith, 1959).

In an interview with Glynis Horning published in the *Natal Mercury* on 20th February 1979, Margaret stated, 'My dear, I knew nothing about fish when I met my husband – I'd been brought up at Indwe far away from the sea and sometimes even the taps ran dry. I had a positive fear of water!' (Oceanographic Research Institute archives).

Margaret was not a natural diver and only learned to swim at the age of 11 years.

'I learnt to swim at Port Elizabeth by floating out of my depth and being too proud (or too stubborn) to call for help, so I swam. ... And so as an adult and an Ichthyologist I could swim but I lacked the porpoise-like love of the water that characterises children brought up near the sea' (Fargher, 2003).

Margaret would go on to become an accomplished scuba diver and for many years would dive at every opportunity in order to observe and catch fishes.

JLB did not initially approve of Margaret's diving but the many valuable specimens that she collected soon changed his mind. William also developed into 'an experienced diver and underwater hunter of fishes', according to an article by JLB Smith published in *The Times of London* on 22nd January 1955.

JLB Smith often paid tribute to his wife's work. In the acknowledgements for *The Sea Fishes of Southern Africa* (1949), he states:

'My wife has been my full-time partner from the beginning and has been artist, adviser, buffer, critic and secretary, and is one of the most skilful collectors of fishes with many devices of her own. She has shared with me many hardships and sustained me when my courage has failed. But for her spirit, energy and unflagging enthusiasm this work could hardly have reached completion in any reasonable time.'

In contrast to this fulsome praise for Margaret, what JLB fails to mention is the contribution of his first wife, Henriette, who had sustained him during his formative years as an ichthyologist. Although Henriette had considerable artistic talent and was well known for her creativity, there is no evidence that she illustrated any of his scientific papers during his marriage to her between 1931, when he first published on fishes, and their divorce in 1937.

According to one of the artists on the 1946 Mozambique expedition, Denys Davis (1986), Margaret 'was always cheerful, meeting needs, coping with crises, foreseeing difficulties, explaining arrangements, smoothing ruffles, never ruffled herself, her special charm pervading all'.

The excellent illustrations of Mozambique fishes produced by Margaret Smith and her co-artists made it possible for Portuguese East Africa (now Mozambique) to issue, in 1951, the first set of postage stamps in the world that depicted marine fishes in their natural colours. The set of 24 stamps, ranging in value up to 50 escudos, depicts a range of tropical Western Indian Ocean fishes including butterflyfish, puffers, lionfishes and wrasses (Eshmeyer & Bearse, 1974).

During her travels Margaret became fluent in Portuguese and, in addition, learned to read French, Italian, Spanish and Dutch. She gave radio talks in English and Afrikaans in South Africa and in Portuguese in Mozambique, Brazil and Portugal. Margaret also appeared on television in Portugal, the USA, New Zealand and Réunion, and in several television films in South Africa, including the famous documentary, *They called him Doc*, broadcast by the SABC in 1976. According to Maylam (2017), JLB Smith was equally adept at languages[4] and, while in Mozambique, he learned Portuguese and subsequently delivered a lecture in the language in less than four weeks (although Margaret confided to this author that it took them 10 years to master the language). During the 1940s and 1950s JLB regularly corresponded with his Mozambican friends in Portuguese (letters in the Rhodes University Archive).

The legendary charm and vivacity of Margaret, teamed with her lively intelligence and gung-ho approach to life, was to serve as a lifelong foil to the taciturn and introverted JLB, and both were to shine more brightly as a result.

---

4   Samantha Weinberg (1999) claimed that JLB Smith could read 16 languages and speak eight but I think that this is an exaggeration. Other sources suggest he could 'only' read seven languages (English, Afrikaans, Dutch, Portuguese, German, French and Italian) and speak four fluently (English, Afrikaans, Portuguese, German), with a smattering of Italian. He also had an excellent grasp of Latin.

CHAPTER 8

Agony and ecstasy
Dramatic discovery of the first coelacanth

EIGHT MONTHS after their wedding, and while Margaret was pregnant with William, they landed their biggest catch: the first coelacanth. This event changed their lives forever. On 3rd January 1939 the Smiths were reading their Christmas mail at their lagoon-side cottage, the Blue House, in Knysna when Margaret said that she felt shock waves coming from her husband. She looked up and could see a drawing of a fish on the letter that he was reading. He had received a letter from Marjorie Courtenay-Latimer, Director of the East London Museum, that read:

> 'Dear Dr Smith, I had the most queer-looking specimen brought to notice yesterday … . It is coated with heavy scales, almost armour like, the fins resemble limbs.'

Marjorie Courtenay-Latimer's famous sketch of the first coelacanth.

He stared at a sketch that came with the letter,

'… at first in puzzlement, for I did not know any fish of our own or indeed any seas like that; it looked more like a lizard. And then a bomb seemed to burst in my brain, and beyond that sketch and the paper of the letter I was looking at a series of fishy creatures that flashed up as on a screen, fishes no longer here, fishes that had lived in dim past ages gone, and of which only often fragmentary remains in rocks are known' (Smith, 1956).

The image resembled drawings of fossils in books that he had read on palaeontology. He soon realised he was looking at a coelacanth, a prehistoric fish that scientists believed had gone extinct millions of years ago.

JLB whispered to Margaret, 'This is from Miss Latimer, and unless I am quite off the rails she has got something that is really startling. Don't think me mad, but I believe there is a good chance that it is a type of fish generally thought to have been extinct for many millions of years' (Smith 1956). Margaret did wonder about her husband. Had he perhaps had too much sun? He was a man who seldom spoke without thinking first, and this was quite the most extraordinary thing she had ever heard him say (Smith, 1956; Bell, 1969).

Marjorie Courtenay-Latimer and the mount of the first coelacanth by Robert Center.

Smith (1956) later wrote:

'It was as if the stage had been set for the coelacanth. I was in contact with the various museums, had by constant visits and voyages established cordial personal relations with trawler crews and the firms that ran them, had widespread contact with anglers, partly because I was one myself, and my brain held not only a rapidly increasing and almost comprehensive knowledge of the fishes living in our waters, but also a sketchy panorama of the long line … of fascinating fishy creatures … from remote ages past. … My peculiar photographic memory had recorded that the fossil Crossopterygii were described in Volume II of the *Catalogue of the Fossil Fishes of the British Museum*, published in 1891.'

His instinct told him this was a 'living fossil', a member of an ancient group of fishes that was thought to have gone extinct over 65 million years ago. Every detail that Marjorie had sent him seemed to confirm its identity, but he was also aware that finding a living coelacanth was utterly fantastic and highly unlikely.

Even though his main interest was in living fishes, he had read widely on fossil fishes, and now he wanted to know more. He sent a telegram to Keppel Barnard, Director at the South African Museum in Cape Town, asking him to urgently send him a copy of volume 2 of Arthur Smith Woodward's authoritative *Catalogue of the Fossil Fishes in the British Museum*, which Barnard promptly did (Smith, 1956; Bell, 1969); the book arrived on 6th January 1939 (Thomson, 1991). After studying this book, Smith was more convinced than ever. 'If this fish was not a coelacanth, it was something very much like it' (Smith, 1956).

He was in a difficult situation. As an 'amateur' ichthyologist, he was afraid that he would make an embarrassing mistake; a wrong identification would ruin his reputation. He sent a telegram to Miss Courtenay-Latimer, 'Most important preserve skeleton and gills fish described'. The reason why he wanted these organs is that they are soft and decompose when an animal dies, and are therefore not preserved in the fossil record. He realised that, if he had the soft organs, he could study aspects of this ancient fish that had never been studied before. But it was too late. Despite her best efforts, Marjorie had been unable to preserve the internal organs of the fish because the museum did not have enough preservative for such a large specimen. The soft parts had all rotted and been thrown away (Smith, 1956; Bell, 1969; Weinberg, 1999; Bruton, 2015).

Though he was almost convinced by Miss Courtenay-Latimer's description and her sketch, JLB couldn't risk announcing the find without seeing the fish itself. He resolved to travel as soon as possible to East London, about 580 kilometres away over rough roads, to see for himself what remained of the fish and to satisfy his curiosity. But he first had to finish marking examination papers for the University of South Africa. He wrote to Miss Courtenay-Latimer again:

'Your fish is occasioning me much worry and sleepless nights. It is most aggravating being so far away. I cannot help but mourn that the soft parts of the fish were not preserved even had they been almost putrid. I am sorry to say that I think their loss represents one of the greatest tragedies of zoology, since I am more than ever convinced on reflection that your fish is a more primitive form than has yet been discovered. ... Your fish has the general external features of a Coelacanthid, fishes common in early times in northern Europe and America. Whether or not it is a new genus or family I can determine only on examination, but I feel sure that it will make a great sensation in the Zoological world' (Smith, 1956).

The next day he received another letter from Marjorie:

'I strove to do all I could to preserve it. As I found the work too much for me, I had it taken to Mr. Center and got him to do all the heavy work ... There was no skeleton. The backbone was a column of soft white gristle-like material, running from skull to tail – this an inch across and filled with oil' (Smith, 1956).

The reference to a soft backbone made of gristle intrigued Smith and he became still more convinced that the fish, impossible as it might seem, was a living representative of a group of extinct fishes. He wrote again:

'Many thanks for your letter and for the parcel of three scales. They leave little doubt in my mind about the nature of the fish, but even so my mind still refuses to grasp this tremendous impossibility. The discovery is going to be a real zoological sensation.'

He had long felt a premonition that he would one day discover a remarkable sea creature, and it appeared to be coming true! But he remained very cautious:

'Those were awful days, and the nights were even worse. I was tortured by doubts and fears. What was the use of that infernal premonition of mine if it was just going to lead me to make a scientific fool of myself?' (Smith, 1956).

Smith later learned that the first coelacanth fossils had been found by a Swiss-American palaeontologist, Louis Agassiz, who described a new species of extinct fish, *Coelacanthus granulatus*, from a fossil of Permian age found in a road cutting in England in 1836. Agassiz coined the name, *Coelacanthus* (Greek for 'hollow spine') as he had noticed that the tail fin was supported by hollow spines; *granulatus* refers to the rough ornamentation on the scales. Agassiz was a well-respected palaeontologist who later established the Museum of Comparative Zoology at Harvard University in the USA. Despite his stature as a scientist Agassiz, like many scientists of his day, did not accept Darwin's theory of evolution by natural selection and believed that species were created by 'ideas in the mind of God'. He also wrongly proposed that coelacanths were closely related to the armour-plated placoderm fishes that lived over 300 million years ago, but the British palaeontologist Sir Thomas Huxley[1] correctly placed them with the lobe-finned fishes.

Louis Agassiz, the Swiss-American palaeontologist who discovered the first coelacanth fossils in England in 1836.

Over the next 150 years many more coelacanth fossils were found, all dating from 420 million to about 65 million years ago, when the coelacanth fossil record ends[2]. It therefore made sense to assume that the coelacanth lineage had died out with the dinosaurs (and many other creatures) after the great Cretaceous extinction about 65 million years ago. Three species of extinct coelacanth have been found in southern Africa. Robert Broom found fragments of *Whiteia africanus* (160 million years old) in 1905 in the Free State, and Brian Gardner found scales of *Coelacanthus dendrites* (175 million years old) in 1973 in Namibia. In 2015, Rob Gess from the Albany Museum and Michael Coates from Wits University described a new species of estuarine coelacanth, *Serenichthys*

---

1 Interestingly, Thomas Huxley launched his celebrated scientific career with a study on the Portuguese man-of-war or blue-bottle, based on specimens that he collected in the sea off Simonstown [Simon's Town] in South Africa (Siegfried, 2007). Although Huxley was one of Darwin's strongest supporters, and was nicknamed 'Darwin's Bulldog', he also revealed a tinge of jealousy that he had not thought of evolution by natural selection, 'How extremely stupid of me not to have thought of that' (Huxley & Huxley, 1947).

2 A very small percentage of dead animals become fossilised as many conditions have to be met simultaneously in order for a dead animal to become a fossil. Furthermore, only a tiny fraction of those forms that are fossilised are ever discovered by humans, usually in the surface layers of the earth's crust on land, rarely under the oceans. As Richard Dawkins (2017) remarked, 'I personally would consider it an honour to be fossilised, but I don't have much hope of it'.

kowiensis (360 million years old), based on over 30 specimens found on Waterloo Farm near Grahamstown (Gess & Coates, 2015), close to where JLB had regularly walked. But no fossils of the modern coelacanth in the genus *Latimeria* have been found.

Serenichthys kowiensis, the extinct, estuarine coelacanth found by Robert Gess near Grahamstown.

The respected South African fishing company Irvin & Johnson (I&J) played an important role in the discovery of the first coelacanth. Like many long-established fishing companies, Irvin & Johnson started out as a sealing and whaling company. The two founders, George D Irvin and Charles Ocean Johnson, were both experienced seamen who participated actively in sealing and whaling. According to the veteran marine journalist Lawrence Green (1958), Johnson was known for his foul temper and rough justice. Once the skippers of two of his whale catchers decided to have a last drink before leaving Cape Town for the Antarctic. As a result, their ships collided in Table Bay and had to put back to port for repairs. Johnson hit one of the men with his fists and was fined five pounds for assault. 'I'd like to pay another five and give the other fellow a hiding', he told the magistrate, who then fined him again for contempt of court!

Interestingly, from 1936 onwards Keppel Barnard had arranged for I&J fishing boats in Cape Town to collect unusual fishes for the South African Museum (Gon, 2002, 2007). For several years the enthusiasm and co-operation of the fishermen increased the annual number of accessions into the museum's collection to thousands. JLB Smith himself went out on I&J trawlers from Cape Town and Port Elizabeth in the 1940s to examine their catches while doing research for his book, *The Sea Fishes of Southern Africa* (Bell, 1969; Gon, 2004).

An I&J steam trawler, *Nerine*, skippered by Captain Hendrik ('Harry') Goosen, and built in Grimsby, England (C Chapman, pers. comm., 2018), caught the first living coelacanth off the Chalumna River mouth to the south-west of East London on Thursday, 22nd December 1938. The trawler was named after the guardian sea nymph that was sent, in ancient mythology, to rescue shipwrecked sailors. The name is appropriate, as at the outbreak of the Second World War in 1939, the *Nerine* was commandeered by the South African Navy and, after being painted grey and fitted with a 3-inch gun, assumed duty as a minesweeper. In November 1941 she played a key role in the rescue of survivors from the wrecked liner, *Dunedin Star*, off the remote coast of South West Africa (now Namibia) (Spargo, 2008).

The steam-powered trawler, *Nerine*, that caught the first coelacanth.

Hendrik Goosen, interviewed in East London in 1986 and 1987, recalled that 22nd December 1938 had been a stormy day with a cold-water upwelling reaching onto the continental shelf. He had landed a meagre catch but decided to shoot his side-trawl once more about 5 kilometres offshore of the Chalumna River mouth, where he would not normally fish, at a depth of 40 fathoms (73 metres), to catch some 'edibles' for sale and 'inedibles' for the East London Museum and aquarium, as was his habit. In the course of his career, Captain Goosen collected many unusual specimens for the East London Museum and the JLB Smith Institute of Ichthyology (now SAIAB), including the rare circular seabat (*Halieutaea fitzsimonsi*), slender snipefish (*Macroramphosus gracilis*) and the very rare picarel (*Spicara australis*) (Bruton, 1990). That particular day's catch included 2½ tonnes of 'inedibles' (sharks and rays), several bizarre deep-sea fishes, and one unusual large blue fish.

In 30 years of trawling, Goosen's crew had never seen such a fish. When they showed it to Goosen, he commented, 'It was so beautiful, at first I wanted to set it free, but I knew I had to keep it' (*Sunday Times*, 14.1.1990). 'It was pale mauve blue in colour with silvery markings'. To his surprise, he found that it was still alive. 'He stretched out a hand and prodded it, then leapt back with a great start, for the creature heaved itself up and lunged at him with fearsome teeth, narrowly missing his hand' (Bell, 1969). It is to his

Captain Hendrik Goosen.

eternal credit that Goosen kept the coelacanth. In fact, he separated it from the pile of sharks and manhandled it towards a bin containing water. Unfortunately it was too large for the bin and died on deck.

After Hendrik Goosen died of a heart attack in relative obscurity in East London on 14th January 1990 at the age of 85, Marjorie Courtenay-Latimer argued that he had not been given sufficient credit for the capture of the coelacanth.

> 'Without Captain Goosen, there would never have been a coelacanth. He caught the first specimen ... The JLB Smith Institute of Ichthyology in Grahamstown also owes him a great deal. It wouldn't have had many of its valuable specimens had it not been for Captain Goosen's keen interest' (M Courtenay-Latimer, *Sunday Times* 14.1.1990).

However, Goosen's contribution has been generously acknowledged in all publications on the coelacanth, both local and international (e.g. Smith, 1956; Bell, 1969; Bruton, 1990, 2015, 2017, 2018; Thomson, 1991; Weinberg, 1999).

At quarter to ten on the morning of that fateful day, Marjorie Courtenay-Latimer received a call on her newly installed telephone from the manager of I&J to say that they had collected some fish for her. Her father, Eric Latimer, reported in his diary that day:

> 'Today Margie came home full of excitement about a wonderful fish. She is very worried because she says it is so big and [she] has nothing to put it into – it is too big to go into a bath. She says Capt. Goosen off the Trawler *Nerine* rang up to say there was a ton and a half of sharks brought in if she wanted anything she could fetch them. At first she said she was too busy because she had been busy cleaning and articulating the fossil bones from Tarkastad. Then she decided she would go to the harbour and wish the crew a Happy Christmas.
>
> 'On the trawler she met an old Scots crewman who helped her look through the haul of fishes. "I picked away at the layers of slime to reveal the most beautiful fish I had ever seen ... It was five foot long, a pale mauvy blue with faint flecks of whitish spots; it had an iridescent silver-blue-green sheen all over. It was covered in hard scales, and it had four limb-like fins and a strange puppy-dog tail"' (Anon, 2004a and b; A Smith, 2004).

In Marjorie's report to the Board of the East London Museum dated 9th February 1939 she recorded, 'At first I thought it was a lung fish and then I realized that I didn't know what it could be'; this is not surprising, as her main fields of expertise were birds and plants. But her naturalist's instincts told her that it was something special, so she decided that 'the only person who would help me without a laugh would be Dr JLB Smith of Rhodes University', and sent a letter and sketch of the fish to him in Grahamstown on 23rd December 1938, two days before Christmas.

Richard Greenwell (1989) of the International Society of Cryptozoology (a society that studies animals whose existence is questionable), sketched the event as follows:

> 'The day was December 22, 1938. In Europe, the clouds of war continued to gather following Hitler's takeover of Austria and Czechoslovakia. In isolationist and complacent America, Hollywood was putting the finishing touches to *Gone with the Wind* and *The Wizard of Oz*. And in East London, South Africa, a 32-year-old naturalist named Marjorie Courtenay-Latimer was putting the finishing touches to the mounting of a fossil reptile in its new display case at the East London Museum. At 10 a.m. the telephone rang. It was a call that was to change Courtenay-Latimer's life – and the history of zoology – forever.'

As Smith was on holiday at the time in Knysna, recuperating from an illness but also marking examination papers, Marjorie's letter was forwarded to him there, but only arrived on 3rd January 1939, 12 days later. The sketch that she enclosed, which showed the main diagnostic features of the fish, such as its bony head, the extra lobe on the tail fin (which she called its 'puppy dog tail'), lobed fins and large scales, has become one of the most iconic doodles in the history of zoology, comparable to Darwin's historic 'I think!' diagram of a family tree.

Marjorie had a desperate time trying to preserve the large fish, which weighed 57.6 kilograms and, after trying the hospital mortuary and the local cold-storage depot, she trundled it on a borrowed handcart, with the help of her assistant, Enoch Elias, over 2 kilometres from Upper Oxford Street to Nahoon View Road, where a part-time taxidermist, Robert Center, worked. By now the bright blue scales had faded to dull grey and the fish had started to rot. Although they wrapped it in cloth soaked in formalin, the soft organs soon decomposed and were discarded, for which she was later unfairly criticised. She had little choice at the time as her museum focused mainly on dry displays and was very poorly equipped for preserving large, wet specimens. As Center had no idea what a living coelacanth looked like, he mounted the paired, lobed fins pointing downwards, like limbs, which resulted in journalists coining the nickname, 'old four legs'. We now know that the coelacanth does not 'walk' on its lobed fins but hovers above the bottom, with the paired fins performing exquisite sculling movements.

By 9th January 1939 Marjorie had not as yet heard from Smith and was becoming very anxious. She was also experiencing trouble at the museum, as her father observed:

'Margie is furious with Dr Bruce-Bays[3]. She says she cannot understand him, he is most annoyed about the fish – says it is a Rock Cod and she is foolish making such a song about it, when Dr Smith sees it he will laugh at her and he couldn't be bothered with the thing. Margie is very upset and worried – she persists that she is sure it is something wonderful … I have become interested in this fish story and wonder how it will end' (E Latimer diary, 7th January 1939).

Forty-four days elapsed between JLB's reading Marjorie's first letter and his finally being able to examine the specimen in East London and confirm its identity – this must have been agony for him! He eventually arrived at the East London Museum on 16th February 1939 and rushed to see the strange fish.

'Although I came prepared, that first sight hit me like a white-hot blast and made me feel shaky and queer, my body tingled. I stood as if stricken to stone. Yes, there was no shadow of doubt, scale by scale, bone by bone, fin by fin, it was a true Coelacanth. It could have been one of those creatures of 200 million years ago come alive again' (Smith, 1956).

Smith said to Marjorie, 'I always knew somewhere, or somehow, a primitive fish of this nature would appear'. Another of his 'premonitions'!

During their early relationship there was some needle between Margaret

3 Dr James Bruce-Bays was a local medical doctor who was the Chairman of the Board of the East London Museum at the time.

Smith and Marjorie Courtenay-Latimer. Marjorie was incensed when Margaret later claimed that she was 'out shopping' when JLB arrived at the museum to inspect the coelacanth for the first time (Thomson, 1991). She insists that she arrived at work very early that day in order to be present for the big occasion. She was also annoyed when Margaret said that she had not appreciated the importance of the coelacanth – yet she was the one who had saved it for science. In later years, however, they built up a very cordial relationship and attended meetings and conferences together.

Dr Bruce-Bays, Chairman of the Board of the museum, then arrived. He had not met JLB Smith before and seemed visibly surprised that this lean fellow (dressed in field khakis as he had been out collecting fish earlier that morning) was the revered fish expert.

'I am slight and thin and had then hardly any grey hairs; in fact, despite all I have endured there are too few even now. His features did not change, but his eyes and that queer power of reading the thoughts in other men's minds told me exactly what was in his. What! Is this skinny little fellow your expert? In those clothes I must have appeared very young to that dignified and portly old man, far too young to be able to give so startling an opinion about this fish. He would have to weigh this matter very carefully indeed before permitting the Museum to be involved in any fiasco from youthful enthusiasm. ... the many ramifications of the discovery soon convinced him that it was not just an old fish but something of very much greater importance. He forgot my apparent youth, my lack of flesh and my clothes, his doubts had clearly evaporated, and his parting words and handshake were warm, almost enthusiastic' (Smith, 1956).

Soon news of the discovery reached the media. Smith tried to keep it secret until he had published his description of the new species, but he had no hope of doing so as the East London Museum needed the publicity. Newspapers and radio stations throughout the Western world broadcast the news and put the museum, East London and South African science on the world map. On 20th February 1939 the *Eastern Province Herald* trumpeted, 'Best Fish Story in 50,000,000 Years. One of the Most Sensational Scientific Discoveries of the Century'.

JLB Smith in 1939.

Cape Times

MONDAY, FEBRUARY 20, 1939

SENSATIONAL CAPTURE OF PREHISTORIC FISH OFF CAPE COAST

Media coverage in early 1939 on the capture of the first coelacanth.

The commercial value of the first coelacanth also soon became apparent to the Board of the East London Museum, and some of its members were keen to sell it to raise funds for their impoverished institution. Early in June 1939 Marjorie was asked by Bruce-Bays to type a letter; but when she read its contents, she refused to do so. The letter was addressed to the British Museum and offered the coelacanth for sale for £5,000 (Ribbink, 2004). Marjorie also informed the Board, in a very forthright manner that, if the letter was sent, she would resign immediately. To her surprise, Bruce-Bays backed down immediately, but the issue was raised again in July 1939 and this time the Board asked JLB Smith's advice. He told them that the coelacanth's value 'was beyond any sum of money, and it would always draw world-wide attention' to their museum (Smith, 1956; Bell, 1969). This time the matter was settled; the coelacanth would stay.

There is no doubt that this was a wise decision as the discovery of 'old four legs' put the East London Museum on the world map and provided considerable impetus for the development of ichthyology and museology in South Africa. Furthermore, some patronising colonial attitudes were challenged by the decision to keep the specimen in South Africa rather than send it to a well-established European museum, where it would disappear into their vast collections. Throughout his career almost all the fish specimens that JLB Smith and his collaborators collected in Africa stayed in South Africa, although donations or loans of material were occasionally sent abroad, as is customary in taxonomic research.

On 22nd February 1939 the East London Museum sent the specimen by train to Grahamstown, under police guard. It was placed in a special room in the Smiths' house. 'It had a curious, powerful, and penetrating odour, an odour that in the coming weeks was always to pervade our lives, awake or asleep' (Smith, 1956). His household was drilled in fish protection measures: the fish was never to be left alone and, if there was a fire, it should be saved before anything else.

'Steenbras', the house that JLB Smith had built in Gilbert Street, Grahamstown, where he described the first coelacanth in 1939 and where most of the illustrations for the first edition of *The Sea Fishes of Southern Africa* were prepared from 1945 to 1948.

Smith faced an ethical dilemma. Could he rightfully claim the fish as his own, and go ahead and describe it himself, or should he share this responsibility with others? He is firm in this regard in his writings:

'One curious feature of this whole affair was that at no time did I look upon it as anything but my own. There was no question in my mind that I had to take full responsibility for the decision of the identity of this creature. ... It was perhaps due to that curious premonition that fate had prepared this occasion for me, and that, come what may, I must face it alone.... I knew that I had to go on and take the decision alone. It was do or die. It was indeed characteristic of all my work on fishes that right from the very start I struggled alone, possibly because no help was available even had I wanted it, but certainly because I am what my wife calls a "Lone Wolf" and work best on my own' (Smith, 1956).

JLB's admission that he preferred working on his own is telling, and points to a conscious decision to exclude other possible input, such as that of Barnard. When he published his major treatise on the coelacanth, he did not cross-reference to anyone else's work in the entire document, which is almost unheard-of in scientific publications.

From January to June 1939 he and Margaret worked furiously on the description of what would later be regarded as 'the zoological find of the century' (Greenwell, 1990) and 'the greatest biological sensation of the 20th century' (Balon, 1991). The manuscript describing the fish was submitted to a scientific journal just four days before their son, William, was born. It was a baptism of fire for the young wife, and the prelude to 30 years of hard work and absolute dedication as assistant to JLB Smith. Smith later wrote:

> 'It was an intense and stressful period. We had no social life, business and financial affairs took a back seat, and our food reached its destination over and between sheets of manuscript. We had no conversation, no thoughts, no ideas nor eyes, for anything except the Coelacanth, all day and all night. We could never forget it, certainly not with that smell' (Smith, 1956).

When he dissected the fish JLB insisted that Margaret should witness the entire process, bone by bone, 'in case something happened to him and she had to continue his work' (SATV documentary, 1976). During this painstaking work Smith was delighted to discover that the modern coelacanth shared many features with its extinct relatives, and the unchanging nature of its external anatomy over millions of years became increasingly apparent. For instance, he discovered a fine chain of sensory bones just behind the head that had previously been found in ancient, fossilised coelacanths, but not in any other fish.

Smith published his first, single-page note, with one illustration, on the discovery of the first coelacanth, 'A living fish of Mesozoic type', on 18th March 1939 in *Nature* (Smith, 1939a), followed by a four-page article, 'A surviving fish of the order Actinistia', with five illustrations, in the *Transactions of the Royal Society of South Africa* (Smith, 1939b). He named the fish *Latimeria chalumnae*, after Marjorie Courtenay-Latimer and the Chalumna River, and it was placed in a new fish family, the Latimeriidae; its common name is the 'Indian Ocean coelacanth'.

On 16th March 1939 John Roxborough ('JR') Norman (1939), ichthyologist at the British Museum (Natural History), read a paper on Smith's discovery to the Linnean Society of London, the same august body that had first heard about Darwin's theory of evolution by natural selection back in 1858. After Norman's presentation, Sir Arthur Smith Woodward, then Director of the British Museum (Natural History) and the author of the definitive catalogue of fossil fishes that Barnard had sent to Smith, commented on the similarity of the living coelacanth to fossil forms, such as *Macropoma*. He added that the coelacanth was possibly the most important zoological discovery since the Australian lungfish, thought at first to be an amphibian, which had been discovered in South America (1836), Africa (1837) and Australia (1869) (Thomson, 1991; Weinberg, 1999)[4]. There was no doubt about Smith's discovery now – it had entered the mainstream of scientific discourse.

Smith published a further note, 'A living coelacanth fish from South Africa', in *Nature* (Smith, 1939c), and then his major 106-page monograph, 'A Living Coelacanthid Fish from South Africa', with 19 figures and 44 plates, in the *Transactions of the Royal Society of South Africa*[5] (Smith, 1939d). He provided a remarkably complete description of *Latimeria chalumnae*, especially considering the state of the specimen.

Carl Hubbs (1968), the leading American ichthyologist, stated that Smith's description of the first coelacanth was 'perhaps the most meticulously detailed account ever accorded a fish specimen – at least of a posthumously exhumed carcass'. It is extraordinary that JLB Smith, a self-taught ichthyologist with only 17 scientific papers on fish to his name thus far in his career, was able to master the anatomy of a strange fish so quickly and competently. His anatomical description of the coelacanth was only superseded by the extremely detailed descriptions and drawings published by a team of French scientists 20 years later.

Dr EI White, FRS, the pre-eminent fish palaeontologist in Britain who was Keeper of Geology and then the first Keeper of Palaeontology at the Natural History Museum in London, became a thorn in JLB's side at this time as he ridiculed the colonial amateur's efforts. Smith was particularly infuriated when White pre-empted by one week the publication of his first description of the modern coelacanth in *Nature* by publishing a popular article entitled, 'One of the most amazing events in the realm of natural history in the twentieth century', in the *Illustrated London News* on 11th March 1939 (White, 1939), in order to

---

4 Modern lungfish were known for over a century before the first living coelacanth was discovered and they initially filled the 'missing link' gap in evolution between fishes in the sea and the tetrapods (four-legged animals) on land. The first Australian lungfishes were collected from the Burnett River through the initiative of a bushwhacker, William Forster, and were sent to the curator of the Sydney Museum, Gerard Krefft. The mysterious beast was known colloquially as the 'Burnett salmon', but no-one was even certain that it was a fish. It was initially named *Ceratodus forsteri* but is now called *Neoceratodus forsteri*. The genus *Ceratodus* was erected by Louis Agassiz, the same scientist who described the first coelacanth fossils.

5 JLB Smith was a staunch supporter of the Royal Society of South Africa and was elected a Fellow early in his career, in 1935, at the age of 38 years, mainly in recognition of his work in chemistry.

snatch some of the glory[6]. White also appeared to belittle remote scientists with some colonialist one-upmanship: 'The report of this discovery was made some time ago, but was treated with scepticism by the experts – they are only too familiar with deliberate hoaxes or the misplaced enthusiasms of the unin-formed to place credence in such reports until supporting evidence is available'. The international media nevertheless went into a feeding frenzy over the coela-canth discovery and it received banner headlines from New York to Sri Lanka, London to Buenos Aires. The *Auckland Star* in New Zealand headlined their front-page article, 'Loch Ness Outdone'.

JLB Smith had to rely on the nomenclature developed by palaeontologists for the bones of coelacanths when he described the first and second specimens of the modern species, and soon realised that there were different schools of thought as to the names of the different bones. He decided to avoid the 'battle of the names' and followed an alternative course – he gave the bones numbers, and allowed others to fight over their names. This did not diminish scientific respect for his work. Many years later, in 1953, when the eminent Danish coelacanth palaeontologist Dr Jürgen Nielsen visited Grahamstown, the Smiths suggested that he should visit the East London Museum to view the first coelacanth. Nielsen's response, 'Quite unnecessary. The descriptions and photographs of the various structures in your monograph on the first coelacanth are more than adequate. I have no need to see them for myself' (M Smith, 1969).

Others, too, heaped praise on Smith and his discovery. Michael Lagios and John McCosker (1969) labelled him an 'adventurer and ichthyologist' and stated that 'no living organism has so dramatically affected the public consciousness and scientific imagination as *Latimeria chalumnae*. For scientists it provided a unique opportunity to gaze backward at evolution, through its living tissues, at a lineage dating to the early Devonian.' A prominent American ichthyologist wrote to Smith, 'Now I can die happy for I have lived to see the great American public excited about fish' (Smith, 1956).

---

6 This was not the only time that politics was to intrude into the coelacanth story. Many years later, when American marine biologist Mark Erdmann and his wife, Arnaz, on honeymoon in Indonesia in Sep-tember 1998, encountered a coelacanth in a market in Manado, they didn't immediately realise the significance of their discovery and allowed a friend to post information about it on Facebook. Mark stated that he was subsequently caught up 'in a web of politics and turf battles which basically committed me to secrecy' for the year following the discovery. While Erdmann's formal description of the Indonesian coelacanth was in press in *Nature*, the formal naming of the new species was rudely pre-empted in March 1999 by a French catfish specialist, Laurent Pouyard (1999), who published a description of the new coela-canth's DNA and its general anatomy, and also gave it a name, *Latimeria menadoensis*. As Pouyard's description fulfilled (although barely) the requirements of the International Rules of Zoological Nomenclature, his pirated name stands. And so the intrigue of the coelacanth continues.

In his later writings and interviews Smith (1956) stated that he immediately recognised the fish depicted in Marjorie's rough sketch (by the combination of unusual characters, rather than by any one character) as a member of a long-extinct group of fishes, the coelacanths. Others dispute this claim, calling it 'a created myth', saying that he would not have had sufficient knowledge of extinct fishes at the time to make this positive identification, especially at his holiday home in Knysna and away from his library. They argue that he would have had to consult palaeontologists in Grahamstown (or Cape Town) before he could be sure. What they ignore is Smith's intellect and his photographic memory – and the fact that he also had a library in Knysna. He had, in fact, previously read extensively about fossil fishes.

Alan Hodgson and Adrian Craig (2004), in a history of the Zoology Department at Rhodes University, state:

'Van Hille [Dr JC van Hille] always considered that Alice Lyle never received credit for her achievements. He also believed that she played a critical role in the identification of the first coelacanth (*Latimeria chalumnae*) in 1938. In a letter to Miles dated 30 April 1980 van Hille wrote: "The zoo lecturer you refer to was Alice Lyle, she was a dear! It was actually she who identified the coelacanth. Miss Latimer, of the East London Museum saw that it was something quaint and kept it in formalin in her bath [sic]. She sent a little sketch to J.L.B. who was on holiday in Knysna and was slow in reacting. Eventually he took the sketch to Omer-Cooper [Head of Zoology at the time] who also had no idea. Alice came in to bring them tea and saw it and said 'I have seen it before'. She studied in Bloemfontein (Grey University College, which became the University College of the Orange Free State) where the emphasis was on vertebrates. Omer was more of an Entomologist and Smith a Chemist. So Alice got the Cambridge Natural History from the library and there was a good picture of the coelacanth. I [van Hille] have this story from Omer and always think of it when in all the books and articles it mentions that J.L.B. identified the coelacanth."'

This unfortunate allegation, which questions the credibility of JLB Smith as a scientist, can easily be dispelled as the East London Museum, JLB Smith Institute of Ichthyology (now SAIAB) and the Rhodes University Archive have copies of the correspondence between Smith, Courtenay-Latimer and Barnard from early January 1939, in which it is clear that Smith suspected from the outset that the specimen was a coelacanth. When he received Woodward's *Catalogue of the Fossil Fishes in the British Museum* from Barnard (before leaving Knysna for East London via Grahamstown), he was able to confirm his suspicion. Furthermore, the original letter from Marjorie Courtenay-Latimer to JLB Smith was forwarded unopened from Grahamstown to Knysna, so staff in the Zoology Department would not have seen it before Smith. There is no record of Smith showing the sketch to Omer-Cooper while in Grahamstown, in transit to East London, but it is possible (though unlikely) that it eventually found its way to the Zoology Department where Lyle may have seen it, and later commented that she recognised the drawing.

This does not mean that Smith, who was a practising ichthyologist with a superb memory and a first-class intellect, had not recognised it first himself. Peter Jackson, an undergraduate in Zoology at the time who later became an ichthyologist, remembers Lyle 'as very knowledgeable about zoology in general and an excellent undergraduate teacher' (Hodgson & Craig, 2004), but she was not a fish specialist and there is no reason to believe that she would have been more likely to recognise the coelacanth than JLB Smith.

The Smiths did call in at Grahamstown *en route* to East London (Smith, 1956; SATV documentary, 1976) and it is likely that during this stop-over JLB consulted books on fish palaeontology in the Department of Ichthyology and possibly the Albany Museum to confirm his hunch, which would have been the normal thing to do. For instance, Gunther's *History of Fishes* was in the Albany Museum library then (N Tietz, pers. comm., 2017). In fact, he and Margaret were delayed in Grahamstown for a week as heavy rain had made the unpaved road to East London impassable (Smith, 1956; Bell, 1969), so he had plenty of time to consult the relevant literature.

At the time, the Professor of Geology at Rhodes University College (RUC) was Edgar Mountain (from 1929 to 1949). JLB might have spoken to him, and he might also have spoken to Professor JVL ('Jack') Rennie, who joined the Geology Department at RUC in 1931 and founded the Geography Department in 1936, lecturing on palaeontology to third-year students (John Rennie, pers. comm., 2016). However, it seems unlikely that JLB would have consulted with faculty members, both because he had fallen out with the Zoology Department, and there were no experts on fish palaeontology in the department at that time.

Jack Rennie carried out research on fossil plants from the upper Devonian portion of the Witteberg Group, largely from a black shale layer in the Witpoort Formation, and published this work with Edgar Mountain in 1942 and 1967 (R Gess, pers. comm., 2016). Interestingly, this is the same rock formation in which Robert Gess of the Albany Museum later found fossils of an extinct estuarine coelacanth that he named *Serenichthys kowiensis* (Gess & Coates, 2015). Jack Rennie

Jack Rennie in 1934.

appears (with his son, John) in some of the photographs of the second coelacanth when it was returned to Grahamstown on 31st December 1952 in the military Dakota, as he was a family friend (W Smith, pers. comm., 2016) and was invited to be present.

Kirk-Spriggs (2012) further perpetuated the allegation, in an obituary on Brian Stuckenberg, ex-Director of the Natal Museum:

> 'While an undergraduate he [Brian Stuckenberg] undertook considerable work for James Leonard Brierley Smith (1897–1968), the renowned South African ichthyologist accredited (probably bogusly, see Hodgson & Craig 2005: 5) with the identification of the first extant coelacanth (*Latimeria chalumnae* Smith).'

He then makes a comment that would appear to draw attention to Smith's eccentricity, and so, perhaps, his credibility:

> 'When summoned to tea with "Fishy Smith" (as he was known to his students) one day, Brian [Stuckenberg] found him barefoot, up a tree eating fruit and was invited to join the feast!' (Kirk-Spriggs, 2012).

In his recent history of Rhodes University, Paul Maylam (2017) states, 'Van Hille believed that Lyle played a critically important role in identifying the coelacanth early in 1939 and was never given due recognition for this'. The problem with this argument is that, although Alice Lyle joined the Zoology Department at

RUC from the University of Fort Hare in the late 1930s, and was Acting Head in 1936, JC ('Bob') van Hille joined the Zoology Department only in October 1940 (Hodgson & Craig, 2004) and had not as yet arrived in Grahamstown in early 1939; this means that he could not have been a witness to the event and his views would have been based on hearsay[7].

Perhaps this is a case of lingering jealousy on the part of the Zoology Department, that one of the greatest zoological finds of the 20th century was made on their doorstep by an amateur zoologist employed in the Chemistry Department. It is difficult to believe that a man of Smith's integrity and intellect would (together with his wife) have fabricated the conversation that he had with Margaret when he received Courtenay-Latimer's first letter on the coelacanth in Knysna, and which he relates in detail in *Old Fourlegs* (Smith, 1956), in numerous other publications, as well as in several radio and TV interviews. And it is a pity that this allegation has been perpetuated in the histories of Rhodes University, which JLB Smith served with such distinction. He was not only an award-winning chemistry researcher but also brought international recognition to the university through his epochal research on the coelacanth and other marine fishes.

After the death of Hendrik Goosen in January 1990 the *Sunday Times* reported Marjorie Courtenay-Latimer as saying:

'… the dates of the dramatic events which followed the "discovery of the century" were altered to cover up Professor Smith's delay in identifying the fish'. She claims in this article that "she never blamed Professor Smith for it was Mrs Smith who faked the account of the coelacanth's discovery. In the book [*Old Fourlegs – The Story of the Coelacanth*], most of which I believe she wrote, it was stated that I got the first wire from JLB Smith on January 3. It wasn't, it was January 9. I have my original notebook to prove it."'

---

7   Bob van Hille was still lecturing in the Zoology Department at Rhodes University 26 years later when this author was an undergraduate there (1966–1968), and went on to serve that department for over 50 years. He was yet another example, with Billy Barker, Edgar Mountain, JLB Smith and many others, of the longevity of Rhodes' academics.

For the record, Margaret Smith stated emphatically in the early 1980s that she did not write one word in the *Old Fourlegs* book; it was all JLB Smith's work. Margaret also admitted that, compared to her husband, she found writing difficult, and it is inconceivable that she would have been able to record JLB's first-hand experiences in *Old Fourlegs* with such emotion and detail. It is also regrettable that some of Marjorie Courtenay-Latimer's comments in later life do not accord with the written record.

JLB Smith (1956) later said that he had anticipated that there would be an 'initial storm of scorn and disbelief' when he announced the discovery of the coelacanth, even though he had already established himself as a respectable ichthyologist in the international community by 1938. As it turned out, his announcement of the capture was accepted by most foreign scientists, except the previously mentioned EI White of the British Museum (Natural History) in London, but was met 'with complete disbelief' by local scientists and some members of the general public and the media. 'One prominent American scientist wrote to say that he had been called up late at night by the editor of an important paper who told him that they had got a report from South Africa that a live Coelacanth had been found. He supposed it was just hot air. This man asked who had said so. He replied "a man named Smith". "J.L.B. Smith?" "Yes." "Well, then, I think you should be safe to go ahead and publish"' (Smith, 1956).

When Smith wrote in confidence to Keppel Barnard at the South African Museum on 7th January 1939 about the coelacanth, Barnard's reply was 'couched in such incredulous and facetious terms that it served only to increase my fears of the reactions from a wider field' (Smith, 1956). But when Smith sent him further information 10 days later, Barnard's reply 'was now really startled and no longer facetiously incredulous' (Smith, 1956; Summers, 1975). In the meantime, Barnard had mentioned Smith's letters in confidence to the Director of the South African Museum, Dr ED Gill, who had himself worked on fossil fishes and published an important paper on extinct lungfishes. Gill was apparently of the opinion that Smith was 'dangerously deluded' (Thomson, 1991).

When the Smiths triumphantly visited the Albany Museum to share the excitement of their discovery with the Director John Hewitt, an expert on spiders, scorpions, reptiles, amphibians and archaeology, they '... were met with a stony face – how could JLB have made such a terrible mistake. When JLB asked, "Have you seen its picture?", Hewitt replied, "Yes, of course, that's just a Kob with a regenerated caudal"' (MM Smith, 1979). This was the man who had originally encouraged Smith to pursue his studies on fishes. The next day the Smiths met Cornelius Liebenberg, a botanist in the Albany Museum, who '... was most upset, placed his hands on my husband's shoulders and said, "What on earth made you do this dreadful thing? ... This coelacanth nonsense. You'll never again be able to hold up your head in any scientific community". "But it is a Coelacanth", Smith insisted, to which Liebenberg replied, "No, man, it can't be. Old Hewitt says it isn't, and if he says it isn't, then it can't possibly be one"'.

These responses were disconcerting to the Smiths as Hewitt was a respected zoologist, who had already been Director of the Albany Museum for 29 years, and would continue in this post for another 20 fruitful years. Liebenberg eventually recanted and was an important link in the chain that led to Smith being invited to write *The Sea Fishes of Southern Africa*, as he knew that Smith had already started writing a book that would help anglers to identify their catches (MM Smith, 1969). It seems that any animosity between Smith and Hewitt was soon repaired as JLB later served on the Council of the Albany Museum during Hewitt's reign as Director.

After the coelacanth saga JLB also developed cordial relationships with the East London Museum and, in his capacity as Honorary Curator of Fishes, attended the official opening of the museum's new building by the Administrator of the Cape, JG Carinus, on 28th November 1950, together with Dr Jack Rennie of RUC (G Morcom, pers. comm., 2017). According to Nancy Tietz (pers. comm., 2017), Smith was an effective Honorary Curator at the museum who visited and regularly corresponded with Marjorie on fish and museum issues into the late 1960s. Susan Jewett, then Research Associate, Division of Fishes, Smithsonian Institution in Washington DC, who visited the East London Museum in October 2003, commented that it had one of the best collections of displayed fish that she had seen anywhere, partly a consequence of the collaboration between Courtenay-Latimer and Smith.

On 7th June 1939 the Director of the South African Museum (now the Iziko South African Museum) in Cape Town, Dr Edwin Leonard Gill, offered the services of their expert taxidermist, James Drury, to re-preserve, restore and re-mount the first coelacanth specimen, as well as to create a mould from

Marjorie Courtenay-Latimer and Hendrik Goosen with the Drury mount of the first coelacanth in the East London Museum, ca 1940.

which further castings could be made. This was necessary as the first mount by Robert Center in East London had not been satisfactory, and there was a risk that the fish would rot. Gill offered this service at no cost as the Museum was content with 'the honour of being entrusted with the job and the first right to do a good replica' (Summers, 1975). This offer was accepted by Courtenay-Latimer and Smith and the fish was despatched by train to Cape Town on 19th August 1939, with Marjorie as escort. Gill tactfully asked Marjorie not to 'watch over Drury's doings all through, for he dislikes even more than I do having people watching him at work' (Summers, 1975). Marjorie returned to East London on 3rd September 1939, the day Britain declared war on Germany, but amid all the chaos and fear of that time she was thankful that the coelacanth was in safe hands in Cape Town.

After months of painstaking work Drury completed the new mount and the coelacanth was returned to the East London Museum in December 1939, where 'the Board of Trustees expressed great pleasure at Drury's work' (Summers, 1975).[8] Drury's mount is still on display in the East London Museum. Astonishingly, the mould of the coelacanth, which Marjorie had claimed from the outset, was only returned to the East London Museum 14 years later in 1953 after years of correspondence (Summers, 1975).

---

8 Drury (1942) wrote an interesting report on his mounting of the coelacanth but his most famous, if controversial, work had been done earlier, between 1906 and 1924, when he had made plaster-of-Paris moulds of 68 living San people (Bushmen). His first cast was made from a living subject, a seated boy playing a musical instrument. The casts were displayed in a diorama at the South African Museum until 2001, when the display was dismantled following protests from the Khoisan community and others who said that it represented a time when Bushmen were treated like specimens in a museum.

Inevitably, after the announcement of the discovery of the first coelacanth off East London, other prior sightings of the prehistoric fish came to light. Margo and George Branch (pers. comm., 2016), highly respected marine biologists from the University of Cape Town, revealed that Margo's uncle, Arnold Lundie, a professional biologist, had once caught a large blue fish with white spots and lobed fins off the Transkei coast near Umtata Mouth in the 1920s. Arnold was from a family of scientifically astute botanists, medical doctors and experienced anglers, but none of the family members recognised the fish as anything special. They cooked and ate it, noting that it had an oily flavour, like a shark. Years later, when the capture of the first coelacanth was announced, they realised that 'their fish had been a coelacanth with the typical shape and colour'.

A trawlerman in Durban reported that six large fishes resembling the coelacanth had been netted off the coast of KwaZulu-Natal many years ago but the specimens had not been kept or photographed. Another man reported to JLB Smith that he had once seen a coelacanth washed up on the beach near Gonubie, and Leonard Thesen (of the Knysna ship-building family) claimed that, in 1925, he had done a painting of a coelacanth on a curtain that had hung in his seaside cottage in Plettenberg Bay in the 1920s based on a fish washed up near Knysna. He claimed that severe arthritis would have prevented him from doing this painting after the mid-1930s, but later research by Robin Stobbs (1996a) revealed that it had been painted after 1938. As the Thesens and the Smiths knew each other in Knysna, one wonders why the painting was not brought to Smith's attention earlier. Rumour has it that Leonard Thesen could not understand what all the fuss was about and sought to deflate the importance of the coelacanth's discovery.

A more credible claim of a coelacanth sighting, off Malindi in Kenya, was made by GF Cartwright of Zimbabwe. In a letter dated 3rd August 1953, he wrote to Smith:

'One day I had swum out and had my harpoon gun. I looked down into the water and just below my sandshoed foot I saw a large fish. It was heavily built and probably weighed from 100 to 150 lbs and I thought how just too comfortably my foot would fit into its mouth. It was totally unlike any other fish I had seen or saw afterwards. It looked wholly evil and a thousand years old. It had a large eye and the most distinguishing feature was the armour-plated effect of its heavy scales ... It had a baleful and ancient appearance. I decided that I should attempt a head shot and with luck might secure the fish. My gun was not quite as powerful as it might have been as it had only two rubbers. … the harpoon struck the fish but did not penetrate.'

In his reply to Cartwright dated 10th August 1953, Smith wrote,

'I have read your letter many times and weighed up carefully what you have said, and at the moment I can see no reason at all why it should not have been a Coelacanth. A great deal of what you say would certainly fit a large Rock Cod, but then a part makes it extremely unlikely. I have never believed that the Coelacanths live only at the Comoros, indeed I have quite a fair amount of evidence from other parts, and it should not be forgotten that after all the first one came from South Africa. If ever you see another I do sincerely hope that you will have a chance of getting it, though I should imagine that even a bullet would have quite a job to penetrate his thick scale armour. You would probably have more chance of the harpoon penetrating if you shot at him from behind, but even then you would have to be close-by.'

Smith later met Cartwright in Harare (Salisbury) and, after hearing his story again, concluded that he '… could think of no other fish, apart from the Coela-canth, that looked like the one that Mr Cartwright had described' (Bell, 1969).

Perhaps the most unusual report was the remarkable case of the 'silver coelacanth'. In 1964 a chemist, Dr Ladislao Reti, bought a 10-centimetre long silver ornament from a priest who had it hanging in his church in Bilbao, Spain. It was apparently an *ex voto*, an offering given in fulfilment of a vow. The ornament is an accurate depiction of the coelacanth, with large scales, a big, bony head and lobed paired fins, yet a silversmith estimated that it had been made about 100 years earlier. Two explanations have been offered for this mystery: it was modelled on a coelacanth caught near Spain, perhaps in the Mediterranean Sea or Atlantic Ocean, or it was copied from a coelacanth seen in the Comoros (Fricke, 1987; Thomson, 1991; Weinberg, 1999).

JLB Smith favoured the latter explanation:

'If the silver coelacanth is genuine, as it could be, then it could easily have arisen from someone who had voyaged in early times to the East and seen the fish at the Comores – for in those days, over a long period, all the ships called at Anjouan Island (then known as Joanna). …. Eastern races are famous for their skill as silversmiths. All along East Africa they have plied this art for

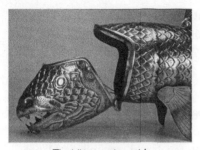

The 'silver coelacanth'.

centuries, and the model could have been made by one of these men in that area. The Portuguese were the first white voyagers in those parts, and odd Spaniards often went with them. One of them might well have acquired this model and taken it to Europe. At any rate, I firmly believe that some of those early voyagers had at least seen a Coelacanth. I think this very much more likely than that the ornament was based on [a] specimen from the Mediterranean' (Smith, 1956; Bell, 1969).

JLB Smith was also inundated with weird queries and requests for information from laypeople who believed they suddenly had access to an expert on 'old things'. One woman wrote to say that she had an old violin, could he please tell her how valuable it was? A man with a pirate's map offered to share the profits with Smith if he could help him find the buried treasure marked on the map! (Smith, 1956; Bell, 1969). Smith was also asked to identify unusual shells and a 'fish-monstrosity' with 'a face of a monkey, short legs, and an eye in the top of its head' (Smith, 1956), probably a josef, *Callorhinchus capensis*. He was also, of course, accosted by ultra-religious people who 'roundly reproved me for ignoring the Bible in my preposterous statements about millions of years, and did I not know that the theory of evolution was evil' (Smith, 1956). Sadly, Margaret disposed of the contents of the 'Crackpot files' before she died.

The capture of the 1938 coelacanth was a classic example, in the field of science, of a 'black swan' event: an unforeseen circumstance that came as a total surprise and then had major 'downstream' consequences; a geopolitical equivalent is the 'Arab Spring'. If the cold-water upwelling had not caused the coelacanth to venture into unusually shallow water, and Captain Hendrik Goosen had not shot one last trawl off the Chalumna River mouth on that fateful day in December 1938, JLB Smith would probably have remained an amateur ichthyologist, the Ichthyology Department and Institute in Grahamstown would probably not have been established there, and ichthyology would have followed a very different course in South Africa, almost certainly based in Cape Town, Port Elizabeth or Durban.

CHAPTER 9

Marjorie Courtenay-Latimer
Pioneering museum director

MARJORIE EILEEN Doris Courtenay-Latimer led an extraordinary life that is related in full elsewhere (Bruton, 2019) – only a rough sketch is provided here. She was born two months prematurely on 24th February 1907 in East London and weighed a mere 680 grams at birth. This impossibly tiny baby grew into a frail but lively child with a deep interest in the natural world. She survived early encounters with a tiger (escaped from the local circus), a cobra, and a full panoply of childhood diseases, all the while developing into a precocious little naturalist with a special interest in flowers and birds.

Her father observed of her, 'She is naturally gifted with a flare of finding things and knowing by instinct what is wanted or where to look for what she wants'. Despite her family's frequently moving from one small inland town to another at the behest of her father's employers, the South African Railways, Marjorie had by the age of nine amassed collections of bird's eggs, beads, butterflies, succulents and stone implements. She sent these treasures to an expert, Dr J Brownlee, in King William's Town, who was mentoring her in nature studies. 'Latimer be patient', he said to Marjorie's father, 'this child will go far in her natural gift of the beautiful. God grant her the health.'

In Marge's 16th year, after the family had moved back to East London, Dr George Rattray, then Headmaster of Selborne College, visited the Latimers to talk about their daughter, whose brilliance in natural history was now well known. 'He says they are striving to get a Museum established in East London and feels that Margie would be a wonderful person to work for it', wrote her father. Later he would add, 'She has one great wish and that is to work in a Museum'.

Marjorie Courtenay-Latimer at the age of 24 years during her first year as Director of the East London Museum in 1931, wearing her nurse's tunic.

On 4th May 1931 she was interviewed by the museum committee for the job of Curator at the East London Museum. Marjorie wore a straw bonnet and a dress decorated with the bluebells of Scotland, 'looking like a country bumpkin compared with the beautiful, nicely dressed other women who were applying for the job' (Jewett, 2004). One of the committee asked her if she knew anything about the platanna, and she gave him 'chapter and verses' (Anon, 2004b).

Marjorie was always destined to make her mark in biology and, despite her lack of formal training in ichthyology, fulfilled her early promise by playing a key role in the discovery of the first coelacanth.

The East London Museum can trace its origins back to 1921 when a group of interested people met with the Mayor, Captain J Neale, and Deputy Mayor, the medical doctor Dr James Bruce-Bays, to suggest the building of a museum for East London and to form a museum society. The first purpose-built museum was opened on 23rd September 1931 at the top of Oxford Street. A new museum building was officially opened on 25th November 1950, with JLB and Margaret Smith among the official guests, and was expanded in 1983 and again in 2006 (Morcom, pers. comm., 2017)

Marjorie Courtenay-Latimer started work as Curator of the East London Museum in mid-1931 for the princely sum of £2 per month. The museum had recently acquired its first permanent premises and she worked furiously laying out the new museum's displays in time for the official opening on 23rd September 1931. At this event the founder, Dr Bruce-Bays, said '… the museum was going far with such a charming and able girl and that the arduous task before her would be swept along in her enthusiasm and charming personality'.

Montage of Marjorie Courtenay-Latimer and the original East London
Museum (1931–1950), with the first coelacanth and the *Nerine*.

Marjorie was keen to ensure that the museum's displays reflected topics
that were important to East London, including the ethnography of the local
indigenous people and the marine biodiversity along the adjacent coastline
(Courtenay-Latimer, pers. comm., 1984; Bell, 1969). The displays that she
inherited included a bottled piglet with six legs, 12 photographs of East London, six stuffed birds (largely eaten by dermestid beetles) and prints of Xhosa
war scenes. On her second day at work she apparently arrived with an axe and
hacked up the 'terrible, terrible' display cases and started to gather new natural
and cultural history material for the museum (Anon, 2004a and b).

The new East London Museum, opened in 1950.

Marjorie Courtenay-Latimer (far left) with five of her sisters in the 1940s.
From left: Marjorie, Elsie (behind), Patricia, Lorna, Norah and Joan.

Marjorie later (1996) commented, 'The Museum collection was very sad: all kinds of odd specimens … I interviewed fishing clubs and the manager of the fishing trawlers to save material for me, and in no time beautiful marine material was brought in.' She also added to the museum's collection some old dresses, china and jewellery, beadwork dating back to 1858 collected by her mother, and her own bird eggs and stone implements. On weekends and holidays she collected flowers, shells, butterflies, moths and further ethnological material, and in 1935 her great-aunt, Lavinia Bean of Port Elizabeth, donated to the museum what is reputed to be the only intact dodo egg in the world. This precious egg was given to Miss Bean by descendants of a sailor who had been shipwrecked on Mauritius. A replica of the egg is still on display in the museum, with the original safely stowed away under lock and key. Its identity has never been authenticated using DNA or surface ultrastructure techniques as the museum does not want it to leave the premises.

On 6th December 1933, while collecting shells and seaweeds on the beach near Igoda Mouth, Marjorie met JLB Smith for the first time. 'A spry man, almost drowned by his baggy shorts, with startling blue eyes and a thick bristle of sandy hair, had come up to her and asked what she was doing' (Weinberg, 1999). Eric Latimer recorded in his diary that day, 'She was charmed with him, said [they] had a long chat, he was camping at Igoda. He is very interested in fish, but unfortunately the Museum only has a few bad specimens, but he has offered to help her with any she may care to have classified, which she is very excited about, because she has no books on fish at all.' She later wrote, 'JLB Smith … of all the scientists I met as a young girl struggling with meagre funds in a small Museum, always gave encouragement and never criticism' (Courtenay-Latimer, 1969).

Marjorie stated in an article, 'My story of the first coelacanth' (1969), that her involvement in the coela-canth drama began in 1911 when, at the age of four years, she gazed out across Algoa Bay from her grandmother's house in Port Elizabeth and developed a fascination for Bird Island and its lighthouse out in the bay. She had to wait 25 years before she could eventually visit the island at the age of 29 years, with her mother and father, spending six weeks there collecting birds' eggs, fishes, sponges, seaweeds and seashells for display in the East

Marjorie Courtenay-Latimer in 1952.

London Museum. It was there that she met Captain Hendrik Goosen, skipper of the *Nerine*, who came ashore to inspect her collections, and agreed to take them back to East London for her. Thereafter Goosen regularly set aside material that he caught while trawling, and notified Marjorie of his catches when he returned to port in East London.

Marjorie was briefly engaged to a certain Alfred Hill, but it didn't last long; as he said, 'no wife of his [was] going to be climbing trees and chasing birds' (E Latimer diary, 30th April 1929). She was also once engaged to Eric Wilson, son of Robert Wilson, founder/manager of the Wilson's Sweet Factory in East London, where 'Wilson's XXX Mints' were produced. Robert Wilson was on the Board of the East London Museum, and sponsored a field trip to Tarkastad where the 170-million-year-old fossil of a mammal-like reptile was excavated. Robert Broom named it *Kannemeyeria wilsoni* after Wilson in 1937 (it is now synonymised with *K. simocephalus*), and it was this fossil that Marjorie was busy mounting when she received the historic phone call from Goosen in December 1938. Eric Wilson died of pneumonia before he could marry Marjorie (not in a military skirmish, as previously reported; Bruton, 2017). After Eric's death, Marjorie decided that she would not marry, but would devote the rest of her life to 'her' museum, of which she was Director for 42 years until 1973. Marjorie's involvement in the discovery of the first coelacanth is related in detail elsewhere in this book.

As young women Marjorie and Margaret attended conferences as '... girls together. ... If they all went to a conference, JLB would sleep in one room and the girls would share another and "get up to mischief"' (N Tietz, pers. comm., 2017). Marjorie had been named William's godmother, and her life and those of the Smiths would be forever interwoven. In her later years, Marge 'became increasingly jealous of Margaret's successes' (N Tietz, pers. comm., 2017), although they remained good friends.

Marjorie Courtenay-Latimer in her office at the East London Museum in about 1960.

Marjorie was a founder member of the Border Historical Society and the Border Wildflower Association and received many honours and awards, including an Honorary Doctorate from Rhodes University in 1971 with the citation 'for having built a cultural institution of which East London, the Eastern Cape and South Africa can be proud and for her important contributions to South Africa's scientific and cultural life'. She also received the Freedom of the City of East London in 1974.

On the occasion of the 50th anniversary of the discovery of the first coelacanth in 1988 the hotel group Sun International sponsored Marjorie on a trip to the home of coelacanths, Grande Comore, where she was treated like royalty by Comorian officials. On this trip she collected shells, studied wild flowers and met people in the villages who told her 'tall stories' about coelacanths.

In 1998 the South African Mint produced a gold coin to commemorate the 60th anniversary of the discovery of the coelacanth and presented the first coin to her at a glittering ceremony in the new Two Oceans Aquarium in Cape Town.

In 2003 clay casts of her footprints were placed in 'Heroes Park' in Quigney, East London, alongside those of icons Nelson Mandela and Walter Sisulu, and the jetty where the first coelacanth was landed has been named 'Latimer's Landing'. Another remarkable accolade was the renaming of Oriel Hall at Rhodes University as Courtenay-Latimer Hall.

After she retired, Marjorie spent 15 happy years at her holiday cottage, 'Mygene', at Witelsbos in Nature's Valley. She eventually returned to East London, to a small house in Vincent next door to the one in which she had grown up, where she took up sculpting and painting flowers on ceramic tiles. She was working on a bust of JLB Smith when she heard of his suicide, and was unable to complete it (Jewett, 2004). She had accumulated a significant collection of coelacanth memorabilia as well as Wedgwood porcelain, including a plate depicting the coelacanth, made in 1963 to celebrate the 25th anniversary of its capture. Marjorie remained professionally active well into her nineties, attending museum and conservation conferences – a remarkable achievement for someone who had been such a frail child. She died of pneumonia in East London on 17th May 2004 at the age of 97.

Marjorie's contributions to science and museology were hailed the world over (Thomson, 1992; Weinberg, 2000; Anon, 2004a and b; Oliver, 2004; Pearce, 2004; Smith, 2004; Bruton, 2015, 2017, 2018a and b), and the Border Historical Society published a special edition of their journal, *The Coelacanth*, with tributes by her friends and colleagues (Batten, 2004; Bursey, 2004; Jewett, 2004; Tietz, 2004; Watson, 2004). In addition to her major contributions to museology and natural history in South Africa, Marjorie is remembered in the name of the Indian Ocean coelacanth, *Latimeria chalumnae*, the genus *Latimeria* (as in *Latimeria menadoensis*), and the family, Latimeriidae.

CHAPTER 10

William Smith

Larger than life

WILLIAM MACDONALD Smith, JLB and Margaret's first and only child, was born in Grahamstown on 25th June 1939. Glynis Horning (1979) later reported on an interview with Margaret:

> 'By the time Margaret's son was born, she was as involved in fish as her husband, and William arrived in the world with not even a bootie to his name – his parents had forgotten to buy them in the excitement of the coelacanth discovery'.

In his Foreword to this author's book, *The Annotated Old Fourlegs. The Updated Story of the Coelacanth*, William wrote:

> 'We arrived at almost the same time – the coelacanth in December 1938 and I, six months later. I was told that during the months preceding my arrival it was all hands to "the fish" so when I was born there were no baby clothes (thank heaven for a granny). Fortunately I was not born with scales as some had predicted! My earliest recollections were of two parents who did nothing but work, both at university and at home (which I assumed all parents did). This, no doubt, was one of the reasons for their great success. And this shaped me so that when I chose a life partner, it had to be someone with whom I could share life and work and I was lucky enough to find Jenny.
> 'It was only some years later that I realized that JLB and Margaret were not like other parents. Dad was incredibly bright (considered at the time to be one of the three greatest minds South Africa had ever produced) and, as a result, he had only select friends. He hated parties and small-talk, and

people were scared of him. As a youngster growing up it was impossible for me to win at anything – he always came out on top, which was tough but I had to learn to cope. This made me the person I am today' (W Smith, 2017).

William attended St Andrews Preparatory and Secondary Schools in Grahamstown and then completed his last two years of schooling as a boarder at Union High School in Graaff-Reinet, where he matriculated in 1956. He attended St Andrew's College barefoot, as his father said that it was 'unhealthy for a young boy to wear shoes'. Throughout his life JLB Smith was of the opinion that closed shoes are bad for your health and he preferred to wear open sandals, even on the most formal occasions (such as a visit to the Prime Minister). William's nickname at school was 'Rorfie Smith' (I Sholto-Douglas, pers. comm., 2016; J Rennie, pers. comm., 2017).

William (pers. comm., 2016, 2017) has said that he had a different but special childhood. The Smith family was always on the go, mostly outdoors, walking along endless beaches, hunting in rock pools for obscure specimens, or talking to fishermen as they stood in the surf or when their ski boats returned to shore. His childhood was also unusual in that his father was bent on forcing his somewhat eccentric views on diet, exercise, work ethic and diligence onto his son, whereas Margaret strove to offer him a 'normal' childhood.

According to John Rennie (pers. comm., 2016), a childhood friend of William's – and son of a family friend, Professor JVL ('Jack') Rennie, Head of Geography at Rhodes University College (RUC) in the 1940s – William was forbidden to play with toys 'for fun', but he did have a stash of old Dinky toys hidden in the hedge in the garden, with which he would play when Smith was away. JLB did encourage 'educational play' and bought William a crystal radio set, which he thoroughly enjoyed and used to the full. William also showed signs of being a budding scientist. One of the 'experiments' that he did in the garden was to dip the tails of chameleons to varying depths in a bottle of black ink so that he could identify the individual lizards in the garden.

William Smith as a teenager, on a fishing expedition with his parents.

John Rennie also recalls:

'One Christmas holiday Wm being older by a year or so organized the Hewson boys and me to form a gang/club. We had been watching a nest of owl chicks growing up from white fluffy stage in a small quarry off the old bay road a little beyond the Leather Institute and now the later much newer residences. We became "The Owls" with Wm's guidance for those few holiday weeks and from rudimentary Latin I think even I had at least one shirt with embroidered owl on the pocket and motto "Strages Enim Semper" hopefully correctly meaning "Owls For Ever"!' (J Rennie, pers. comm., 2017).

The Smith family's fervour for collecting specimens seems to have rubbed off on William's friends too. During his Christmas holidays in 1961 John Rennie collected a strange fish at Mpekweni, east of Port Alfred, and took it to JLB Smith for identification. 'I picked up the tiny fish at the water edge, only about 6 or 7 centimetres long, before the green sand whelks cleaned up'. He also found a dead 3-metre long oarfish on the beach that day (John Rennie, pers. comm., 2017). JLB Smith found that the strange fish belonged to a new species, which he named the scaly sandlance, *Bleekeria renniei*, after John Rennie. This is a rare species that is only known from the Eastern Cape coast between East London and Port Alfred and from the Seychelles (Smith & Heemstra, 1986).

William's childhood friend Glyn Hewson remembers:

'William, their son, and I became close friends those school years; I had a few days with the three of them down at Knysna, staying in the famous Blue House (kept away the mosquitoes, so it was said), a prototype of the somewhat gaunt style which we had got used to next door [in Grahamstown]. Wonderful days of boating on that magnificent estuary, camping overnight at Featherbed, below the one Head which they owned, sampling the strictly-separation-of-protein-and-starch diet presented rather expedition style. Fish, fish and more fish. Sweetened bread rusks with guavas. Coffee. William and I were ravenous and I certainly ate my delicious fill at mealtimes.

'I remember the downstairs rooms filled with files and papers, press cuttings, photographs and sketches, watercolours and Indian ink pens as well as the inevitable bottles of specimens and a plethora of expedition equipment. ... All overlaid with the patina of Margaret's exuberant commentary, stories and humour. JLB was very preoccupied for the most part; but there were moments over meals when he would ask leading questions and, like her, make an observation or tell a story from the fund of experiences which they had had. I travelled the world. William and I had some good times growing up: exploring the hills around Grahamstown ...; linking up our bedrooms with a marvellous kind of crystal-set communication wire; writing letters while the Smiths were in the Seychelles – receiving replies in envelopes awash with the most exotic stamps; being intrigued a few years later on by the brilliant success of William's extra Chemistry lessons for first year students (his mother passed on her gift of exceptional teaching). Recognising a niche in the market. ... A powerful personality in a 6' 6" frame garbed usually in shirt and shorts under a white chem coat just on his knees with lime green fluorescent ankle socks disappearing into size 12 leather shoes was not easily ignored' (G Hewson, unpublished memoir).

William commented in the 1976 SATV documentary about his father that he 'had a wonderful childhood' during which his dad taught him 'how to fish, how to dig things', but also said, 'I didn't think he was a very good father' as 'he was difficult'. 'If I got home and we hadn't fought for three hours, mom would take my temperature.' Apparently Margaret had to act as the 'shock absorber' between the two as William was the only one of the four children from two marriages who had the strength of personality to stand up to JLB Smith.

'He was single-minded to the point of being unbelievable', said William later of his father, 'and while this was a formula for success, certainly, it was not the route to happiness. As a child, living with that intellect was very difficult; I could never win. ... His behaviour, with hindsight, was in danger of breaking me. But it didn't, and I wouldn't change him for anything' (William Smith, cited in Weinberg, 1999).

William Smith the angler.

99

Kathleen Heugh (pers. comm., 2017), eldest daughter of Tony Heugh, a student in JLB's last Chemistry class, provides further insight into William's boyhood:

> 'The story that sticks in my mind is how William used, as a young boy, [to] visit my father in his university room, begging for a sweet/s and terrified that either JLB or Margaret would find out [and afterwards he] would need to brush his teeth and then ask Tony whether he could smell anything on his breath! This had to do with the abstemious and minimalist life style of the Smiths and JLB's conviction that people did not need to consume volumes of food, but rather train their bodies to endure very meagre portions (fresh vegetables or fish mainly I believe …). William had to learn how to endure weather changes – he only ever wore shorts and a thin shirt – no shoes, winter, summer, in the cold, wet or heat!'

At the age of 15 William participated in his parents' epic 1954 fish-collecting expedition to Kenya, Seychelles, Aldabra and Dar es Salaam. This was a life-changing experience for the young man as he was able to visit exotic places, do dangerous things, fish and dive to his heart's content, and endure with his parents the hardships of field research. During this trip Margaret had to keep an eagle-eye on the adventurous young man in the hostile East African environment.

William with Margaret Smith (in pith helmet) on the 1954 expedition to East Africa.

Keith Hunt, Registrar at Rhodes University from 1986 to 1995 and a neighbour of the Smiths in Gilbert Street while he was Warden of Jan Smuts Hall, commented:

'William was fed a strict vegetarian diet (+ I guess some fish!) & he used to come to the kitchens of Jan Smuts where the matrons used to feed him! I got to know the family better when William was a first year student in Smuts [Jan Smuts Hall, where Keith Hunt was Warden]. He was as large as life & very noisy! He began his teaching career in Smuts – giving classes in 1st year chemistry – I suspect on notes from JLB! Poor Billy Barker who was prof of chemistry seemed unable to handle the big classes from a discipline point of view – hence the need for extra lessons' (Keith Hunt, pers. comm., 2016).

William, whom Nancy Tietz (pers. comm., 2017) described as 'a huge Margaret', had a stellar career, like his father. Although, from the outset, he decided that 'I never wanted to live in my [parents'] shadow and tried to be my own person' (W Smith, pers. comm., 2017). After matriculating he studied at Rhodes University where he obtained his BSc and BSc (Hons) degrees, both with distinction, graduating in 1961. It was during his second year at Rhodes (1959) that he realised that he had a talent for teaching.

At that stage, the Professor of Chemistry at Rhodes University was still the redoubtable Billy Barker, who had ousted JLB Smith in the race for the Chair of Chemistry 34 years earlier. Barker, a brilliant researcher, was a poor lecturer and had no control over his classes, which often degenerated into riots. The more serious students were reduced to a desperate search for textbooks or other ways of making sense of the subject. The students would chant 'Billy, Billy', stamp their feet, and roll balls down the stairs, resulting in a very unscholarly atmosphere (John Rennie, pers. comm., 2016, 2017; J Maree, pers. comm., 2017).

George Cory, who had strongly endorsed Barker's appointment, should have known better than to appoint into a teaching post a brilliant researcher who was a poor lecturer, as he himself had experienced substandard teaching during his stint at Cambridge University. For instance, in his lectures on 'heat', Sir William Napier Shaw, the famous meteorologist, mumbled at the blackboard and his students couldn't make head or tail of what he was talking about. Sir Joseph John ('JJ') Thomson, the Nobel laureate in physics who discovered the electron, also muttered incoherently during his lectures on electricity and filled the blackboard with mathematical formulae that did not add up (Shell, 2017).

Into the pandemonium of Barker's lectures, and to the relief of a concerned student body, strode William Smith, who saw an 'edupreneurial' opportunity. Towards the end of Barker's career, in 1959, William – who had a thorough understanding of chemistry – approached Jack Rennie of Geography and asked him to make a space available where he could give informal lectures on chemistry to students, even though he was still a student himself. He started by tutoring his girlfriend in chemistry but, by the end of the year, he had attracted a class that was big (about 80 students) and lucrative enough for him to buy his first car from the proceeds – a brand new turquoise Volkswagen Beetle (J Smith, pers. comm., 2017)!

William with his new Volkswagen Beetle, bought from the proceeds of his teaching.

According to Johann Maree, who attended William's lectures:

'His lectures were interesting, he talked with confidence that built up our confidence in turn, and he told us what we needed to know. I remember writing to my parents asking them for the money to pay for William's lectures and promised them a first class pass if they gave me the money. I received the money and I passed Chemistry 1 with a first!

'William's personality was almost larger than life. William himself was a large person and his personality matched his physique. He was self-confident and always gave the impression that he knew what he was talking about. He was a good talker with the ability to explain complex things in a simple way. He was also a warm person so that one could warm to him easily' (J Maree, pers. comm., 2017).

In 2017, William wrote:

'When I discovered JLB's disinterest and disdain for film and television, I knew I had found my own passion. When I produced my first movie as a student he was convinced I would become a criminal. Fortunately he was wrong or at least I never got "caught" but despite being perplexed, I think he would have been proud.'

William and his cine equipment.

Journalist Audrey Ryan has an interesting memory of the lighter side of William's life as a student at Rhodes University in the early 1960s:

'I do remember one occasion when he was a student. I was asked to organise and compere a fashion show for Child Welfare in a local theatre using the Rhodes Rag Queen and her Princesses as models. I had a great idea. The cherry on the top was lingerie, the final item. William – now a great, strapping student – would be my model. It was a dark secret. Only Margaret Smith was in the know. Between us we managed to find a beautiful (size WXX) nightgown and slippers to fit and a lovely scarf for his head. His make-up was perfect, and I taught him to walk and move like [a] model. The script was a big build up to this, the final item, the music was sexy and sweet and then … in swept

William, smiling and twirling as to the manner born. It was a triumph. The audience howled and clapped. I was watching JLB who had been persuaded by Margaret to come. After a moment of complete astonishment he opened his mouth and roared with laughter, an unusual and heart warming sight.'

William left Rhodes at the end of 1962 and completed his MSc in Chemistry in seven months at the present-day University of KwaZulu-Natal in Pieter-maritzburg in 1963. Although he registered for a PhD at this university, he real-ised that, unlike his parents, his interest lay in business, not in academics. He initially joined the giant chemical company African Explosives & Chemical Industries (AECI) (which had previously supplied his father with explosives to catch fishes) in their Work Study Group in Modderfontein. Here he devel-oped several unique concepts, including a patented safety fuse that is still used worldwide. He then joined Afrox (African Oxygen Ltd) for two years, becom-ing Technical Manager at the age of 29 years; but the teaching bug kept biting and he moved into the supplementary education arena.

Over the next 38 years (1968 to 2006) William was to become a household name in South Africa. He started by developing a 'Pre-University School' that prepared students for their first year and, despite some initial opposition, within five years the concept was adopted by all the major universities in South Africa. He was first to introduce the use of closed-circuit television in educa-tion in South Africa in 1968. Through the 'Star Schools' programme (which included the printed media) he developed supplementary tuition to high-school learners in Mathematics, English and Physical Science. In 1970 he ran the first multiracial school, despite problems with the authorities. This service was expanded to include winter and spring holiday programmes, pre-exam classes, matric revision sessions and 'Saturday Schools' covering the sylla-buses of all the different examining bodies, in all the major centres, using some of the country's top teachers on a part-time basis.

Although William's educational radio and television broadcasts were enormously successful, he really excelled in face-to-face teaching in the class-

Margaret and JLB Smith at
William's MSc graduation in 1963.

room. His demonstrative personality coupled with carefully crafted lessons led to his becoming an extremely popular and successful teacher, with over 12,000 students passing through his hands each year.

Because of the success of his educational programmes, William was forced in 1980 to develop big-group teaching methods, and eight-hour sessions with suitable breaks were implemented. His ability to succeed in this format evoked disbelief among educationists until they saw for themselves that it worked. In October 1980 he offered his 'Science Revision Weekend' in the Wits University Great Hall. An hour before the event over 1,500 students had packed the venue and, by starting time, over 3,000 had to be turned away.

In 1981 the pressure to reach still more students prompted William to develop the 'One-Person TV Production Studio', in which the presenter controlled the whole production himself. This system produced many hours of high quality and very effective educational material for television at a fraction of the normal cost. The studio attracted worldwide interest and he was invited to address educational and television broadcast suppliers in Japan (Sony Corporation), the USA and Europe, and hosted visits from educationists from Australia, Canada and elsewhere. Sponsorship from the Barlow Foundation resulted in the construction in 1990 of the first television studio that could broadcast quality educational programmes live; this led directly to the development of the 'Learning Channel', a South African TV channel dedicated to primary and secondary education.

In 1990, backed by Hylton Appelbaum, then Executive Director of the Liberty Life Foundation, William introduced the world's first interactive television educational broadcasts in which viewers were able to phone in live and have their problems solved on air, while they watched their television screens. His TV channel was not only cost-effective but also very user-friendly as it allowed any good teacher to become a presenter. Sponsorship from Liberty Life, Barlows and the Argus group of newspapers meant that this service could be provided free by the SABC.

By 1992, 13 hours a week of William's syllabus teaching material was being broadcast on SABC TV, and printed support material was appearing weekly in newspapers with a combined readership of 1.7 million. By 1995 over 1,000 schools had purchased educational programmes on tape for use in the class-room, and William led the world in phone-in educational programmes. By 1997, 600 hours of interactive live educational broadcast developed by William and his team was being broadcast on SABC 2 and 3, and over 2,000 schools were receiving their educational video tapes. In 1998 he was voted one of the top three television presenters in South Africa and, between 2000 and 2002, he pioneered educational broadcasts to 28 African countries, reaching over 100 million people through regional radio stations. In the midst of all this, he was also a co-presenter, with Jeremy Mansfield, of the popular television quiz show, 'A Word or 2'.

William Smith doing what he does best, teaching.

William wrote several study guides on physical science and developed 'The Island System' method of teaching physics, which was widely hailed as one of the most exciting advances in the field for years. He also created several mathematics teaching programmes, and in 1984 his 'Basics Mathematics' video was rated in the United Kingdom as the world's best educational programme on video. Through his highly successful 'Let's Speak Afrikaans' radio programme, which had the highest listenership of all SABC English Service programmes at the time, he also taught thousands of South Africans how to speak this language. He soon became known as 'South Africa's favourite schoolmaster' (McGregor, 2010).

He received the 'Impumelelo Gold Award for Innovation' in 2005, the 'Golden Plumes' award from the SABC and recognition from the South African Association for the Advancement of Science in 1992. He also won South Africa's highest professional teacher award, the Technotron/Barlow Rand/University of Pretoria 'Teacher of the Year' award on 17th May 1991.

This award, for the 'most innovative and inspiring science teacher in the country' is the highest professional award given to a teacher in South Africa and was worth R50,000. In 2003 Johnnic Communications bought *The Learning Channel* and William's specialised studios were moved to the SABC headquarters in Auckland Park. William retired from educational broadcasts in 2006.

William and his second wife, Jenny.

William has two children, David and Lee-Anne, with his first wife, Jenny, from whom he was divorced in 1976. He and his second wife, also Jenny, have three daughters, Helen, Jessica and Bronwyn, who all live in Perth, Australia. William and his second wife, Jenny became very well-known for their development of the 150-hectare Featherbed Nature Reserve on the Western Heads at Knysna. 'The Heads' are two enormous sandstone cliffs that stand like sentries on either side of the entrance to the Knysna Lagoon from the sea. In addition to the cliffs, which offer spectacular views out to sea, the Western Head also has extensive milk-wood forests and large caves. JLB Smith had bought the Western Head in the 1950s using profits from his book, *Old Fourlegs*, primarily to protect access to his favourite fishing spot, Duiker Rock (later known as 'JLB's Rock'), in the Narrows. He later also acquired Featherbed Bay, and William inherited and extended these properties. The Western Head and Featherbed Bay received South African Heritage status in 1987.

Radio journalist, Audrey Ryan (1997), who worked briefly with the Smiths, has an interesting memory of the Knysna Heads:

'My final memory is a gentle one. I was on a visit to Margaret in Knysna some years after her husband's death. William was there and the two of us went fishing on the Heads across the lagoon belonging to the Smiths. It was a great day. I don't think we caught much, but I do remember in late afternoon saying to William that I had had a strong sense of his father's presence as we moved around, and he turned to me and said that he too had felt the same thing. Not surprisingly really, for JLB was a great fisherman, long before he became a great Ichthyologist.'

By retaining the Western Head in a near-pristine state, so that it could provide habitat for rare animals such as the Knysna loerie, blue duiker and black oystercatcher, William developed a reputation as a committed conservationist. He spent most of his free time in the 1980s and 1990s building up the facilities and services on this stunning natural site, pioneering 'ecotourism' long before it became fashionable. Together with the *John Benn* luxury floating restaurant (named after a famous Knysna port captain), two ferries (*Spirit of Knysna* and *Three Legs*) and a custom-built paddleboat, *Paddle Cruiser*, Featherbed Nature Reserve became one of the major tourist attractions along the famed Garden Route. The ferries took visitors back-and-forth to the nature reserve as well as on cruises on the lagoon and past sight-seeing attractions such as The Heads and 'JLB's Rock'. In 2008, after 25 years managing and developing this unique but demanding enterprise, William and Jenny sold the Featherbed Nature Reserve, together with the tourism business, restaurants and five boats to the mining magnate, Kobus Smit, who is continuing the Smith legacy.

CHAPTER 11

Room to breathe

The difficult war years, and a new beginning

In 1942 JLB and Margaret Smith started a long battle to improve JLB's ailing health.

'For many years the aftermath of the East Africa campaign led to continued ill-health, the precise origin of which baffled those I consulted. In succession they took away my teeth, my tonsils, and my appendix; but I have no harsh feelings towards those who assisted at my partial dismemberment, and am rather grateful that they did not focus their attention on any other organs as well' (Smith, 1956)'.

Samantha Weinberg (1999) commented:

'But he was determined not to give in to death, and so he didn't. Instead he developed a proactive method of fighting his illnesses. He walked for long distances every day. ... He also changed his diet. Using his knowledge of chemistry, he analysed how the stomach worked, what got digested and where, and came up with one of the first food-combining diets. He refused to mix proteins and carbohydrates: he never ate meat with vegetables, or bread with butter or cheese. People thought he was crazy. His sandwiches, remembers Jean Pote, used to consist of two pieces of cheese with some apple wedged between them.'

According to Margaret, 'They paid great attention to diet and exercise, not eating "dead" [processed] food and walking every day'. Margaret would claim, somewhat hyperbolically, that in the last 25 years of his life, JLB had walked the equivalent of twice around the world! Smith would regularly walk 8 kilometres before breakfast and then, with the whole family, 40 kilometres on a Sunday, always at a fast pace. Walking became a fetish with him but it probably saved his life and turned him into a very fit man. He even went for the occasional jog, as in Durban on the morning of 26th December 1952 – 'At dawn I went for a quick run along the beach' (Smith, 1956) – during the anguished wait for an airplane to fetch the second coelacanth.

About 20 years later (1961) Smith wrote to Carl Hubbs at the Scripps Institution of Oceanography in California: 'Incidentally I have a body on which the 1914–1918 war left its marks. It is something like an ancient car held together in unorthodox fashion and capable of running only on the highest grade of super-octane fuel. This makes my tropical expeditions rather hard going, but they go' (Hubbs, 1968). Hubbs also recounts the following incident at a 1958 conference in the USA: 'As a group of us was walking out to lunch, anticipating some of the food for which New Orleans is acclaimed, Jack Randall in the lead suddenly said, "Hey, you guys, let's go over that way", whereupon our South African guest spiritedly retorted, "What do you mean by calling me 'a guy'; I shall not walk with you any farther." But he relented and we all partook of a delicious seafood lunch. Though he had already told us repeatedly of his rigorously limited diet, he overindulged so prodigiously that he promptly suffered an attack of acute indigestion, and called, almost to the point of insistence, for an abrupt change in the hourly schedule of the whole conference to fit into his own condition!'

JLB Smith (second from right) with (from left) Gilbert Whitley, LP Schultz and Carl Hubbs.

JLB regained his health to such an extent that he and Margaret were able to withstand the hardships of the arduous fish-collecting expeditions that they organised up the East African coast and to the Western Indian Ocean islands in the late 1940s and 1950s. At the age of 70, shortly before he committed suicide, he was still working long hours and walking an average of 50 kilometres per week (MM Smith, 1969) and was more agile and younger-looking than men many years his junior.

John Wallace, ex-Director of the Port Elizabeth Museum and an expert on sharks and rays, who worked briefly with the Smiths in Grahamstown, commented:

'JLB and Margaret went for a "constitutional" walk each day at about 5 pm. I accompanied them. After some days I got used to JLB concentrating on keeping fit, walking at a pace that as a young man I struggled to maintain and which left Margaret far behind. He would stop long enough for her to catch up before setting off again into the distance!' (J Wallace, pers. comm., 2017).

'William remembers that no day passed without extensive walks, so much so that he hates exercise to this day' (J Smith, pers. comm., 2017).

The intervention of the Second World War gave JLB Smith some breathing space to consider his future. He continued to meet his teaching obligations in the Chemistry Department but found that his research on fishes was occupying more and more of his time and attention. His mind was also strongly focused on his project of finding another coelacanth with all the soft anatomy intact while, at the same time, surveying the little-known fishes of East Africa, where he predicted the coelacanth lived.

As he was unable to travel beyond the borders of South Africa during the war, he focused on making fish collections along the Eastern Cape and Transkei coasts. He continued to produce publications on chemistry, mainly on the essential oils of South African indigenous plants, and he produced three textbooks on chemistry: *Numerical and Constitutional Exercises in Chemistry* with M Rindl (1941, second edition in 1943), which was also published in Spanish (1955); *A Simplified System of Organic Identification*, with an American edition in 1943; and *A System of Qualitative Inorganic Analysis* (1941), with second (1943), third (1944) and fourth editions (1949).

At that time his colleagues' opinions of him differed. He was described by many as very determined and single-minded, and only prepared to tolerate the inefficiencies of others if they served his own needs. Many regarded him as aloof and arrogant; yet others, as cold and austere, even frightening; but, to his close friends, he was kind and generous. One colleague commented that, to be a fisherman, you have to be a romantic, but scientists are not romantics. In JLB Smith, however, he found someone who managed to combine the romanticism of an angler with the realism of a scientist. Many agreed that JLB didn't, in general, like people and that, with his penetrating blue eyes and piercing stare, he would often intimidate them.

Shirley Bell experienced the kind and generous side of JLB's personality, and his ability to inspire others to reach their full potential:

'... I researched material for articles when I became editor of *Field and Tide*, and JLB showed interest and wrote to me about them, and that's how my friendship with the Smiths began. He would write to me while they were away on trips. It was so interesting for me and such a privilege. So it was quite strange for me to hear later how autocratic he could be ... I just saw this endlessly helpful, concerned, generous-spirited man who had a huge reputation, but had somehow noticed me and my little efforts and decided I should now go back to studying and find out who I was, and who had a scientist wife who was also generous-spirited and supportive' (S Bell, pers. comm., 2017).

JLB Smith had no enthusiasm for wars. 'As a scientist I can never view with any pleasure the apparent ease with which some politicians appear to contemplate war, and the spending of countless millions on destruction and death, while they will in peace-time hedge and jib at a few thousand pounds for a scientific endeavour.' The aftermath of the Second World War did, however, benefit his research, as South Africa (like other countries) realised that there was a strong need to invest in science and technology to promote future economic growth. Scientific research had become a national priority and science a matter of international prestige. Soon after the war ended, Prime Minister Jan Smuts appointed Basil Schonland as his Scientific Adviser with a mandate to advise the government on research development and co-ordination. Following his recommendations, the Council for Scientific and Industrial Research (CSIR) was formally established on 5th October 1945 (Kingwill, 1990). This was the funding agency that would soon make it possible for Smith to devote himself full-time to ichthyology.

Immediately after the war the burden on JLB Smith became almost unbearable. Like any scientific discipline, chemistry is a demanding subject, especially if one chooses to combine teaching and research. The rapid development of organic chemistry, shortages of staff, escalating teaching loads to returning servicemen, and Smith's burgeoning career in ichthyology, eventually forced him to make a decision on his future. He chose fish research, realising that this was a wide-open field with many opportunities. His ambition to capture an intact coelacanth also influenced his decision, as he was convinced that research up the east coast of Africa would reap rich rewards.

This was a difficult decision for Smith as he loved chemistry and, judging from his correspondence with other organic chemists, now stored in the Rhodes University Archive, he continued to show an active interest in the subject well into the 1950s. He also enjoyed interacting with students but realised that, if he pursued a research career in ichthyology, his teaching would probably fall away – in this he was right.

He had taught chemistry at Rhodes University College (RUC) for 24 years (1922–1946), six years longer than Cory (1904–1922), and two years longer than his subsequent ichthyology career would last (1946–1968). There was, however, considerable overlap in his two careers, as he first published on fishes in 1931 and continued to have an interest in chemistry until 1956. This overlap period therefore lasted for 25 years, more than half his active life span as a scientist.

JLB Smith and George Cory were, of course, not the only organic chemists in South Africa who went on to achieve fame in other fields. They also include Professor C van der Merwe Brink (President of the CSIR), Dr WS Rapson (Scientific Adviser to the Chamber of Mines) (Warren, 1977), Professor Reinhardt Arndt (President of the Foundation for Research Development) and Professor Christoph Garbers (President of the CSIR) (Mike Brown, pers. comm., 2017).

Smith's life now became very complicated. On 30th September 1946 he resigned from the Department of Chemistry, but his resignation only took effect from 1st January 1947 and he then took nine months' leave (partly unpaid) from the Chemistry Department in order to work full-time on fishes until his CSIR grant came through. On 16th May 1947 he was appointed Professor of Ichthyology by RUC, heading up a brand-new department, with the proviso, 'though working in the Department of Zoology, Dr. Smith be independent of the Professor of Zoology'. Technically, from 16th May to 30th September 1947, he was simultaneously a Senior Lecturer in Chemistry (on leave) and a Professor of Ichthyology.

That same year the CSIR awarded Smith a Research Fellowship in Ichthyology and funds for travel and, later, for clerical assistance and publications. Rhodes University College appointed him as a Research Professor[1] and provided equipment and accommodation in an old wood-and-iron building in Artillery Road that had been used as a military barracks during the South African War (1899–1902). Some of these buildings dated from 1828, nearly 120 years earlier, and they came in for criticism from an early historian of the university, Ronald Currey (1971):

'The troops left for the front, and once more the Drostdy buildings, with the horrid recent additions, were left unoccupied. So they remained for the next five years. (Traces of the red-brick scourge, now decently shrouded in whitewash, are to be found tucked away in odd corners of the present, so different, buildings. The most significant of these remnants now houses the Ichthyology Department).'

It was a very humble habitat for the epochal scientific events that would unfold there over the next 22 years. According to Margaret Smith (1987), 'It consisted of one room, then two, then the old Zoology building, when Zoology moved, housed the Department of Ichthyology for 25 years'. JLB Smith refused to abandon the old building as he said that it would be too time-consuming to leave but, after he died, 'Rhodes was to supply a new building, as the other was too old, too cramped and a tinderbox'.

---

1   It would be 10 years before another South African institution (the South African Museum in Cape Town) would create a full-time post for an ichthyologist (Gon, 2002).

Margaret Smith was appointed as a Scientific Associate in the Department of Ichthyology, a position she held until after JLB's death in January 1968. The funds provided by the CSIR and university were not sufficient, however, to cover all the costs of their numerous fish-collecting expeditions and JLB and Margaret had to raise further support, financially and in kind, from private donors and local officials in the countries they visited.

The original Department of Ichthyology in Artillery Road at Rhodes University College.

The CSIR's research grant to Smith of £800 per annum included no pension or other benefits. At the same time, he lost the government pension that was due to him after 25 years of university teaching as he had resigned before reaching retirement age, and refused to claim that he had retired from teaching on medical grounds. This combination of circumstances would cause financial stress to the Smiths in later years and even forced them to send many letters to angling clubs asking them to provide financial assistance for their research. Rhodes University College, too, was having financial problems; it nearly went bankrupt in the late 1940s due to the global depression, the aftermath of the Second World War and an internal crisis (Gon, 2001; Maylam, 2017).

The research grant to Smith by the fledgling CSIR was one of the best investments they ever made. Another, equally far-sighted investment made by the CSIR at the time was to the Telecommunications Research Laboratory (TRL) at the University of the Witwatersrand. One of its staff, Trevor Wadley, arguably became South Africa's greatest inventor, our own 'Thomas Edison'. [2]

---

2   Wadley had served in the Signal Corps during the Second World War and made major contributions to the development of radar, building on the work of Basil Schonland (1896–1972), then Director of the Bernard Price Institute for Geophysical Research at the University of the Witwatersrand (Bruton, 2010, 2017), who would later establish the CSIR and become Chancellor of Rhodes University. Wadley invented the Wadley Loop (a unique circuit for cancelling frequency drift); one of the first practical broadband radios in the world; the Ionosonde (for probing the ionosphere with radio waves); the first crystal-controlled radio in the world that could be set to a consistent frequency; a Transistorised Receiver (which is still a very popular radio receiver among radio hams) and a Rack-Mounted Receiver (which was extensively used by the BBC for its international radio broadcasts) (Bruton, 2010, 2017). Most importantly, he invented the Radio Tellurometer, the most accurate distance-measuring device in the world for over 30 years, which was used in over 60 countries and earned South Africa massive amounts of foreign exchange (Bruton, 2010, 2017).

South Africa's science and technology glitterati during the 1940s and 1950s also included HJ van der Bijl (1887–1948, establishment of Eskom and Iscor, co-inventor of the thermionic valve) and Dr JH van Eck (1887–1948, establishment of Eskom, Iscor, Sasol and the Industrial Development Corporation). JLB Smith knew, and was admired by, all of them.

In October 1946 Smith wrote to the CSIR, informing them that he intended to resume his search for the coelacanth off East Africa. They approved the idea in principle and appointed a committee (to JLB's horror) to plan the way forward. Smith, of course, wanted to hunt for the coelacanth alone but the 'powers that be' had more grandiose ideas for a comprehensive oceanographic expedition, with the capture of a coelacanth being only part of the objective. When this idea proved to be too expensive, Smith reminded them of his simpler and less expensive plan, but eventually the whole initiative was 'bureaucratised' out of existence.

CHAPTER 12

Grit and determination
The epic East African expeditions

JLB SMITH had long wanted to write a book on South African sea fishes for anglers but realised that he did not have the funds to publish it. In 1945 an interesting series of events led to the breakthrough that he had been seeking. He had the good fortune to engage with Hugh le May, who first came to South Africa from England during the South African War and made his fortune in the mining industry; he eventually settled in Lourenço Marques (now Maputo) in Mozambique. A keen angler, Le May was frustrated, as Smith had earlier been, by the fact that there were no good books available for him to identify the fishes that he caught. Having happened on a willing author, he offered to finance the research and production of such a guide to fishes. This collaboration between Smith and his benefactor Hugh le May was to launch a classic of South African natural history.

Smith realised that it was pointless trying to produce a book on 'South African' fishes alone, as fish do not respect political boundaries and many species along the south-east coast of Africa have their origins and main populations further north, off East Africa or in the western Indo-Pacific region. If he was to resolve the taxonomic relationships of southern African fishes, and understand their distributions, he would need to have a better understanding of East African fishes as well. Furthermore, he knew that the Western Indian Ocean and its islands had been subjected to very little research at that time, and he had also predicted that the main population of coelacanths would be found there. All these factors pointed to the need for him to extend his research effort into East Africa.

The Smiths and the Le Mays formed a special relationship, and Hugh le May's son Basil joined the Smiths on their second expedition to Mozambique in June–July 1946. He proved to be a good field-worker, and also an excellent entertainer. After the expedition JLB wrote to him, thanking him for his help and recommending that he should pursue an acting career in Hollywood (Gon, 2001). Three years later Smith named a new species of moray eel after him, *Lycondontis lemayi* (now synonymised with *Gymnothorax flavimarginatus*), 'for his appearance in party dress at the Smiths' house in Lourenço Marques!'

With the new Department of Ichthyology established (1947), and finances for a book on the fishes of the region now secured, the puzzle pieces were starting to fall into place and Smith immediately accelerated his programme for a series of intensive fish-collecting expeditions along the coasts of South and East Africa. These expeditions included the following:

- 1946: Pondoland coast.

- 1946: Southern Mozambique, Lourenço Marques and Delagoa Bay (now Maputo Bay).

- 1948: Southern Mozambique, Inhaca Island to Bazaruto Island. In an article that Smith (1958) later wrote on the fishes of Inhaca Island, he commented '… we have identified more than five hundred and sixty species from around Inhaca, of which some two hundred and thirty known species had not previously been recorded from Southern Africa. We discovered there more than twenty new to science.'

- 1949: Southern Mozambique, Inhaca Island, Machangulo, Ponte Torres and Ponte Abril.

- 1950: Central and northern Mozambique, the first expedition north of 20°S, from Beira to the Lurio River, with Pinda Reef (14° 10'S, 40° 40'E) being their main target. On this expedition Margaret nearly died of food poisoning and they came within a whisker of being wrecked on Pinda Reef, yet they managed to collect and record large numbers of fishes (Smith, 1956; Bell, 1969).

- 1951: Northern Mozambique, including Mozambique Island, Pinda Reef, Ibo and the Quirimbas Archipelago (Kerimba Islands) from Porto Amelia to Cabo Delgado. During this trip, the Smiths traversed very wild territory and encountered strong winds, treacherous currents and a tidal ebb and flow that exceeded four metres. There were no telecommunications or food supply-lines, and drinking water was extremely scarce. At Pinda they stayed in the famous lighthouse (the tallest in East Africa) for several weeks, also using it as a makeshift laboratory. Later in the trip they lived aboard a stout little diesel-engined wooden cabin cruiser, or *vedeta*, provided by the Portuguese authorities. They were joined on this expedition by their 13-year-old son, William, and by photographer Peter Barnett from Durban. They were constantly in fear of marauding prides of man-eating lions, as described further on (Barnett, 1953; Bell, 1969).

Peter Barnett and Margaret and JLB Smith enjoying a rustic meal on Ibo Island on the 1951 Mozambique expedition.

On this trip, Smith seriously contemplated doing the 200-kilometre open ocean journey from the African mainland to the Comoros in the little vedeta – an archipelago he had already identified as a possible site for the main coelacanth population (Smith, 1956; Bell, 1969). 'Whenever I planned any expedition and studied charts, always my eyes and mind would stray to the Comores, those mysterious blobs in the blankness of the seas, like drops left behind from a dripping Madagascar torn from the body of Africa' (Smith, 1956). Standing at Cabo Delgado one day, JLB said to Margaret, 'Come on, lass, let's go to the Comoros'.

Even though he had no compass or detailed chart (the Admiralty charts he had with him were printed in 1877!), he reckoned that he would be able to navigate there and back using his watch and the sun and stars, a hare-brained scheme for such a practical man. The seas around the Comoros are treacherous, with vicious currents and strong winds, and it would have been a hazardous and probably calamitous trip in a small boat. Fortunately,

Margaret's common sense prevailed and Smith had to abandon his absurd plan and admit that the odds were against them. Throughout their many expeditions Margaret's persuasive influence and common sense, always urging JLB to do the sensible thing, is obvious, and it probably saved his life on many occasions. She was, indeed, the power behind the throne, the rational mind when the sometimes flaky scientist became frenetic, and a strong support when the man who often questioned his own worth needed a shoulder to lean on (Bruton, 2017).

• 1952: Zanzibar, Pemba Island and Kenya. Margaret took an English-Swahili phrase book with her to make communication easier. These coasts had never been explored by scientists before and the local inhabitants showed great interest in the Smiths' strange endeavours. In Zanzibar, JLB solved the riddle of 'a large water snake' in a reservoir by identifying it as a giant longfin eel, *Anguilla mossambicus*.

• 1952: South African coast at Plettenberg Bay and Knysna, and the rugged coast from the KwaZulu-Natal border to just north of Port St Johns, covered on foot. They also surveyed several previously unexplored estuaries.

• 1953: Southern Mozambique, including Inhaca, Inhassoro, Bazaruto, Vilanculos, Ponte de Barra Falsa, Inhambane, Vila Joao Belo and the Bay of Lourenço Marques (now Maputo Bay). More than 80 new distribution records and several species new to science were collected. One of the reasons why Smith decided to visit Bazaruto was because a traditional Mozambican fisherman had once told him that, to the south of Bazaruto, he had caught a huge, oily fish with soft flesh and no proper skeleton, and with the same large scales and queer fins as illustrated in a reward leaflet that Smith had issued to encourage fishermen and officials to bring any coelacanth catches to his attention (Bell, 1969). After searching in vain for coelacanths at Bazaruto, Smith concluded that, if one had been caught there, it would probably have been a stray from further north.

• Seychelles and the islands and atolls between the Seychelles and the African coast, including Aldabra, ending in Dar es Salaam. On this trip Smith joined local fishermen in a dug-out outrigger canoe (*galawa*) for a day of deep-water fishing in treacherous seas using traditional long lines, and caught several deep-water snappers that were previously unknown from the African coast. William Smith, now 16 years old, was part of this expedition.

- 1956: Their last expedition was to Pinda in Mozambique. This expedition was initiated by the colonial Mozambique government, which invited Smith to carry out experimental fishing in northern Mozambique using the line-fishing method he had learned in Shimoni, Kenya, on the previous expedition (Smith, 1957). Smith used the opportunity and the vessels provided by the authorities to collect shallow-water reef fishes.

Pinda Lighthouse, the tallest in East Africa, where the Smiths set up
a camp and laboratory on their 1951 Mozambique expedition.

All these expeditions were instigated and organised by JLB Smith in the manner of a latter-day Percy Harrison Fawcett, the British geographer who forsook the comforts of English gentility in order to lead exploratory expeditions into the jungles of Amazonia in Brazil between 1906 and 1925. The words used by Percy Fawcett's son, Brian, to describe his father apply equally to JLB Smith:

> '"Fawcett the dreamer", they called him. Perhaps they were right. So is any man a dreamer whose active imagination pictures the possibilities of dis-covery beyond the bounds of accepted scientific knowledge. It is the dreamer who is the investigator, and the investigator who becomes the pioneer.
> … True, he dreamed; but his dreams were built upon reason, and he was not the man to shirk the effort to turn theory into fact' (Fawcett & Fawcett, 1953).

The various fish-collecting expeditions that the Smiths carried out would not have been contemplated by ordinary people. They covered vast areas of

unknown and hostile terrain where transport, logistics, food and water supplies and communications were a nightmare, yet they performed first-class
research and brought back to Grahamstown large collections of carefully
labelled fishes, many of them also meticulously illustrated.

Margaret Smith, Peter Barnett and JLB Smith on the 18-metre motor launch
loaned to them by the Portuguese authorities that served as a temporary home,
laboratory and artist's studio during the 1951 expedition to northern Mozambique.

A photographer/writer, Peter Barnett from Durban, accompanied the
Smiths on their 1951 expedition to northern Mozambique; it was a life-
changing experience for him. He provides valuable insights into the
hardships and tensions that accompanied this expedition in his colourful
memoir, *Sea Safari with Professor Smith* (1953). After a year of exchanging
letters with JLB Smith about his possible participation in the expedition,
Barnett was granted an interview with Smith in Grahamstown. He over-
nighted in a local hotel; then, puffing away on his pipe, waited outside the
hotel the next morning for Margaret Smith to collect him. Margaret arrived
in a brightly-polished vintage Plymouth. 'An even-featured, sturdy woman
of about thirty-five got out, and marched briskly into the hotel. A moment
later she reappeared, patently looking for someone. I ventured a cautious
"Good morning"'. Within minutes she had asked him to put his pipe out as,
'The professor does not like the smell of smoke in the car'.

Barnett (1953) described Margaret as follows:

'She was of medium height, with a powerful, well-set body. Her face, untouched by cosmetics, was intellectual and strong, with heavy eyebrows, and eyes the colour of granite. She had a clear, sunburned skin. I learned later that she came from sturdy Scots-Afrikaner stock. ... She was the youngest in the family and was made [to] rough it by her elder brother from the earliest days of childhood – invaluable origin and training, I found out later, for the prospective wife of an ichthyologist' (Barnett, 1953).

His description of JLB Smith is equally revealing:

'He was not at all like my conception of a professor. The savant, as such, has always conjured up for me mental pictures of mild-mannered men with far-away looks. But Professor Smith was lean, he had a patriarchal visage, lean cheeks, and deep hollows at the temples; he seemed to me the epitome of perennial youth. He sat as straight as a guardsman; I felt that this man would retreat not an inch in compromise. His shrewd blue eyes were as clear now as in youth, and he gave the impression of great superiority over the uncertainties of smaller men. His movements were quick and decisive and his grey hair was short, in a brisk crew cut. He wore a light, off-white suit, and a black tie with a stiff white high-low collar. I had many times read, in novels, of gimlet eyes but this was the first time I had actually seen the real thing. They were blue, penetrating, and coldly speculative. They gave the impression of immense force of character, and single-minded purpose' (Barnett, 1953).

The interview was brisk and efficient. 'The professor offered me a seat and questioned me. I knew that he was summing me up. He has a habit of not looking at you directly as he talks, but swings around suddenly, fixing his gaze on you. This has a startling effect, almost as if he has caught you not paying attention in class. ... He is a master speaker, making his points with the practised ease of the professional lecturer' (Barnett, 1953).

Three weeks later Barnett received a letter from JLB Smith informing him 'with no great enthusiasm' that he would accompany the Smiths on the expedition. The Smiths and Barnett flew from Durban to Lourenço Marques on 29th May 1951 and then embarked on the motor vessel *Lurio* for Mozambique Island. The *Lurio* was a steel-hulled vessel with a shallow draught so that she could negotiate the many shallow sand bars that are typical of the inshore coastal waters of Mozambique.

William Smith also participated in this expedition, at the age of 12, during his Standard 8 year at school.

'William has good memories of his time on this expedition. The highlights were collecting a specimen new to science, *Bathygobius william*, riding turtles, coming face to face in the water with the massive grouper (National Geographic apparently had to cage the fish to prevent it from appearing in every picture) and missing 6 months of school' (J Smith, pers. comm., 2017).

Within the first day Barnett encountered Smith's diligent approach to expeditionary work.

'I soon found him to be an ingenious character, meticulous in detail and with a plan in everything he did. He never gave a direct order. He always passed an opinion and left one with the feeling that you could act to the contrary if you só desired. Disconcertingly he was usually right in his "opinions". … Professor Smith, like Lewis Carroll, numbers every letter he writes, files everything, and had listed every article, down to the smallest box of pins, in the fifty-odd pieces of baggage that we took on the expedition. His list, for example, would read "Box 48; ¾ down right-hand side: extra forceps in metal sheath"' (Barnett, 1953).

The expedition also revealed many of JLB's character traits. 'It was never Professor Smith's habit to praise because he said, "When a motor runs smoothly there is no need for repair – for comment. And when faulty, it has to be licked back into perfect running order"' (Barnett, 1953). He was remarkably friendly and courteous to the local Mozambican people, both adults and children. When they arrived on the island of Ibo JLB Smith leaned down to talk to a young boy standing with his mother onshore, 'whereupon with screams and babbling away in the native tongue he rushed around his mother's skirts in an effort to escape. We learned later that the word he was screaming amounted roughly to "Cannibal". It seemed he had been told that all white men ate human flesh. The professor's interest convinced him that he was the chosen' (Barnett, 1953). Smith also showed uncommon sympathy for the Portuguese lifestyle. They arrived at Ibo at about two o'clock but 'the professor decided that to land immediately would be unfair as the officials were at siesta', so they did some fishing.

JLB's relentless work ethic surfaced throughout the expedition, and he did not care for creature comforts in the field. He once caught Barnett relaxing briefly after lunch. 'Have you any work to do?' he asked. 'Yes, I most certainly have, but I've just had lunch', Barnett replied. 'Relaxation?' Smith fired back, 'But you relax when you sleep, and you'll relax forever when you're dead. In the meantime we've got work to do.' On another occasion Barnett dozed off while fishing. Suddenly he felt a sharp tug on the line and struck, only to find that the professor had pulled the line to wake him up.

At other times Smith questioned his own work ethic and longed for a more leisurely lifestyle. In 1948 he wrote to a high-ranking friend in Mozambique, Commandante Tomas Vitar Duque, Port Captain in Lourenço Marques, 'Sometime when life is not quite so full we intend to come to be able to enjoy some more leisurely things that you offer. I should love to idle for a few days on the beach at the Polana or at Inhaca, and not always feel work driving me away.' Although this was a highly unlikely scenario, and never took place, it does reveal the mental conflict that he was experiencing at the time.

Later in life JLB Smith was happy to acknowledge his weaknesses. In an article published when he was 59 years old, he wrote:

> 'Advancing years have brought me solace, for with my relatively frail body my purely male pride is no longer outraged by having to acknowledge that my wife is physically more powerful than myself. Nevertheless it took years of skilful propaganda on her part to remove the hurt that she could handle weights beyond my lift and could row a boat under conditions where I would be helpless except at risk of serious internal strain' (Smith, 1997, reprinted from 1956).

Throughout the 1951 expedition Smith constantly admonished Barnett for his pipe and cigarette smoking. On one occasion, on a small coral atoll near Cabo Delgado, they were suddenly attacked by a swarm of malarial mosquitoes. As they fled along the beach, Barnett noticed something interesting: JLB himself took a few puffs in an effort to escape their tormentors. 'The professor paused for one second to light a cigarette, puffing smoke wildly in a vain attempt to gas the mosquitoes, and gasping invective at how horrible it tasted.'

Although it seems unethical today, Smith made extensive use of cigarettes as a means to encourage rural people to collect fishes for him. 'He invariably kept tins of cigarettes to barter with fishermen for their catches' (Barnett, 1953).

In an article entitled 'Magic Cylinders', he extols the virtues of taking cigarette rewards on expeditions to remote parts of Africa:

'The parts where we usually do our work are quite beyond the reach of ordinary supplies, and cigarettes are of far more value for our work than money, for fishermen and others will make an effort to give service and to bring specimens for cigarettes that hardly any money would tempt them to do.

'It is most important to have entire uncleaned fish as specimens, and in hot climates it is very difficult to get fishermen to keep them like that for more than a short time. Cigarettes proved the only way. ... Cigarettes are indeed the most potent means of maintaining discipline and constant willingness in the servant retinue, without obvious force, that we know. In Mozambique most of our natives are Government sailors or policemen, some excellent and intelligent. It is my policy to give regular rations of cigarettes and matches. There was rarely any misbehaviour, but when it occurred, it was pointed out. There was no scolding, the culprit was merely overlooked on ration day, and it was never necessary to repeat the penalty' (Smith, 1955b).

In *Old Fourlegs*, Smith further comments, rather crudely, that he always took several hundred cigarettes with him when he travelled '... in wild parts. They are a wonderful open sesame to primitive hearts' (Smith, 1956).

The Smiths' rigid exercise regime also impacted on Barnett's laidback lifestyle:

'I remembered how we had walked one afternoon to continue the filming of the San Sebastian *Fortaleza* [fort]. The professor and Margaret Smith walked fast, the theory being that not only is walking a means of transport, but one must also derive the benefit of exercise from the action so as not to waste time. ... My fairly easy-going approach to life was not at one with Smith the martinet. This personality clash coloured and influenced our association even in the most mundane and normally unimportant matters.'

Barnett (1953) also noticed that the Smiths did not enjoy their East Africa expedition in the way that most people would enjoy an outing into tropical Africa:

'Enjoyment in their busy lives comes from the inner satisfaction of accomplishments and hardships that they endure willingly in the pursuit of scientific knowledge. ... I felt that no matter what I did, I would become entrangled [sic] in the complexities of the professor's will. However as we talked on and on, I began to understand a little more about this man, an extreme egotist, sublime in the certain knowledge of the supremity [sic] of his own intellect, which had been proved throughout his academic career in universities from Stellenbosch to Cambridge. Once he told me that he had known the Queen Mother personally when she was Lady Bowes-Lyon and how he had, as a young man, been driven down the Strand in a Rolls-Royce and not ... allowed to alight to make a purchase. The chauffeur did that for him. "You see me now in rough khaki clothes, he said, and therefore find it hard to visualise such vastly different circumstances."'

On the island of Ibo, Barnett also learned about some of Margaret's unusual interests:

'We spent about an hour walking about this tiny island and discovered another fort. I have never met anyone so fond of forts as Margaret; she would walk for miles if she knew she would find some rambling remains over which to climb and speculate. I was never sure whether it was a love of history or an innate pugnacious spirit which brought forth her tirades on bloody battles of yore.'

He said to her, 'You would have made a fine general, or leader of those bands of Yugoslav girl guerrillas I knew during the war'. She smiled and said nothing (Barnett, 1953). Once he asked Margaret whether, as a scientist, she was also an atheist. She replied, 'The world of nature is too ordered and the creatures I study too lovely to be created haphazardly, by mere chance'.[1]

---

1 But Margaret had confused evolution by natural selection with mutation. Like a misprint in a book, a random mutation is unlikely to lead to improvement (but it sometimes does). Mutations are random and by chance and have no bias towards 'improving' a plant or animal. In contrast, evolution by natural selection is very directional and not by chance and is unquestionably biased towards an improved ability to survive.

On this expedition Margaret explained JLB's work ethic to Barnett:

'The professor demands a standard of work and behaviour far above the capabilities of the normal man. Many of his former students are today successful men; they often come back to visit him, now as friends and to laugh over all they went through at his hands in their student days. His students fell into two distinct groups, those that liked him and those that didn't. Those who liked him were, in his own opinion, those who WORKED. ... He made things difficult for the others and would waste no time on them. Therefore if he is taking this trouble about you, he must see something worthwhile in you' (Barnett, 1953).

Of all their fish-collecting expeditions, probably the most rewarding was the extensive 1954 trip to Kenya, the Seychelles, Aldabra and Dar es Salaam. Smith (1957) describes their visit to Aldabra in revealing detail:

'Probably because of the remoteness and difficulty of this region, Aldabra has received little attention from the marine biologist, indeed less than twenty species of marine fishes have been recorded from there. Three days were spent at Aldabra and we employed every possible moment in intensive collecting of fishes by every possible means, including explosives, poison, nets, spears and lines, by which means we obtained at least ten thousand specimens of numerous species and acquired a fairly comprehensive knowledge of the fish life of that area at the time of our visit.'

Ten thousand fishes in three days! That is wholesale slaughter, by any measure. In a bizarre way ichthyologists are fortunate in that their quarry, among the lower vertebrates, tends to be lumped with the invertebrates, which entomologists and arachnologists don't hesitate to collect by the thousands. This is in contrast to the other vertebrates, the amphibians and reptiles, and especially the birds and mammals, for which it would be difficult to justify collecting even a few dozen specimens. There is no doubt that the Smiths made optimal use of rare opportunities to collect fishes in remote places, often in bizarre ways, and went to great lengths to record and preserve the specimens for long-term study, but collecting *on this scale*, especially in areas like Aldabra that now enjoy strict protection, would be unthinkable today.

The huge collections of fishes included many new range extensions and species unknown to science. Most importantly, the artists were able to record the live colours of many of them, which was essential for the major book on the sea fishes of southern Africa that Smith was planning. 'An important conclusion that JLB reached at this time was that many fishes, even small, apparently feeble species that were previously only known from the Pacific Ocean, also occur off Africa and have a very wide Indo-Pacific distribution. On the basis of these findings an American ichthyologist concluded that the great Indo-Pacific 'was just one little puddle after all!' (MM Smith, 1969).

Margaret (1959) later recalled working with William on this expedition:

'In 1954 came the highlight of my underwater work. With a bit of feminine manoeuvreing I managed to have my 15 year old son, William, included as a member of our expedition to Kenya, Seychelles and the islands north of Madagascar. Six foot tall, strong and healthy, no phobias to overcome, well trained in our work, and loving it, he made an ideal diving companion. During this expedition for a month we lived aboard a small 40ft fishing vessel. We travelled close on 2000 miles through some of the loneliest seas of the world, where the only land in the vast open Indian Ocean is a few tiny specks of islands north of Madagascar. My son and I worked as a team, and we had many experiences and adventures. ... The tide was rising fast, William and I had been hard at it for nearly three hours, and were just picking up the last few specimens before returning to the boat, when millions of tightly packed small silvery whitebait suddenly came along and surrounded us. ... Within a minute or two we were surrounded by huge fish snapping up the silvery morsels ... William and I sat spellbound. We were merely parts of the scenery, for fish of up to 20 to 80 lb. would come shooting straight towards us, and within inches of our masks suddenly veer away. It was a never to be forgotten scene: Kingfish, rock-cods, barracudas, tunnies and even a shoal of shy exquisite torpedo-shaped rainbow-runners' (MM Smith, 1959).

In all his field work JLB Smith was very ably assisted by Margaret who, without any prior training in the field, threw herself into the study of fishes and eventually, by force of circumstances, illustrated most of his publications. As fishes lose their colour soon after death, it is essential that the artist should be in the field

Margaret illustrating fish and JLB examining specimens on the 1951 expedition to Mozambique.

with the fish-collecting team so that notes can be made of the live colours. Taking four fish artists plus Margaret and a photographer with him on his expedition to Mozambique in June/July 1946 underlines the importance that JLB Smith placed on illustrating fishes (Gon, 1996).

Glyn Hewson, who arrived in Grahamstown with his family on 1st March 1951 and lived next door to the Smiths in Gilbert Road, remembers helping Margaret after one of the early 1950s expeditions:

'At one point during these early years, I had a vacation job for two weeks helping Mrs Smith classify and sorting the huge numbers of fish which she and her husband brought back from East Africa after each expedition. I have a cherished memory of those hours and hours of not very exciting work made so memorable because she knew so much about so many of those fish. She would chat away with such excitement and humour lacing information with anecdotes and stories about the expedition ... I was fascinated by her meticulousness and I had the feeling that there was just nothing which she could not do. I remember her talking about the frenzy when they had just received a whole lot of new fish; or just after there had been a controlled explosion. How fast and accurately she had to work to record colours and details for those masterpieces which she would then create. The consummate artist. Correct down to the last scale' (G Hewson, unpublished memoir, 2004).

He also remembered the readiness with which the Smiths shared information on their latest expeditions with the Grahamstown public:

'Both she and JLB were wonderful lecturers. Invariably, after an expedition, there would be the chance to go down to the General Lecture Theatre and hear an enthralling account of months up the East coast with slides and maps and even displays on view. Margaret was exceptional on these occasions. I will never ever forget her ability to make her fish pop out of her talk and swim in front of you. She would chuckle and chat about them like intimate acquaintances, which of course they were: "now look at this fellow; what is so special about him is the shape of this fin .... And the reason for this is of course, that …" or "this little one is so beautiful but don't be misguided, he can be very nasty; if you look closer …"'

During the East Africa expeditions Margaret Smith not only acted as the chief artist but was also responsible for supervising the other artists, entertaining visitors, organising the cooking, making arrangements for eating and accommodation, and negotiating (initially using sign language) with the locals for fresh produce. This was a time-consuming and frustrating task in remote areas where there was no electricity and food was scarce, as she also had to play a full role in fish collecting, both from shore at low tide and in deeper water from boats. Once the fish had been collected she also had to help sort, illustrate, preserve and catalogue them, and develop her skills in fish identification.

In a talk given in Grahamstown in 1951 she described the conditions under which the team had to work on the East African expeditions:

'All this work was exhausting and on return to the lighthouse they could not rest as in that hot climate fishes spoil in a very short time. Dirty and tired they often worked right through to nightfall without stop or food. After that, photographic work had to be done in pitch darkness in a small, smelly outside room with lions about. Having perpetually to be on guard while working is a severe strain. The sun is dangerous, and there were plenty of wild animals, leopards, lions, snakes, also poisonous flies, mosquitoes, parasites of many kinds, leprosy, and other diseases. The continual fear of lions on shore was especially wearing. On the water there was always anxiety and danger, storms, sharks, and currents and especially the terrible stonefish' (Rhodes University Archive).

JLB and Margaret Smith sorting fish on Quisava Island during the 1951 expedition to northern Mozambique.

Suntan lotions were not available in the 1940s so JLB made his own lotions or placed a strip of plastic over his lower lip (which looked very strange) to reduce the risk of skin cancer (W Smith, pers. comm., 2017).

In a letter to M Tannebalm (from Keatings Pharmaceuticals, who had donated medical supplies to the Smiths) dated 21st August 1956, JLB Smith recalled the threat posed by lions in northern Mozambique:

> 'Although building and harbour construction are proceeding fast this is still very much the wilds and only a few hundred yards from the Village is jungle where wild beasts abound. One farmer in the area killed [over] fifty lions last year, they plague all these people, and natives are constantly being taken by them. The peninsula of Nacala is one of their most notorious haunts, and nobody ventures out after dusk.'

During an expedition to Pinda in 1950 Smith (1951) commented '… and the cook-boy tells you the food is cold and that he must go as the lions took that woman over there last night'.

In northern Mozambique they also encountered shallow reefs that were teeming with eels:

> 'As far as the eye could reach, there were eels, big and small, crawling and gliding all over the reef, some of them four or five feet long. Wherever you trod, eels shot out from under your feet, or heads with fang-lined mouths popped out of holes and were hastily withdrawn. It was like walking in a snake park. … [On] one occasion, my son had bent down to examine something in a pool, when the head and forepart of a huge Silver Conger came vertically out of a hole between his legs; he leapt a good three feet into the air!' (Smith, 1968b).

They also had encounters with giant pythons. On Vamizi Island in northern Mozambique the Smiths left two local sailors, who couldn't keep up their walking pace, to rest in a clearing in the jungle:

> 'When we did get back to the sailors, they were pale with fright and almost fell on our necks with relief. They told us that soon after we had left them, an enormous python had uncurled itself from a nearby tree

and, according to their story, had adopted a most threatening attitude. Lacking any weapon, they had apparently been almost paralysed with fear, but the creature eventually slipped away' (Smith, 1968b).

On their expeditions they were also vulnerable to contracting bilharzia, hookworm, typhus, malaria, blackwater fever and fungoid infections (Smith, 1968b), and even suffered from pawpaw poisoning!

'It was not until some time later that I discovered that my indisposition had been due to papaw [sic] poisoning. We had been short of all fruit except papaw which grew well at Palma and both of us ate freely of these succulent delicacies, as we considered them. I have since found that papaw, despite its reputation of being easily digested, causes severe abdominal pain in some people. My wife, however, ate freely of them for a long time without any digestive disturbance, except that they turned her skin so yellow that when we returned to civilization the first doctor we met was convinced that she had jaundice. It was more than ten years before she lost that yellow tinge!' (Smith, 1968b).

This was surely an exaggeration!

CHAPTER 13

Sea and shore dangers
Taking risks

WHILE JLB never learned to dive in spite of a lifetime's involvement with the denizens of the deep, Margaret, who had grown up far from the sea (as JLB had done), without access even to a swimming pool, was up for the challenge.

In 1952, by now thoroughly committed to the world of ichthyology, Margaret learned how to skin dive with the help of members of the Durban Undersea Club. Her first tentative dive with goggles in Mozambique later that year opened her eyes to a whole new world:

'We waded out, I put my goggles in position, and with my heart pounding …
I put my face underwater. My breath caught up as it always did but as the new world I had entered opened up before me, my wonder, excitement and curiosity pushed the physical discomfort into the background until I could hardly spare the time to take my head out of the water and breathe.'

She was hooked and from then on took every opportunity to dive.

In January 1961, at the age of 43 years but still strong and slim, she had lessons with the experienced diver Gary Haselau, who taught her how to scuba dive (Bell, 1987)[1].

Margaret described in her own inimitable style what she saw on one particular dive in Mozambique, as if the fishes were all personal friends, and from the perspective of an artist who tried to capture their colour patterns:

---

1 Weinberg (1999) incorrectly states that Margaret first learned to scuba dive in Hawai'i at the age of 60.

'I saw unicorn fishes come nosing around the corner, rock-cods scavenging in the crevices, a sparkling shoal of Caesios passed me on business bent (elegant streamlined fishes clad in glorious blues and yellows) … there was the easily identified neat little *Chromis dimidiatus* [chocolate dip] whose front half is a rich deep brown and back half contrasting white, for all the world as if he'd forgotten to put on his trousers … his first cousin, *Ternatensis*, and *Pomacentrus opercularis* … handsome fish depending on good features rather than gaudy colours to express his personality … other coral fishes in transparent blues and greens … a long scintillating mauve coral fish … *Anthias squamipinnis*, loveliest little jewels of the sea – shapely bod, elongate elegant fins and colours that defy reproduction. As they flash below in the blue water the general impression is that of lining gold with mauve glints and the brightest of yellow … I never see them without a catch in my throat at their beauty' (MM Smith, 1959; Richards, 1987).

Margaret did have some scary moments while diving, including a close encounter with a giant moray eel while snorkelling with William:

'We watched in fascinated horror while he eyed us, first with the left eye and then with the right as he turned his head from side to side … [We] were buffeted by breakers on the outer rim of the coral reef where I swallowed gallons of water … and a very scratched and bruised ichthyologist decided that sometimes one had to pay a high price for one's specimens' (Richards, 1987).

She was also attacked by barracuda while snorkelling off Malindi in Kenya. Margaret eventually stopped scuba diving in her 60s (Richards, 1987).

Peter Barnett documented many of the dangers that they encountered on their 1951 Mozambique expedition. For instance, when they arrived on the Island of Mozambique, he commented wryly that it 'is not a popular picnic spot' as it is 'inhabited by thousands of snakes'. Of Pinda he remarked, 'This was lion country, and to move into the bushlands without firearms and a guide invited possible death, especially at night'. Not far from the lighthouse the local people were constantly terrorised by lions that broke into their huts at night. 'On one occasion two Blacks were asleep in their hut when a lion broke in. Other members of the village heard the screams of the terrified occupants and managed to frighten off the lion [by] making a great din

Margaret Smith follows JLB and the bearers as they make their way through a narrow fissure and dense forests to the marine coast in northern Mozambique in 1951.

with drums and empty tins. The two escaped with minor wounds only – that time' (Barnett, 1953). When Smith visited Mozambique Island in December 1952, he found that a close relative of his friend, the Port Captain, had been eaten by a lion. In *High Tide* he wrote, 'Even to this day (1960), the postal service from Port Amelia depends mostly on African runners and at times they and the letters have disappeared, taken by lions' (Smith, 1968b).

In *Old Fourlegs* Smith (1956) commented further on the lions:

'Almost every night they tore open the natives' flimsy huts and savagely choked their last frenzied screams. It was horrible to hear the triumphant roar that accompanied a kill; we even had one of the brutes come and cough at us early one morning from the top of a thicket-clad cliff as we worked on the reef below. In the morning we would find their pug marks near our bedroom window. It was not pleasant.'

Barnett's first encounter with the deadly stonefish was a memorable one. While they were wading along a coral bank, JLB called him over to see a particularly vividly-coloured fish. While staring at it, he noticed 'a peculiarly shaped piece of coral looking itself almost like a fish. Part of the coral resembled fins, a tail, and with some stretch of the imagination, even a wide, dead-white mouth. Something made me look up and I saw that the professor was smiling. "You have just seen your first stonefish", he said.'

Smith stabbed the fish with a spear, lifted it out of the water and carried it to a dhow where he laid it on a cross beam. He then depressed the warty skin around the dorsal spine with the spear to make the poison well out. Suddenly a stream of yellowish liquid squirted high into the air and directly into one of Barnett's eyes! Smith screamed out an order and Barnett fell backwards into the water, fully clothed, and kept his head underwater with his eyes open for as long as he could. Mercifully, no pain followed and he was not blinded.

JLB Smith with a stonefish on the 1951 expedition to Mozambique.

Luckily for him, the neurotoxic venom of the stonefish is only deadly if it enters the blood stream.

The true stonefish, *Synanceia verrucosa* (family Scorpaenidae), known as *sherova* in Mozambique, has 13 dorsal spines, and at the base of each spine are two large venom sacs, one on each side. When the fish is tramped on, the skin surrounding the spines presses the venom sacs and the venom is injected through needle-sharp spines, like a snake's fangs. The venom causes swelling almost immediately and excruciating pain that is so severe that the victim may become demented and lose consciousness (Barnett, 1953). True stonefish are regarded as the most dangerous fish in the sea as their stabs can be fatal to an adult human within two hours (Smith, 1949). The stab of the false stonefish, *Scorpaenopsis diabolus*, which is in a different subfamily of the Scorpaenidae (scorpionfishes) to the true stonefish, causes intense pain for one to three hours (unless treated) and is probably responsible for reports that the 'much-maligned' stonefish is not as dangerous as it is made out to be.

At the time of Smith's expeditions, the only effective method of treatment for a stonefish stab was to immerse the wound in water that is as hot as the victim can tolerate for at least 90 minutes, which denatures the protein in the venom and causes it to lose its toxicity. Experiments by Australian scientists have shown that the venom rapidly loses its power if it is bathed in water at 50°C (Smith, 1968b). Subsequent research has shown that a mild acid or alkali also reduces its potency, and an injection of a solution of emetine hydrochloride in water quickly relieves the pain (Barnett, 1953; Smith, 1968b). Because of the danger of stonefishes, the Smiths and Barnett wore leggings and heavy, tin-lined boots when they waded along coral banks in Mozambique.

When JLB was stabbed by a stonefish near Pinda in 1950, Margaret was forced to treat him using the painful 'hot water' method, and almost certainly saved his life. Smith described the agony he had to endure in his book, *High Tide*:

'During my life I have endured a good deal of severe pain, but nothing comparable with this appalling agony. … half-fainting I staggered about, unable to keep still, until my wife gave me an injection of morphine. After some time this diminished the sweating and made me sleepy, but had no effect on the pain. About three hours after the stab, my wife decided to try hot water, and within one minute of immersing the hand, the effect was dramatic. The agony was reduced to just a bad pain. … We continued the hot water treatment for some hours and the pain gradually eased … The swelling of the hand and arm increased to a maximum after three days, extending even above the elbow. … Two weeks later, my arm was back to almost normal size, but could not be used. … Even three months afterwards, the hand was still weak [and] remained weak for several years.'

Glyn Hewson also described the dramatic talk that Margaret gave about this incident:

'I will never ever forget an audience of some 400 people rivetted in silence as she told of JLB's unexpected encounter with the world's deadliest fish: the stone fish. How a man came in one evening with a basket of fish on his head and told them that he had found a stone fish for them; in excitement how the professor had put his hand up to help take the basket down; in so doing, how his hand was spiked between thumb and index finger by one of the spines of the stone fish which was sitting on the very top of the pile. Within seconds, how he had crumpled to the ground where he writhed in agony as he slipped towards a coma. She systematically tried everything she knew but none of the antidotes or injections had any effect. In near panic and with rising despair, she filled a syringe with almost boiling water and injected into the puncture. It saved his life. His recovery was complete except that there was always a slight stiffness in that area of the hand thereafter.'

Margaret herself was stabbed by a scorpionfish which, while not as deadly as a stonefish, is worth avoiding (as this author himself has experienced).

While they were at Pinda, JLB attended the funeral of a local fisherman who had succumbed to stonefish poison, and he and Margaret treated a local woman who had also been stabbed:

'The woman was lying on a grass mat writhing and emitting little moans from deep down in her throat. Her foot was already swollen and turning black at the puncture. Margaret Smith ordered that a tripot of water be boiled over the open fire, and while the men were arranging [this] the woman was moved into a crude lean-to shelter. As soon as the leg was disturbed her moans became screams terrible to hear, and then gradually subsided again to long monotonous whimpers as she was laid [down] to rest. A villager brought the pot of hot water to where the woman lay. One man gripped the leg at the calf, while a woman knelt with the patient's head in her lap. The leg was raised, the pot tilted and the foot immersed in hot water. ... The woman screamed and tried to free herself and more men were required to hold her down. They repeated this treatment for many hours, pausing only to reheat the water. When we left the pain seemed to have subsided as she no longer moaned. Later I learned that she had, at that stage, mercifully fainted. But she lived and we saw her again next day lying on the sand under a tree near her hut' (Barnett, 1953).

Despite all the hardships, Barnett learned a great deal about fishes from the Smiths:

'There was a fish which the professor called "comic opera". Its colouring seemed to be of no definite pattern. It was as if an artist in complete abandon had experimented with pure colour, from iridescent reds to jet black. Its expression was that of constant amazement, no doubt at its own absurdity, and its mouth was shaped and red-lipped, like an old Clara Bow' (Barnett, 1953).

The unusual dietary habits of the Smiths were also revealed to Barnett on the expedition:

> '… the professor handed round cold chicken and bread, the latter for me alone as he considered "dead food … unworthy of his palate". Food is very important to the Smiths, and as they train like prize fighters, there is no room for compromise as far as their diet is concerned. Basically it is an excellent diet, but it eliminates eating for pleasure and places everything on a scientific basis' (Barnett, 1953).

As anyone who has worked in the tropics knows, you acquire exotic pets along the way. In a dingy hotel in Porto Amelia, Margaret was seen swatting flies and carefully placing them in a glass tube. When the other guests questioned her about this peculiar behaviour, she responded by opening a box and lifting out an enormous, hissing chameleon, which she had caught and tamed. At this stage, any suspicions that the other guests might have had about the sanity of the South African scientists were finally confirmed. Sadly, the chameleon came to a sticky end as quarantine regulations at South African Customs forbade its entry into the country, and it was duly pickled.

Barnett also learned that the reason why all the intricate travel, fishing and accommodation arrangements worked so smoothly on the expedition, even in the remotest reaches of Mozambique, was the goodwill that the Smiths

Margaret Smith with a lizard in Mozambique in the 1940s. She loved exotic animals.

had generated there during their previous expeditions, followed up by prolific letter writing. Between the expeditions they spent many hours writing to everybody who had helped them; from porters to local fishermen (*marinheiros*), hotel managers to launch skippers, port captains to lighthouse keepers (*chefe de farol*), administrators to governors, everyone received a letter of thanks (Barnett, 1953; MM Smith, pers. comm., 1980). Largely through Margaret's affability, the Smiths made friends wherever they went on their expeditions. JLB's main contribution to this cordiality was to share the fish discoveries that he made with officials and local people, and to ask them questions about fish.

Back in Grahamstown after the 1956 expedition to the Seychelles, Margaret set about illustrating their vast collections of fishes, many of them new to science. She co-authored a book on the *Fishes of the Seychelles* with JLB, producing a phenomenal 938 illustrations, of which 344 were in full colour. Many of these excellent illustrations were used in later editions of *Sea Fishes*. Margaret also co-authored and produced 233 new colour paintings for *Fishes of the Tsitsikamma Coastal National Park* (Smith & Smith, 1966), as well as figures for JLB Smith's articles on fishes in the 1960s in the *Standard Encyclopaedia of South Africa, Animal Life in South Africa* (edited by Sydney Skaife) and the *Afrikaanse Woordeboek*. One of her first major solo works was the description and illustration of the common marine fishes of South Africa for the *Ensiklopedie van die Wêreld* (MM Smith, 1975).

The Smiths' commitment to their science, as evidenced by their tireless exploration of the East African coastline, enduring months of almost intolerable living conditions and often putting their lives at risk, resulted in a rich haul of material that would enhance fish collections in South Africa and become the basis for a range of future publications.

CHAPTER 14

Bombing and poisoning fishes
Effective but controversial short cuts

EARLY IN his collecting career, JLB Smith decided that the most effective way of collecting fish was to bomb them. Though he could swim, he never learned to snorkel or scuba dive, unlike Margaret and William, but contented himself with gazing at underwater life through glass-bottomed buckets while he 'blasted' the reefs.

> 'Having selected an area I would go off with explosives in a small boat and examine the bottom through a glass-bottomed bucket. ... there is nothing more wonderful and exciting as treasure after treasure comes aboard, some quite new to African seas, many new to science. ... But we got results, wonderful results, thanks to explosives, thanks to Messrs. African Explosives and Chemical Industries, who have kindly provided this means, covering our work for many years' (Smith, 1958a).

JLB Smith preparing explosives for bombing fishes on an expedition to Xai-Xai in Mozambique in 1946.

In a 1953 popular article on their fish collections at Pemba Island, north of Zanzibar off the coast of Tanzania, he writes:

> 'We made a rapid survey up and down this channel. Through a glass-bottomed bucket, the steeply sloping coral-clad banks clearly showed teeming fish-life, clouds of flashing fingerlings and the stealthy shadows of their larger brethren coming and going. I had a wonderful view of a large shoal of grotesque Unicorn-fish, their quaint horns and white-edged tails clearly visible, swimming in a level sheet some fathoms down.
>
> 'Soon I found a place where a spur of the island broke the surface and formed a wide eddy. Watching through the glass [glass-bottomed bucket] I sent down a large bomb with 25 seconds of spitting fuse. We shot off over the edge of the shallows and waited – 20 … 25 … BOOOOOM! – off she went; a few seconds and up boiled the big hump of dirty water, and then a shout from the boys, for up came the fish – fish of all kinds, big and small, shining and sparkling in gorgeous hues, rolling in the boiling foam. … On this brief intense voyage there was no leisure and little sleep, but my exhaustion was tempered by the wealth we had blasted from Pemba's coral-clad reefs, privileged as we were to be the first to bring them to the light' (JLB Smith, 1955b).

JLB's explosives were sometimes used to frighten away dangerous animals. Once, off Tekomaji Island near Palma in northern Mozambique, he and his two assistants were precariously perched in their tiny wooden dinghy when they were suddenly surrounded by six giant hammerhead sharks. Smith nonchalantly chased them away by tossing small homemade bombs at them. On another occasion in the same area he once found himself staring into the slit eyes of a giant shark in shallow water, with no explosives handy:

> 'I had just got off a hump into thigh-deep water when suddenly the wind dropped, the water smoothed, and I found myself literally face to face with a blunt-nosed brute of a shark – a good seven feet long. We faced one another for a split second, then I found myself back on the rock in the middle of the channel, with no clear recollection of whether I had run, jumped or flown there.'

Smith had managed to obtain permission from the Portuguese colonial authorities in Mozambique to use explosives (and poisons) to catch fishes. This he considered necessary as nets are useless over coral and rocky reefs, and many fish species are not attracted to bait, whereas explosives and poisons allowed him to catch even the smallest, most secretive species.

'There are many places in the sea where fishes live in numbers where you cannot fish with lines, use nets, or even poison. In deep reefs and among coral heads where fierce currents rage, there is only one method for the scientist – explosives' (Smith, 1958a).

He further justified the use of explosives as follows:

'Practically every fish in the sea must die a cruel and violent death – that is nature. But it is ludicrous to suggest that fishes have any fear of explosives – they cannot have. I have thrown dummy bombs with fuse attached, and watched – fish do not flee from these in fright, instead hundreds come round and snap at the stream of shining, dancing bubbles of gas. When a real bomb is used, the fish do not even move away, they continue swimming, quite unconcerned, then in a fraction of a second they are dead, without pain or fear, a wonderful end for any creature. I wish I could count on one like that' (Smith, 1958a).

The powerful pressure wave produced by an underwater explosion stuns or kills fishes without damaging them unduly, and causes them to float to the surface, where they can easily be collected. Smith had studied explosives and poisons after the First World War and had an above-average knowledge of these deadly methods, but he does not elaborate on this knowledge in any of his publications. He blasted thousands of fishes out of the water and even hoped to catch coelacanths in this way (Smith, 1956, 1968a). He not only detonated explosives in midwater but also on coral reefs.

'To get the fishes from the coral heads, explosives provide a short cut. The blast breaks open the coral, kills or stuns the fishes and causes a current to boil upwards and carry them to the surface, where they float for a time' (Smith, 1951).

Smith even persuaded the Portuguese authorities to store large amounts of dynamite that he had somehow managed to post to them in Mozambique. In a letter dated August 1953, Mario Emilio Azinhals de Melo, Chief of Staff, Quartel General in Lourenço Marques, informs him, 'I beg to inform you that I have already received the explosives, which you mentioned in your letter dated 11th August, and they have been stored in the Lourenço Marques magazine at your orders for the period for which you think it is necessary'. But this arrangement would go sour; he later heard from the Portuguese authorities that they had destroyed his valuable hoard of dynamite as, not surprisingly, it was considered to be a hazard! (Rhodes University Archive).

In his Preface to the 1949 edition of *The Sea Fishes of Southern Africa*, Basil le May recalls the use of blast fishing during a fish-collecting expedition at Inhaca Island in 1946:

'We had been given permission to drop some hand-grenades over the sandstone ledge, which shelved perpendicularly for about fifty feet, at the southern end of the island and where numerous fishes of many colours glided but would not take bait. Professor Smith and I were ashore and Mrs. Smith and Francis Spence cruised up and down in my father's motor boat ready to net the dazed fish. After the first grenade, several fish came up and those within reach were recovered. Suddenly, in great excitement Professor Smith told me to jump in and get "that *Aurora borealis*" – or so the name sounded to me. As I had just been discharged from the Army, I was used to travelling light and was reluctant to dive in, in my only khaki shorts and shirt. When I explained my predicament to Professor Smith he said, "Take your clothes off!" To this I replied, "What about your wife?" and without hesitation he answered, "Don't worry about her, science comes first!". I duly jumped in and caught the fish, but while attempting to hand it to Professor Smith it recovered and swam away!' (B le May, 1949).

In his notes on 'Underwater explosions' in the introductory chapters to *The Sea Fishes of Southern Africa*, Smith (1949) again justifies the use of explosives:

'But recent carefully controlled experiments have yielded rather surprising results in the matter of submarine explosions. It has been found that a blast of such intensity as to disable a submarine has no effect on fishes

145

more than 200 feet away, and that Mollusca such as oysters more than 50 feet away from the explosion centre are apparently unharmed. It is curious that the effect is the same whatever the amount of explosive employed, for there is little difference in general effect on marine life whether 10 lbs. or 2,000 lbs. of dynamite be detonated. A shock powerful enough to be felt on a boat 10 miles away had no observable effect whatsoever on fishes only 25 feet away from the explosion.'

Later, Smith (1959, 1970) tried to convince his readers and marine conservationists that using explosives does no permanent harm to the marine environment:

'In recent times, several persons in prominent positions have made public statements indicating the use of explosives in killing fish as cruel or otherwise to be deprecated. There is a good deal of sentimental misunderstanding about this matter, especially on the part of those without actual experience. Apart from my own widespread experience and experiments, extending over many years, scientists in the USA have investigated the various aspects on a considerable scale. It is quite incorrect to state that the method is cruel. There is no anticipation whatever on the part of the fish and death is instantaneous and certainly painless. The killing range of the detonation in the sea is surprisingly limited for fishes of ordinary size, for it has been shown that those more than 80 yards [about 73 metres] away from even an enormous explosion are rarely affected. As far as my observations go, the use of explosives in the sea apparently works no permanent harm. On investigating areas which I had bombed in various parts of East Africa, the fauna was found to be completely regenerated after a lapse of one or more years, with much the same order of population as initially.

'It is my considered opinion that in the hands of a competent and experienced scientist this is one of the most humane as well as one of the most efficient methods of securing valuable specimens without any permanent harm to the fauna. Not only does this method secure easily and in perfect condition, fishes that cannot be got by any other means, but it rapidly gives qualitative and quantitative information about fish populations that would be difficult to acquire by any other method in even far greater time. The chief drawback lies in the use of explosives by unskilled persons of low mentality, for disastrous accidents result, but it is only where authorities are lax, or where there is no prohibition, that such persons secure explosives.'

In *High Tide* he repeats these comments, adding, 'No purely Museum scientist is in any position to express views about this matter ...' (Smith, 1968b).

Needless to say, not everyone, this author included, agrees with Smith, as there is ample evidence to show that explosives can cause long-term damage to coral reefs. Robin Stobbs (1997) visited the sites off Shimoni near Kenya's southern border in 1953, a year after the Smiths had dynamited extensively for fish in this area. The local fishermen showed him 'numbers of clearly visible shallow craters which they identified as places where JLB had exploded charges the previous year'. It has been estimated that coral reef damage from explosive blasts may take up to 35 years to recover fully, as reef growth is a few millimetres annually. Yet JLB Smith states in *Our Fishes*, 'In our work off East Africa I was able to visit and study exact spots where I had bombed a year or more previously. It was interesting to see that in each case the fish life had apparently returned to normal' (Smith, 1968a). Smith, however, was not a diver and could not reliably assess the impact of his explosives in water deeper than a few metres.

According to Margaret (SATV, 1976), JLB made cunning use of explosives, carefully studying the underwater terrain before deciding on the length of fuse to use. Their biggest enemies while using 'bombs' were birds and sharks, which quickly snapped up their prized specimens, and, in the case of the sharks, also exposed the divers to danger. He needed to make optimal use of their limited time over remote tropical reefs, and to efficiently winkle fishes out of deep crevices and coral heads. He did this with great success, and laid the foundation for the world-class fish collection that is now in the possession of the SAIAB. However, these methods are prohibited today.

Using explosives was not completely safe and the research team experienced some mishaps, as JLB Smith was unquestionably a risk-taker. In a caption to a photograph taken during their 1951 expedition to northern Mozambique, he wrote, 'Silhouette Island, where bombing fish caused an island to disappear' (Barnett, 1953).

Because of his lifelong struggle with ill-health, Smith developed a rather cavalier attitude towards his own mortality, which often also caused him to ignore the safety of others. On their 1951 expedition to northern Mozambique, while driving along a bush track between Mocimboa da Praia and Cabo Delgado, they unexpectedly encountered a large bush fire. Unable to turn around, they decided to drive through the fire. 'Barnett and I sat on the gelignite to keep it down. ... The last twenty or thirty yards, we dashed through an actual wall of flames' (Smith, 1968b). Except for singed eyebrows, they survived unscathed but, when they arrived at Cabo Delgado, JLB inspected the heavy load of gelignite that they were carrying and remarked that '… it was strange we had not blown up in the heat and ragged bumping as we sped through the forest fire' (Barnett, 1953). Smith often sat in a tossing boat with a pot of boiling water nestled on top of the open flame of his Primus stove while stores of paraffin, petrol and TNT lay nearby (Barnett, 1953).

During this expedition they had another frightening experience, 'Once we sat with half a ton of Ammon gelignite at the foot of the mast of our small motor vessel while a dry storm raged all round, the lightning almost continuous, and we discovered that the lightning conductor had been removed for painting, and not replaced!'

But their most hair-raising experience took place at Aldabra island during the 1954 East Africa expedition:

'In 1954 my wife, our fourteen-year-old son and I made a two thousand mile voyage in a fifty-foot motor fishing vessel from Seychelles through all the small banks and islands north of Madagascar to Mafia and Dar es Salaam. The first day out the sea was rough, and while lashing our explosives more firmly I was flung down a hatch on my back. It seemed like the end, as my legs were dead, but I slowly recovered, though with awful pain, and was able, with help at first, to do my bombing. … It was just on low tide, and we had only a short time. In the boat I had a hundred and fifty pounds of AE&CI Ammon gelignite. A fifty pound bomb was ready with a thirty-five second fuse. I was sitting on one fifty pound box and, having selected my spot, dropped the bomb, when my wife, a powerful oarswoman, rowed hard for the side. We moved only very slowly and then to our horror a sweep of the tide came round, scooping us back like a gigantic hand, right back to where the bubbles came up.

'There was nothing we could do. Then it came, a terrible crash, I was whirled through the air, roaring water raged all round and I knew it was the end. The gelignite in the boat must surely have gone off with such a shock – anyway death that way was quick. But it did not and I was most annoyed that it was taking so long to die, for I went on struggling in the bubbling water. Suddenly my head broke through into the sun, I looked round, there was my wife, and our friend, clinging to the waterlogged boat – also still alive. I swam to them, grabbing and stuffing into my shirt pocket a lovely little fish, later proved new to science.

'When I looked into the boat I saw to my amazement that the gelignite was still there … My wife and I looked at each other and just laughed. It was incredibly comical to still be alive after all that. … Incidentally, after my return, it was found that my fall had broken one of my vertebrae – but it had healed itself. The fall had also dislocated something in my back that gave me pain. Not long after the Aldabra shock I suddenly realized I was free from the pain – the bomb had shaken the dislocation back into place, but I doubt whether this method is likely to become popular as a remedy for such complaints' (Smith, 1958a).

William (pers. comm., 2017) recalled this experience:

'The whole trip was carried out with military precision. Sixteen-hour work days, every day, avoiding cyclones and reefs, and I watched in horror as the boat carrying both my parents was blown into the air by an underwater explosion when the current unexpectedly changed direction. There was 20 kilograms of unexploded gelignite in that boat! That was the day I nearly became an orphan.'

JLB was clearly aware of the dangers of explosives as he once said to Flora shortly before they left on an expedition, 'If we don't come back, please look after William' (I Sholto-Douglas, pers. comm., 2016). He may generally have used explosives carefully and effectively, but one wonders what impression he made on local fishermen who witnessed this brutally efficient method of 'fishing'? He does discuss the ethical issue of the impression his methods created in 'the minds of primitive people' and was obviously concerned about it. He wrote:

'One of our great troubles in using explosives in our work was the way in which we excited the natives, who, with their primitive tackle and traps, rarely got much. They saw this white man throw a small object into the sea, there was a boom and a splash, and sometimes the water would be covered with lovely fish. How easy and simple it appeared' (Smith, 1956).

His use of explosives was certainly effective. He reported on an expedition to Pinda in 1950:

'On one occasion I put down a large bomb in deepish water on a reef where natives commonly fish from canoes. Among those killed was a large black fish (*Macolor niger*), some specimens of 15 lbs. This is a predatory fish, a flesh-eater, with large mouth, and yet the natives of that area, with fishing tradition of several hundreds of years, did not know it and had never seen one, though it must have been there all the time' (Smith, 1951b).

He observed (1955) that within three months, he was able to collect more species of fish off Zanzibar than Colonel Lambert Playfair, author (with Albert Günther) of the standard treatise on Zanzibar fishes, who had collected there over 'many years'.

Explosives can now be made from readily available ingredients, such as diesel fuel, nitrogen-based soil fertilisers and the powdered urea foam that is used in boat building, mixed with small amounts of gasoline and gunpowder (Stobbs, 1997). Recipes for explosives are readily available on the internet, so they are potentially available to anyone. As a result, their use is increasing despite the fact that they are banned.

Today, blast fishing with explosives, together with deep-set gill nets targeting sharks, represents one of the major threats to marine animal communities in the Western Indian Ocean (and elsewhere). Blasting is arguably the most sense-less form of fishing as, if it is used incorrectly, it instantly destroys coral and rocky reef communities that may have taken millennia to develop. Branching corals, such as *Acropora* species, are particularly vulnerable to blast fishing as they are reduced to useless rubble. In addition, this fishing method is indis-criminate and wasteful as many fishes and invertebrates that humans do not use are also killed (Richmond, 2011; Bruton, 2016).

While diving in the *Jago* submersible at depths of 170 metres off Grande Comore in 2008, coelacanth researchers Hans Fricke and Jürgen Schauer felt the jolt of dynamite depth charges being discharged by fishermen near the water surface. If the typical pattern of 'development' of rural fisheries is fol-lowed in the Comoros, i.e. the replacement of traditional methods – harvesting fishes and other aquatic animals relatively sustainably, mainly because of their inefficiency – with dynamiting and deep-set gill nets, this will represent a serious threat to coelacanths and other marine life (Bruton, 2016).

On their 1951 expedition, in addition to doing their own collecting, the Smiths also frequented local fish markets and inspected the catches from the traps and nets of local fishermen, often finding valuable specimens. JLB usually worked with the *marinheiros* out at sea, 'bombing' fishes, whereas Margaret worked inshore.

'Margaret Smith was dressed in a bright green romper affair, which caused much consternation among the local populace and whom she watched merrily out of the corner of her eye. Slung across her left shoulder and hanging low on her right hip she carried a canvas pouch. This was divided into sections, in each of which reposed sundry jars and test tubes. A long pair of tweezers clung to the pouch and about her waist was strapped a large hunting knife. … Margaret Smith recognised the more precious [fishes] immediately and these were put into test tubes taken from the canvas pouch. Some were so minute that they were picked up with tweezers' (Barnett, 1953).

She would take a group of *marinheiros* with her along the beach to sample small fishes in intertidal pools at low tide, using a fish poison made from the 'pounded bark of a forest tree' (Smith, 1968b), and known as *warrula*. This is made by local people by stripping and pulping the bark of the warrula tree, also known as the fish-poison-vine, *Tephrosia vogelii*, a small tree that is indigenous to and wide-spread in tropical Africa and is extensively used to kill insect pests as well as fishes (Bruton, 2016). After blocking any outlets from an intertidal pool with rocks, Margaret would scatter handfuls of the pulp onto the pool and then stir it with a *warrula* branch. Within minutes the fishes would start swimming erratically and

Margaret Smith in fish-collecting gear on an expedition to Mozambique in 1951.

then flap about helplessly on the water surface, where they could be scooped up with a hand net.[1]

In addition to explosives and poisons, Smith used some other unconventional methods to collect fishes.

'I had to go and get the material myself, and for many years I tramped shores, searched the rock-pools, talked all sorts of people into collecting, went to sea with line boats and lived through the misery of trawlers in bad weather. Once I found a colony of cormorants' nests accessible, and as soon as a parent had fed a baby, I made it disgorge and got some most interesting and unexpected specimens that way. Hunting one's own material takes you off the beaten track, to natural beauties known to few, as well as to unpleasant, unhealthy and uncomfortable places. You meet many queer people and you learn a good many things besides ichthyology' (Smith, 1949b).

In a 1997 *Ichthos* article, journalist Audrey Ryan mentions that JLB Smith even used a gun 'for shooting specimens out of the water', and Smith (1951b) mentions that they removed live coral heads and broke them up with hammers to retrieve the small fishes hidden inside.

The use of rewards to encourage fishermen to catch coelacanths was also novel and somewhat controversial, but it did serve to raise awareness about fish, and JLB's £100 reward led directly to his securing the second coelacanth specimen. His example was soon followed by others: the French doubled the reward (for a live coelacanth) to £200 in 1953 and the American government offered $5,000 for a specimen, a hefty bounty for any fish over 60 years ago. In 1975 the Steinhart Aquarium even offered a reward of a two-week round trip to Mecca for a lucky Muslim coelacanth fisherman!

---

1   *Warrula* may also refer to various tropical climbing plants that have been introduced into Africa from Asia and the Pacific islands, such as beach-poison-vine, *Derris trifoliata*, which was formerly used as an organic pesticide to control agricultural pests and is still used in rural areas as a fish poison. Other plants that are widely used to produce fish poisons in tropical Africa include the physic nut tree (*Jatropha curcas*, also an introduced alien species), various euphorbias, especially milkbush (*Euphorbia tirucalli*), violet tree (*Securidaca longepedunculata*), snake bean (*Swartzia madagascariensis*) and tamboti (*Spirostachys africana*). The African dream herb (*Entada rheedii*), whose large brown seed pods (entada beans) are often found along the East African coast, is also crushed and used as fish poison (Bruton, 2016).

Coelacanth photographed by the late Peter Timm in the iSimangaliso Wetland Park in Zululand in November 2000.

Portrait of a coelacanth taken by Laurent Ballesta in the isiMangaliso Wetland Park in Zululand.

View of Diocesan College in 2018, with Devil's Peak in the background.

Brooke Wing at Diocesan College ('Bishops') in Cape Town where the science classrooms in which JLB Smith studied from 1912 to 1914 are located.

Groote Kerk in Somerset West where Henriette's father was the Minister.

The 'Ou Pastorie' in Somerset West where the Pienaar family lived during JLB Smith's marriage to Henriette Pienaar.

The Drostdy Tower at the entrance to Rhodes University.

JLB Smith's fold-up canvas boat, which he used on the Knysna Lagoon, on display in the Knysna Angling Museum.

Entrance to the JLB Smith Collection Management Centre in the South African Institute for Aquatic Biodiversity in Grahamstown.

'JLB's Rock', his favourite fishing spot in the Narrows at Knysna, where he nearly drowned in 1955.

William Smith in his broadcasting studio in the 1980s.

Model of the steam trawler *Nerine* with the side-trawl net that was used to catch the first coelacanth in December 1938, on display in the East London Museum.

'Latimer's Landing' (left) in the Buffalo Docks, East London, where the first coelacanth was landed.

Marjorie Courtenay-Latimer and Hendrik Goosen outside the East London Museum at a function in 1988 to mark the 50th anniversary of the capture of the first coelacanth.

Ecological diorama created by Marjorie Courtenay-Latimer in the East London Museum.

Marjorie Courtenay-Latimer with her dog Cindy and Nancy Tietz in October 2003.

Marjorie Courtenay-Latimer with the miscellaneous items that she collected on her trip to the Comoros in June 1989.

Four postage stamps commemorating the discovery of a living coelacanth, issued by the South African Post Office in 1989.

Marjorie Courtenay-Latimer in her doctoral robes from Rhodes University on the front cover of the June 2004 edition of the journal of the Border Historical Society, The Coelacanth.

Marjorie Courtenay-Latimer with her unique dodo egg in 2004.

The Smiths' house at 9 Gilbert Road, Grahamstown.

Margaret Smith's home at 37 Oatlands Road in Grahamstown, where she lived with her sister Flora.

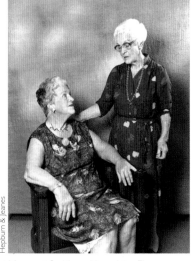

Hepburn & Jeanes

Margaret Smith and her sister, Flora Sholto-Douglas, in 1986.

Ishbel and Ian Sholto-Douglas at their home in Grahamstown in 2016.

Dakota 6832 at Ysterplaat Air Force Base in the colours she wore during the epic flight in 1952.

Dakota 6832 in retirement at the Ysterplaat Air Force Base in Cape Town.

30 th December 1952 - 1992

40th Anniversary of the Dakota
Flight to the Comoro Islands
to Fetch the Coelacanth
MALANIA ANJOUNAE

RSA 16c RSA 30c
RSA 40c RSA 50c

00017

Commemorative cover issued in 1992 to celebrate the 40th anniversary of the flight of the 'Flying Fishcart', Dakota 6832.

Double outrigger canoe (galawa) used by traditional fishermen in the Comoros, off the south coast of Grande Comore.

Display of some of JLB Smith's personal possessions at SAIAB.

JLB Smith's faithful Bergheil folding plate camera that he took on his East African expeditions.

JLB Smith's two popular books on fishes, *Our Fishes* and *High Tide* – both published posthumously in 1968 in English and Afrikaans.

Rare colour painting of a fish by JLB Smith; the yellowhead butterflyfish, *Chaetodon xanthocephalus*.

Front covers of the 14 editions of *Old Fourlegs*, which was eventually published in five English editions and nine foreign language editions.

Drury mount of the first coelacanth on display in the East London Museum.

Eugene Balon

Coelacanth specimen in the Muséum National d'Historie Naturelle de Paris in which the flesh has been cleared and the bony and cartilaginous skeleton stained to reveal its structure.

Hans Fricke

Jürgen Schauer and Mike Bruton extracting a tissue sample for DNA analysis from the first coelacanth in the East London Museum in 1987.

Hans Fricke, Mike Bruton and Jürgen Schauer with the first coelacanth in the East London Museum in 1987.

Karen Hissmann

The spectacular front door of the Ichthyology Institute (now SAIAB), designed and carved by Maureen Quin in 1976.

Front entrance to the South African Institute for Aquatic Biodiversity (SAIAB) after it became a National Facility of the National Research Foundation in 2004.

The new Collection Room building of the SAIAB, built in 2003; **Inset:** Part of the enormous fish collection at SAIAB.

View of the JLB Smith Collection Management Centre at SAIAB.

The new Department of Ichthyology & Fisheries Science at Rhodes University, established in 1981.

A melancholy Margaret Smith after she received her honorary doctorate from Rhodes University in April 1986.

Tesza Musto with Margaret Smith in February 1987.

Christine Flegler-Balon and Carolynn Bruton chatting to Margaret Smith in February 1987.

Margaret Smith after receiving 'The Order for Meritorious Service Class 1: Gold' from the State President, PW Botha, in February 1986.

Margaret Smith House at Rhodes University.

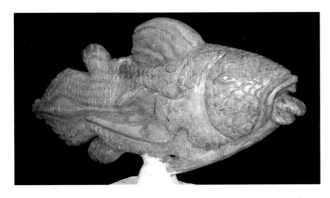

Soapstone carving of a coelacanth in Moroni, Grande Comore.

Professor Hans Fricke with a dried coelacanth on Moheli Island, Comoros.

Mike Bruton (left) and Robin Stobbs in discussion with a coelacanth fisherman on Grande Comore in 1987.

The Sea Fishes of Southern Africa by JLB Smith (1949).

Smith's Sea Fishes by JLB Smith (1977).

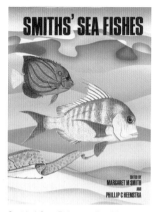

Smiths' Sea Fishes, edited by Margaret Smith and Phil Heemstra (1986).

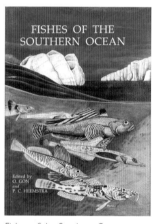

Fishes of the Southern Ocean, edited by Ofer Gon and Phil Heemstra (1990).

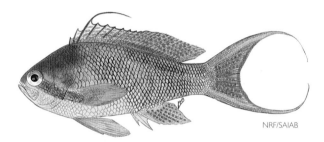

NRF/SAIAB

Sea goldie, *Anthias squamipinnis*, illustrated by Margaret Smith for *The Sea Fishes of Southern Africa* (1949).

NRF/SAIAB

Lycodichthys antarcticus, illustrated by Dave Voorvelt for *Fishes of the Southern Ocean* (1990).

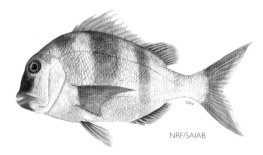

NRF/SAIAB

Englishman, *Chrysoblephus anglicus*, illustrated by Dave Voorvelt for *Smiths' Sea Fishes* (1986).

Examples of books on fishes published through the original Department of Ichthyology, JLB Smith Institute of Ichthyology and South African Institute for Aquatic Biodiversity.

An Illustrated Guide to the Freshwater Fishes of the Zambezi River, Lake Kariba, Pungwe, Sabi, Lundi and Limpopo Rivers by Rex Jubb (1961).

Freshwater Fishes of Southern Africa by Rex Jubb (1967).

Pocket Guide to the Freshwater Fishes of Southern Africa by Mike Bruton, Peter Jackson and Paul Skelton (1982).

Fisherman's Favourites. Fish, Seafood and Seaweed Recipes by Carolynn Bruton and Liz Tarr (1992).

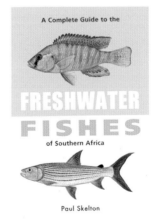

A Complete Guide to the Freshwater Fishes of Southern Africa by Paul Skelton (2001).

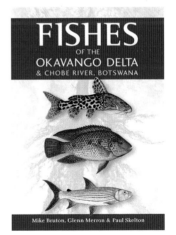

Fishes of the Okavango Delta and Chobe River, Botswana by Mike Bruton, Glenn Merron and Paul Skelton (2018).

Books on the coelacanth and related topics by Ichthyology staff and other authors.

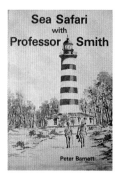

Sea Safari with Professor Smith by Peter Barnett (1953).

Old Man Coelacanth by Shirley Bell (1969).

The Biology of Latimeria and Evolution of Coelacanths, edited by Jack Musick, Mike Bruton and Eugene Balon (1991).

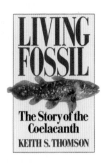

Living Fossil – The Story of the Coelacanth by Keith Thomson (1991).

The JLB Smith Institute of Ichthyology – 50 Years, edited by Paul Skelton and Johann Lutjeharms (1997), with a drawing of a barb in pride of place.

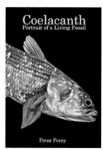

Coelacanth – Portrait of a Living Fossil by Peter Forey (1998).

A Fish Caught in Time – The Search for the Coelacanth by Samantha Weinberg (1999).

The Four-legged Fish by Mike Bruton (2000).

Die Jagd nach dem Quastenflosser – Der Fisch, der Aus der Urzeit Kam by Hans Fricke (2007).

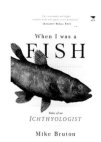

When I was a Fish – Tales of an Ichthyologist by Mike Bruton (2015).

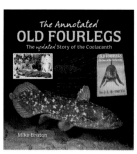

The Annotated Old Fourlegs – The Updated Story of the Coelacanth by Mike Bruton (2017).

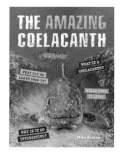

The Amazing Coelacanth by Mike Bruton (2018).

CHAPTER 15

Jubilation

Publication of *The Sea Fishes of Southern Africa*

IN 1940 the publication of Austin Roberts' famous *The Birds of South Africa* had introduced the concept of natural history field guides that documented the wildlife of a particular region. This book had inspired mining magnate and keen angler, Hugh le May, to think about producing a similar book on southern African sea fishes, but he realised that this would require the skills of a scientist. He discussed the idea with his Johannesburg accountant, Bransby A Key, another keen natural historian. On 26th September 1945 Key wrote to JLB Smith and outlined Le May's idea for a book with colour illustrations that would resolve the confusion surrounding the scientific and common names of local fishes. 'One fish for example had no less than 14 common names around our coast' (MM Smith, 1987). Key also indicated that an amount of £1,000 would be made available by Hugh le May for the production of the book (Smith, 1956; Bell, 1969; Gon, 2001).

After careful thought, and while conducting research for the planned book, Smith accepted Hugh le May's offer but told him that £1,000 would not be enough. Le May's financier Key replied that finding a competent author was much more important than any budgetary issues, and that funds would be made available. Key then contacted John Voelcker, the leading businessman who had been involved in the production of Roberts' bird book through what came to be known as the *John Voelcker Bird Book Fund*, and persuaded him to join the fish book venture (Gon, 2001). In 1946 they created a trust, the *Sea Fishes of Southern Africa Book Fund*, which was chaired by Voelcker, with Key as the Honorary Secretary. Other members included Hugh le May, Guy Carlton Jones and James H Crosby, all leading businessmen. In late 1947, as part of the fundraising campaign, the Smiths exhibited the colour plates that had been prepared for the book in Johannesburg and raised a further £9,000 (Gon, 2001).

JLB and Margaret Smith worked extremely hard in the late 1940s to complete the first *Sea Fishes of Southern Africa* book. Margaret's responsibilities, apart from protecting 'the professor', included attending to the voluminous correspondence, answering every letter received no matter how trivial, cataloguing the rapidly growing library holdings, and producing the endless illustrations of fishes. As the fish collection and library holdings increased, the fledgling Department of Ichthyology ran out of space. According to Peter Jackson (1996), Joseph Omer-Cooper, Professor of Zoology at Rhodes University College (RUC) at the time, likened Ichthyology to 'the camel that asked its master if it may put its head inside his tent during a desert storm, and little by little got more and more of itself inside until it eventually occupied the whole tent'.

Jackson (1996) witnessed this phase of their work:

'At that time they were very much alone. Apart from the young artists I cannot remember anyone assisting them for very long in their ceaseless beaver-like preparation of the book … Smith's single-minded zealotry had earned him a reputation of eccentricity among his colleagues, but to a young student the dragon was his wife. Her role as a helpmeet in those days is well documented but what is less known is the Cerberus-like vigilance with which she protected her husband's person. Students seemed to exist for the express purpose of "wasting the Professor's precious time" as she put it. "What do you want to see him for?" she would demand, with a stare that would freeze a basilisk. "Let them come in, lass" would come a quiet voice inside the famous cottage on Rhodes campus where they worked. With a hissed "Don't be too long, now" she would grudgingly admit me to the presence'.

Nancy Tietz (pers. comm., 2017) had a similar experience:

'When one visited the Ichthyology Department in the old wood & iron building one did not get much further than Doris Cave, the library and the coelacanth (*Malania*) near the entrance. In the company of Richard Liversedge [then Director of the McGregor Museum in Kimberley] on my first visit I was received by Margaret in what was known to all at Rhodes as the "Inner Sanctum" while Richard was allowed to approach the Professor in what was known as the "Holy of Holies". After that JLB would come through to see me in the Inner Sanctum (Margaret's laboratory) but when

I moved to Grahamstown I was always ushered into the Holy of Holies, much to my surprise I might add.'

Having provided financial support for the production of the book, Hugh and Basil le May later also offered support for a new building for the Department of Ichthyology after Hugh visited Grahamstown in November 1947. He was appalled by the cramped and unhealthy working conditions in the Department of Ichthyology that he had helped to establish. At that time Smith occupied the study of Professor Joseph Omer-Cooper, Head of Zoology, and was promised the use of a garage on campus to store his priceless fish collection (Gon, 2002)! Smith explained that he had often complained to the College authorities that the poor state of repair of the building interfered with his research, and had repeatedly asked for better accommodation. In a letter to Le May dated 4th March 1948 he wrote, 'I have never had a decent place to work in ... always had to manage in corners'.

Judging by correspondence 20 years later between Margaret Smith and Basil le May, Hugh had quietly but effectively convinced the authorities at RUC and the CSIR of the importance of supporting JLB's work. The Le Mays' support and generosity, both moral and financial, could not be ignored at a time when RUC was virtually bankrupt (Gon, 2001; Maylam, 2017). This, combined with Smith's productivity as a scientist, his success as a fundraiser and the huge publicity generated by the first coelacanth, made it clear to all concerned that it was time to establish a Department of Ichthyology and provide a decent building to house it. RUC was effectively JLB's employer and also covered the operating costs of his Department, and the CSIR provided his research grants.

However, in the late 1940s the relationship between Smith and Hugh le May started to sour. Hugh le May's offer to fund a new laboratory for Smith eventually fell through due to disagreements between the two men and the precarious state of the South African and world economies (Gon, 2002). Their relationship reached a new low on 16th November 1948 when Smith wrote to Le May, 'Please don't send me any more unpleasant letters. I think you have been misunderstanding me. I am not chasing after you for money.'

The main point of contention was that Le May did not want any publicity to accompany his donations (to the book or the laboratory), yet Smith insisted on going public with plans to acknowledge Le May's donations to both projects. A plan for Le May to sponsor the establishment of a field laboratory on Inhaca Island in Mozambique also collapsed when it became clear that it was to be named after him (Gon, 2002). JLB Smith did not seem to comprehend that Le May was a very modest man who shied away from publicity and disliked flattery. In contrast, Smith regarded publicity as a means to obtain more support for his work, and wasn't averse to the occasional use of flattery. Gon (2002) argues that flattery was 'an integral part of his personality'; he liked to please his benefactors and could not stop himself from doing so (with the encouragement of Margaret).

In spite of their dislike of publicity, the Le Mays' contribution to ichthyology was generous and sustained. In 1969 Margaret Smith would write to Basil, who had by then taken over the chairmanship of the book fund, to ask him for financial support for the new Ichthyology Institute. He acceded to her request and also accompanied Margaret on her first visit to the Department of National Education, which eventually led to the Institute's being established as a Declared Cultural Institution (effectively a national museum funded by the government).

In one of the more bizarre episodes in JLB's life, and in the midst of publishing his *magnum opus*, Le May's potential sponsorship of a new fish research laboratory at RUC was cancelled when Smith unexpectedly resigned from the College in November 1949 to take up a position as Director of the Natal Museum in Pietermaritzburg. He then promptly changed his mind when the museum refused to accede to his various conditions of employment, decided to stay in Grahamstown, and asked the College to take him back (which they did)!

Smith described this career move, as if it had already happened, in a letter dated 14th November 1949 to Frank Reid, who edited the newsletter of the Cape Town school, Bishops.

'After having initially turned it down, I eventually accepted the invitation of the [Trustees] of the Natal Museum to become director of that institution, and shall take over from the beginning of next year. It has been quite a wrench uprooting here, but there are so many opportunities for my researches in Natal and so many people who have for long been eager that I should come there, that work has won. At some later date I shall be making on behalf of the Museum an official announcement about the plans I have for developing various lines of research.'

But he did not leave Grahamstown, and continued working there until his death nearly 20 years later!

Smith realised that it would be impossible to prepare a book about sea fishes without artists to illustrate the fishes. His first attempt to illustrate his own research papers in 1931 had met with ridicule, but he practised hard and managed to illustrate all his own work until 1941. The scale and expectations of the new book project demanded illustrations well beyond JLB's capacity, and he realised that he would have to adopt a different, more ambitious strategy. It was his dictum that 'A good illustration is better than a whole volume of text'.

Much later, Margaret recalled the events, and the results thereof:

'When we received the letter early in October 1945, J.L.B. said that he could not possibly write the book. I told him he had to write it if only to publish the dorsal and anal fin formulae key that he had evolved to identify fishes. He replied that it was impossible as every fish should be illustrated. "Well", I said, "I will do it". He laughed and said, "You took three weeks over the last drawing and there are over 1 000 fishes to be drawn." I piped down a bit! I asked if the Trustees would pay for the illustrations and he said, "Yes, if necessary". I replied, "There is an Art School at Rhodes", so we decided he could write the book.

'We went right through that Art School and only two out of 24 students, Valeria de la Harpe and Pat Parkin, stayed the pace. I remember Pat telling me that the Art School was very scathing about her being a "fish-artist". J.L.B. replied that they would all be forgotten except the so-called fish-artist. Other artists included Denys Davies, a geology student, and Hester Locke, a newly married young woman from the Training College. Her contribution was far greater than the number of illustrations she did, as she helped me, especially at Lourenco Marques, to run the house, feed the artists and look after my small son. The artists worked hard. They got 5 shillings for a drawing and 10 shillings for a painting.

'After I had been correcting drawings and putting in scales for 18 months, I had 12 pencilled drawings ready for the artists to ink in, but they were unable to do them because of examinations. So in desperation one afternoon I took up the pen and found to my amazement that my hand was steady. From that day, I never looked back as far as illustrations were concerned. At the end of that year, after Pat and

Denys had written their examinations, they worked full time at drawing for a while. Then they left, and I did the remaining drawings and
paintings for the book.

'Each illustration took from 8 hours to 68 hours. I remember one
species had a green body and red spots. They were all done in water
colour and I dared not let the green and the red touch. It took me
60 hours to paint. If I had to do that now, I would use waterproof ink
for the red dots and paints for the green background and I would take
far less time. Another fish, a sole, had 8 000 scales. I did the scaling for
24 hours (three full days). JLB pointed out that you would not be able
to see the scales once it was reduced, and that I should just indicate
them. I replied, "I couldn't. I either had to do the thing as it was or not
at all" (MM Smith, 1987).

Margaret, speaking of a university student artist who was 'very good at colours but
useless at scales', said:

'She got tired of drawing scales so just did "wiggle, wiggle" with scales and
you can't do "wiggle, wiggle" with scales, you have to count them.

'To work out how many scales to fit in you have to use trigonometry,
calculating by triangles. One fish was very troublesome, I said to JLB that
if I could cheat I'd get it … and you know what that fish had done, it had
cheated, it had put in one extra scale! So I went through it scale by scale,
found the extra scale and drew it in.

'Painting fish as they are collected also means that the artist must be
very quick, for fish rapidly lose their colours. … You learn to be very careful
because reds fade to purple, blues go to green and some lose their colours
completely when they die' (Richards, 1987).

Hester Locke (1986), one of the artists recruited by Margaret, recalls those
early days:

'In the spring of 1945 I became the first member of a small team of part-
time artists who joined Margaret Smith in the enormous task of
preparing the illustrations needed for a comprehensive publication of
the ichthyological research by Dr JLB Smith. This work became the

definitive *Sea Fishes of Southern Africa*. As Dr Smith … was still a full time senior lecturer in the Department of Chemistry at Rhodes, his fish research was done in his limited spare time and the collection was housed partially at his home at the top of Gilbert Street. This meant that the trainee artists had to work in the Smiths' living room or, in good weather, on the shady verandah.

'My own introduction to scientific illustration was a rude shock. From a background of child art centres and teacher training courses in creative painting, I had to learn a new terminology and quickly acquire fine-motor skills previously undreamed of. Most important of all, I had to learn to observe and recognise subtle variations of e.g. body line. I had to practise measuring accurately and to count with infinite care, items which indicated species specific data. No longer could I sketch a few casual crescent shapes to indicate scales: each scale had its own serial position and the exact number was imperative. Soon the team members began to invent new tools to replace our crude maths instruments. No. 10 sewing needles replaced the metal points of dividers, etc.

'As some of the specimens, notably the deepsea fishes, were very dark in colour, taking accurate counts became a nightmare. Naturally "Doc" and Margaret carefully checked all our pencil work before we were allowed to ink it in. As no colour washes are permitted in line drawings, we had to use dots to indicate dark markings or shading. This tedious task had us all sighing with frustration. As we graduated to working in colour, life became much more exciting and by mid-year in 1946 we were rewarded with an invitation to join the Smiths on an expedition to Mozambique.

'Throughout this period the artists aimed to complete one drawing per day, and every night we proudly pinned our finished products to the dining room wall. To add to the interest in our work we were allowed to join a few of the collecting trips, e.g. we went to Inhaca one day and experienced … firsthand the stress of making swift colour notes before the colours faded, all in a boat that was rocking and dipping. This sight of the exquisite jewelled creatures which came out of the water gave us new concepts regarding the iridescent quality of the colours on fishes. … I count these many exciting tasks and events amongst some of the most meaningful experiences' (Locke, 1986).

Peter Jackson who in 1972, late in his long and interesting career (Jackson, 2010), was appointed a Senior Research Fellow in the JLB Smith Institute of Ichthyology, had obtained his BSc from RUC in 1948. During his undergraduate years he went on several fish-collecting trips with the Smiths along the Eastern Cape coast, at the time that the artists were preparing paintings for the first edition of *Sea Fishes*. He remembers:

> 'Because of his fear of fire destroying all this work, the spare room of the Smiths' house in Gilbert Street was totally devoid of all furniture except for a large, much-travelled suitcase in the centre. In this the drawings, each covered with tissue paper, were placed when completed. We would sometimes sit around this in a circle on the bare floor, while an illustration was passed from hand to hand with the Professor expounding on the fish depicted and Margaret, if asked, telling about a drawing, colouring or mounting technique' (Jackson, 1996).

A strange ritual indeed!

John Day, Professor of Zoology at the University of Cape Town until his retirement in 1974, graduated from RUC in 1930 during Smith's tenure as a Senior Lecturer in Chemistry. In his review of marine biology in *A History of Scientific Endeavour in South Africa*, he remembers a visit to the Smith household in Grahamstown:

> 'I visited him and his new wife, Margaret, just after the war and found the lounge littered with specimens and paintings, for his wife and students from the arts school had illustrated practically every species in colour' (Day, 1977).

The Sea Fishes of Southern Africa by JLB Smith was printed by the *Cape Times* and published by the Central News Agency on 25th June 1949. In this edition Margaret Smith illustrated 685 species, Patricia Parkin 98, Denys Davies 90, Hester Locke 26 and Valerie de la Harpe 13, with JLB Smith providing many ink drawings.

For subsequent editions of *Sea Fishes*, new artists would join the team – some under the direct tutelage of Margaret – and would go on to forge distinguished careers in the field of fish illustration. Elizabeth Tarr joined the Ichthyology Institute as a Research Assistant in 1973 but Margaret soon recognised her potential as an artist. After participating in a fish research expedition to the Okavango Delta in Botswana, during which she took colour notes on live fishes, she developed her skills and became a highly competent fish artist. In 1982 Jean-Michel Vinson, an accomplished natural history artist, joined the Institute staff and worked for a year on drawings for the revision of the *Sea Fishes* book. Dave Voorvelt then joined the Institute in 1983 to help complete the revision and soon showed excellent talent and devised several new illustration techniques of his own. Elaine Heemstra was appointed as an artist in 1988 and also made a significant contribution. Even though each artist had their own individual style, and worked in different media (water colour, acrylic or inks) each could be relied on to render scientifically accurate illustrations (Voorvelt, 1996).

Liz Tarr and Dave Voorvelt, expert fish artists.

JLB Smith regarded the first edition of his book as 'an experiment', writing:

'It is a strictly scientific regional monograph embracing the results of 20 years of intensive research, but was deliberately written to be usable by the ordinary man. Both phrasing and terminology were simplified as far as possible, without loss of scientific standard. An accurate and detailed illustration was prepared for practically every species, certainly of every one any ordinary person is likely to see. There are 1,270 separate illustrations, each of which took from 8–50 hours of drawing work. ... In addition there appears for the first time in this book a unique universal key, quite simple in operation, by means of which any ordinary man may track any fish known, and even recognise as new any not yet recorded. ... Each illustration was checked four times, each fin and scale count, and other scientific data, four times. There were three sets of proofs and each was checked by three different groups of people. The Index contains close on 100,000 names and they were checked and cross-referenced six times in all. With twenty years of intensive research as a background, over 30,000 hours of work in compilation by all who took part, crowded into three ½ years of solid labour, were necessary to produce this one book.'

In his notes on 'How this book was made' in the 1953 edition of *The Sea Fishes of Southern Africa*, JLB Smith observes:

'It is in many ways a pity that by some odd chance the systematic study of fishes has often been left to scientists not able to comprehend the wonder of the living creatures, and concerned only with the purely taxonomic aspects of form and structure of dead material in bottles. This has resulted in an unfortunate gap between angler and systematist, probably wider than in any other popular branch of natural history. As an angler, the author of this book was from youth eager to learn about the fishes he encountered, but found the existing literature baffling and unsatisfactory. Faced with no alternative but to master the subject, he set out to do that.

'Where this book differs from most others is that it gives the ordinary man the power to track by scientific methods in a few moments any fish already known from our waters, and to recognise as such any not yet recorded. While this is perhaps its most important feature, at the same time it may be stressed that this work is essentially a full scientific revisional monograph summarising the results of research on our fishes to date. The descriptive scientific detail may to other workers at first sight appear rather meagre, but a combination of description, keys and accurate illustration covers every important scientific character in every species it has been possible to examine' (JLB Smith, 1953).

Judging by the Foreword written by the President of the CSIR, Basil Schonland, when the 1949 edition of *Sea Fishes* was published, Smith had achieved his objective:

'As a comprehensive and critical scientific revision of the marine fishes of this region it will be a standard work of permanent value. It will also be of great interest to the large number of people who are not specialists in fishes but who are interested in knowing more about the types, habits and distribution of those they see and catch. The author has devoted much ingenious care to making this book one which the layman can use and enjoy. He has provided an original and easily-operated means of identifying any fish so far known in our waters. His wide knowledge of their habits and of the lore of fishermen shows itself on every page and makes interesting and exciting reading' (Schonland, 1949).

Although the first edition of *Sea Fishes* was relatively expensive (52 shillings and six pence; about R2,593 in today's currency), despite the subsidisation of the costs of the colour plates by the *Sea Fishes Trust*, it was very well received by the public, with the first 5,000 copies selling out in four weeks (Gon, 2002). As Humphry Greenwood (1968) later wrote in an obituary to JLB Smith, 'There is probably no other ichthyologist who can claim to have [had] queues forming outside bookshops on the day his regional monograph was published'. The new book was soon dubbed 'the angler's bible' and the eminent American ichthyologist, Carl Hubbs (1969), described it as a 'sumptuously illustrated compendium'. Other tributes poured in: '... you have attained a permanent position in South African history as one of our great men' (SG Shuttleworth); '... the finest piece of work I have seen for a long time ... invaluable to all workers in the field of ichthyology' (TC Marshall); and '... a monumental work that assures you a permanent place among the few who have contributed much to the furtherance of the knowledge of our fauna' (SH Skaife) (Gon, 2002).

The first edition of *Sea Fishes* had a massive impact on scientists and lay-people alike. In their correspondence stored in the Rhodes University Archive the Smiths recall many incidents:

'A friend travelling in the Karoo spent a night at a country hotel. He was surprised to see the manager's wife in deep study of the "Sea Fishes", and asked her if she used the book much. "Oh, yes," she said, "often. You see, people get tired of eating the same kind of fish all the time, so I hunt up other names for the menus" (Smith, 1961).

'We have had many hundreds of letters from all over the world from scientists and laymen who use the book. They include officers and crews of steamers which cover the seas of the globe, and traders and officials on islands equally remote. Scientists who worked in the remote Pacific wrote to say that it was the first book opened in tracking any unknown fish there. ... No matter to what remote country I travel, the book is there to greet me. Constantly it brings stories, and often laughter. ... Another friend, who is a collector of natural-history books, visited a famous book shop in London and asked to see what they had in his line. The manager took him to an inner store where his best pieces were kept and, producing a book, said: "This is the finest publication in natural history from any part of the world." It was the "Sea Fishes'" (Smith, 1961).

The *Book Fund* made a modest profit of £350 and published a second edition of the book in May 1950 (with a print run of 500 copies), and an enlarged and revised third edition in 1953. The fourth edition (1961) was brought up-to-date with a synoptic index, and a fifth edition was published in 1965. In 1977 a new edition was published by Valiant Press under the title *Smith's Sea Fishes of Southern Africa*, still with JLB Smith as the sole author.

Later editions (following the initial 1949 edition) were illustrated by Moira Lambert, Patricia Parkin, Elizabeth Tarr, Jean-Michel Vinson, Ann Lefebvre, Elaine Heemstra and Dave Voorvelt.

Thereafter, a completely revised, multi-authored edition of the book, renamed *Smiths' Sea Fishes* (to recognise the contributions of both Smiths), co-edited by Margaret Smith and Phil Heemstra, was published by Macmillan in 1986, Southern Book Publishers in 1995 and Struik Nature in 2003.

Despite the success of the book, Smith was bitter about the effort that it had taken for it to be financed. In a letter dated 22nd September 1949 to Professor TA Stephenson in England, he wrote:

'The whole thing, from before the actual start, has been one long desparate (sic) and grim battle, right to the very end. The money was not just provided …Behind the pleasant words in the introduction lies a whole series of desperate engagements with people whose outlook on life are not yours and mine … I suppose I have become exceedingly ruthless because I was determined to see this work published … I have emerged unscathed, but with few illusions about the princes of commerce and very much tougher than I ever expected I could become … I have had to fight with tooth and claw for all this.'

Sea Fishes is much more than a taxonomic treatise as it includes extensive introductory chapters on fish anatomy, distribution, senses, whether they feel pain, reproduction, growth and ageing, swimming speed, coloration and bioluminescence, respiration, osmoregulation, temperature tolerances, buoyancy, sound production and migrations, as well as on dangerous and venomous fishes, and the effects of fishing. There are also general notes on fish taxonomy, nomenclature and classification as well as on oceanography and the history of ichthyology in South Africa.

Of particular interest to anglers and other laypeople are the general notes on fish biology. For instance, the elf is described as follows in one of the later editions of the book (Smith & Heemstra, 1986):

'Swift and voracious, elf bite viciously and fight well; large fish often jump repeatedly ("saltatrix" is Latin for a "dancing girl"). Elf take almost any moving lure and most flesh. With a shoal of sardines or other small fishes as their prey, they will gorge themselves in a veritable feeding frenzy, regurgitate, and then start all over again. They are, in turn, preyed upon by larger fishes, such as kob and sharks. Elf are delicious eating, both fresh and smoked, but the delicate flesh softens rapidly and does not keep well; excellent bait, especially for line-boat fishing. Van der Elst (1976) has published a comprehensive work on the biology of the elf; spawning takes place off Natal from September to December, hence to conserve the stock, the closed season in Natal is from September to November inclusive.'

Admittedly these notes on the elf are more comprehensive than those for most fishes in the book, as the elf is a very popular and well-known angling fish, but they do demonstrate that, to write a book of this nature, you need to be both a scientist and an angler; a laboratory-based taxonomist would not have had sufficient knowledge of fish biology and behaviour to do so.

Later editions of *Sea Fishes* included less information of interest to anglers as an increasing number of species had to be added. An interesting exception is the chapter on seabreams (family Sparidae), which includes popular angling species such as riverbream, carpenter, fransmadam, santer, dageraad, stumpnose, roman, slinger, musselcracker, blacktail and steenbras. This chapter, written by the two Smiths, still includes extensive biological information.

Sea Fishes set a new standard for a scientific publication that is useful to scientists and also accessible to the lay public. It is used by scientists, anglers, aquarists, hobbyists, commercial fishermen, spearfishermen, divers and naturalists in southern and eastern Africa and throughout the Indo-Pacific region, as many of the tropical species are shared by the Indian and Pacific Oceans.

John Wallace, previously the Director of the Port Elizabeth Museum and a Board member of the Ichthyology Institute, remembers:

'In 1964 I joined the penultimate voyage of the *RV Anton Bruun*. … On board were twenty scientists, many from the USA. I was not surprised to see them using the *Sea Fishes of Southern Africa* as their prime reference – we were in the SW Indian Ocean after all. But I was most impressed to learn that even in California this book was used for teaching tertiary level ichthyology "because it was the best illustrated book of its sort, in the world". Although many of the species would have been different, it was an invaluable reference work for higher level classification' (J Wallace, pers. comm., 2017).

The number of marine fishes known from South Africa had increased from fewer than 200 (recorded by Andrew Smith in 1849), to 260 in 1897 and 336 in 1901 (by JDF Gilchrist[1]), 670 in 1903 (by L Péringuey), 718 in 1905 (by KH Barnard; Gon, 2002) and to 1,005 species in Barnard's (1925, 1927) two-volume monograph. But the real increases occurred after JLB Smith became involved in marine fish systematics. In the 1953 edition of his *The Sea Fishes of Southern Africa* 1,325 species are recorded, of which 315 (23.8%) are endemics (Smith, 1977), and 1,400 species are recorded in the 1961 edition of the book. In the last edition of *Smiths' Sea Fishes* published by Struik Nature (Smith & Heemstra, 2003) the number of species has increased to over 2,200[2].

---

1 Dr John DF Gilchrist (1866–1926) is regarded as the 'Father of South African ichthyology' in recognition of the pioneering role that he played at the beginning of the 20th century. He was a highly productive scientist and administrator who established the Marine Biological Survey (now the Sea Fisheries Research Institute) and arranged for the purchase of the first sea fisheries research vessel, the *Peter Faure*. He also initiated taxonomic research on our fishes and made the first comprehensive fish collections. But, like JLB Smith, he also had his quirks and eccentricities. At the South African College, where he taught, he had a reputation for being absent-minded. He once passed a lady he thought he knew and courteously raised his hat, to which she indignantly responded, 'Surely, John, you know your own wife?' (Gon, 1993).

2 As there are about 15,000 marine fish species in the world, this is a very diverse regional fish fauna. This high diversity is due to three main factors: the high diversity of habitats, the fact that the fish fauna is composed of species from three major biogeographic zones (Indo-Pacific, Atlantic and Antarctic), and the the high proportion of endemic species (about 13%) (Gon, 1996, 2002).

CHAPTER 16

The second coelacanth

'It was more than worth … all that long strain'

E VER SINCE the capture of the first coelacanth it had become an obsession of JLB Smith's to find the home of 'old fourlegs' and to secure a second, intact specimen. In the late 1940s he planned to organise an expedition specifically to find coelacanths. However, he received little support for this idea, so he changed his plan and broadened the scope of his expeditions to include the collection of all types of fishes, while always keeping an eagle eye out for coelacanths and talking to local fishermen about them. In 1948, in his quest for the next coelacanth, he had a leaflet printed in English, French and Portuguese, the main European languages used in East Africa at the time. The printing of the leaflets was partly sponsored by the proceeds of an exhibition on the coelacanth that Marjorie Courtenay-Latimer had organised at the East London Museum. The text in the leaflet is simply written and would have been intelligible to most readers, but the postal address given for Smith ('Rhodes University, Grahamstown, Union of S.A.'), seems a little thin!

The £100 reward poster.

On the leaflet Smith offered a £100 reward (sponsored by the CSIR), a considerable amount of money at that time ('equivalent to a year's salary for most people in Africa', Bergh *et al.*, 1992; 'half the price of a small car at the time', Spargo, 2008), for the capture of a second coelacanth. This was another example of his unconventional yet practical thinking. It must have felt strange for the new leaders of the CSIR, bent on launching cutting-edge South African science onto the international stage, to approve this zany project. The leaflets were distributed throughout East Africa on the Smiths' expeditions, to officials, fishermen, traders and boat skippers, anyone who might encounter a coelacanth. It was a great delight to the Smiths when they spotted their leaflets stuck to the walls of lighthouses and huts in the remotest parts of East Africa.

Local fishermen found it hard to believe that anyone would pay £100 (10,000 escudos) for one dead fish, but from then onwards the coelacanth became known as 'Dez Contos Peixe', literally the 'Ten Thousand (escudos) Fish' – or the 'Hundred Pound Fish'. It is interesting to note that French colonial officers in Madagascar and the Comoros showed far less enthusiasm for distributing Smith's reward leaflets than did their Portuguese counterparts in Mozambique (Smith, 1956; Bell, 1969). JLB's incentive campaign paid dividends during his search for the coelacanth, but it may have hampered later conservation efforts to reduce fishing pressure on the natural populations of this species. In an international coelacanth conservation campaign launched by the famous German researcher, Professor Hans Fricke, this author and others in the late 1980s and 1990s, CITES (the Convention on Trade in Endangered Species of Wild Fauna and Flora) was persuaded to list the coelacanth on Schedule I, which means that it may not be traded for commercial gain.

When Smith examined the first coelacanth, he realised immediately that it was not a deep-water fish (Smith, 1956; Bell, 1969). It had hard scales, a heavy, bony head and strong fins with spines as found in typical reef fishes, and it was brightly coloured, like other shallow-water fishes. It also had moderately large eyes like those found in fishes that live in well-lit waters. By contrast, deep-water fishes are typically dark in colour, often black or grey, and have soft bodies with no or few scales, soft rays in their fins, and light bones. Their eyes are either enormous and very sensitive, with giant pupils, or they have disappeared completely, and they often have huge jaws and small though expandable bodies for taking occasional large meals. Furthermore, many deep-sea fishes are bioluminescent – capable of producing light biologically through the excitation of an enzyme, luciferin.

Smith speculated that the first coelacanth, caught off East London, was a stray from further north that had drifted southwards on the south-flowing Mozambique/Agulhas Current. He deduced that coelacanths are mainly tropical fishes that live further north, and therefore decided to mount expeditions along the East African coast in an effort to find more of these fishes. Smith (1956) presented his reasoning in very user-friendly terms in *Old Fourlegs*:

'When I looked at that fish, even the first time, it said as plainly as if it could speak: "Look at my hard, armoured scales. They overlap so that there is a three-fold thick layer of them over my whole body. Look at my bony head and stout spiny fins. I am so well protected that no rock can hurt me. Of course I live in rocky areas, among reefs, below the action of the waves and the surf, and, believe me, I am a tough guy and not afraid of anything in the sea. No soft deep-sea ooze for me. My blue colour alone surely tells you that I cannot live in the depths. You don't find blue fishes there."'

Smith also hypothesised that the coelacanth is a tough, rocky-reef-dwelling, ambush predator (Smith, 1965), and once again he was right. This represents an extraordinary example of how a scientist (and angler) with a keen eye for detail can decipher the living habits of an animal from its anatomy. This was despite the fact that the first coelacanth had been caught in an atypical habitat, and the second from an unknown habitat off Anjouan. Smith's knowledge of living fishes allowed him to make far more accurate predictions about their likely habitat preferences and hunting behaviour than El White or other scientists, whose expertise lay mainly in the study of extinct fossil fishes or preserved modern fishes.

In addition to rocky reefs off the East African mainland coast, Smith also proposed that coelacanths may live off the Western Indian Ocean islands, in particular off the huge, ancient island of Madagascar. Because of the continuity of the Indian Ocean environment, the marine fish fauna off Madagascar has lower levels of endemicity than its land animals, and many of its fish are shared with other Western Indian Ocean islands and the African mainland. On his last expedition to Cabo Delgado in northern Mozambique, Smith had looked longingly across the Indian Ocean towards the Comoros, about 200 kilometres away, and speculated that coelacanths might occur there. In an article published posthumously in the *Standard Encyclopaedia of Southern Africa* he even imagined 'natives feasting on succulent coelacanth steaks on a remote Madagascar shore' (Smith, 1971; Spargo, 2008).

Smith's conclusion that coelacanths most likely live among rocks in areas that are remote from zoologists, but at moderate depths accessible to traditional hook-and-hand-line fishermen in the tropics of East Africa, was supported by the British scientist JR Norman (author of the authoritative *History of Fishes*). Norman suggested that 'long-baited lines perhaps hold out the best chance of catching fresh specimens' (Norman, 1939). Most coelacanths have, in fact, been caught by hand-line fishermen (Bruton & Stobbs, 1991; Nulens *et al.*, 2011), and we now know from Hans Fricke's work that their depth preferences in the Comoros range between 100 and 800 metres. As the average depth of the oceans is 3,688 metres, coelacanths are relatively shallow-water fishes.

In contrast, other fish experts from England, particularly EI White, as well as from France and Denmark, concluded that the coelacanth was a fish of the deep abyss, and fruitless expeditions were mounted by Jacques Millot in collaboration with Jacques-Yves Cousteau (co-inventor with Émile Gagnan of the aqualung) and his *Calypso* crew in 1954 and 1963 to find them in deep water. Alas, Cousteau, or 'Captain Planet' as he had been nicknamed, who had probably seen more live fish under the sea than any other human at the time, was destined never to see a living coelacanth in its natural habitat. The only live specimen that he ever saw was the eighth coelacanth known to Western scientists, which was caught on 12th November 1954 off Mutsamudu and kept alive in an overturned boat for 24 hours.

As an angler, Smith (1956) was even able to predict correctly how a coelacanth would play, once hooked; they would be dogged fighters, like rock cods and groupers. Traditional Comorian fishermen who have caught coelacanths know immediately when they have hooked one by the reactions of the fish. Unlike oilfish or sharks, which tug hard and fast, they described how *gombessa* (their name for the coelacanth) are comparatively slow and tenacious, like groupers (*sahali*), and may take up to two hours to bring to boat.

Although JLB Smith was the first to offer a reward for a coelacanth, he later strongly discouraged this practice after numerous coelacanths had been caught by traditional fishermen (and then bought or confiscated by the French authorities). The French had offered a reward of $280 for a dead specimen and $560 for a live one. Cousteau, who also disapproved of this policy of offering a reward to catch a rare fish, commented that Comorian fishermen had practically abandoned fishing for food, instead going 'fishing for money'; and he lamented, after the capture of the eighth specimen, '... two more wealthy fishermen joined the local coelacanth aristocracy' (Gon, 1998).

In a letter to the editor of *The Times of London* published on 4th June 1956, JLB Smith stated:

'Investigation indicates that the coelacanth evidently frequents a certain depth zone, so that the available Comoran habitat for coelacanths must be restricted. All the evidence indeed indicates that there cannot be any high population of coelacanths there. If, as is quite likely, these are the only coela-canths in existence, there may well be only a few hundred of them in all. In the last three years the French have got ten specimens, more than enough for full scientific investigation. Science and the world are no longer crying for dead coelacanths. The only excuse for further hunting of coelacanths at the Comores is that mankind may be able to see one alive in an aquarium.

'It is disturbing that no habitat for coelacanths other than the Comores has been found. Nothing has transpired about the international expedition, and apparently no coelacanths have been taken in these three years other than by the lines of native fishermen, induced by large rewards to concen-trate on hunting coelacanths. If a herd of dinosaurs were discovered in some remote jungle the world would rightly recoil in horror from a policy of rewarding natives to slaughter as many as possible. The situation of the Comoran coelacanths is in reality no better, and the present policy is debasing a once important scientific quest to the level of senseless slaughter of one of our most precious heritages in biology. The French own the Comores, but the coelacanth belongs to science and to mankind. ... The policy of rewarding natives for catching coelacanths should immediately be reversed, or modified, to that of a severe punishment for killing one.'

As can be imagined, this letter was not well received by the French.

In September 1952, during their long fish-collecting expedition to Kenya and Tanzania, the Smiths mounted an exhibition of some of their catches in Zanzibar and distributed their reward leaflets. There they met Eric Ernest Hunt, skipper of the schooner *N'duwaro* ('billfish' in kiSwahili), who traded between Tanzania and the Comoros. Hunt was no ordinary mariner. He was born in London in 1915 to a respectable family and schooled at Eton. He was a dashing, handsome man whom some described as 'a dead ringer for Errol Flynn (only shorter)' (Weinberg, 1999). He was a qualified engineer who first came out to East Africa in 1935 as a motor mechanic and then ran a ferry service on Lake Victoria. At the outbreak of the Second World War he enlisted with the Royal

Electrical and Mechanical Engineers and served in Abyssinia and East Africa, where he received citations for bravery.

After the war Hunt decided not to return to England, forsaking the comfortable life of an English gentleman to go adventuring off the east coast of Africa (Weinberg, 1999; McGregor, 2015). With progressively larger vessels, he traded tea and coffee, spices, cloths and cloves. He was also an accomplished aquarist who set up aquaria for freshwater and marine fishes in his home in Zanzibar and had a particular interest in the strange lifestyles and breeding habits of freshwater killifish (*Nothobranchius* species). Like Smith, his passion for fish arose from a love of angling. He was also greatly concerned about the destruction of marine life through the uncontrolled use of pesticides, long before environmental activism became popular (Stobbs, 1996b).

Hunt showed real interest in the coelacanth, questioned the Smiths in detail about their quest, and took copies of the reward leaflets to the Comoros on his next trip. The Smiths, in the meantime, travelled to Kenya to collect fishes, and then called in at Zanzibar on their return. There Margaret met Hunt again and, as they parted, he joked, 'When I get a coelacanth, I'll send you a cable'. They both burst out laughing but Margaret did remark to Smith later, '... that man is all there, I think we can rely on his judgement if ever he gets a coelacanth; he is sound' (Smith, 1956).

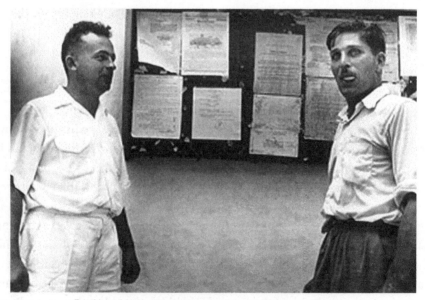

Eric Hunt (right) with the coelacanth reward poster in Zanzibar.

The Smiths returned from their 1952 expedition in relative luxury aboard the *Dunottar Castle,* one of the 'old ladies' of the Union-Castle fleet. This may seem strange to modern scientists but it was the only way in which they could travel back to South Africa with their large fish collections[1].

On board the *Dunottar Castle* in the 1950s a bugler would have called the guests to meals and the scrumptious menu would have included turtle soup, parsnip fritters, roasted pheasant, Melton Mowbray pork pies, Dover sole, foie-gras, truffles, plover's eggs, cock's kidneys and crayfish tails. Lawrence Green, a regular voyager on the 'lavender liners' in the 1940s and 1950s, mentions that the turtle soup was made from the flesh and fat of the green turtle, *Chelonia mydas,* simmered for three days with basil, thyme, parsley, celery and tomatoes. Some ships had cows, hens and chickens on their poop decks to provide fresh food (Green, 1958).

They are likely to have had little appetite for the ship's entertainments (cinema, tombola, dancing and card games), let alone its epicurean menu. It would not be surprising if they had stayed in their cabin during meal times (wearing their khaki outfits) and warmed up a tin of pilchards and peas on their primus stove for dinner! They would also no doubt have pored over and organised their expedition notes and carefully plotted out the process of archiving and illustrating the fishes that they had collected once they returned to Grahamstown. Little did they know that their carefully laid plans would soon be thrown into complete disarray!

When the *Dunottar Castle* slowly slid over the bar into Durban harbour early in the morning of Wednesday, 24th December 1952, the Smiths must have breathed a sigh of relief. Their expedition had been hugely rewarding, but they were very glad to be back in South Africa and away from the heat and hardships of the tropics. Smith (1956) commented at the time, 'It will be a long time before anything gets me back to the tropics'. But their relief would have been short-lived because soon – that very same day, even before disembarking – they would

---

1 The beautiful Union Castle liners, called 'mailships' as they carried the international mail bags, had lavender-coloured hulls and scarlet, black-topped funnels, and plied the seas between South Africa and Britain between 1900 and 1977. The smaller Union Castle liners, including the *Dunottar Castle,* which could sail through the Suez Canal, were known as 'intermediate ships' and provided a round-Africa service. It helped that the Smiths had developed a very good rapport with the manager, agents and captains of the various Union Castle liners on which they travelled. As a result, they received a hefty discount on their tickets as well as special services, including access to cold storage facilities (for their large fish collections) and to the communications room, from which they could make phone calls and send telegrams.

be involved in another mad scramble to secure a coelacanth specimen and, unbelievably, JLB Smith would be back in the tropics within a few days.

Three weeks after Eric Hunt had said goodbye to the Smiths in Zanzibar, he was moored in Mutsamudu on the north coast of Anjouan island in the Comoros and was brought a coelacanth specimen! It had been caught by a traditional fisherman, Ahamadi Abdallah (elsewhere referred to as Achmed Hussein and Achmed Hussein Bourou), using a hand line from a dugout canoe on 20th December 1952. This happened to be a big day in the Comoros, as the islanders were preparing for the Compétitions Sportives de l'Archipel, the annual sports festival, to be held on Mayotte. The principal of the primary school in Domoni, Affene Mohamed (who would later become the Comorian Minister for Cultural Affairs under President Ahmed Abdallah), also happened to be the captain of the Anjouan soccer team, and in preparation for the prestigious event, he visited the local hairdresser near the fish market for a shave. As he passed through the market, he recognised the fish as the one illustrated on the reward leaflet; the fish, the fisherman and the schoolteacher duly hitched a ride in the government truck transporting the soccer team as far as Mutsamudu, where, according to *radio cocotier* (the Comorian term for 'bush telegraph'), Hunt's ship was moored. The fish was a small male, 135 centimetres long and weighing 37.5 kilograms (Smith, 1956; Nulens *et al.*, 2011; Bruton, 2015). In *Old Fourlegs* Smith (1956) dramatically describes how the fish was manhandled for 25 miles (40 kilometres) along steep mountain paths across deep valleys and through dense forests but the reality is that the journey was carried out in a government truck.[2]

Eric Hunt immediately preserved the fish as best he could and sent a telegram to Smith, 'HAVE FIVE FOOT SPECIMEN COELACANTH INJECTED FORMALIN HERE KILLED 20TH ADVISE REPLY HUNT DZAOUDZI'. The telegram took four days to reach Smith, finding him still on board the *Dunottar Castle*, newly docked in Durban.

Smith was thrilled by the news but very anxious. How certain could he be that Hunt had identified the fish correctly? Did Hunt have enough preserva-

---

2 This author can confirm that it is *very* mountainous and densely forested terrain, having travelled this route with two Canadian ichthyologists, Eugene and Christine Balon, and Robin Stobbs, while they were studying a migratory goby, in between coelacanth researches on the island. *En route* they passed through Bambao, where coconut husks were used as fuel to heat water in an ancient perfume processing plant; the delightful aroma of ylang-ylang permeated the air. Indiana Jones-style, they clambered down vine-strewn cliffs and ancient ladders to reach the fishes deep down in the valley of the Tatinga River.

tive to save the soft parts? He didn't even know where Dzaoudzi was until one of the ship's officers looked it up and told him that it is on the small island of Petite-Terre (or Pamanzi) off the main island of Grande-Terre (or Maore) in Mayotte, Comoros. It was also the location of the French colonial administration of the islands, and had an airstrip.

Smith then received another telegram from Hunt that increased his anxiety: 'CHARTER PLANE IMMEDIATELY AUTHORITIES TRYING CLAIM SPECIMEN BUT WILLING LET YOU HAVE IT IF IN PERSON STOP PAID FISHERMAN REWARD TO STRENGHTEN POSITION STOP INJCETED FIVE KILO FORMALIN NO REFROGERATOR STOP SPECIMEN DIFEFERNT TOURS NO FRONT DORSAL OR TAIL RENMANANT BUT DEFINITE IDENTIFICATION HUNT'.

Not only were the French authorities threatening to seize the fish, but it was different from the first specimen, which fuelled his doubts as to whether it was a coelacanth at all.

Most people, after an exhausting expedition to the tropics, would have settled for a delayed trip back to the Comoros to retrieve the second coelacanth, but Smith's sense of ownership of the specimen after his extensive reward campaign, and his determination to be the one to describe it, dictated that he must go back and retrieve it immediately. Even before disembarking at Durban, he started preparing to fly to the Comoros. Captain Smythe placed the ship's telephone on the bridge at his disposal and helped in every way he could, even providing snacks – cheese, dried figs, Brazil nuts – for Smith to take on board whichever aeroplane could be secured to fly him to fetch the fish. The hastily devised plan was now for JLB Smith alone to fly back north, with Margaret continuing her journey on the *Dunottar Castle* to Port Elizabeth, and then by road to Grahamstown with the fish collections.

Margaret tried to persuade JLB to allow a French scientist, Jacques Millot, from Madagascar to examine the second coelacanth in the Comoros. JLB had previously met Millot, head of the French Scientific Research Institute in Tananarive, at a conference in Johannesburg, but he would have none of it. It was *his* fish and he would be the first to identify and describe it.

Smith was exhausted after his long expedition but he now had to find the energy to face up to this new challenge. After 14 long years he finally had another coelacanth – but how could he get to the Comoros over the Christmas holidays in time to save the fish? Later he wrote, 'It was an awful time. I can stand a good deal, but find suspense wearing, for while my imagination helps my work it clouds my life' (Smith, 1956).

While JLB was trying to arrange an aeroplane (there were, of course, no commercial flights from South Africa to the Comoros at the time), he and Margaret were invited to a series of teas and meals in Durban. He wrote of one such outing:

> 'We were probably deadly guests at that luncheon, but our charming hosts were old friends, considerate and expert at making even corpses feel at home. Even so their tasty food almost nauseated me. There was fish, but I could see only Coelacanth. It was a hot day, and there was a specially delicious cold drink; but I could think only of formalin' (Smith, 1956).

The week of Christmas 1952 was one of the most frustrating times in Smith's life. Initially he tried to obtain permission to use a Sunderland flying boat from 35 Squadron at Durban Bayhead, or even the more ponderous Catalina, which would have resulted in a slow journey, but nothing came of this (Bergh *et al.*, 1992). He then spent hours on the telephone trying to persuade various decision-makers to provide an aeroplane 'to take a mad scientist to a foreign country to fetch a dead fish', as one journalist later wrote. At one stage he had an angry exchange with a senior military officer, who, quite reasonably, asked him what a fish had to do with the armed forces. Smith replied that it was of national importance. '"What! A fish! Of national importance?" "Yes! A fish", I barked back, so firmly that he listened again … He concluded by assuring me that I had as much hope as trying to get a plane to the moon' (Smith, 1956).

Has such an extraordinary series of phone calls ever been made by a scientist to a parade of senior politicians, all in the pursuit of a single, dead fish? He phoned the President of the CSIR, senior government officials, Members of Parliament, the Ministers of Economic Affairs, Internal Affairs, Transport and Defence, all during the Christmas holidays! Only a remarkably determined man who was totally convinced of the importance of science would have dared to follow this course. Most people thought that he was crazy to attach such importance to a fish.

Margaret advised him to go for broke and phone the Prime Minister, Dr Daniel François ('DF') Malan, but Smith was loath to do so. He had had a bitter experience with the previous South African Prime Minister, Jan Smuts, who had a keen interest in science, had served as the President of the South African Association for the Advancement of Science in 1925 and was elected a Fellow of the Royal Society in 1930. Smuts was a towering figure in international politics but had a reputation for putting the needs of foreigners ahead of those of his own people. In 1945 Smith had asked him to provide a military aeroplane to collect fishes killed by a submarine disturbance off Walvis Bay in South West Africa (now Namibia) but Smuts refused even to meet him (Smith, 1956).

Malan and his National Party had defeated Smuts in the 1948 general election on the platform of apartheid. Malan himself was a minister of the Dutch Reformed Church, devout and sternly Calvinistic, and seemed unlikely to hold enlightened views on science. Smith was aware that leaders of this same church held the view that the theory of evolution was in direct conflict with the teaching of the Bible and that it should not be taught in schools. He doubted that Malan would be sympathetic to his cause.

Eventually, after exhausting all other possibilities, and with the mediation of Dr Vernon Shearer, Member of Parliament for Durban, Smith phoned the Prime Minister at his holiday retreat in Strand, near Cape Town to ask him to supply a military aircraft to fetch the fish in the Comoros. After initially talking to Malan's wife, Maria, Smith received a call back from Malan at 23h00 on the evening of Friday, 26th December 1952. Smith later learned that Malan had returned his call because he realised that the author of *The Sea Fishes of Southern Africa*, which he had at his bedside, was the self-same scientist now so desperately in need of help.

Smith set about persuading Malan that the collection of the second coelacanth was an issue of 'national prestige', a phrase which seems rather quaint today; but he was right. As long afterwards as 1998, the discovery of the coelacanth was judged to be of sufficient national importance to justify the issue, by the South African Mint, of a gold coin depicting 'Old Fourlegs', and in 1989 the South African Post Office issued four postage stamps commemorating the discovery. This was only the second set of South African postage stamps to honour science, the first being the stamp issued in February 1979 that celebrated Antarctic research and depicted Trevor Wadley's Radio Tellurometer.

The Prime Minister listened patiently to Smith's plea, which he made in perfect Afrikaans, and then said:

'Your story is remarkable, and I can see at once that this is a matter of great importance. It is too late to try to do anything tonight, but first thing in the morning I shall get through to my Minister of Defence to ask him to allocate a suitable aeroplane to take you where you need to go.'

Smith (1956) later recalled,

'As I put down the receiver, I felt dazed, like a man reprieved on the very scaffold, like somebody suddenly jerked from the hollows of hell to a high hill-top in heaven.'

Early the next morning Malan instructed the Chief of the South African Defence Force, Lieutenant-General CL de Wet du Toit, to provide a suitable military aircraft to fly Smith to the Comoros to collect the coelacanth.

Many years later there was an amusing sequel to this dramatic saga. After the publication of the new edition of *Smiths' Sea Fishes* in 1986, Margaret Smith and this author formally presented a copy to the then Minister of National Education (later State President of South Africa), FW de Klerk, at the Union Buildings in Pretoria. He thanked us for the gift and laughingly said, 'I will keep it next to my bed in case I receive an urgent call from you'. He clearly knew about the incident with Malan 34 years earlier, such is the power of the coelacanth story (Bruton, 2015, 2017)!

The aeroplane chosen to take Smith to the Comoros was a Douglas C-47 Dakota, a reliable propeller-driven plane with Pratt & Whitney engines, a cruise speed of 333 kilometres/hour, and a range of 2,400 kilometres.[3] The 'Flying Fishcart', as she was nicknamed by the *Pretoria News*, is now the only Dakota in its class that can still fly.

The navigator on the historic flight, Willem Bergh, was another example of a chemist who had changed tack and became accomplished in another field. He had originally obtained his MSc from the University of Pretoria and taught chemistry at the Military Academy at Saldanha Bay before becoming a

---

3 Dakotas were first produced by the Douglas Aircraft Company in December 1935 and are regarded as some of the most versatile transport aircraft ever made. About 400 DC-3s (and their military counterparts, the C-47s), many of them over 70 years old, are still flying today as a testament to the durability of the design. The plane that took Smith to the Comoros, Dakota 6832 KOD ('King Oboe Dog' to early air controllers), was commissioned in 1944 and was still doing maritime and general transport work for 35 Squadron in the 1990s, 40 years after the coelacanth flight and well into her 50th year. She was eventually 'retired' to the Ysterplaat Air Force Base in Cape Town as a living display.

navigator in the Air Force and eventually retiring in 1983 with the rank of Lieutenant-General.[4]

Dakota 6832 with a crew of six flew to Durban from Swartkops Air Force Base in Pretoria early on the morning of Sunday, 28th December 1952. Smith (1956) described his first meeting with the crew at Stamford Hill Aerodrome in Durban: 'When the door was opened three huge Air Force officers emerged and came over towards us. ... They were all covertly scanning me closely; what was in this skinny little fellow to get a Prime Minister to send a special plane to look for a fish?' After a breakfast of coffee and litchis, Smith boarded the plane. When the crew were ready for take-off the pilot, Commandant Jan Blaauw, asked Smith if he was ready, to which he replied that

Lieutenant Duncan Ralston, a crew member on the historic flight of the 'Flying Fishcart' in December 1952.

yes, he was, but were they? The contrast between Smith's scrawny frame and his assertive manner was a surprise to the burly Air Force stalwarts, but they soon learned that there was more to him than met the eye. When Smith learned that they had only 11 litres of drinking water on board, he delayed the flight and insisted that they take another seven litres 'in case they were forced down in the tropical wilderness of Africa' (Smith, 1956; Bell, 1969).

At 05h00 they were finally on their way to the Comoros (Smith, 1956; Bergh et al., 1992). After refuelling in Lourenço Marques and overnighting in Lumbo in northern Mozambique, they flew out over the Indian Ocean in the direction of Dzaoudzi. During the flight, to the amazement of the crew, Smith suddenly appeared in the cockpit with a bowl of freshly-made fruit salad of pineapples, paw-paws and bananas (filched from the hotel pantry in Lumbo) sprinkled with sugar and dried milk, followed by cheese and biscuits.

They approached the small, primitive airstrip at Pamanzi in trepidation, not knowing whether they would be able to land. The strip had been built about 10 years earlier, during the Second World War, by South Africa's Union Defence Force when they occupied the island (Bergh et al., 1992). They buzzed the airstrip and realised that they would have to land uphill, towards a

---

4   Other crew members also had distinguished careers. Lieutenant Duncan Ralston achieved the rank of Major-General and Peter Letley (Captain) became a Brigadier. Commandant Jan Blaauw flew American P5 1D Mustang fighter-bombers during the Korean War (1950–1953) and was awarded the American Silver Star for rescuing a comrade, Vernon Kruger, who had been shot down.

small volcano, with no chance of going round again. But a Dakota with a competent crew is a highly versatile aircraft and they landed without mishap. Smith commented at the time:

'The situation was typical of most of my life, either heaven or hell, seldom anywhere between. When I asked my wife to marry me, I said I did not know if I could bring her happiness, but I could at least promise that she would never be bored; and she has eased many a tight corner by reminding me of this with a smile, often a very grim one. Here it was again. Could anything be more ridiculous? In my maturity I had staked virtually my whole life on the identity of a fish I had not seen. … I wanted only one thing, and that was to see the fish, to know if I was a fool or a prophet' (Smith, 1956).

Eric Hunt had rushed to the airstrip. 'Where's the fish?' demanded Smith. 'On my boat … It's true, don't worry', Hunt replied. But Smith was in agony. What if it wasn't a coelacanth? What an embarrassment that would be to him and the Prime Minister who had supported him! Soon they were on Hunt's schooner and a coffin-like box was shoved in front of them. They all stared at 'Doc' Smith.

The historic photograph of JLB Smith shortly after he had identified the second coelacanth on Eric Hunt's schooner at Pamanzi, Mayotte, on 29th December 1952. Eric Hunt is on the far left and Pierre Coudert on the right in front.

Later, on his arrival at Durban airport, Smith would relate – in a speech that has claimed its place in the annals of South African history – what transpired: that after the box had been opened and he had knelt down to look at its contents, he could confirm that this was a coelacanth, albeit a different species from the specimen found in 1938.

When Smith realised that the specimen was indeed a coelacanth, his first thought was that Dr Malan would not be embarrassed by his generosity. Then he knelt down to examine the fish carefully. Fourteen of the best years of his life had gone into the search for this second coelacanth and here beneath his hands his dream had come true at last (Bell, 1969). What's more, he had proved his critics wrong. The coelacanth is not a fish that lives 'in the inaccessible depths of the ocean', as White, Millot and others had forecast, but an inhabitant of relatively shallow, rocky reefs in the tropics in a place where trawl nets would be difficult to use and baited hand lines would be more efficient, as he (and JR Norman) had predicted (Norman, 1939; Smith, 1956; Bell, 1969).

Although Smith was elated with the catch, he was disappointed to find that the specimen had been badly mutilated during the salting process. While Hunt had been away searching for formalin in Mutsamudu, his deckhands had hacked the fish open lengthwise like a kipper and had destroyed parts of the brain and other organs, but they had fortunately followed Hunt's instructions and not discarded the rest of the internal organs.

As he took a closer look at the fish in the box, Smith noticed that the second coelacanth was missing its first dorsal fin as well as the 'puppy-dog' tail in the middle of the tail fin, and decided that it must be a different species from the first. He told Eric Hunt that he planned to name it *Malania hunti* but Hunt demurred and told him that he was honoured by the suggestion but would prefer that it should be named in honour of the French territory where it had been caught; Smith then settled on the name, *Malania anjouanae.* This initial hunch that the second coelacanth was a different species from the first speci-men would later prove to have been wrong: research revealed that the dorsal fin had probably been bitten off by a predator, and that it was, in fact, the same species as the first spec-imen, *Latimeria chalumnae.*

Smith was later to discover some fascinating features about this coela-canth. The gill arches looked like jaw bones, which indicated that

The second coelacanth, showing the missing first dorsal fin and missing middle lobe of the tail fin.

these structures have a common origin, and the notochord along the back, as in sharks and rays, proved to be a hollow tube made of cartilage, the forerunner to a bony backbone. He confirmed that the limb-like fins had their own bony internal skeletons and that the fish had no lungs, but a swim bladder filled with fat. In the intestines he found the remains of prey fishes that he estimated to be at least 15 pounds (6.8 kilograms) in weight, confirming that the coelacanth was a powerful predator.

JLB Smith photographing the second coelacanth in 1953, with the assistance of Margaret.

Before they departed from Dzaoudzi, Smith fired off telegrams to Malan and the CSIR, and they took a few photographs, one of which, showing Smith with the second coelacanth, Hunt, the crew of the Dakota, Governor Pierre Coudert, the fisherman Achmed Hussein Bourou and some local inhabitants, has become an iconic image in the history of ichthyology. Another rarer photograph shows the crew, Captain Hunt, one French official and JLB Smith standing next to the Dakota, with Smith in typical field gear – khaki shirt and shorts, rain coat and shoes without socks! Before they were allowed to escape, Governor Coudert invited them to join him for a sumptuous banquet '… with toasts of wine, vintage brandy and glorious chocolate cake' (Bergh *et al.*, 1992), but Smith would have none of it as he wanted to finalise the ultimate 'fish-jacking'. They quickly hustled the fish on board the Dakota and began the long return journey to Durban.

Coudert was later rapped over the knuckles by the French authorities for allowing Smith to escape with the precious scientific specimen (Weinberg, 1999), which was really the property of France. But as Smith said to him, 'If this one had been found on the steps of your Residency, sir, I would have come for it, for it is mine'. As was the case with the first coelacanth, Smith had no hesitation in claiming the second fish. 'In my own mind I felt no ethical uneasiness about going for this fish, rather the reverse, for even though this Coelacanth had been found in French waters, it was mine by every right' (Smith, 1956). He had spent 14 years searching for it and, at that time, he knew more about the importance of the coelacanth than anyone else.

Soon after leaving Pamanzi with the precious booty, the Dakota crew played a trick on Smith:

'Suddenly Captain Letley stiffened and began to write down a message which he passed to the Commandant who read it, glanced at the Professor, and then read it again and passed it over to him. With dismay the Professor read that a squadron of French fighters had left Diego Suarez even before the South Africans had taken off from Dzaoudzi. They intended to intercept the Dakota and force it to land on Madagascar. "How fast are they?" he wanted to know. "Much faster than we are", said the Captain. "Think they'll catch up before we get to Lumbo?" He nodded. "Any hope of escaping in a cloud?" "Radar", said the Captain. "Well", said the Professor, "I'm not giving up my Coelacanth. I don't believe they'd shoot us down if we refused to turn back. I don't know how you chaps feel, but I'm not going back"' (Smith, 1956).

Grins split the men's faces and their chuckles told him that he was having his leg pulled (Smith, 1956; Bell, 1969). Playing jokes on one another is an effective way of relieving tension on a long flight but this was a brave hoax to play on Smith, an intensely serious man on a deadly earnest mission.

At one stage during the return flight one of the crew happened to visit Smith in the back of the plane where he found him huddled over his portable primus stove, trying to light it so that he could make the crew some hot coffee. It took the intervention of the Captain and the Commandant – who told him that the fish would be blown to bits if he continued – to stop him (Bergh *et al.*, 1992).

During the return flight, Smith asked the crew to record their thoughts when they had first been informed about the mission. Commandant JPD Blaauw (pilot) said: 'It must be a pretty important fish if the Prime Minister is prepared to give an aircraft and a crew to some hare-brained scientist to fetch it'. Captain P Letley (co-pilot) commented: 'My reply (as you requested) cannot be written down. Anyway I enjoyed the trip'. Lieutenant WJ Bergh (navigator) complained: 'I was all set to go on a special visit (my girlfriend) for the week-end, I did not like the idea very much at first. I had to cancel all arrangements by phone and said, "Somebody caught a fish that should long since have been dead!" The trip was, however, so enjoyable that I was all for staying at Dzaoudzi.' And Lieutenant Ralston summed up all their feelings with: 'Not very impressed at first and was doubtful whether it was the correct fish. Professor Smith's enthusiasm is infectious, and I have found this an extremely enlightening trip.'

For all their scepticism, when JLB wept on seeing the coelacanth, the six crewmen could sense the historic significance of the occasion and wept with him in sympathy and relief. They had become a team (Bergh *et al.*, 1992).

On their return to Durban with the fish on Monday, 29th December 1952, Smith gave an epic radio interview at 22h00 on the tarmac at Durban Airport with George Moore of the SABC, wherein he recounted the dramatic moment when he first saw the fish:

> 'I could not bring myself to touch it and I asked them to open it, and they did and I knelt down to look, and I'm not ashamed to say that after all that long strain, I wept … for it was true … it was a coelacanth – and what was more wonderful, a species different from that of 1938 – another coelacanth. It was more than worth while all that long strain' (Smith, 1956; Bell, 1969).

This now famous interview is etched in the memories of those who heard it. His speeches on the coelacanth were always charged with passion and emotion and left little doubt in the audience's minds that the study of fishes, and science in general, is a vital ingredient of human endeavour and essential for the progress of society, but this one surpassed all the others. He was later told that all SABC programmes had been rescheduled that evening to accommodate his interviews. Having given the English interview in a state of near collapse, Smith then repeated the interview in Afrikaans. It was clear to listeners that he was totally exhausted, almost shell shocked, which made them even more appreciative of his effort.

Smith received hundreds of messages in response to this broadcast. One such letter from an anonymous fan read:

'Dear Dr Smith, Thank you for one of the most moving broadcasts it has ever been my privilege to hear, and for not pleading exhaustion as an excuse at a time when you might well have done so. Thank you indeed for sharing with us, the listeners, your hour of triumph. With you we were, each one of us for a few moments, hare-brained scientists in quest of a dead fish; with you we wept on the deck of a boat at the islands which we shall probably never see. Thank you, and God bless you. From one of the many' (Smith, 1956).

It's doubtful that any scientific event in South African history can have had such an emotional impact on people until, perhaps, the drama of the first human heart transplant by Christiaan Barnard and his team at Groote Schuur Hospital in Cape Town on 3rd December 1967.

On their first night back in Durban, Smith insisted that the coelacanth in its coffin should sleep next to his bed in the Snell Parade Barracks, with a special detail of Zulu guards on duty outside.

In order to thank the Prime Minister for his support, Smith flew with the coelacanth from Durban to Grahamstown and then straight on to Cape Town. Although he had already broken nearly every rule in the Air Force's books, including perhaps an unwritten one about lighting a primus stove while airborne, he chanced his arm again and asked Commandant Blaauw if his wife, Margaret, and son, William, could accompany them on the flight from Grahamstown to Cape Town and back. 'It would be highly irregular, of course, highly irregular, and I don't think it has ever been done before, but then everything about this flight *has* been highly irregular' (Smith, 1956; Bell, 1969). The crew and the Smith family duly departed for the Cape of Good Hope. On the way they swooped low over the 'Blue House' in Knysna and dropped a plank (attached to a small parachute) on which was inscribed a message to JLB's eldest son, Bob, that they were taking the coelacanth to show to the Prime Minister!

The crew of the Dakota, despite their fatigue, still had a further mischievous prank to play on the Professor. As they were flying over Bredasdorp, Captain Letley suddenly pointed to his earphones and jotted down an incoming radio message. He passed it to Commander Blaauw, who solemnly read it to Smith. 'Message from Dr Malan', he said, 'He thanks you very much for having taken the trouble to come so far, but he does not wish to see the fish and wishes you a safe return to Grahamstown'. Although Smith was extremely disappointed, he showed no sign of it and put the message into his pocket. 'Well, we've come so far that we might as well lunch in Cape Town and go back early in the afternoon.' Then he saw their wide grins and realised that they were teasing him again, knowing full well that the only thing that would have turned him back would have been an order from the Prime Minister himself! (Bell, 1969).

They landed at Ysterplaat Airforce Base in Cape Town where they were met by the Cape Commander-in-Chief, Colonel Louis du Toit, who told them that Dr Malan had invited them to lunch and to spend the day with him and his wife in Strand. JLB Smith, as always, wore a flannel suit with open-toed sandals. At the function, the Malans' daughter, Marietjie, followed the Professor around, much interested in all the fuss, and called him 'Oom Vis' ('Uncle Fish') (Bell, 1969). The coffin containing the fish was placed in the shade of a tree and opened. Mr and Mrs Malan, and Margaret Smith, who was also seeing it for the first time, looked on curiously. Then, with a twinkle in his eye, Malan said, 'My, it *is* ugly. Do you mean to say that *we* once looked like that?', to which Smith, to whom the coelacanth was a thing of great beauty, replied, 'H'm! I have seen people that are uglier.'

Commandant Jan Blaauw (centre) flanked by Margaret and JLB Smith, with William on the far right, with the coelacantha and the crew of the 'Flying Fishcart' at Ysterplaat Air Force Base in Cape Town on 30th December 1952.

Smith gave Malan a scale from the beast, which was promptly placed in the family archives, and later in the afternoon gave a short talk to the hundreds of people who had gathered to see the famous fish. William Smith (2017) commented many years later, 'While Dad was showing the fish to the Prime Minister, I got a much better deal by being taken to the Air Force base – to a teenage boy, fighter planes were much more exciting than an "old fish"'. William was even caught giving an impromptu press conference on the coelacanth at the military airport (Richards, 1987).

Like George Cory before him (Shell, 2017), JLB Smith was often subjected to actions or comments that were intended to 'pop his bubble' and mock his achievements. In his account of this event Professor John Day (1977) couldn't resist the temptation for a little humour:

JLB Smith showing the second coelacanth to the Prime Minister, Dr DF Malan, at the Strand on 30th December 1952.

'... then on to Cape Town and the Strand where he laid his find at the feet of Dr Malan. When the box was opened there were tears in his eyes and those of the guardian policeman as he named the second coelacanth *Malania anjouanae*. Maybe the formalin was too strong for the policeman but there can be no doubt of Smith's great emotion. Later discoveries of many more coelacanths by Professor Millot, who organized a panel of experts to describe the complete anatomy of the coelacanth, showed that the differences between *Latimeria chalumnae* and *Malania anjouanae* were due to mutilations but to Smith must go the credit of finding the home of the coelacanths. The native fishermen of the Comoros are indifferent. "Oh, yes", they say, "we catch quite a few on long lines set on deep rocky slopes around the islands but they are too oily and not good eating"' (Day, 1977).

According to Jenny Day (pers. comm., 2017), John Day

'was never very complimentary about JLB. I think John was a bit derogatory about the fact that JLB was really a chemist, and something of an amateur ichthyologist in JHD's opinion, and also a publicity seeker. I seem to remember that JHD considered JLB to be a splitter – certainly with regard to the coelacanths.'[5]

---

5 In taxonomic circles 'splitters' are scientists who tend to describe new species that are later found to have already been described, or who (sometimes unnecessarily) split existing species into two or more new species.

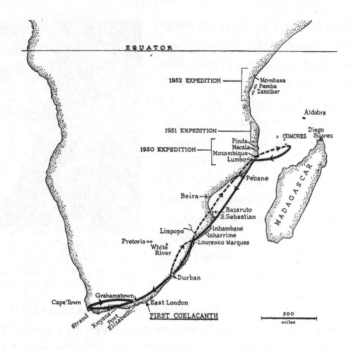

Map published by JLB Smith in *Old Fourlegs*, showing the route flown by Dakota 6832 from Durban to the Comoros, back to Durban, then to Grahamstown, Cape Town and back to Grahamstown.

After they took off from Ysterplaat on their return to Grahamstown they swooped low over the *Dunottar Castle* in the Cape Town Docks and then made a slight detour over Dr Malan's house to drop copies of the morning newspapers, which had banner headlines on the coelacanth coup, and waved to the Prime Minister standing on the lawn. When they arrived in Grahamstown they were met by a group of VIPs, including the mayor, Councillor McGahey, and Marjorie Courtenay-Latimer. 'She kissed me before them all, and nobody was embarrassed, not even myself' (Smith (1956). Then the exhausted crew were finally able to fly back to Swartkops Air Force Base near Centurion, just in time to attend the SAAF's New Year's Eve Ball (Bergh *et al.*, 1992).[6]

John Rennie recalls the arrival of the second coelacanth in Grahamstown on 31st December 1952:

6   The return flight took 34 hours and 5 minutes (22 hours in the air) and covered more than 7,400 kilometres across three countries! At £40 per hour in the air, the flight cost over £1,360 at a time when a new car cost £500 (Bergh *et al.*, 1992). Further details on the historic flight are provided by Smith (1956), Bell (1969), Bergh *et al.* (1992), Stobbs (1993, 2002) and Bruton (2015, 2017, 2018a, b).

'Margaret [John Rennie's wife] and I were ... at the Grahamstown airstrip to witness the Dakota arrival and Margaret recalls the almost theatrical appearance of JLB alone first and then with Margaret and then perhaps with William, the pilot and the crew and so on at the cabin door and the steps to be photographed thoroughly and suitably for publicity' (J Rennie, pers. comm., 2016).

Sadly, about two weeks after these stirring events, another drama unfolded in the unforgiving seas around the Comoros – Hunt's schooner, *N'duwaro*, sank during a cyclone in mid-January 1953. The cyclone also devastated the island of Dzaoudzi; if the coelacanth had been caught two weeks later, the Dakota would not have been able to land. Hunt survived this sinking but died at sea 39 months later on 3rd May 1956 when his next vessel, *Hiariako*, an elderly, two-masted, 120-ton schooner (Thomson, 1991), sank after striking the shallow Geyser Bank midway between Mayotte and Madagascar.[7]

Smith heard from Hunt several times between the two shipwrecks. In a letter dated 1st June 1955, written from Majunga, Hunt reported on the latest coelacanth finds:

'By the way the last one [coelacanth] caught i.e. the large female about three months ago, was caught by one of my crew, and only about a couple of hundred yards from the schooner. ... The eggs were rather like those in a chicken, being in a cluster of varying sizes and three large well formed ones presumably ready for dispatch. A young fellow there broke one open and sucked it, the colour was yellow as a chicken's, and he described the flavour to be the same. Next morning the fish left for Paris.'

---

7   *Hiariako* was carrying 14 crew, 11 passengers, and 30 tons of cargo (article by JLB Smith in *Grocott's Mail* 28.5.1956; Weinberg, 1999; Stobbs, 1996c; Bruton, 2015). Two members of his crew and three female passengers eventually reached Grande Comore safely, after drifting for 17 days in a rowing boat, but Hunt was lost at sea, along with all the other passengers and crew, just 10 months after his marriage to his young wife, Jean Fowler. After the *Hiariako* ran aground Hunt had apparently tried to tow both the rowing boat and a raft using a small, outboard-powered dinghy, but this was unsuccessful. He then left in the dinghy, Shackleton-style, with a French passenger and the cook, to seek help in Mayotte.

    Before Hunt left on his last voyage he had told a colleague that he was planning to collect some freshwater fish in the Comoros. He had also said that this was probably his last voyage as he would be selling his schooner, retiring to Majunga on the north-west coast of Madagascar with his young wife, and starting a business there collecting and trading in freshwater and marine fishes and aquarium plants (Stobbs, 1996c). Sadly, these exciting plans never came to fruition.

The media frenzy after the capture of the second coelacanth exceeded that after the first. The *New York Herald Tribune* screamed 'Air Race to Save Dead Fish Stirs Scientists Here', the *Times of Malta* announced 'Malan Sends Plane to Collect Reputedly Extinct Fish', and the Karachi *Dawn* proclaimed 'Missing Link Found!'. The coelacanth and the Comoros had entered the global lexicon.

Smith ended this episode with a salutary warning. In a report published in the *The Times of London* on 2nd January 1953, he wrote:

'It is a stern warning to scientists not to be too dogmatic. We have in the past assumed that we have mastery not only of the land but of the sea. We have not. Life goes on there just as it did from the beginning. Man's influence is as yet but a passing shadow. This discovery means that we may find other fishlike creatures supposedly extinct still living in the sea.'

CHAPTER 17

Mending bridges
International collaboration on the coelacanth

WITH THE completion of his self-appointed tasks of describing the first and second coelacanths and finding their true home, Smith had bridges to mend. He knew the French were upset about the fact that he had snaffled a valuable biological specimen from under their noses, an act that precipitated what Hubbs (1968) later called 'a period of active non-cooperation'. As Margaret wrote in 1969, 'He always maintained that the first Coelacanth had given him more than any one man could hope for in a lifetime, and that it would have been incredibly selfish to have kept the second to himself'. Before he left Pamanzi, Smith promised Coudert, the French Governor of the Comoros, and Hunt that he would offer a further reward of £100 for a third specimen and that this specimen would be 'donated' to the French. Although this offer pleased the French, it was rather cheeky considering that the specimen he would be offering would, just like the second one, be landed in French territory (Nulens *et al.*, 2011).

Smith wanted to smooth over ruffled feathers and contemplated two plans: one was that he would send the second coelacanth to the USA where it could be dissected by a team of comparative anatomists; or, secondly, he would hand it over to French scientists, as it had been caught in French waters. Fortunately, neither plan needed to be carried out as a third coelacanth was caught in September 1953, also off Anjouan, and a steady stream of specimens was subsequently caught by traditional fishermen off Grande Comore, Anjouan and Moheli islands (none have ever been caught off Mayotte). The French subsequently prohibited foreign scientists from searching for coelacanths in their waters and proposed instead that an international expedition under French leadership should continue to conduct coelacanth research. This ban lasted until the Comoros gained their independence on 6th July 1975.

Back home, the second coelacanth was displayed to the public in the Grahamstown City Hall on 9th January 1953. Grahamstown's only traffic officer, 'Archie' Archer, stood in attendance in full uniform, tears streaming down his cheeks from the formalin fumes, as he directed the human traffic that filed past the 'smelly cadaver'. Professor Jack Rennie recalled, 'It reminded us of King George V's death in 1936 when we had processed past the catafalque where his coffin was lying in state'. The coelacanth was later also available for viewing at Smith's laboratory.

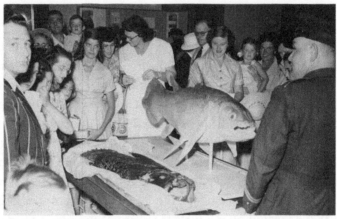

The second coelacanth specimen on display at a Civic Reception hosted by the City of Grahamstown on 9th January 1953. The cast of the first coelacanth was on loan from the East London Museum.

'During this time we estimated that not less than twenty thousand people came to look at old man Coelacanth. Not many humans have achieved that in death. It reminded me of Lenin in his glass coffin, or dead royalty in state' (Smith, 1956).

Smith also commented:

'A coelacanth can do strange things to scientists. My wife and I posed for photographs and became ciné and television stars. I would leave broadcasting engineers fixing a tape machine in my office to face more flash-bulbs or to wave the Coelacanth's fin for a ciné. We were told that within three days a television record from our laboratory had been shown all over America, and later we got letters from scientist friends in remote places like Japan, Alaska, and Timor to say they had seen us on the screen. ... In this process an obscure and highly scientific term became part of the common speech of mankind.'

At about this time Glynn Hewson, a neighbour in Grahamstown, wrote:

'With the dramatic discovery of the coelacanth at the end of 1952, its seemed as if the world found special time for Gilbert Street and the department down the road. Suddenly one morning there was a TV crew outside on the street, or there would be people knocking on our front door to ask where the Smiths lived. And such was the nature of the relationship between our homes that Margaret Smith thought nothing of asking us to host guests from abroad who had come to see the Smiths or enquire about some aspect of the coelacanth story. Their house and lifestyle did not easily accommodate such intrusions!

'The celebrated palaeontologist, Eigil Nielson of Copenhagen, was one such visitor who gave an outstanding public lecture on coelacanth fossils of Greenland: Thursday, August 6, 1953. Another was the writer and author, Quentin Keynes (a nephew of John Maynard Keynes, so he was quick to tell us!) who arrived *en route* to the Comore islands on his first trip and then, on his second, in the company of a man with dark hair and eyes (the son of Laurence Olivier, so he was again quick to tell us!).'

In October 1953 Smith attended a meeting in Nairobi of the Scientific Council for Africa, with Jacques Millot and Maurice Menaché from France and Alwyn Wheeler and EB Worthington from England to discuss future research on the coelacanth, but exactly the same impasse occurred as had taken place seven years earlier in South Africa, when the CSIR had wanted to organise a general oceanographic expedition, as opposed to Smith's more narrowly focused plans. Smith now proposed an expedition with the express purpose of catching coelacanths whereas the others favoured a broader oceanographic survey that would include a coelacanth search. Once again, Smith's obstinate pursuit of a narrowly defined goal bumped up against the broader, more holistic approach adopted by the staff of large, state-aided institutions. Both points of view had their merits, but the scientists could not reach consensus.

Maurice Menaché, Jacques Millot, EB Worthington and JLB Smith at the meeting of the Scientific Council for Africa in Nairobi in October 1953.

Smith told the other delegates that he would not join an oceanographic investigation but that his knowledge and experience would always be at their service. He then informed them that he would continue with his own plans for hunting coelacanths and described how he would try to keep one alive in a large decked boat that had been partially filled with sea water. According to Smith (1956), the tense meeting in Nairobi had its lighter moments:

'We were discussing personnel and equipment for the vessels, and it was established there would be quite a number of scientists and assistants on each. One Frenchman said, "It weel be necessairy to provide a wench on each ship." This certainly shook the Britishers. As they looked up sharply I could see in their faces the unspoken comment, "It may be the tropics, but really …." I said mildly, "He means winch"; and there was some laughter, which the French at first did not understand.'

Although the Nairobi delegates had not supported Smith's proposal, he nevertheless had a deep feeling of contentment after the get-together. The home of the coelacanth had been found, as he had predicted, in the tropics of the Western Indian Ocean in relatively shallow water. The French had obtained their own coelacanth (the third, in September 1953, with six more being caught in the Comoros in 1954), and plans were under way for international research on the fish. He felt that he had met all his obligations regarding 'old fourlegs' and could concentrate again on his work on the other marine fishes of East and South Africa. He also realised that he would be able to keep his second coelacanth specimen as there was no longer a need for it to be sent away for international study.

As it turned out, from 1953 onwards the French ban thwarted any plans Smith might have had to hunt for coelacanths in the Comoros and Madagascar. One year later, in November 1954, French officials in Mutsamudu used the method proposed by Smith to keep a coelacanth alive and made the first observations on a living fish (Millot, 1955b); the front page of

Le Monde was proudly headlined, *Notre Coelacanthe!* ('Our Coelacanth'). The fish, a 41-kilogram immature female, was captured off Mutsamudu at 20h00 and kept in a small sunken boat from about 23h30 to 15h30 the next day (Nulens *et al.*, 2011). The people of Mutsamudu spent the night dancing and singing to celebrate this momentous event (Smith, 1956; Bell, 1969) but Millot ignored the festivities and was able briefly to study the live fish just before it died, noting that it avoided bright light and readily took fresh fish.

In 1953 the *Daily Mirror* in London announced that the London Zoo had prepared a special large aquarium and offered a reward of £1,000 for a live coelacanth. In *Old Fourlegs* JLB Smith (1956) expressed his desire to have a live coelacanth on display:

> 'It had long been my ambition to catch a Coelacanth alive so that the ordinary man could see it in an aquarium, and be given the opportunity to look back to the kind of creature that lived hundreds of millions of years ago. There is probably no other true scientific story which has given the ordinary man so clear a vision of what is meant by time, and to have a live Coelacanth on view would round it off in a way that H.G. Wells would certainly have appreciated. It was in one sense his idea of a "Time Machine" come true.'

JLB's appeal for a coelacanth to be seen by 'the ordinary man' in an aquarium was echoed by Marjorie Courtenay-Latimer in 1998 and by this author too, on several occasions since 1997.[1]

French scientists acquired most of the next 25 coelacanths caught in the Comoros, and by late 2011, 45 coelacanth specimens had been lodged in museums in France (the largest number in any country) with a further 10 in Madagascar.

---

1 Today (January 2018) this author is more inclined to encourage the display of robotic coelacanths in public aquaria, considering that the technology now exists to make very realistic swimming models.

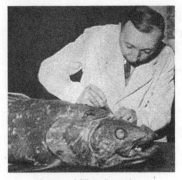

Jacques Millot dissecting a coelacanth in Paris.

Of those whose capture locality is known, 215 of the 299 'African' coelacanth specimens have been caught off the Comoros (Nulens *et al.*, 2012; Bruton, 2015, 2017). Jacques Millot, James Anthony and later Daniel Robineau made extremely detailed studies of coelacanth anatomy and published their results in a series of scientific papers and a comprehensive, three-volume monograph, 'L'Anatomie de *Latimeria chalumnae*', between 1954 and 1978 (Millot, 1953, 1954a, b, c; 1955a, b; Millot & Anthony, 1958, 1965, 1974; Robineau 1976; Robineau & Anthony, 1971, 1973; Millot *et al.*, 1973, 1975, 1978). It was perhaps the last great accomplishment in formal descriptive anatomy; the great Victorian tradition of highly detailed descriptions had ended and the era of quick, short descriptions had begun.

In 1954 and again in 1963 Jacques Millot, in collaboration with Jacques-Yves Cousteau and his team on the dive ship *Calypso*, searched for coelacanths using electronic flash photography off the Comoros, Seychelles and Aldabra, but without luck (Smith, 1956). In 1954, an Italian dive team led by Franco Prosperi secretly (and illegally) dived off Mayotte and claimed to have photographed a live coelacanth, but the photograph that they published in Paris and London turned out to be a fake – it was an inflatable coelacanth! In the 1960s, 1970s and 1980s further coelacanth research expeditions were launched to the Comoros from Britain, France, Canada, the USA and Belgium, some of which tried to catch live specimens, once again without success.

Smith was right about coelacanths occurring in Madagascar, but the first specimen from there known to Western scientists was only caught on 5th August 1995, in gill nets laid for sharks near Anakao, 30 kilometres south of Soalary (Heemstra *et al.*, 1996; Nulens *et al.*, 2011). This was nearly 43 years after the first Comorian coelacanth, although these fish have almost certainly been caught by traditional fishermen in both localities for centuries (Stobbs & Bruton, 1996). The Madagascar coelacanth was recognised by Dominique Couttin, a visitor to Anakao, in a fisherman's catch. She bought it for US $6 and donated it to the Institut Halieutique et des Sciences Marines at the University of Toliara. To date (October 2017), 13 coelacanth specimens are known from Madagascar, the third most after the Comoros (215) and Tanzania (officially 63, but probably more than 80). Madagascar has also yielded a rich bounty of coelacanth fossils; extinct species in the genera *Coelacanthus, Piveteauia* and *Whiteia* have all been found in Triassic deposits there.

In June 1956, in the first publication on coelacanth conservation, JLB Smith wrote a caustic letter to *The Times of London* suggesting that the French had sufficient specimens and that their present policy is 'debasing a once important scientific quest to the level of senseless slaughter of one of our most precious heritages in biology', but he got a robust response. Gavin de Beer, Director of the British Museum (Natural History), responded the next day, 'When Professor Smith states that science and the world are no longer crying for dead coelacanths he forgets that, while he may possess a specimen, other museums such as this have need for one, and have been promised specimens by our generous French colleagues'. On 5th June 1956 the *New York Post* nevertheless supported Smith with an article headlined 'Senseless slaughter of rare fish assailed'.

The following week Millot weighed in, 'If Professor Smith were an anatomist he would realize that, for an extensive study ... of the kind we are pursuing ... a dozen specimens are hardly sufficient', and then directs a sharp jab at Smith's controversial fish-collecting methods, 'In particular they [the Comorians] must be credited with having protected the coelacanths from being dynamited with depth-charges, which, though hardly believable but nevertheless true, Professor Smith twice proposed to do'.

In 1963 Smith wrote a dramatic article entitled, 'The Atomic Bomb and the Coelacanth', in which he stated, 'In my view there is a very real danger that this priceless heritage from the past may suffer extermination unless steps are taken to prevent it'. Also in 1963, on the 25th anniversary of the first capture, he gave a rousing speech during which he appealed for the formation of an international society to conserve the coelacanth. Unfortunately, nothing came of his proposal but, in April 1987, during a later coelacanth research expedition to the Comoros, Eugene and Christine Balon, Richard Cloutier and this author founded the Coelacanth Conservation Council/Conseil pour la Conservation du Coelacanthe (CCC) in a café in Moroni. The CCC subsequently played a major role in cataloguing coelacanth catches and promoting and co-ordinating coelacanth research and conservation internationally.

In *Old Fourlegs* JLB Smith speculated that '... the coelacanth doubtless sheds its eggs inside a special case, quite possibly like those produced by some sharks and rays. Who will be the first to find one?' (Smith, 1956). In arguably the biggest *faux pas* of his career, he did not accept the gift of the 29th coela-canth, a 65-kilogram female caught in 1962 off Mutsamudu, when it was offered to him by Dr Georges Garrouste of Madagascar, on the basis that his coela-canth work was done. He recommended that they should rather send it to the American Museum of Natural History (AMNH) in New York.

Coelacanth yolksac juvenile found inside a pregnant female dissected at the American Museum of Natural History.

Fourteen years after receiving this coelacanth specimen, and eight years after JLB Smith had died, scientists at the AMNH finally dissected it and, to their amazement, found a litter of pups inside the pregnant mother! For once JLB Smith's prediction had been wrong: the coelacanth contained five embryos, the first evidence that the coelacanth is a live-bearer, not an egg-layer, like most fish. In fact, coelacanths have a very advanced breeding strategy as they produce a few, very large eggs (the largest of any fish, about the size of an orange) and have the longest gestation period (about 36 months) of any animal, 12 months longer than that of the African elephant. They give birth to a few large juveniles (not more than 36, according to our present knowledge) that resemble the adults. The AMNH discovery was announced by James Atz in an article enti-tled '*Latimeria* babies are born, not hatched' (Atz, 1976) and in 1979 the Amer-ican Museum donated a cast of one of the embryos to the Ichthyology Institute in Grahamstown.

In 1965 the French decided that they had enough coelacanths, moved their operational base from the Comoros to the Muséum National d'Histoire Naturelle in Paris, and handed over the responsibility for the distribution of further coelacanth catches to the Comorian authorities. The Comorians were delighted, and instituted a practice whereby fishermen were obliged to sell coelacanths to the government in return for a reward of £100. Thereafter, international coelacanth research became decidedly collaborative and was characterised by 'coelacanth détente' from the 1970s onwards, when coelacanth specimens were exchanged as goodwill gifts between the Comoros, France and other countries. The era of coelacanth diplomacy was, in fact, initiated by Millot and Anthony when they donated the 15th coelacanth, a 125-centimetre female caught off Grande Comore in July 1956 (Nulens *et al.*, 2011), to the British Museum (Natural History) in London, where it is still on display today. Since then the French have officially donated coelacanth specimens to Japan, Algeria, China, Kuwait, South Korea, South Africa and even the United Nations in New York.

In July 2017 an exhibition featuring the coelacanth was held in Kaikyokan, a modern aquarium in Japan, to commemorate the 50th anniversary of the arrival of their first coelacanth. This specimen was a gift from President Charles de Gaulle to M Shorikim, Head of the Yomiuri Newspaper Company, in recognition of his cultural contributions to France and Japan.

Multi-national collaboration has since become a feature of coelacanth research and several multi-authored books and journals have been published on their evolution, genetics, anatomy, physiology, demography, feeding, breeding, locomotion, behaviour, habitat preferences and conservation (McCosker & Lagios, 1979; Suzuki *et al.*, 1995; Balon *et al.*, 1988; Fricke *et al.*, 1991; Musick *et al.*, 1991a, b; Benno *et al.*, 2006; Hissmann *et al.*, 2006; Ribbink & Roberts, 2006; Nulens *et al.*, 2011; Bruton, 2017a).

Margaret Smith (centre) showing the second coelacanth to Robin Boltt (left) and Burke Hill, Senior Lecturers in Zoology at Rhodes University, in 1966.

On the 40th anniversary of the capture of the second coelacanth a 'Coela-canth Banquet' was held at Natal Command in Durban, organised by Professor Mike Laing, which Shirley Bell (pers. comm., 2017) described as 'one of those crazy, wonderful, unlikely occasions. … It was like finding oneself back in a different era of history.' Twenty-five people attended, including most of the crew of Dakota 6832. On arrival the guests were served the same 'treat' (chocolate cake and red wine) as a frustrated JLB Smith had spurned when he arrived at Dzaoudzi to collect the fish. Willem Bergh showed Shirley his notebook from the epic flight and regaled her with stories of the precarious landing and take-off in Dzaoudzi. Brigadier JH Pretorius, Officer Commanding: Natal Command, together with William Smith, unveiled a plaque:

> *This plaque commemorates Professor JLB Smith who stayed the night of 29 December 1952 in Room 47 of this Headquarters Building with the Coelacanth* Malania anjouanae, *after they had been flown from the island of Pamanzi in the Comores by SAAF Dakota 6832.*

CHAPTER 18

Growth of a legend

Significance of the coelacanth

THE COELACANTH story captured the imagination of scientists and laypeople alike worldwide and helped to raise awareness of how little we know about marine life. As Richard Greenwell (1990) of the Society of Cryptozoology put it:

> 'In a way, the story of the coelacanth, besides being scientifically important, represents the perfect human drama. The old fish, the sea captain, the young naturalist, the desperate professor, the prime minister, the Air Force crew, and the impossibility of it all becoming possible. I doubt if any novel or movie script could fully capture the personalities of the individuals or the dynamics of the story.'

The discovery and description of the first coelacanth had another interesting impact, that of confirming the predictions made by palaeontologists:

> 'Although work on fossils had reached a high level, there always remained, at least in the mind of the ordinary man, a certain degree of doubt as to whether scientists' reconstructions of pre-historic creatures from fossil remains could be taken seriously. Did not the imagination of the scientist at times outrun his discretion? The discovery of the living Coelacanth has helped to dispel such doubts, for it has shown in convincing fashion how almost uncannily accurate have been the deductions and reconstructions of the palaeontologists' (Smith, 1949).

The discovery of extinct and living coelacanths also helped to support the Darwin/Wallace theory of evolution by natural selection, *inter alia*, by appearing in the fossil record at the right time[1]. It has also focused attention on that crucial evolutionary step when animals left the comfort of the sea and ventured into harsh environments on land. The crucial question in this regard is: why leave the water? The probable reason is that fishes were subjected to constantly increasing predation pressures from larger, faster or more powerful fish predators and had three choices: get bigger and faster, remain small and slow and cover yourself with armour (as many ancient fishes did), or leave the water. Those that 'chose' the latter took one of the boldest steps in evolution, but they were only able to do so by taking some of their salty *alma mater* with them in the form of their blood and cell fluids. This transition required not only massive changes in body form but also substantial adjustments to their physiology, behaviour, feeding and breeding. Of course, it was not only the fishes that underwent this monumental retooling to live on land – the crustaceans, molluscs and several other groups did so too. But the vertebrates, led by the ancestors of the lungfishes and the coelacanths, have achieved it in the grandest fashion (Dawkins, 2009; Bruton, 2015).

Ultimately, the story of the coelacanth is about the survival of a group of fishes over hundreds of millions of years, against almost insurmountable odds, and through four major extinction events. They first evolved at least 170 million years before the dinosaurs appeared and outlasted them by surviving the Cretaceous extinction 65 million years ago. The coelacanth lineage also teaches us a great deal about ourselves and how we evolved. After all, we are nothing but advanced fishes. As Dawkins (2017) has said, 'If a time machine could serve up to you your 200-million-greats-grandfather, you would eat him with *sauce tartare* and a slice of lemon. He was a fish.'

It is now thought that fishes evolved into four-legged animals on land between 380 and 365 million years ago, about 40 million years after the first coelacanths evolved. At the beginning of this period all backboned animals were fishes but, by the end of it, there were many amphibians and reptiles on land (Dawkins, 2009; Bruton, 2015). The latest genetic evidence suggests that the lungfishes are closer to the main line of tetrapod evolution than the coelacanths, although this conclusion is still being debated, but the recent deciphering of the coelacanth genome has provided valuable insights into

---

1   The British biologist JBS Haldane (1964) was once challenged to name a single discovery that would falsify the theory of evolution. 'Fossil rabbits in the Devonian', he answered. So far not a single fossil has been found out of place in the evolutionary record, one of the many proofs of evolution.

this crucial step in evolution (Amemiya *et al.*, 2013). The lungfish genome, which is apparently far more complicated, has not as yet been deciphered.[2]

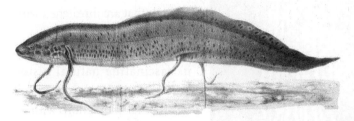

The African lungfish, thought to be closer to the origin of four-legged animals than the coelacanth.

Some supporters of Darwinian natural selection suggest that plants and animals are beautifully adapted to survive and reproduce in modern environments, but they are partly wrong. Neo-Darwinians, with the benefit of DNA and other genetic evidence, point out that modern organisms are actually adapted to survive in their *ancestors'* environments, with which they co-evolved. The genes that survive, and are passed on through innumerable generations, add up, in effect, to a description of what it took to survive *in the past* (Dawkins, 2017).

Rapid environmental changes wrought by humans therefore represent a severe threat even to the most exquisitely adapted organisms, and particularly to the most specialised ones, such as the coelacanth. Humans have brought about many changes to the environment of the coelacanth, including global warming, plastic and insecticide pollution, alterations to predator and prey populations, direct mortalities of coelacanths (although fishing pressure by traditional fishermen is thought to have had a negligible effect; Bruton & Stobbs, 1991), and the environmental impacts of blast fishing, poisoning and the destruction of coral reefs.

Both the Indian Ocean and Indonesian coelacanths are listed as 'critically endangered' in the international *Red List of Threatened Species*, which implies that they will probably go extinct if the conditions that threaten them continue to prevail. Notwithstanding this assessment, modern coelacanths will

---

2   The closest known fossil to a 'missing link' between an amphibian-like fish and a fish-like amphibian is an extraordinary creature called 'tiktaalik', discovered in the Canadian Arctic by Neil Shubin and Edward Daeschler, which has a crocodile-like head on a salamander's trunk with a fish's scales and tail (Shubin, 2007).

Stainless steel sculpture by Uwe Pfaff of the coelacanth with the profile of a man inside, highlighting the interrelated destinies of coelacanths and men.

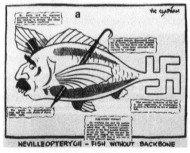

The British Prime Minister Neville Chamberlain was lampooned in this cartoon for being a backboneless politician for his appeasement of the Nazis.

likely outlive humans. The coelacanth has become, for many people, a symbol of hope and optimism. For marine conservationists, it is *the* representative of all marine animals that are threatened with extinction, the 'panda of the seas'.

The coelacanth is famous not only for its fascinating natural history but also because it has a rich cultural history in terms of its interactions with humans. Few fishes have intersected with human culture in as many ways as 'old fourlegs'. Over 5,000 scientific and popular publications have been written on the coelacanth (Nulens *et al.*, 2013) as well as innumerable press articles. The coelacanth has been celebrated in irreverent prose by Ogden Nash, in song by Charles Rand, through the visual arts by *New Yorker* cartoonist Robert Day, and cinematographically in *Creature of the Black Lagoon*, a Hollywood blockbuster based on the drama of the discovery of the second coelacanth (Bruton, 2017). The word 'coelacanth' even entered public parlance when 'a prominent member of the British Parliament ... in attacking an opponent, called him a "Coelacanth" on the grounds that from his long silence in that august assembly it was a surprise to find him still alive' (Smith, 1956), and was used by *Time* magazine when it described Richard Nixon as a 'Coelacanth of American anti-communism'.

In 1973, eight years after Winston Churchill's death, George Lichtheim described him as follows: 'In one of his aspects he is a political coelacanth, a prehistoric monster fished up from the depths of the past (thus he appears to British left-wingers, who are nonetheless secretly proud of him).' In everyday language the word 'coelacanth' is used, a bit unfairly, to refer to people who are old-fashioned and struggling to survive or, more appropriately, to animals or people that have risen phoenix-like from oblivion (Fricke, 1997), or to those who have been left behind by modern advances.

Pair of 40 Comorian franc coelacanth stamps signed by JLB Smith.

There is no doubt that JLB Smith's gift for publicising the coelacanth helped to raise its (and his) public profile and made it a familiar symbol around the world. Coelacanths have appeared on the postage stamps of at least 22 countries, including six where they are known to live (Comoros, Indonesia, Madagascar, Mozambique, South Africa, Tanzania) and 16 where they do not! Not surprisingly, the Comoros has issued the most coelacanth stamps (12 sets). In 1989 South Africa issued four postage stamps showing the coelacanth, JLB Smith and Marjorie Courtenay-Latimer examining the first specimen, the JLB Smith Institute of Ichthyology (now SAIAB), and the *Jago* submersible. Further examples of the cultural significance of the coelacanth are discussed by Fricke (1997) and Bruton (2017).

Coelacanths have also appeared on money. The 1,000 CF (Comorian franc) banknote and 55 CF coin depict the coelacanth, as do a 10 euro coin issued by France, a 2 meticais coin from Mozambique and the 1,000 and 4,000 kwacha coins from Zambia. South Africa minted a 24-carat gold commemorative coin showing the coelacanth in 1998 to celebrate the 60th anniversary of the first capture and, in 2013, a 10-cent silver coin was issued to commemorate the establishment of the iSimangaliso Wetland Park.

Coelacanths have also been the subject of cartoons highlighting the threats of nuclear bombs, air pollution or the impact of humans on the natural environment and, more happily, to celebrate the dramatic evolutionary step by amphibious vertebrates from water onto land or the evolution of biodiversity. The coelacanth has also been used in works of art, books, plays and crafts as a symbol of surprise, rarity, survival and primitiveness, or as a 'living fossil', 'window into the past' or 'time machine'. The South African artist

Five Comorian franc coin depicting the coelacanth.

Hylton Mann used the coelacanth to symbolise our dependence on fossil fuels, like oil and coal. His artwork shows three businessmen staring at a coelacanth egg (the source of life) while a line of coelacanths spirals off into extinction over a barren landscape created by humans.

The coelacanth enjoys such a high profile among the general public that it became the 'full-time Public Relations Officer' of the South African Institute for Aquatic Biodiversity (Bruton, 1996; Gon, 2002). This author even presented a paper at a conference of the Southern African Museums Association entitled 'The coelacanth is a mammal', based not on its taxonomic relationships but on its ability to be milked!

CHAPTER 19

After the coelacanth

Consolidation and renewal

B Y 1953 the Smiths were able to return to their work on the other fishes of the Western Indian Ocean. By now JLB was 56 and Margaret 37 but they still had enough drive and energy to embark upon further fish-collecting expeditions. In 1953 a short collecting trip, which reaped rich rewards, was undertaken from Bazaruto Island southwards to Inhaca Island off Mozambique. This was followed in 1954 by a more ambitious expedition to Kenya (mainly Shimoni), Seychelles (including the outlying Denis and Bird islands), Amirantes (mainly D'Arros and Alfonse), Providence, St Pierre and Astove, and finally to the Aldabra Archipelago (Cosmoledo, Assumption and Aldabra). They were accompanied on this expedition by their son, William, now 15 years old; and, on the latter half of the expedition and in two vessels, by four South African game-fish anglers. The islands that they visited proved to be among the richest areas from which they had ever collected and a great deal of new material, mainly small species, was brought back to Grahamstown. However, lack of space and containers seriously limited their ability to preserve and transport larger specimens.

In 1955 JLB accompanied some South African fisheries industrialists to Angola to study the fisheries potential there. They flew to Luanda and then followed the coast southwards to the town of Moçamedes in a light aircraft. JLB's expert knowledge of fish and fishing, and his fluent Portuguese, were invaluable to the group but his lack of experience in fisheries science probably meant that he could make few contributions in this field. He subsequently published two popular articles on angling in Angola but nothing on the commercial fishing potential there.

In 1956 the Smiths mounted their last expedition to East Africa, to Pinda in northern Mozambique. Here, calm seas and spectacular equinoctial tides greatly facilitated their collecting, and vast numbers of fish were collected and many photographs were taken. Despite the rigours of constant expeditionary work, JLB Smith, now 59 years old, published 14 scientific papers that year, including the first *Ichthyological Bulletin* of the Department of Ichthyology, on the parrotfishes of the Western Indian Ocean.

During their fish-collecting expeditions in the 1940s and 1950s the Smiths formed many firm friendships with the Portuguese authorities in Mozambique. Among their friends they numbered, as Margaret wrote in 1969, '... two Governor-Generals, four Port Captains, Military, Naval and Merchant Navy personnel, administrative officials, journalists, scientists and private persons'. They also established cordial relations further afield, in Kenya, Tanzania and the Seychelles, which greatly facilitated their work. During these expeditions Margaret was the gifted 'public relations officer' whereas the laconic JLB gained favour with their hosts mainly by sharing his expertise on fishes, giving public talks in Portuguese (in Lourenço Marques and Beira), and showing the officials the fishes they had collected.

During all these encounters with officialdom, no matter how formal the occasion, JLB Smith always wore his expedition khakis (usually shorts, but occasionally long flannels), leather sandals and a pith helmet. Margaret also adopted this dour plumage while on field trips with Smith, often wearing khaki shorts (tucked up so that they looked like bloomers) and men's shirts (with large, practical pockets), leather sandals and a pith helmet.

JLB Smith meeting senior Portuguese officials in Lourenço Marques in 1951 in his typical khaki shorts and pith helmet.

The Smiths' fish-collecting expeditions were mainly funded by the CSIR, but funding was also provided by private individuals, angling clubs and companies. The Portuguese authorities were particularly generous, especially in supporting expeditions to the remote, northern parts of their colony. These regions had hardly been explored before and, north of Angoche, remain relatively unexplored even today, except through satellite imagery. The authorities in Kenya, Tanzania (including Zanzibar), Aldabra and the Seychelles also supported their work; these multi-national collaborations were among the first forged by South African scientists in East Africa.

Between expeditions, the day-to-day work of the new Department of Ichthyology at the Rhodes University College (RUC) continued. Journalist Audrey Ryan (1997) had vivid memories of the early days in the Department of Ichthyology as it was in 1953 when she applied for a position there:

'With some trepidation I arrived to be confronted by a tough looking ten year old [William], scowling ferociously and chewing green peas! After that hurdle, the interview with a distracted and exhausted Prof Smith was relatively easy, and I was told to start immediately. The Department of Ichthyology was an old wooden building on the main campus with a small lawn outside – too small to accommodate all the pressmen milling around plus cameras set up to film the star of the show – a great ugly, strange looking fish in a trough filled with preservative of some sort. The building creaked, the offices were all partitioned and everywhere was the smell of formalin and fish. My meeting with Margaret was the start of a long friendship and my admiration for her at that time was tremendous. There were people from all over the world to be greeted and charmed; an exhausted and often irritable husband to care for; and a small boy who also wanted her attention.

'The pressure on the Smiths was enormous and at times poor William would get the worst of it as we heard the roar "Get that damned child out of here" and Margaret would remove his offending presence, until the next time. My work consisted of typing out all the articles and letters from throughout the world that were being clamoured for – never a dull moment to start with. … Margaret was kept busy protecting her husband from the curious, and charming the scientists and the press.'

Pat Long (1997), who also worked in the Department of Ichthyology in the early 1950s as a scholar and student, remembers:

'Another job I had was to file letters. This was interesting, as the correspondents were from all over the world. The letters that especially interested me were those from … the Emperor of Japan who was an *amateur ichthyologist*. The Professor (as we called him) was interested in all sorts of things not concerned with fish, and I remember one letter he wrote to the trainer/coach of the Springbok rugby team, advocating some method of play that he thought would improve their chances of success.

'The deadliest job … was typing fish catalogue cards. Along the top I had to put the fish's number. As far as I can remember, this consisted of four numbers: dorsal spines followed by dorsal rays and then anal spines followed by anal rays, e.g. 11 14 3 12. Then the Latin names, etc. It seemed to me that every species had a unique number, and I got quite good at predicting which species went with which number, especially the eels.

'Across the short passage from Mrs Smith's door … was a little room. For a short while, a beautiful girl called Felicity Mather-Pike worked in this room. When she was shown her workplace, she asked Mrs Smith if she could pretty it up a bit, as she found the stark white not to her liking. Felicity and her current boyfriend spent the weekend painting the cupboards red and white and putting up pretty curtains with a pattern to match. On the next work day, we all held our breath, but nothing happened for a few days. Then came a day when the Prof had to go into Felicity's room for something. "This is a scientific research laboratory, not a lady's boudoir" he stormed at the top of his voice. "Who gave you permission to paint this room? And can I smell perfume?" Felicity's replies were inaudible and what the outcome of the Prof's rage was, I can't remember, but I certainly quaked in my shoes that day. And yet he was always unfailingly kind to me and I had no fear of him. Provided one did one's best and didn't do anything silly, he was tolerant.

'Some of the respectful fear people had for the Prof was instilled in them by Mrs Smith. She would say, "The Professor wouldn't like …; The Professor likes …; the Professor gets angry when …" and so we learnt to be careful and keep out of his way and treat him with the utmost respect.

'I was paid a shilling a day as a school girl, and at the end of the holidays the Prof would call me into his office to pay me. One pay day he asked me what I intended to do with the money and seemed surprised when I said that I was going to buy as many Mozambique fish stamps as the money would allow. I was so proud of those stamps because the Smiths were instrumental in getting the Mozambique government to issue them.

'Mrs Smith had a rich and throaty voice and said that she was very interested in music (I was a music student) and would love to sing in a choir, but she had devoted her life to helping the Professor with his work and wouldn't do anything which took her away from that. She knew how to project her voice and told me how she could call the Professor or fishermen across large stretches of water in Mozambique and make herself heard without shouting.

'The Smiths had a house in Gilbert Street ... The side of the house furthest from the street faced a quarry, and the Prof was afraid of flying rocks damaging his walls, so the whole side was faced with corrugated iron. People thought this was an expression of the Prof's eccentricity, but it looked sensible to me.

'Mrs Smith told me that as a child William wasn't allowed toys. Boxes, blocks, wood, string, nails, tools, etc. were permitted, but no ready-made toys from a shop. He certainly wasn't a deprived child though, and when he was older, he rigged up a working telephone between their house and the Hewson's house down the road so his mother and Mary Hewson could chat without using the GPO lines' (P Long, 1999).

Glyn Hewson (unpublished memoir, Rhodes University Archive) also recalls the Department of Ichthyology in the early 1950s:

'Through my school years I frequently visited the old Ichthyology Department. I loved it. Long, white walled and rambling with a wide verandah and no pretensions at all, it was filled with fascination. I remember a major part of it being a huge long room, like a small hall, subdivided by partitions. Communication was instant; voices merely floated over the tops of these divides. Not that there was a lot of chatting. Most communication was fairly direct and to the point, especially if it emanated from the inner sanctum at the far end of the huge room: the office and work space of the Professor.

'Displays, photographs and maps adorned the partition walls – who did all the calligraphy labels and titling – Margaret Smith of course – just yet another talent she had taught herself! Can you have an affection for a distinctly unattractive smell? Certainly! A mere whiff of formalin and I am back there: walking between the shelves of fish steadily sorting, talking over a cup of tea, reading yet another pamphlet or book or press cutting on a display. Travelling the world.

'Those press cuttings! One of the jobs which I had, as a twelve year old, in the time after the sensation of the coelacanth, was the sorting and compiling of all the news cuttings about the event. … There was a note of severity in Margaret Smith's voice when she was talking to me about how they wanted to have the cuttings mounted in the files, "Remember Glyn, a cutting without a source is useless to us". … She brought some through one morning and said with one of her infectious peals of laughter, "You must look at this, it's wonderful, – the Professor loved it." … And of course it was the now celebrated cartoon of the coelacanth addressing a bemused scientist against the background of key events of 1952 (upheavals in Korea, Malaya; the Cold War and Mau Mau) with the acerbic comment, "If this is the best you can do in 50,000,000 years, throw me back".

'Grahamstown boasts practically the oldest newspaper in the country: *Grocott's Daily Mail.* Famous for its little printer's blapses here and there. Intrinsically a part of the character of the publication. Very Grahamstonian. Very eccentric. Everybody wrote letters and made comments on ranges of issues. Including JLB Smith. Especially while on expeditions, we would be regaled with letters detailing the news of what was happening. With their constant focus around JLB, they did not lack egotism and often brought chuckles to my parents as they read about the adventures of "… the intrepid Professor and Mrs Smith".

'On another occasion when Grahamstown had one of its colossal forest fires on the Mountain Drive there were a number of people out fighting the fire. He wrote about it and commended the effort which had been made, but also commented, "I contemplated becoming involved, but decided that my hands were more valuable to Science than fighting fires". That's just the way he was: blunt, utterly focussed and unrelentingly prioritised. He had this gift though for stopping at moments and directing a question or a comment because he was interested, because in his own way he cared and made you worth his while. There was a sense of privilege in that. I asked him for a testimonial towards the end of my university career. It was written and delivered the next day: warm, affirmative and insightful. Margaret was that way too' (Hewson, pers. comm., 2017).

Grocott's Daily Mail is more than a newspaper, it is an institution, the oldest continuously published family newspaper in South Africa. The letters and articles that JLB Smith published in *Grocott's* (as well as in the *Eastern Province*

Herald) covered a wide range of subjects. They included how to start a trout farm or make fish food from trawler waste, Japanese exploitation of South African tunny stocks, the exploits of Cousteau, how to settle an argument on the size reached by fishes, the electrical shocks produced by fishes, stonefish and lionfish venoms and their treatment, and how to sex a fish.

He also wrote about the habits of sea urchins, how the weather affects fishing, whether fishes feel pain, how to treat spider, sea snake and mamba bites, unusual behaviour in octopuses, the danger posed by blaasops and button spiders, the biology of crabs and lobsters, traditional fishing methods and the economics of angling.

Nor did he limit himself to matters ichthyological. He also wrote on race relations, how to determine whether a watermelon is ripe, the chemical properties of milk, and the dangers of pasteurised milk. It seems that the citizens of Grahamstown had an unquenchable appetite for anything that Smith wrote.

JLB was even happy to share with readers of *Grocott's* his method of packaging and sending fishes worldwide: 'Each fish is wrapped in soft paper, then with cloth damped with formalin, and all were packed in a special flat tin made and soldered by Messrs Cockcrofts of Bathurst Street'. He also reported that one parcel of preserved mullet that he sent to Australia in February 1950 had taken two years to arrive but that the receiver found, 'The specimens are in excellent condition, so well packed that they have remained damp throughout this long period in transit'. All these articles are preserved as press cuttings in the Rhodes University Archive.

Like many Grahamstonians (this author included), JLB Smith was himself an enthusiastic reader of *Grocott's* and insisted that it should be sent to him while he was away on expeditions in remote parts of East Africa. In an article sent to the newspaper from Ibo in northern Mozambique, published on 4th July 1951, he explained,

'To reach us the paper goes by train to Lourenço Marques, then by steamer to Port Amelia. From there it is taken by native runner 60 miles through country teeming with crocodiles, lions, leopards, elephants, buffalo and other pests. Once opposite the island the carrier waits for low tide and wades in all about 7 miles from one mangrove swamp to another until he reaches here.'

In another *Grocott's* article dated 2nd July 1956 Smith is sanguine about the criticism levelled at him by the British palaeontologist EI White, and refers to two statements he had written in the Foreword to *Old Fourlegs* (in anticipation of criticism), 'I do not mind. No man is a god', and 'That criticism will serve the useful purpose of making it plain to the man in the street that *Old Fourlegs* is not a scientific treatise but a human story, which is all to the good'.

In late 1951/early 1952 blasting took place in the quarry near to the Smiths' house in Gilbert Street, which resulted in dust and even rocks falling on their house. One rock fell right through the roof, but fortunately no-one was injured. JLB, drawing on his knowledge of explosives to support his arguments, mounted a vocal campaign through *Grocott's* to force the quarry to operate safely. In an article published in the newspaper on 14th December 1951 he also wrote, 'Freshly crushed silica dust is as slow and deadly as leprosy – worse, there is no cure for silicosis'. But he faced legal hurdles because when the plans for the house in Gilbert Street were approved on 27th March 1951, there was a condition that stated, 'Council cannot accept responsibility for any damage that may be caused to the property to be erected because of its close proximity to the municipal quarry'.

After 1957 JLB and Margaret Smith did not mount any further expeditions together beyond the shores of South Africa and settled, for the first time since their marriage 20 years earlier, into a semblance of a stable home life. An important role that Margaret played during this phase of JLB's career was to create situations in which he could relax a little, take a break from his strenuous work schedule, and refresh his mind. It was not an easy task as JLB was driven by a

Marlin in 1959, JLB's faithful shadow and companion until the end.

fierce compulsion that few could comprehend. He acquired a series of dogs, all named after fish, first Snoekie, then Sharky, Tiger and Mako, and eventually Marlin, a terrier that Margaret described as a 'funny, chubby, ugly little dog' (1976 SATV documentary), who became his constant companion and shadow to the end. Whenever JLB was on top of the world, Marlin would walk in front of him with his tail wagging, but when JLB was stressed or depressed, Marlin would walk behind him with his tail between his legs. Marlin would also go fishing with JLB, perched in the prow of his aluminium boat, *Blikkie*, or nestled in the bilges of his innovative, fold-up canvas boat, as they traversed Knysna Lagoon.

Although active fish collecting by the Smiths had ended, specimens still continued to pour into the Department of Ichthyology, testimony to the enthusiastic network of anglers, aquarists, divers, holidaymakers and beachcombers whom they had inspired to become amateur fish collectors. This collecting network was instigated, not only by the famous *Sea Fishes* book, but also by the many popular articles in magazines and newspapers, in English, Afrikaans and

JLB Smith speeding across Knysna Lagoon in his aluminium boat, *Blikkie*, with Marlin in the prow.

Portuguese, that JLB Smith published, as well as his frequent radio broadcasts.

As Margaret wrote in 1969, 'It [JLB's books and popular articles] turned hundreds of South Africans into amateur ichthyologists, continually on the watch for interesting and valuable specimens which they report or send in from all points of South Africa's long coastline'. In 1957 the South African Minister of Posts & Telegraphs even granted the special privilege of free postage of all fish specimens sent to the Department of Ichthyology! This public tradition of donating fish specimens to 'Ichthyology' in Grahamstown, continues today (although at a lower intensity) and has resulted in the discovery of numerous new distribution records and new species, genera and even families of fishes.

Margaret Smith sorting fishes in the congested Collection Room of the original Department of Ichthyology in 1966.

One remarkable success of this tradition was the discovery in Port Elizabeth of a new species, genus, family and suborder of stingrays by a journalist from the *Eastern Province Herald*, Dave Bickell, who wrote under the pen name *Izaak*. JLB Smith had previously corresponded with Bickell about a vessel for his coelacanth search in July 1953 and about the possible establishment of a marine reserve off Port Elizabeth in June 1967.

The sixgill stingray, *Hexatrygon bickelli*, found by Dave Bickell.

Bickell described his remarkable discovery in an *ICHTHOS* article in 1986:

'It happened to my wife and [me] while walking along the Summerstrand tideline one evening. We spotted a stingray, and my first thought was to move it out of harm's way in case someone injured a foot on its spike. When I turned it over I saw it to be something that I had never seen before. I checked Smith's book and could not find a description of it, so I contacted the Port Elizabeth Museum, and Malcolm Smale collected it and sent it to the J.L.B. Smith Institute. It proved to be not only a new species but a new family of stingrays. Professor Margaret Smith and Dr Phil Heemstra who worked on it kindly gave it my name (*Hexatrygon bickelli*).

'I often wonder how many scientific treasures are lost because the finder has not taken the trouble to check it in Smith's book. … When Smith's book was first published in 1949 it was hailed by scientists and laymen alike as a masterpiece. A big achievement of the book was its bringing closer together the angler and the scientist. The angler realised how much his alertness could benefit science. So he kept his eyes open to help add to man's knowledge of the sea and its creatures. And Professor J.L.B. Smith was the right man to be at the head of things. His enthusiasm and immediate reaction to any specimen sent in, no matter how valuable or mundane, was a great incentive to anglers to look for more. … Our present knowledge of the life in the water around us owes much to the inspiration the non-scientist has derived from *The Sea Fishes of Southern Africa* and the living memory of the great man who produced it' (Bickell, 1986).

The sixgill stingray, as found by Bickell, is a flabby, heavy-bodied fish that is unique among rays in having six pairs of gill slits rather than five. It grows up to 1.7 metres long, has a rounded pectoral fin disc and a long, triangular and flexible snout that it probably uses to probe for food in the bottom sediment. Its jaws are greatly protrusible to allow it to capture buried prey, and it has a tiny brain. Specimens have since been caught in the South China Sea and off Hawai'i, and it is thought to inhabit upper continental slopes and seamounts at depths from 500 to 1,120 metres. It gives live birth, with litters of two to five pups. An extinct relative, *Hexatrygon senegasi*, lived during the Middle Eocene (49–37 million years ago) (Heemstra & Smith, 1980; Smith & Heemstra, 1986).

The discovery of the sixgill stingray is a remarkable example of the successful collaboration between laymen and ichthyologists. From a taxonomic point of view it is an even more astonishing discovery than the coelacanth as it is regarded as the most primitive of all known stingrays and required the establishment of a new suborder and family (Hexatrygonoidei and Hexatrygonidae; Smith & Heemstra, 1986) to accommodate it, whereas *Latimeria chalumnae* required only a new family (Latimeriidae) that fitted into an existing suborder and order (Coelacanthiformes).

Other rare fish that were sent to JLB Smith by Dave Bickell included an onderbaadjie (*Lampadena hectoris,* now *Lampanyctodes hectoris;* December 1956), redtail filefish (*Pervagor scanleni,* now *Pervagor melanocephalus;* December 1957; initially named after AR Scanlon of Rhodes University) and a Cape sandlance (*Ammodytes capensis,* now *Gymnammodytes capensis;* June 1960).

Another amateur whose association with Smith led to a contribution to science was Arland Read, son the late art entrepreneur Everard Read. Arland was a 'gillie' (fishing assistant) to JLB Smith as a 12-year old in Knysna. Thirteen years later he sent a fish that he had speared off Durban to Margaret Smith and received a typically positive response, 'Your DERMATOLEPIS has been giving me plenty of trouble, but don't worry it is always the most interesting things that give one the most trouble! ... The species ALDABRENSIS has been known only from Aldabra, Mozambique Channel and now this specimen of yours. It is truly a remarkable achievement for you to have speared one of these so far south' (MM Smith, *in litt.,* 2.5.1968). For some reason, the Smiths always spelt fish species' names in upper case in their letters.

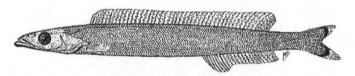

Cape sandlance, *Gymnammodytes capensis.*

Margaret Smith developed a filing system in which the names of their individual and institutional contacts worldwide were carefully stored in alphabetical order, like a library catalogue. In their correspondence (now stored in the Rhodes University Archive) there are some strange letters. For instance, on 14th September 1960, JLB enquired from the District Surgeon in Elliotdale whether he could provide details on the death of a child who had ducked his head into a tidal pool 'when a small fish shot into its mouth and became wedged in the throat, from which the child died before it could be got out'. In this letter he also asked the District Surgeon for any records of fatal injuries caused by devilfish [lionfish] stabs along that coast.

CHAPTER 20

Fishy correspondence
One man's fish is another man's *poisson*

T HE SMITHS were famous for replying promptly to every letter that they received and also for thanking donors of fish specimens or photographs. On 22nd February 1958, JLB wrote to Mr J Davey of Umzinto:

> 'It was very good of you to send all this information about the Duckbill Sting Ray that you caught. It must have given you a good fight, the few I have had on my line have proved exceedingly difficult to kill. This particular species is found over most of our coast from the Cape right through to Delagoa Bay, though not many fall to anglers. It is a great pity that you did not keep one of the young specimens which we should have valued greatly for our collections. Can you tell me the approximate size of the young and were they much the same shape as the mother?'

JLB Smith's response to anglers' queries was often supplemented by advice on how to improve their fishing success. On 26th August 1958 he responded to enquiries by LA Pretorius of Flagstaff about the senses and food preferences of trout:

> 'Apparently all fishes have a sense of smell, of varying power. Generally speaking, fast moving fishes such as trout rely more on sight than on smell in catching food. At the same time trout apparently have quite a keen sense of smell, since it appears to be well established that they find the smell of human hands unpleasant, and when trout are caught on bait such as worms, repeated experiment has shown that if one handles the bait in rubber gloves, results are better than otherwise. I have also been told by several experienced

trout fishermen that they never tie or handle flies except with gloves. ...
As far as is known a trout's eyesight is good, but that only within a limited
range. That is, while he may see and be frightened by a moving object
some distance off, he can distinguish details only fairly close by. However,
it is advisable to keep low down and concealed when fishing for trout in
still clear water. ... Most food found in all but very large trout consist of
insects of some kind and it would appear that the trout probably prefers
moving bait, which would show that it is still alive.'

On 5th March 1959, he wrote to Mr C Cousins of Grahamstown:

'This is a fine specimen of the famous Bonefish, which has been made
famous by Zane Grey. It is found in almost all tropical seas throughout the
world, preferring shallow mangrove and sandy parts. A great fuss is made
of it in America, but we get even finer specimens on our South and East
coast. It is only very rarely found as far as south as the Western Cape, being
a truly tropical fish. The photograph is returned herewith.'

On 11th April 1960 JLB received an enquiry from Rabbi AH Lapin of the United
Hebrew Congregation of Johannesburg, 'In recent months there has been
imported into the Union from Norway sliced pieces of what is known as
"Saithe". Could you tell me whether this fish has scales?' JLB answered, 'Yes,
the saithe, *Gadus virens* [now *Pollachius virens*] does have scales, as well as fins,
both of which are required for a fish to be kosher'.

Smith often added notes about the culinary properties of fishes to his letters.
On 23rd March 1960 he replied to JA Steyn of Green Point in Cape Town:

'Thank you for your letter recently received together with the drawing. This is so good that it leaves no doubt as to the identity of the fish
which is: GONORHYNCHUS GONORHYNCHUS. No. 102 in my
book on South African fishes. It is a fish that lives in fairly deep water
and is known as SANCORD by the trawlers, which often catch them at
the Cape and on the South Coast. It is not at all rare, and not really
worthwhile to take a great deal of trouble about sending, though you
might perhaps send it to the South African Museum at Cape Town. I
am very much obliged to you for taking the trouble to send this
description and drawing, it could well have been a rare fish which we

should have been greatly pleased to have
had. So next time you get anything out of
the way, please notify us again, we shall be
pleased to hear from you. This fish,
strangely enough, is quite good eating, and
grows to about 2 feet in length.'

Saithe, *Pollachius virens*.

In a letter to D Paton dated 3rd February 1964, he gave advice on fish preservation:

'I have little doubt that this is ALECTIS CILIARIS, No 527 in my book.
The illustration given there is of a fish larger than yours and considerable
changes take place with growth. The cross bars on the body vanish with
age. This is quite a rare fish, specimens are only occasionally seen and
curiously enough although it extends right through the Indian Ocean
and into the Western Pacific as well, specimens are more common in
South Africa than in East Africa. If possible next time you encounter any
rarity of that size, please try to catch it. If you have nothing else just put
it in a small plastic dish with salt; that will preserve it sufficiently for
identification at least. Otherwise try to get a little methylated spirits, mix
four parts to about one of water and use that.'

JLB was always happy to share his knowledge of fishes, in very concise and
easy-to-understand terms. On 21st February 1957 he wrote to MHH Partridge
in Salisbury (Harare):

'The temperatures at which fish normally feed depend on the temperatures
to which they are accustomed. Fishes generally live and feed within a range
of 8–10°C, that is 17 or 18°F. Outside that range they generally do not feed
and cannot reproduce. Some fishes feed all the year round, others apparently feed very little during very hot or very cold weather. ... The reading
of scales in determining the age of fishes is not at all easy except where there
is a considerable difference between winter and summer temperatures. In
the tropics where there is little variation it is sometimes extremely difficult
to find any difference in the annulation on the scales. As far as the age of
game fishes is concerned, scales may sometimes be used, but in other cases
that is almost impossible and this is generally done by means of the otoliths
or earbones.'

The Smiths occasionally received letters from persons who were frustrated by not receiving an immediate response, but they were always polite in their replies. On 13th February 1967 JLB replied to a letter sent on 1st February 1967:

'This is the first we have heard about the fish you mention. We have a rigid routine covering the receipt of specimens at this Department. On arrival they are immediately entered into our Accessions book with all details of donor, locality etc. and the same day an acknowledgement of receipt is sent. If I am here the identification and other details are included in the letter. If not the specimen is placed either in deep freeze or preservative to await my arrival.'

JLB then indicated that the specimen, which was supposed to have been hand-delivered, had never been received, and recommended that future specimens should be sent by post as the South African Post Office would deliver any parcel weighing up to 22 lbs (10 kilograms) free to the Department of Ichthyology if it was labelled 'Fish specimen'.

Both JLB and Margaret Smith were positive ambassadors for South Africa in their correspondence with scientists and anglers abroad, and regularly sent gifts to these friends and acquaintances. On 21st November 1967, JLB wrote to Marie-Louise Bauchot in Paris:

'I am having sent to you a South African journal named PANORAMA for 12 months. This is a reflection of life in South Africa … well illustrated and produced and I think you will find it interesting. Also there will be coming a package of special fruit which you have had before. Please accept these as a token of my appreciation of the very great amount of trouble which you continually take in assisting my work and which I do appreciate very greatly.'

They also reached out to other scientists in need. Dr H Aldinger of Stuttgart, Germany, mentioned in a letter to him (31st March 1950) that the coelacanth scale that Smith had sent him during the war had been confiscated by the censors and that he had 'regretted this loss deeply'. On 15th May JLB wrote to Dr Aldinger:

'It was a great joy to receive your letter of the 31st March last, and to know that all is well with you, or at least as well as can be expected after so great a catastrophy [sic] as this last war. As a scientist I do sincerely regret such indiscretions, and wish that man could settle his differences by more sane methods. I regret very much indeed that you have suffered such great loss of books and other personal possessions, and it is a great pleasure to be able to send you a copy of the monograph on the Coelacanth as a very slight contribution towards the regeneration of your library.'

Coelacanth scale.

A considerable amount of JLB's correspondence during the 1950s and 1960s was concerned with his health. On 6th November 1950 he wrote to a medical doctor friend, Dr WF de Villiers, a urologist in Port Elizabeth, that 'possibly as a result of the neurotoxin of our friend the Stonefish, but possibly also merely because of A.D. I think it would be advisable to have an overhaul by some specialist who deals with heart'. Dr De Villiers referred him to a cardiologist.

On 23rd March 1951 Smith wrote again to Dr De Villiers, this time about his problematic kidney:

'Casting back over my life, I had a very severe fall when I was about 17. Travelling at night on a bicycle downhill at between 30 and 40 miles an hour [48–64 km/hr], I hit an unknown gate and was flung about 50' [15.2 metres] through [the] air, coming down on my back, and though fortunately protected by a roll of blankets, this was as you can imagine a severe bang which knocked me unconscious. Although I came through relatively unharmed and actually walked about 30 miles until the bicycle was repaired, and then rode another 100, I recollect during my years before and around the twenties suffering from considerable pain in the region of the right kidney, which did not incapacitate me and which medical advice dismissed as without significance.'

On 30th May 1951 he wrote again:

'Pleased that you think the kidney is functioning properly, and just hope that our gloomy view on the right ureter will not hurry me unduly into the grave. I have more or less constant pain in the right kidney region, have had it for many years, and now that you think it likely to be a result of scarring, it doesn't worry me. Actually and possibly because of that, the bouts last

[a] very much shorter time than ever before, as now I can say, "Wa to you, I know it isn't a stone or a blockage, its just that old tissue and you can't scare me" and it just retreats into its hole, growling.'

The day after Smith wrote this letter he set off on his next expedition to northern Mozambique. While exploring the vicinity of Vamizi Island he experienced intense pain of a new kind.

'The infernal wind continued to rage and that afternoon after returning to Kifuki I was taken with an acute attack of internal trouble with severe pain, which had all the characteristics of a complete intestinal obstruction; no pleasant experience in so remote a spot' (Smith, 1968b).

On 25ᵗʰ February 1953 he wrote again to Dr De Villiers:

'I have for some time been suffering from internal trouble quite probably resulting from an earlier operation. ... The trouble is in the transverse colon which appears either to be adhesive to the old operation scar or to be suffering from some degree of constriction. ... The symptoms are almost continuous discomfort in the region of the scar, aggravated very much by any hard straining such as rowing and [lifting] fish from the water with a net. It has proved extremely aggravating in our field work.'

In a letter dated 26ᵗʰ May 1958, he hints that he is aware that he has a defective kidney:

'During that time I developed an uneasy pain in the right back between the pelvic bone and the lower ribs. It is more discomfort than anything else and may well be muscular. For some time it has been coming and going, and as it is in the region of my defective kidney I naturally wonder as I seem to feel off-colour when [that] part is uncomfortable'.

The doctor recommended a low-calcium diet:

'Take plenty of fluids, other than milk. Restrict the use of milk, cream, ice-cream; Do not eat any dried fruits, nuts, chocolates or sea foods; Butter can be used freely, but cheese is forbidden.'

The ban on eating seafood must have been difficult for Smith to accept.

On 3rd June 1958 Smith again writes to his doctor and provides some insights into the state of his health:

'Any medical man has a hard life and at times must wonder very forcibly why he ever took it up. However, I think that you must receive some satisfaction and compensation from the very sincere appreciation that you repeatedly receive from persons like myself, whose body is a machine to be kept functioning for a definite purpose. It is difficult to express to you how much I do appreciate your continual consideration, concern and kindness in looking after my defective organism. Yesterday was a great mental relief in that I hope still to accomplish quite a good deal before all the pipes close up, and that would be specially hard now that my mental powers are probably higher than they ever have been or are ever likely to be.'

On 22nd July 1960 he shared a thought with Dr De Villiers, who was experiencing his own medical problems:

'How true it is that "Others he saves, himself he cannot help". How little others know of what lies behind success and achievement and the price that these exact from human souls.'

In a letter to De Villiers' wife on 12th December 1961, he wrote: 'It is a very great comfort to me to be able to come to your husband as I did yesterday when in great need. I count myself very fortunate to have "discovered" him, for life becomes quite a problem at my age and to have someone who is able, and who will tell you honestly what is wrong with your insides, is of tremendous importance to someone like myself.'

In fact, JLB's doctors never determined during his lifetime that he had only one functional kidney.

Now that their major expeditions were over, the Smiths became totally absorbed in sorting, identifying, illustrating and publishing the results of their research on the vast collections they had made in East and South Africa. Their initial plan was to produce a companion volume to the *Sea Fishes*, this time on the fishes of the Western Indian Ocean, but this goal was never achieved. At one stage JLB Smith even considered abandoning his cosy nest in Grahamstown and taking up an appointment at the Natal Museum in Pietermaritzburg (as mentioned in Chapter 15), which was closer to the East African coast. He told a Trustee of the museum that he was planning a major work on the fishes of the Western Indian Ocean (WIO), which would be '... at least 4 times the size of my current volume and would probably occupy 6–10 years' (Skelton & Gon, 1997).

In 1950 he received a grant of £1,800 for the WIO book project from the CSIR and, in 1955, he received a further grant of £5,000 but used these funds, quite legitimately, for the *Ichthyological Bulletin* series (Gon, 2002). In the introductory pages to the 1953 edition of the *Sea Fishes* book he wrote:

'A vast collection of East African fishes and many hundreds of valuable photographs and colour sketches have been assembled. There is at present in preparation a Companion East African Volume, in the same scale as this, and as fully illustrated, so as to cover the fishes of the whole Western Indian Ocean' (Smith, 1953; Skelton & Gon, 1997).

As it turned out, this was wishful thinking. By the end of 1956 Smith realised that he had underestimated the enormity of the project and expressed doubts that he would ever be able to finish it (Gon, 2002). On 1st December 1959 Dr Stephan Meiring Naudé, President of the CSIR, wrote to Smith, suggesting that he should relax his work load and stating that his '... work is of such inestimable value to the country that you owe it to South Africa to take good care of yourself'. Yet, on 12th June 1967, just six months before his death, Smith still wrote to Dr Meiring Naudé that he was hoping to '... live long enough to complete [the project] as it is likely to be the biggest work of all', and referred to it as the '*Sea Fishes of Mozambique*', which suggested that he had scaled down his vision for the WIO book.

The Smiths and their collaborators subsequently produced a series of well-illustrated and carefully researched scientific papers on the taxonomy and distribution of Western Indian Ocean fishes, family by family, which were published in the *Ichthyological Bulletins of Rhodes University*, financed by the CSIR, starting in 1956[1]. By the time of JLB's death in January 1968, they had produced 32 well-illustrated reviews in the *Ichthyological Bulletin* series with a total of 682 pages, 100 pages more than the original *Sea Fishes* book; these Bulletins are available in two bound volumes (Smith, 1969, 1973). They had, therefore, achieved their goal from the scientific point of view, but the Bulletins were not designed for use by laypeople.

Margaret and JLB Smith examining colour plates of parrotfishes prepared for the first *Ichthyological Bulletin of aRhodes University* in 1956.

Their *Fishes of the Seychelles* (Smith & Smith, 1963), in contrast, was 'designed to be of optimal value to anglers, skin divers, and other naturalists as well as scientists'. This book was published by Cape & Transvaal Printers and covers 880 species, of which 95% are also found in other areas of the tropical Western Indian Ocean (Skelton & Gon, 1997). *Fishes of the Seychelles* was a further step in the direction of producing a WIO book. The Smiths chose the Seychelles as almost all the fishes there (92%; Smith & Smith, 1969) also occur widely in the west Indo-Pacific Ocean, so the book was useful to people fishing, diving or researching in any part of this large region. In reality, *Fishes of the Seychelles* was little more than an illustrated catalogue of the fishes of that archipelago as it did not include any

---

1 Smith started this new series after a disagreement with the Royal Society of South Africa and its then President, Dr SH Skaife, over its editorial policies. He suggested to Skaife that, '… when dealing with a scientist of his reputation, reviewers should be told to submit their report within two weeks and that they should be limited to rejecting the work or accepting it without any changes'. These conditions were unacceptable to the Royal Society as the peer review of publications is a cornerstone of modern science.

Portrait of Phil Heemstra by artist Dave Voorvelt.

anatomical descriptions, notes on fish biology or identification keys. As a result, it did not have the gravitas of the comprehensive *Sea Fishes* book or the many authoritative *Ichthyological Bulletins*.

Fishes of the Seychelles was intended to be an adjunct to the *Sea Fishes* book as it mainly covered fishes of the Western Indian Ocean to the north of South Africa (Smith & Smith, 1963). Many tropical fish species in *Fishes of the Seychelles* were re-illustrated by Margaret and her co-artists from fresh material, and the cost of these new colour plates was covered by the CSIR and private donors (Smith & Smith, 1963). This book was in great demand internationally and was reprinted in 1965 and again in September 1969, with the addition of further species, especially sharks, rays and clupeoids (herring-like fishes), courtesy of a generous grant of R5,000 from the Rhodes Foundation Trust.

The Smiths' dream of producing a book on the fishes of the Western Indian Ocean was eventually realised by Ichthyology Institute staff and their collaborators many years later. The first step was taken by Phil Heemstra, then Senior Curator of Marine Fishes, who contributed 16 family revisions to the *FAO Species Identification Sheets for the Western Indian Ocean and Red Sea* (Heemstra, 1984). In 2004, after a great deal of further field and laboratory work, Phil and his wife, Elaine, a Senior Artist in the Ichthyology Institute, published *Coastal Fishes of Southern Africa*, with all-new illustrations of over 400 fish species from coastal waters less than 200 metres deep (Heemstra & Heemstra, 2004).

Then, in early 2018 SAIAB published *Coastal Fishes of the Western Indian Ocean*, edited by Phil Heemstra (now Curator Emeritus at SAIAB) and a 'who's who' of international ichthyologists and illustrators who are all Honorary Research Associates of SAIAB: Elaine Heemstra, David A Ebert, Wouter Holleman and Jack Randall. It is the culmination of the work of more than 100 authors, photographers and illustrators from 16 countries over a period of more than 20 years, with the major contributors including Phil Heemstra, Dave Ebert, Dave Smith, Bruce Collette, Stuart Poss, Jack Randall, Gerry Allen, Helen Larsen, Danny Hensley, Kunio Amaoka, Eric Anderson and Keiichi Matsuura.

This epochal book, which is being published in six volumes, includes accounts of over 3,600 fish species in 260 families and covers the shores of 16 countries in a region extending from the Arabian Gulf and Red Sea in the north to Cape Point in the south and as far east as Kanyakumari, the southernmost tip of India. Interestingly, of the just over 4,000 new fish species described worldwide between 2003 and 2012 (i.e. about 400 per year), 140 were from the Western Indian Ocean and all are included in the new book (Holleman, pers. comm., 2017). As the WIO book only covers coastal fishes in relatively shallow water (less than 220 metres deep), many more treasures are likely to be found in deeper waters in the region in future.

Wouter Holleman.

This book is another multi-national triumph for the SAIAB, building on the long-term vision and legacy of JLB and Margaret Smith.

CHAPTER 21

Old Fourlegs
The best fish book in the world

FROM 1952 onwards JLB Smith was bombarded with requests from around the world to record the dramatic story of the discovery of the first two coelacanths.

In a letter to Frank Reid (an old school friend from Cape Town), dated 31st January 1955, he wrote:

'Instead of getting more staid and sober as I get older I just seem to get involved in more and more fantastic adventures and spend a good deal of my time writing and talking over the radio about them. I am constantly being besieged by overseas firms to write books about these obvious adventures and it is indeed very difficult to steer clear of all these sidelines. Add to this that I am the only really working Ichthyologist in an enormous area of the southern hemisphere and that we have enough material accumulated here, and the most wonderful material at that, to keep me busy for at least 20 years'.

In 1953 he was swept off the rocks by a freak wave while fishing near Knysna and very nearly drowned. In a report on this incident in the *Diocesan College Magazine* (Anon, 1953) it states that '… his chief reaction in the water was intense anger that he should have endured so much in those remote seas [in East Africa] just to come and be drowned on his own doorstep'. When he arrived home and described his narrow escape, Margaret took him to task and told him that he *had* to write up the story of the coelacanth discovery as 'nobody else could write it properly but himself and if he went on like that it might never be written'.

Eventually he succumbed to the pressure and wrote the book, in longhand with a pencil and notebook, in three 10-day spells while floating on the Knysna Lagoon in his boat, accompanied by his dog, Marlin; these were apparently the only circumstances that allowed him to write undisturbed (*Grocott's Daily Mail*, 20th January 1956).

In a Foreword to the first edition, written in August 1955, Smith provides an insight into his psyche at the time:

'This story has been dragged from my reluctant pen by the unflagging determination of my wife, consciously aided and abetted by numerous friends and unwittingly by publishers and literary agents from several countries. In succumbing, for the sake of historical record, it has been my aim to present this extraordinary event as accurately as possible. This has involved the mention of many different persons who played their part in the creation and course of this story. I have spared nobody, least of all myself, which is the extenuation I offer to those inclined to find my descriptive words harsh.

'The general public is apt to regard people like leading scientists or cabinet ministers as almost superhuman and beyond or above ordinary human emotions. They are not, emphatically not, and to scale the heights a man must be prepared to wage an unending, bitter battle with those persistent fundamental weaknesses that constantly plague us all. One friend who kindly read the manuscript [HJ van Eck] asked me if I realised how it revealed myself. I do not mind. No man is a god' (Smith, 1956).

In his Acknowledgements, Smith thanks Margaret: 'To my wife I am indebted for her constant support, for valuable if initially devastating criticism and for numerous illustrations'. It seems that, 18 years into their marriage, Margaret was beginning to assert herself!

JLB Smith starts the book in grandiloquent style:

'These are wonderful times, and it is thrilling to be living now, though it would thrill me even more to know that I could still be here a hundred or a thousand years hence, for this immediate future promises to be of intense interest, even excitement, certainly to the scientist. With a mind constantly reaching towards the potential marvels of the future, it has been my quite fantastic privilege to reveal to the world a living part of the utterly remote past, covering a span of time so great as to be almost beyond the grasp of the ordinary mind. In this process an obscure scientific name, Coelacanth (pronounced "seelakanth"), jumped into prominence and into a permanent place in the common speech of mankind.

'Such things do not happen easily. The appearance of the Coelacanth [he always spelled it with a capital 'C'] was like a giant tidal wave which washed me violently from my path, held me in its grip, carried me along, and set my feet on a quest that dominated some of the best years of my life. It caused me to lead an unusual life, of which many people came to acquire an attractive but distorted picture, seeing in me a scientist who dashed off on eventful expeditions to romantic tropical islands where wonderful fishes new to science were just waiting to jump into my net. They read of me as having almost casually telephoned a Prime Minister to ask for an aeroplane in which to make a sensational flight to fetch an incredible fish that attracted world-wide attention.'

He then sets about dispelling these myths and describing the many obstacles that he had to overcome in identifying and describing the first coelacanth, and finding and securing the second one. It is one of the epic tales of modern science, and a quintessentially South African story – an often melodramatic account of heroism and starry-eyed obsession as Smith details, blow-by-blow, the catching of *his* fish. In the chronicles of South African science, it certainly rivals Christiaan Barnard's epic saga of the first successful human heart transplant.

Old Fourlegs – The Story of the Coelacanth was published by the reputable London company, Longmans, Green & Co. (established in 1724), which had previously published George Cory's six-volume *Rise of South Africa*. *Old Fourlegs* was originally due to appear in April 1956 but printing was delayed by a printer's strike in London and the book eventually appeared in June that year. It took the world by storm. *Old Fourlegs* became an international bestseller and one of the most popular books of science non-fiction in the world at the time.

This was not just a chronicle of discovery but also an analysis of the intimate thoughts of a practising scientist and of the acute frustrations that he experienced while trying to achieve his objective. It reveals a great deal about his character, resourcefulness and determination, and his passion, verging on *terribilità*, to find a second, intact coelacanth specimen. The book also gave many laypeople their first insight into the workings of a scientist's mind, and introduced many people to the arcane disciplines of ichthyology and palaeontology.

Old Fourlegs was eventually published in five English editions and nine foreign language editions (see below) and, in 1993, a braille edition was produced by the South African Library for the Blind. A particularly attractive edition published by Pan Books in 1958 features a full-colour painting of a very toothy coelacanth (incorrectly standing on its paired fins) with the endorsement 'One of the great books of scientific adventure … stranger than fiction'.

Editions of *Old Fourlegs – The Story of the Coelacanth*

1956 English   *Old Fourlegs – The Story of the Coelacanth*. Longmans, Green & Co, London, UK

1956 English   *The Search Beneath the Sea*. Henry Holt & Co, Inc, New York, USA

1957 German   *Vergangenheit steigt aus dem Meer*. Günther Verlag, Stuttgart, Germany

1957 English   *Old Fourlegs – The Story of the Coelacanth*. Reader's Union, London, UK

1958 English   *Old Fourlegs – The Story of the Coelacanth*. Pan Books, London, UK

1960 French   *À la Poursuite du Coelacanthe*. Librairie Plon, Paris, France

1962 Russian   СТАРЦНА ЧЕТВЕРОНОГ ['Starina Chetveronog']. State Publisher of Geographical Literature, Moscow, Russia

1964 Estonian   *Kuidas Avastati Latimeeria*. Eesti Riiklik Kirjastus, Tallinn, Estonia

1965 Afrikaans   *Ou Vierpoot: Die Verhaal van die Selakant*. Tafelberg Uitgewers, Cape Town, South Africa (translated by JLB Smith)

1969 Czech   *Cesta za čtyřnožec Latimérie*. Dillia, Prague, Czech Republic

1970 Slovak   *Cesta za štvornožcom*. Bratislava, Slovakia

1973 Dutch   *Vis op de Loop*. BV Uitgeverij, Nijgh & Van Ditmar, 's Gravenhage, Netherlands

1977 Latvian   *Sencis Četrkājis: Kā Tika Atklāts Celakants*. Apvārsnis, Riga, Latvia

1981 Japanese   生きた化石 ： シーラカンス発見物語. Tuttle Mori, Tokyo, Japan

1993 English   Audio-book *Old Fourlegs – The Story of the Coelacanth*. South African Library for the Blind, Grahamstown, South Africa

2012 English   *The Search Beneath the Sea – The Story of the Coelacanth.*
                 Literary Licensing, Whitefish, MS, USA
2017 English   *The Annotated Old Fourlegs – The* Updated *Story of the Coela-
                 canth.* Struik Nature, Cape Town, South Africa[1]

At that time, no book of non-fiction written by a South African scientist had appeared in so many different language editions, and few rival it even today. Furthermore, *Old Fourlegs* seems to have been the first work of English non-fiction by a South African writer to be translated into Russian, Estonian, Czech, Slovak, Latvian or Japanese, or to be printed in braille for visually-impaired users.

Old Fourlegs was an extraordinary example of JLB Smith's ability to share his enthusiasm for science with non-scientists. Jean Pote (pers. comm., 2014), his personal assistant for many years, has pointed out that Margaret Smith first heard of the Estonian edition when she received a letter dated 4th September 1968 from a 14-year-old schoolboy, Jaan Elken, from Tallinn in Estonia. In an accompanying letter he wrote, 'By the way, the impression of the book was 30 000. The number of Estonians is about 900 000. As the whole impression is sold already, it comes out that every 30th Estonian has got your husband's book!' Similar estimates of the popularity of the book (and the optimism of its publishers) can be made for some other countries. In 1977 Latvia had about 2,485,000 inhabitants; their print run of 65,000 would provide one book for every 38 Latvians. In Russia, where the first print run was 100,000, the population in 1962 was about 122,600,000 and there was therefore one book for every 1,226 Russians!

Old Fourlegs is, of course, far more than just a riveting account of the exploits of a driven scientist. At a time when science was not a strong component of the public consciousness – in South Africa or abroad – it brought science into the living rooms of many thousands of people. Then, through the numerous editions and translations of the book, radio broadcasts by the SABC and the BBC, and Smith's popular articles in local and foreign magazines and newspapers, it raised the profile of South African science internationally and made Smith one of the best known scientists in Africa. This was at a time when South Africa, like many other countries, had learned

---

1   Recently, with the permission of the original publisher and William Smith, and in order to keep the coelacanth story alive, this author republished the entire text of *Old Fourlegs* in a new book entitled, *The Annotated Old Fourlegs – The* Updated *Story of the Coelacanth,* with extensive notes in the margins that comment on Smith's writing and bring the coelacanth story up to date, as do new introductory and concluding chapters (Bruton, 2017).

from events of the Second World War that there was an urgent need to invest in science and technology. Research became a strategic priority and science a matter of national prestige. When the CSIR was formed in 1946 there was little communication between scientists and the general public; Smith was one of the first South African scientists to bridge that gap.

The concept of the 'public intellectual', an academic who enthusiastically shares his/her research results with the general public, was, of course, pioneered at Rhodes University College in the early 20th century by George Cory and ably continued later by Doug Rivett and then JLB Smith. Whereas Cory discoursed on history and Rivett on chemistry, Smith talked fishes. And, like Cory before him, Smith used his technical knowledge of chemistry and physics to master the art of photography, using photographs taken with his faithful Rolleiflex 'Old Standard' twin-lens reflex camera (or lantern slides, in Cory's case) to illustrate his public lectures.

In 1965, Smith delivered a series of popular science talks (in Afrikaans) on SABC radio and said 'Knowing the most wonderful thing in the world is useless if you do not share it with someone'. He also regarded his epic book, *Sea Fishes*, as his 'first big experiment in simplifying science' (Gon, 2002), writing in everyday language with easy-to-use keys that allowed laypeople to identify most fishes.

Other pioneers of the public understanding of science in South Africa included Eugène Marais, Cecil von Bonde, Sydney Skaife[2] and even the politician Jan Smuts. More recently, other South African natural scientists have written their memoirs, including Peter Jackson, Francis Thackeray, Pat Garratt, George Hughes, Brian Huntley and this author, as well as the game rangers/ecologists James Stevenson-Hamilton, Ian Player, Nick Steele, Ken Tinley, Tony Pooley and Paul Dutton.

A post on the 'Goodreads' website dated 5th May 2011, by an American, Luke Farr, illustrates the lasting impact of *Old Fourlegs*:

'As I hurriedly finished packing for my move from my hometown of Eugene, OR, to San Francisco, CA, I realised that I hadn't packed any of my substantial collection of books. I was distraught ... I stood before my book case and decided to select the two most important books I couldn't bear to live without. The first one I pulled off the shelf was 'Old Fourlegs'. While at

---

2   Although he was an entomologist, Sydney ('Stacey') Skaife (1889–1976) wrote popular books on many aspects of natural history for children and adults. They included three delightful 'nature story' novelettes for children, one entitled *Strange Adventures under the Sea* (1964) in which the scientist is 'Dr Smith', portrayed as an old man with a white beard and twirly moustache, and as grandfather of the two child characters, Bunty and Bobby. The other two titles in the series were *Strange Adventures among the Insects* and *Strange Adventures among the Birds*.

times this piece of writing is dated with mild imperialism, and racism, the story it tells is an incredible story of scientific adventure that's rarely heard these days. It's the story of dedicating more than a decade of one man's life towards discovering a second specimen of a fish, and proving to the world that what had been pulled up off the mouth of the Chaluma [sic] River in a trawler's net was indeed a coelacanth.

'The story is inspirational, it's exciting, and for many young people at the time of its writing, as well as the period during which the events of the book took place, it was the inspiration they needed to go out and become scientists and have significant adventures of their own. With each reading of this book, I find my heart soaring at Smith's moment of triumph, I find tears in my eyes as he gives a speech declaring the discovery of the second specimen over the radio to the people of South Africa. The book has been so incredibly important to me growing up, and will continue to be throughout my life.'

In June 1956 Smith presented a copy of *Old Fourlegs* to Dr Malan at the 'Klub Here Sewentien' in Cape Town. The Prime Minister browsed through it with interest, but when he read the statement about himself by Vernon Shearer on page 128, 'He is a tough citizen, believe me, and can take more than most', Malan laughed; Smith assured him that even more critical statements had been made about him elsewhere in the book (*Grocott's Daily Mail*, 25th June 1956). Smith also sent a copy to the Postmaster-General in Pretoria to thank him for the assistance of the Post Office over the years (*Grocott's Daily Mail*, 3rd July 1956). Has any scientist ever done *that* before?

JLB benefited privately from the publication of *Old Fourlegs* as the book and its translations were very profitable. With the proceeds he bought part of a prime piece of real estate in South Africa, the Western Heads at Knysna, which included his favourite fishing spot, now known as 'JLB's Rock', in the Narrows.

JLB Smith presenting a copy of *Old Fourlegs* to the Prime Minister, Dr DF Malan, in June 1956.

The story of the discovery of the coelacanth was also told by Shirley Bell, who first met the Smiths when she was editor of *Field & Tide* magazine, to which JLB contributed a monthly column in the 1950s and 1960s (Bell, pers. comm., 2017). She had previously been editor of *SA*

Fishing and *Ski-scene,* for which Smith had also written regular articles, and later edited his two books, *Our Fishes* and *High Tide,* both published posthumously (Smith, 1968a, b). In 1969, with his encouragement, she published a book for young adults, *Old Man Coelacanth.* The book's title comes from a rebuttal by JLB Smith of the following statement by EI White of the British Museum (Natural History): 'Our living Coelacanth … was a wanderer from deeper parts of the sea to which its kind have retreated in the face of fierce competition with the more active modern types of fishes'. Smith's response was:

Shirley Bell, the Smiths' 'literary daughter'.

'In that long time countless other types of fishy creatures evolved, flourished, and vanished, many of them types that may [have] seemed more suited for survival than our old Coelacanth, but he has outlived them all. He goes plodding steadily on, his needs few and simple, and he will likely still be there when many of these 'active modern types', which are supposed to have driven him to the depths, will be gone and long forgotten. He reminds one of a solitary, tough old man, asking favours of none. Old man Coelacanth. Degenerate? Never!' (Smith, 1956).

Bell ends *Old Man Coelacanth* with the following words:

'In some way, the Coelacanth is still a creature of mystery. No living Coelacanth yet lives in an aquarium for men to see and marvel at, and much of its life history among the reefs and channels of its home can only be guessed at. Yet what wonders were unfolded to men of science and to ordinary folk everywhere when a South African scientist had an "impossible" dream and refused to believe that he could not make it come true. This book is a tribute not only to Old Man Coelacanth who has lived for 320,000,000 years, during which the face of the world has changed many times, but to Professor J.L.B. Smith, who recognised him for what he was and determined to find the home of the Coelacanth for his beloved science.'

CHAPTER 22

Bigger fish to fry

Team building, and the endgame

B Y NOW JLB Smith's international reputation was secure, following the dis-covery and description of the first two coelacanths, the publication of his book, *Sea Fishes of Southern Africa*, as well as numerous scientific papers, and the phenomenal success of *Old Fourlegs*. He received many invitations to attend meetings and conferences abroad, but accepted few of them. In April 1958, at the age 60 years, he attended the first international conference on sharks in New Orleans, where methods for repelling sharks were discussed. It was his first and last visit to the USA. At this conference he met many leading American ichthyologists, including Carl Hubbs. He found himself in great demand. For instance, he was invited by the US Navy to undertake a lecture tour of some of their facilities, but was unable to accept this invitation as he had a standing engagement to meet with Dr António de Oliveira Salazar, Prime Minister of Portugal, in Portugal. He had first met the Prime Minister in Lourenço Marques (now Maputo) during one of the early Mozambique expeditions. They renewed their acquaintance and appeared on Portuguese television together.

In July 1959 JLB Smith embarked on one of his few trips to Europe, visiting museums in Germany, France, Holland, Denmark and Britain to examine the type specimens of fishes from the Western Indian Ocean and meeting scientists with whom he had corresponded. He was also able to help many European ichthyologists with difficult taxonomic problems.

From 1960 onwards JLB Smith did not leave South Africa again and focused his energy on producing publications. In 1963 he and Margaret published *Fishes of the Seychelles*, and in 1965 they jointly authored *Fishes of the Tsitsikama Coastal National Park*, on the fish fauna of Africa's first marine reserve, in both English and Afrikaans editions. For this title, Margaret prepared a further 233 colour paintings of fishes[1]. The Tsitsikamma books covered 189 marine fish species and three freshwater fishes (longfin eel, smallscale redfin and Cape kurper).

JLB commented on the origin of this book in a letter to Dave Bickell dated 19th May 1967:

'The start of this book goes back quite a long way. For many years we have been asked by Booksellers, Anglers and naturalists who find the "Sea Fishes" too heavy to carry around, if we would not consider the publication of a more convenient type of handbook covering the common fishes that most people are likely to see. We always hoped to be able to do this and when the National Parks Board approached us two years ago we saw in this the opportunity for achieving two aims in one book (we [don't] kill birds with stones). There is a lot [that] lies behind this book. We were determined that it should be one of the finest of its kind and have put an enormous amount of work into the illustrations. We determined from the start that these were not going to be the ordinary flat drawings which while very useful for identification are usually mere travesties of the real creatures.'

Margaret's colour illustrations of fishes, all of which were newly rendered from fresh specimens, probably reached their apogee in these books. She used monochrome photographs to record the shape, fins and scalation of the fishes and then tinted the photographs in colour. Another innovative technique that she used to improve the accuracy of her paintings was to copy the scale patterns of fishes on a photocopying machine!

In 1966 and 1967, possibly in anticipation of his impending demise, JLB Smith wrote two popular books on fishes, *Our Fishes* (published as *Ons Visse* in Afrikaans) and *High Tide* (Smith, 1968a, b). The chapters in *Our Fishes* were adapted from a series of radio talks given by Smith on the Afrikaans service of the SABC in 1962, part of a series entitled *Uit die Natuur* (*Out of Nature*); whereas *High Tide* is a collection of popular articles that he had previously had published in magazines in which he describes his adventures collecting fishes along the East African coast, some of which are also mentioned in this book.

In *Our Fishes* Smith shares his remarkable knowledge of fishes and fishing, gained not only as a scientist and angler but also as an inquisitive beachcomber

---

1 Nancy Tietz and GA ('Turkey') Robinson published a companion guide in this series, *The Tsitsikama Shore – A Guide to the Marine Invertebrate Fauna of the Tsitsikama Coastal National Park* (Tietz & Robinson, 1974).

who gleaned information and anecdotes from hundreds of people along the coasts of South and East Africa, and as an active correspondent with fish researchers and anglers worldwide. He discusses dangerous and poisonous fishes, the behaviour, diet, habitat preferences and distribution of many angling species (galjoen, tunny, marlin, stumpnose, steenbras, elf, leervis, musselcracker, dageraad, slinger, dassie, zebra, kabeljou and spotted grunter) as well as unusual fishes, like the coelacanth, klipvis, suckerfishes, eels, seahorses, pipefishes and pipe-horses. His writing style is conversational and highly accessible, and he shares his knowledge without being preachy.

For instance, Smith has this to say about electricity generation in fishes: 'From the study of fossils scientists are confident that even fishes of hundreds of millions [of] years ago had organs that could produce electricity. After all, electricity was always there; man merely discovered it and how to use it; he did not create it.' Regarding the klipvis, he reveals that they are live-bearers, like some sharks, marine catfish and the coelacanth. While discussing the remarkable ability of suckerfishes to cling tightly to rocks in the intertidal zone, he remarks, 'Science is a part of nature. Man is not the only one to use scientific methods or processes to his advantage; many other creatures do this and many did so long before men and his kind appeared on earth' (Smith, 1968a).

He also relates how Somalis use remoras (suckerfish) to catch turtles:

'They catch and keep a stock of live remoras and put a ring round the base of the tail. These they take out in a boat to the reefs where turtles are found. When a turtle is spotted they fasten a line to the ring on the remora and let it pursue the turtle and attach itself to the smooth underside of this animal. ... The turtle is then drawn to the boat with a line' (Smith, 1968a).

Using remoras to catch turtles has also been recorded in Madagascar.

With regard to the seahorse, Smith (1968a) writes:

'Quite often those who see a specimen of the seahorse for the first time exclaim and say that they had thought it was a mythical creature and not a real animal. ... the breeding habits of the seahorse are also upside down and among the queerest in the fish world, if not in nature. It is the female that produces eggs, that at least is normal; but after that normality ends. When the eggs are ripe and ready to be shed the female seeks a responsive male. ... When the female finds her male, the two embrace when ... the female

pushes her eggs into the pouch of the male, where they are fertilised. ...
A large male may take over six hundred eggs. In most animals it is the female
that cares for the young, but the seahorse is way ahead in the matter of the
emancipation of the female.'

Smith encourages readers to carry out experiments (as he often did) to learn
more about fishes. 'The body of this tiny fish [rocksucker] is semi-transparent.
In good light with a lens one can see the heart and chief blood-vessels. You can
actually see the heart beating. I have counted the beats and found the average
to be about 48 per minute.' He also describes unusual angling incidents, for
instance, when he caught a leervis that had swallowed a stumpnose he had used
as live-bait, and landed the leervis without having hooked it. In a discussion on
whether fish feel pain, he mentions the case of a shark that was caught, gutted
and then thrown overboard. Its guts were then used as bait and the *same* shark
was re-caught (Smith, 1968a)!

He also laments the poor use that we make of our marine resources:

'With our great wealth of wonderful eating fish, at the lowest prices in the
civilised world, we South Africans are spoilt. We make poor use of it. We eat
only about 10 lbs. of fish per head per annum, barely ten per cent of the fish
we catch. ... As a nation we are stupid about fish. First class fish has twice or
more the food value of meat. Fish protein is the healthiest and best for us all.'

Later he comments on the palatability of rays, which are regarded as a delicacy
elsewhere: 'We are all too well off; in the matter of eating fish we South Africans
are too fussy', although he also admits to not having been able to eat a slimy
hagfish, a species that is enjoyed by some. In terms of taste, he rates his favourite
fish as red steenbras, elf and spotted grunter, and also describes how to make
innovative and tasty fish dishes, such as 'dassie biltong' and 'geelbek toutjies'
(salted and dried fish fingers, respectively) (Smith, 1968a).

Smith also describes some bizarre incidents at sea that he himself experienced, or that were told to him by others, including attacks by marlin on fishermen in canoes, and attacks on boats by normally docile manta rays and
even by plankton-eating whale sharks. He mentions that an 'innocent' whale
shark was once found to have 'a number of shoes, leggings and leather belts' in its
stomach, and also suggests that giant red steenbras ate some of the passengers
from the wreck of the *Birkenhead* in 1852 (Smith, 1968b).

He inevitably also expresses an opinion on the existence or otherwise of 'sea monsters':

'Some are now not so sure that these are just "tales" for in recent times marine scientists have found a "Leptocephalus"[2] *six feet long*. ... most known eels grow to about ten times the length of their baby "Leptocephalus". This indicates a length of *at least sixty feet* for the adult of this monster baby' (Smith, 1968b).

Smith (1968a) also remarks that 'From a great deal of evidence I have come to believe that some people exude substances [now known as pheromones] whose smell and taste attract sharks and that consequently those people will always be in danger from sharks'. He also expresses the opinion in *Our Fishes*, highly controversial today, that the only way to deal with the 'shark menace' is to fish them to local extinction! 'I have long been convinced that extermination is the only sound method to combat and eliminate the shark menace' (Smith, 1968a). He repeats this advice in *High Tide*: 'Instead of meekly accepting the shark as master of the sea, scientific research should be directed to his complete elimination as a danger, based on the principle of at least local extermination. If enough are killed, the rest will get away and keep away' (Smith, 1968b).

Needless to say, many modern scientists, the author included, do not agree with this point of view, as sharks have an important ecological role to play. Smith not only occasionally showed poor judgement, he occasionally got his facts wrong. For instance, he stated that the yellow-bellied sea-snake, *Hydrophis platurus*, that occurs off southern African shores, lays its eggs on land. This species is a live-bearer and gives birth at sea (FitzSimons, 1962).

Curtis (2015) says of *Our Fishes*, 'The stories in it are of great interest – history and marine biology seamlessly woven together by a rare writer – a scientist who could make himself perfectly understood by the man in the street'. In his book Smith describes some of his most memorable catches. In the early 1930s he landed a huge dageraad off the Tsitsikamma coast:

---

2 A leptocephalus (meaning 'slim head') is the flat and transparent larval stage of an eel. It looks very different from the adult.

'As it lay dying on the rock at my feet it glowed with a series of shimmering colours that held me spellbound. Waves of pink, red, blue, bronze and gold all mixed up passed over that body one after the other. After 40 years that fish remains one of my most vivid memories of the wonderful life of the sea. ... I could not bring myself to mutilate this beautiful creature, but carried it up the 800 ft. cliff and finally to the Albany Museum in Grahamstown. Mounted, it remained on show there until part of the Museum burnt down in 1941' (Smith, 1968a).

The Tsitsikamma coast was one of his favourite fishing spots, as he explains:

'The very deep water at the shore means that the angler can expect to catch not only the usual run of fishes, but that he may constantly hope to encounter the more elusive, rather deep water denizens such as the fabulous Red Steenbras and the Yellowtail. ... The provident angler should in this part always carry a camera, for he never knows when he may make the catch of his life' (Smith, 1966).

Even though he himself was not a diver, Smith regularly interviewed snorkel and scuba divers and discovered that many fish (such as kraaibek) that were thought to be rare because they do not readily take an angler's bait or become snared in nets or traps, are, in fact, quite common underwater. Throughout *Our Fishes* he identifies gaps in our knowledge and encourages readers to fill them.

Shirley Bell wrote to Margaret after JLB's death:

'The way he was towards thousands of ordinary people who admired him so deeply because he always remembered he was a human being first and a brilliant scientist afterwards. That is why his articles were so tremendously popular. He enjoyed sharing what he knew and he discovered, and readers loved this. So many scientists seem to feel that their knowledge is a secret thing not to be shared with laymen – but the Professor wasn't like that' (SAIAB archives).

In his notes on 'The Sea Fishes of Southern Africa Book Fund' in the introduction to the 1949 edition of *The Sea Fishes of Southern Africa*, Bransby Key stated, 'It is intended to perpetuate this fund … and it is hoped to be able to assist the production of a companion volume on the Freshwater Fishes of Southern Africa'. JLB Smith mentions in his correspondence in the 1950s that he intends compiling a book on southern African freshwater fishes, and Margaret stated in 1987, with reference to the 1949 *Sea Fishes* book, 'At the completion of the book we had come to the crossroads. It seemed obvious that we should write the companion volume, on the freshwater fishes of southern Africa. On the other hand for 3 years we had steeped ourselves in marine fishes and it seemed a pity not to use that expertise. … So the decision was made: no freshwater fish' (MM Smith, 1987).

The CSIR and Rhodes University encouraged Smith, as he approached retirement, to build up a team of ichthyologists to expand capacity and continue his work. Several ichthyologists came and went, including Peter Castle; but one, Rex Jubb, stayed for a considerable period of time and made a lasting impact. Reginald ('Rex') Arthur Jubb was born in Britstown, Eastern Cape, in 1905 and educated at Rhodes University, where JLB Smith was his lecturer in chemistry. While at Rhodes, Rex learned about Smith's 'fishy' interests; and after he joined the Rhodesian Civil Service as a meteorologist in 1927, they corresponded, with Jubb sending Smith fish collections.

Rex Jubb with a tigerfish.

From 1952, Jubb published a series of articles on freshwater fishes, including papers on freshwater eels (*Anguilla* species), which were considered to have commercial potential. Jubb retired in 1955 and in 1956, aged 51 years, he was appointed as a Research Assistant in the Department of Ichthyology at Rhodes University. In February 1957 Rex and his wife Hilda joined the Smiths in the department; but, in 1961, space problems necessitated moving their freshwater fish specimen and publication collections, and themselves, to the Albany Museum where Rex worked in a voluntary capacity, although he did serve briefly as Acting Director in

JLB and Margaret Smith with Rex and Hilda Jubb in 1956.

1964/1965. He continued to work at the Albany Museum until the mid-1970s and remained an active correspondent from his home in Port Alfred thereafter.

Jubb's collection of freshwater fishes formed the foundation for the development of the Albany Museum's freshwater fish collection which, combined with the collections from the Iziko South African Museum (dating back to 1875) and the Natal Museum (to 1905), which were later added, eventually comprised over 250,000 specimens. The Albany Museum collection was eventually amalgamated with the National Fish Collection at SAIAB in 2015.

During their time in Grahamstown, Rex Jubb published two important books on southern African freshwater fishes. The first book, inspired by Smith's *Sea Fishes,* was *An Illustrated Guide to the Freshwater Fishes of the Zambezi River, Lake Kariba, Pungwe, Sabi, Lundi and Limpopo Rivers* (1961), covering 105 fish species; and the second, *Freshwater Fishes of South Africa* (1967), covering 166 species, was a worthy companion volume to Smith's *Sea Fishes.*

Jubb described 14 new freshwater fish species between 1954 and 1974 and had three new fish species named after him: *Hypsopanchax jubbi* (1965), *Barbus jubbi* (1967) and *Nothobranchius jubbi* (1979). In 1970 he received an honorary doctorate from Rhodes University for his contributions to ichthyology.

Paul Skelton, third director
of the JLB Smith Institute
of Ichthyology (now SAIAB).

Jubb was a very influential freshwater ichthyologist, who, through his knowledge of the fishes of Zimbabwe, Zambia, Malawi and Botswana, brought to the attention of scientists the diverse ichthyofauna of these regions. He successfully bridged the gap between the Gilchrist/ Barnard era from the 1920s to the 1940s and the modern generation from the 1960s and 1970s.

Rex Jubb died in East London on 25th October 1987 but his legacy lives on. His grandson, Rex Quick, continued the family tradition, completing his MSc thesis in ichthyology at Rhodes University in 1985 and Paul Skelton, who was tutored by Jubb, was subsequently appointed as Chief Professional Officer (Freshwater Fishes), and later Curator of the Freshwater Fish Section, in the then JLB Smith Institute of Ichthyology (now SAIAB). He succeeded this author as the third Director of the Ichthyology Institute (1994–2011).

CHAPTER 23

Tragedy and recognition

Death of JLB, and a flood of accolades

I N LATE 1967 several people noticed that JLB Smith was behaving oddly. That November he handed his secretary, Jean Pote, a bonus cheque that was twice as large as she had expected and, on a visit to East London, he gave Marjorie Courtenay-Latimer a big hug and kissed her on the cheek as he left, something he had never done before. At Christmas he kissed his daughter-in-law, Gerd (Bob's wife), on the forehead – once again, for the first time. He did not, however, change his demanding exercise regime and continued with his daily walks until the end.

In August 1967, two days after returning from a Commission of Enquiry into the Oceangraphic Research Institute in Durban, both the Smiths fell extremely ill, and '… were carried off to hospital … in a comatose condition, mine a deep coma' (letter from JLB Smith to E Parkes, 7th August 1967). The symptoms suggested food poisoning caused by ingesting an insecticide like Parathion, and JLB Smith nearly died from it. Although he returned to work within a few days, he never fully recovered. His blood pressure was unstable and he suffered severe mental depression (Report on the Death of Professor JLB Smith, 31st May 1968, Rhodes University Archive)[1].

On 7th January 1968 JLB Smith committed suicide at his home at 6 Gilbert Street, Grahamstown. Unlike the suicide of another South African natural

---

1 Professor Brian Allanson, Head of Zoology at Rhodes from 1963–1988, described an incident when JLB, Margaret and Marlin walked into his office unannounced and, after cordial greetings, Smith said to him, 'Allanson – don't grow old'. This surprised Brian, as nothing had led up to it, so he replied, 'Well I cannot do anything about not growing old', and the Smiths left. Brian, now in his sprightly 90s and living on Leisure Isle in Knysna, still remembers those strange words.

247

historian, writer and poet, Eugène Marais[2], Smith's was carefully planned and neatly executed. A chemist to the end, he poisoned himself with a lethal dose of cyanide, to which he had ready access. Many years earlier, he had told his chemistry students, in jest, that cyanide would be the 'quickest and neatest way' to die (SATV documentary, 1976). He also remained practical and matter-of-fact to the end, leaving two notes (both of which have disappeared from the Ichthyology archives). The first was addressed to Margaret: 'Goodbye my love, and thank you for a wonderful thirty years. I am going upstairs to the servant's room. Careful. Cyanide'. In a separate statement he had typed: '... For some years I have suffered from severe mental depression ... the sight of one eye has almost gone ... back pressure is proving troublesome ... I live in perpetual fear of becoming bedridden and helpless ... I prefer to take this way out, probably only a brief anticipation of nature' (Weinberg, 1999; MM Smith, pers. comm., 1986). He was cremated in Port Elizabeth and his ashes were buried in Grahamstown on 8th January 1968. His death was mentioned in *Time* magazine and obituaries appeared in many leading international newspapers, including the *New York Times* (Jackson, 1996).

Throughout his ichthyology career, in the field and laboratory, JLB Smith had made extensive use of formalin as a fish preservative. Formalin, a 40% solution of formaldehyde in water, is an effective preservative for museum specimens as it kills bacteria, but it is also highly toxic to humans, as well as being carcinogenic. Smith (1951b) described the hazards of field work during the 1950 expedition to Pinda in northern Mozambique: 'Then you have to start real hard work against time, setting, injecting and preserving the fishes ... Formalin blurs your vision, bites your nostrils and brings agony to every scratch.' We can expect that, with his knowledge of chemistry, JLB would have taken adequate precautions to reduce the risk of formalin poisoning, but this would have been difficult in the rough field and laboratory conditions under which he had to work. It is possible, even likely, that long-term exposure to formalin fumes may have adversely

---

2 Eugène Marais was a long-term morphine addict and suffered from melancholy, insomnia, depression and feelings of isolation. In 1936, deprived of morphine for some days, and depressed after a leading British scientist had plagiarised his research, he borrowed a shotgun on the pretext of killing a snake and shot himself in the chest. The wound was not fatal so Marais put the barrel in his mouth and pulled the trigger.

affected his health in general, and his eyesight in particular.[3]

In the early 1980s Margaret confided to close associates that JLB had told her in early 1967 that he would be committing suicide after he turned 70; this was confirmed by Ian and Ishbel Sholto-Douglas (pers. comm., 2016). It must have been a terrible strain on Margaret not knowing when it would happen. Kathleen Heugh (pers. comm., 2017) remembers that JLB Smith told her father (Professor Jack Rennie) in 1946/1947, more than 20 years before his suicide, '… that he did not believe in being a burden to society and at the point he might come to realise that he might be receiving more than giving to the world, he would take his own life'. Thomson (1991) reported, 'Legend has it that he had announced many years earlier that he had no intention of living past seventy'.

An ex-student, W Norton, wrote after Smith's death, 'I am so glad the Professor had the courage to go when he felt the time had come for him to do so'.

The month before JLB Smith's death, on 13th December 1967, James Hyslop, Vice-Chancellor of Rhodes University, wrote to Smith informing him that the university had decided to offer him the degree of Doctor of Philosophy (*honoris causa*), to be conferred in April 1968. This was a rather belated honour, considering that Smith had served the university with such distinction for over 45 years and, as it turned out, it came too late.

Towards the end of JLB's life his memory loss was palpable as he started to repeat stories, which he had never done before. He had seen some of his friends and colleagues, especially the politician 'Eben' Dönges, become burdens on their families due to protracted illnesses, and did not want to inflict this fate on Margaret. Dönges (1898–1968), South African Minister of Internal Affairs from 1948 to 1961, had been a student with Smith at Victoria College and remained a lifelong friend. He had contracted Alzheimer's disease and his prolonged treatment drained the family coffers until he eventually died on 10th January 1968, three days after Smith, and one year younger than him.

Smith's untimely death resulted in a deluge of remembrances, both generous and harsh. In spite of his tetchy manner, he was loved and admired by many, not least for his empathy and support for those experiencing difficult times.

---

3   The famous South African herpetologist and Director of the Transvaal Museum, Dr VFM FitzSimons, suffered the same fate: formalin fumes virtually destroyed his eyesight.

The Smiths' close friend, Shirley Bell, recalled the friendship JLB had shown her:

'I know his reputation for irascibility, but he was so good to me, and so was Margaret. They made me see new possibilities. I loved being with them. And I loved the stories he would tell (Flora did not like him at all and considered that he had spoiled Margaret's life! She felt that Margaret should have stuck to her intention of becoming a medical doctor). ... I can still remember how shocked I felt when Margaret let me know of his death. I just couldn't associate it with what I knew of JLB, but I think Eben Dönges's deterioration and death had a good bit to do with his decision, as he had this feeling that he might be going the same way after he had had the slight turn that he felt had affected his microscope eye. Margaret was so brave. What unbelievable friends they were to me.'

The depth of Shirley's distress at JLB's death is reflected in a letter from Margaret, dated 23rd January 1968:

'I am sorry that the Professor's death has upset you so much. I know that it was a big blow to you as it was to us but just remember my dear that he wanted it that way. When I feel depressed about it I imagine what it would have been like if he had had a stroke and was now lying helpless and that was a very real danger; in fact he had such strong premonitions that he would have a stroke that it might easily have been waiting for him.'

JLB adopted a philosophical attitude in life that enabled him not only to deal with some of his own demons, but also to reach out to others. In a letter dated 26th June 1967 to Marie-Louise Bauchot, an ichthyology colleague in Paris, he sympathised with her distress and offered this advice:

'I am so sorry to hear of your difficulties. However believe me from my own life I have come to realise that you learn and develop more when you have to work under difficult conditions. While it may be more pleasant at the time to have a smooth path, you learn less of life. I have a saying that one cannot appreciate heaven well unless you have a taste of hell. All the good things in life come from within oneself.'

Allan Heydorn, when he first assumed his post as Director of the Oceanographic Research Institute (ORI) in Durban in 1967, also benefited from Smith's salutary advice. David Davies, who had been the first Director of ORI (1958–1965), had died tragically in a car accident and the person appointed to replace him, John Morgans, didn't last long. Allan inherited an institution in crisis as deadlines had been missed for CSIR research grant applications, and scientists, such as John Wallace and Paddy Berry, were seriously demotivated and wanted to leave. He also learned that there was a distinct possibility that ORI might be closed down, and that a CSIR Commission of Enquiry would be visiting the institution within a month of his arrival to investigate the matter and make a final decision. Allan and his staff worked day and night during that first month, rewriting motivations, drawing up budgets and time schedules, and preparing the submission to the Commission of Enquiry, which was chaired by the President of the CSIR, Dr Meiring Naudé. One of the commission members was JLB Smith (A Heydorn, pers. comm., 2017).

Smith came to see Heydorn in his office shortly before the meeting, and asked him, 'Allan, and how do you feel about this institutional emergency which you were forced to handle so unexpectedly?', to which Allan replied, 'Professor, after the loss of my friend David Davies who [was] such a brilliant first Director, I regard it as a tragedy that things went wrong subsequently and that not only the Institute but also its dedicated staff are now subjected to such a traumatic situation. I am not certain at all that I am up to the job.' Smith looked at him quietly and then said, 'You are quite wrong, Allan. Real growth does not take place at times when everything goes well and according to plan, real growth and development of inner strength only takes place at times of crisis and hardship such as you and your staff are experiencing now. I have seen what you have

JLB Smith and David Davies, both key trendsetters in marine science, at the Oceanographic Research Institute in Durban in 1961. It must have been a very serious meeting for JLB to wear a suit!

jointly put together in a ridiculously short time and I predict that, not only ORI but you as a person, will go from strength to strength as a result of the crisis which you have now been forced to handle' (A Heydorn, pers. comm., 2017). Once again Smith had played his 'strength in adversity' card.

Allan Heydorn also recalled that JLB's

'... wisdom and encouragement meant more to me than can be expressed in words. It was the start of a bond between him and me which existed until the day of his death [sadly, only seven months later]. The Commission gave us the go-ahead to continue, coupled with the so badly required financial support. The crisis also forged a highly productive working relationship between all ORI scientists and myself. And the Institute did grow from strength to strength during the years which followed. Prof JLB Smith remained a father-figure for us and a mentor and advisor. I sought his advice on many an occasion. This included my decision that ORI needed to move from research programmes focussing on individual species, to an approach encompassing holistic ecosystem functioning and the role of individual organisms within the ecosystem. Much greater emphasis was also placed on the importance of land/sea interactions. JLB Smith supported me staunchly' (A Heydorn, pers. comm., 2017).

Many friends and acquaintances were very complimentary about JLB after he died. The South African Ambassador to the United States, HLT Taswell, wrote in tribute:

'We have lost a great South African and an eminent scientist. His magnificent books will long remain a monument to his great research and be read by future generations with the same wonder and admiration that they are today.'

MJ Desparmet, French Ambassador to the Republic of Somalia, wrote to Margaret after JLB's death:

'The news has come to all of us as a shock since Professor Smith beside the admiration we had for him, had become through his letters a kind, helpful if faraway friend linked to us by our common love of nature and sea life.'

John Wallace (pers. comm., 2017), Director of the Port Elizabeth Museum from 1975 to 1986 and a Board member of the Ichthyology Institute, described JLB as '... an intense and dedicated scientist whose life revolved around ichthyology. He was very serious, with no time for frivolous small talk; basically an intro-vert.' Wallace points out too that, in contrast, Margaret was 'an extroverted people-person, a perfect "door keeper" to the lab, who protected JLB from the many who sought access to him. She was, of course, an excellent fish illustrator, without whose expertise JLB's work would not have achieved such inter-national acclaim.'

Wallace, whose speciality was skates and rays, spent some time in JLB's lab where he 'was warmly welcomed by him because he regretted not having been able to devote more time to the skates and rays, which he considered a difficult group. Constructive about my work, he in no way resisted my review of his pioneering contribution' (J Wallace, pers. comm., 2017).

Nancy Tietz (pers. comm., 2017) described JLB as

'Distant, solitary, unless one was talking about fishes, a loner generally, interested and encouraging to young people, impatient with the world around him but knew exactly what was what. Didn't suffer fools gladly except me! (After I'd sent him the measurements and DandA counts of a fish that had been brought into the museum he wanted to see the specimen – we had fried it and eaten it for dinner – he just shook his head and said (words to the effect) next time wait for my response before you do that).'

An angler, Jock Cawse, opined, 'It was always a pleasure to hear of his interests whether it was at a lecture or during an informal chat ... apart from his enthusiasm for his work he was a very kindly person to all who were privileged to know him'; and Val Roux, an ex-staff member, said, 'How I enjoyed his company, his pungent wit and his keen perception'. The well-known angling writer and publisher, Bob Harrison, summed it up by saying, 'It will not be for his achievements that we shall remember him, but for his unending kindness'; and another publisher, RM Hodgson, enthused, 'Our memory of him is one of a very happy personality with a lively mind always dedicated to the work he had on hand at that moment'.

Peter Jackson (1996) had high praise for Smith, the ichthyologist:

Drawing by Dave Voorvelt of Peter Jackson.

'He was certainly the best known ichthyologist in Africa, if not the world at that time ... He was to me, as to most South Africans, the towering figure in ichthyology. ... All in all, Smith, though I was never his student, had a greater influence on my formative years than anyone else. Whatever I wrote was usually modelled on his style. Thus when I wrote a book on Northern Rhodesian (now Zambian) fishes it contained items of information for the interested angler or naturalist, directly inspired by Smith's 1949 book.'

Jackson (1996) also waxed eloquent about JLB's skills as an entrepreneur and marketer:

'Ever the entrepreneur, Smith perceived that the best way to obtain research funds was to get into the public eye and stay there. The coelacanth episode had brought him fame, but his empathy with laymen who loved the sea, especially anglers, earned him his popularity with the man in the street. ... Ever a lone wolf, Smith cared little about the coolness with which his fellow scientists greeted his publicity seeking, which was "not done" in their code ... Smith might have lacked rapport with colleagues and terrified his workers, but though his teaching days were over he was first and last a university don. To him students always came first. From him I received nothing but kindness, courtesy and sound advice.'

Many others echoed this sentiment, and it was this author's experience as well. Underneath the hard exterior was a soft and empathetic core that was especially responsive to anyone in need. Smith's 'publicity seeking' was not in pursuit of personal glory, but he was astute enough to realise that the coelacanth could focus attention on his work and on ichthyology in South Africa, and therefore attract research funding. JLB grappled with journalists throughout his career as he expected them to uphold the same standards of accuracy that he had set for himself, but was often disappointed. He also abhorred sensationalism in science reporting (Smith, 1956).

When Margaret was asked in 1986 what his two main character traits were, she answered, 'His phenomenal memory, and his almost fanatical sense of purpose'. She had written of her husband: 'Characteristically, not prepared to make do with anything second rate and not prepared to risk circumstances over which he had no control and become a burden to anyone, he took matters into his own hands and ended his life' (MM Smith, 1969). She also wrote matter-of-factly to Carl Hubbs that '... she was not surprised, because he always thought that the best time to die was when a man was in the flush of man-hood, before he became a nuisance' (Hubbs, 1969).

As William put it in the 1976 SATV documentary, 'When you've built a career on a brain, and the brain goes, there's nothing left. He wanted to make way for younger people, and he did not want to become a burden on Margaret. He did exactly what he set out to do.' This last observation succinctly summarises JLB Smith's life. However, in the end, not even Smith's formidable will power was enough to reverse the ravages of time. He had already had two minor strokes, the last in 1966, and was feeling desperately tired; it had become obvious that he was losing his lifelong battle with ill health.

CHAPTER 24

Lean as biltong

JLB under the microscope

S MITH ONCE described himself in rather unflattering terms:

> '… a lunatic to whom fish … really is a kind of disease or affliction almost
> like diabetes where one has to have regular injections to keep going. I am
> afraid I have been like this since my earliest youth and I see no prospect of
> ever being cured' (Gon, 2002).

This author tried several times to talk objectively to Margaret Smith about JLB's character but it was a pointless exercise as she regarded him as idyllic, almost godlike, and would never make a negative or even slightly critical or questioning comment about him. To her, everything he did was normal, justified and logical. She accepted his character as it was and adjusted her personality, lifestyle and priorities to fit his needs.

Keith Thomson (1991), in his book *Living Fossil – The Story of the Coelacanth*, described JLB:

> '… a lean and hard man – as spare in his habits as he was in his body. He
> arranged his life to be functional, with no luxuries or frills. His hair was cut
> in a military crew cut, and he cared little about his clothes. He was very care-
> ful about his diet, however, for many years alternating days when the only
> meat he would eat was fish with days when he would eat only fruit and nuts.
> He was moody and intense. He was probably a difficult colleague, too, but at
> the same time respected for his drive and dedication. The one thing he was
> passionate about was fishes, and in this his second wife, Margaret, was his
> constant companion and fiercest publicist … It was a good partnership, and

Smith needed such a partner because most of the time, in his mind at least, the rest of the world was either wrong or contrary, or both.'[1]

JLB Smith tended to be analytical and judgemental. He was prone to long silences and then sudden outbursts that made it clear that he had been listening to, and had analysed, everything that had been said before by others, and had already reached a conclusion about a particular matter long before the conversation had ended. Carl Hubbs (1968) noted that, 'Liberally scattered through "Old Fourlegs" are statements suggesting that the author regarded himself as endowed with powers of telepathy and ESP – along with many other indications of an extremely sensitive, strongly introspective man, vibrant with drive'. Shirley Bell (1969) comments, 'He had long held a firm conviction that he was destined one day to discover some strange and wonderful creature, perhaps even a real sea-serpent'.

Smith's undue preoccupation in *Old Fourlegs* and other publications with detailed descriptions of the frustrations that he experienced during his career is indicative of an acute perceived struggle between himself, the lone scientist, and the world beyond science, which seemed constantly to block his way. He sometimes portrayed himself as a 'lone ranger', single-handedly fending off the scientific apathy of the rest of the human race. In truth, there were many other scientists and science administrators in South Africa at the same time, fighting the same battle.

JLB occasionally – and revealingly – imbued the City of Grahamstown with some of his own traits. In a report to the AGM of the Albany Museum dated 30th March 1954, he stated:

'Grahamstown was no sleepy dorp [town]. It had many characteristics, perhaps the most outstanding of which were that it admired and encouraged hard work and that it equally disliked and got rid of martinets and dictators' (Rhodes University Archive).

Not surprisingly for someone of Smith's loner tendencies and resolute opinions, he was not a keen conference goer, and, the older he became, the less he enjoyed

---

1 Thomson (1991) was quite wrong, however, in another comment on the Smiths, in which he claims that JLB's 'second wife, Margaret, was instrumental in rekindling his old love of fishes'. His love affair with fishes, hatched in his youth, had needed no rekindling. Furthermore, prior to their marriage, Margaret's interests had been chemistry and music, and she had had no prior involvement with fishes or angling.

social gatherings. He also did not enjoy international travel to first-world desti-
nations. He attended only one major fish conference in the USA, the 'First
International Conference on Sharks', organised by the American Institute of
Biological Sciences in New Orleans, during a trip in April 1958, where one of
the themes was, 'Methods for repelling shark attacks'. He did not attend any
of the annual conferences of the prestigious American Society of Ichthyologists
& Herpetologists (ASIH), founded in 1915; nor, throughout his entire career, did
he apparently attend any formal international conferences on fish taxonomy
or zoogeography.

He did attend a few museology, zoology and environmental conservation
conferences in South Africa, usually at Margaret's insistence, and his talks were
not always on fishes. In a rare address to a South African Museums Association
conference in East London in 1955, he was disparaging about the methods of
earlier scientists:

> 'Most of the discoveries in biological science of the past 100 years, especially
> in Zoology, had been recorded in heavy technical jargon, with unnecessarily
> complicated terms. This was not only troublesome to scientists but quite
> beyond the use and understanding of the ordinary man [one of his favourite
> phrases]. Many so-called biologists supposed to study living matters worked
> only with dead things in bottles. ... The days of these complicated treatises
> was passing. Almost all science could be made easy to understand by every-
> body without loss of standard.'

Smith seemed to be far more comfortable in the company of anglers than
scientists, and enjoyed speaking at meetings of angling and underwater
clubs. At these meetings he would mingle with the crowd and happily
share his knowledge and experience, whereas at scientific conferences he
cut a lonely figure and somehow seemed to be insecure, notwithstanding
his international renown.

Nancy Tietz, who attended a conference organised by the National Parks
Board in 1964 at which JLB Smith spoke, remembers him as 'a forceful orator':

> 'He was the first speaker next day. Advised what surveys he would do and with
> his wife would produce a fully illustrated guide to the *Fishes of the Tsitsikamma
> Coast*. He said what he had to say, brooked no argument, and then excused
> himself and Margaret for the rest of the meeting.'

In contrast, Margaret loved the sociality of conferences and meetings, and assiduously maintained a little 'black book' in which she recorded the names, professions and places of abode of everyone she met.

In *Old Fourlegs* JLB admits that his social attitude 'did not always create the most cordial relations'. He had the sort of personality that always made an impact on you, for good or bad; no-one was neutral about him. Decades after he died his ex-colleagues and -students, such as Doug Rivett and Keith Hunt, would become very animated when they spoke about him. Jean Pote stated that he was 'a very hard taskmaster. He didn't allow tea breaks; if we wanted tea, it had to be brought to us at our desks, so we could keep working' (Weinberg, 1999). He also insisted that correspondence should be dealt with while it was still fresh. 'Letters are like fish. If you leave them more than three days, they begin to smell.' Nevertheless, Weinberg's (1999) comment, '... until 1960, when, out of consideration for his always fragile health, he stopped travelling altogether and dedicated himself to his work, and to terrorising his staff and pupils', is overstating the case.

Allan Heydorn (pers. comm., 2017) summed it up well:

'JLB never took kindly to being distracted from his detail work and could be quite taciturn when he felt that he was being disturbed unnecessarily. That enabled him to do such an incredible amount of work in the development of ichthyology in the Southern African realm. For this reason it was easier for him to 'isolate' himself at Rhodes University than it would have been had the Institute been located in Durban or Cape Town. By contrast his live-wire and very sociable wife allowed herself to be distracted far more easily and she could not resist being invited to many meetings which were not really relevant to her field of expertise. I might be wrong, but my impression was that under her directorship, she had to rely on people such as Phil Heemstra to continue with the mission about which JLB was so single-minded. My impression is also that when [Mike Bruton] took over the directorship, [he] had to pull many things together again in order to be able to plot the optimal future course for the Institute.'

There is no doubt that JLB Smith was eccentric, not only in his later years, but even as a young man. His colonial dress code was perhaps inspired by the apparel worn by George Cory. In the field, and even on holiday in

Knysna, he wore practical khaki shirts and shorts, but to the laboratory he almost always wore a thin flannel suit and tie, non-functional apparel for such a practical man, but respectful of the university's formal dress codes at the time. His hatred for shoes extended to the office too, and he usually wore sandals. He expected his employees to dress properly, be formal and courteous and, most importantly, to be *very* efficient and punctual.

During her marriage to JLB Smith, Margaret's house was very sparse, with few (if any) towels, carpets, curtains or cushions, or any kind of décor or decorations. Nancy Tietz (pers. comm., 2017) remembers, 'The décor in the Smiths' house was austere. There were curtains in the lounge but no carpet. There were no curtains in the dining room but the table was properly set with a table cloth, side plates, knife and soup spoon of worn silverplate. The homemade pumpkin soup was served in enamel plates.'

In a speech to the Rotary Club of Grahamstown on 2nd June 1952, JLB revealed the extent of his dietary eccentricity when he talked about experiments that he had carried out on his own body in order to determine an optimal diet. A report of the meeting summarised his unusual regimes:

'After having been in bad health for some time after a serious illness on the coast, he had done a range of experiments with food, including "monofeeding", eating only one kind of food at a time, such as meat, vegetables or fruit. He admitted that some of his experiments were successful, others not, but "after some time there occurred a remarkable improvement in health". He related that they ate little or no refined or "dead" food, such as white bread, refined sugar, but ate as much raw fruit and vegetables as possible. He said that they aimed to obtain sufficient calories from "good proteins" rather than starch. He also said that experts do not support the view "that sugar gives energy". They found the reverse, and it was better to eat protein. The idea that glucose before a game helped a footballer was hardly sound. It was better to take nothing. ... The South African race had become one of the most virile and progressive in the world. It seemed as if the leading races always ate good protein food like meat and cheese and fish' (Rotary Club of Grahamstown report, Rhodes University Archive).

Once again the organic chemist was making his views heard. He even sent recommendations in this regard to the coach of the Springbok rugby team! To some extent he anticipated the 'fad' diets that are now so popular in the 21st century[2].

The Smiths' dietary regime was frugal and unvaried. Even if guests were assured that they were having 'tiger pie' for supper, it was made from fish![3] They had no stove, only a hot plate. John Rennie remembers JLB Smith joining his parents (Professor JVL Rennie and his wife, Beatrix) for dinner in Grahamstown, where a modest spread of bread and cheese was offered. JLB insisted on eating the crusts on either end of the loaf, and also asked for the crusts along the length of the loaf to be cut off for him to eat. This dietary choice was somewhat in conflict with his views, expressed at other times, that he did not eat 'dead', i.e. processed, food (Barnett, 1953), although it's possible he enjoyed the occasional private indulgence: according to Ian Sholto-Douglas (pers. comm., 2016), he had a predilection for 'Silver Leaf' tinned peas!

Sholto-Douglas also revealed that, when JLB and Margaret travelled to Johannesburg where he was to give a talk to the Royal Society of South Africa, they stayed in the plush Savoy Hotel but took their own tin crockery and cutlery into the dining room!

Further evidence of the limitations of the Smiths' menu comes from Mary-Louise Penrith, who remembers joining Nancy Tietz for dinner at Margaret's house one evening. The only course was fish (with no chips), and after dinner they were required to help Margaret with a card index that she was compiling of JLB's publications. Mary-Louise and Nancy were unimpressed as they had intended to go to the movies that night before they were invited to dinner – under false pretences, it would seem. Some correspondents have claimed that even some of the jams and desserts served in the Smiths' household were made from fish!

Nancy Tietz remembers further:

'When young family members went to the Smith household for a meal, "Aunty Mary" told them that they never eat proteins and carbohydrates in the same meal; they eat fish or potatoes, not fish and potatoes. Sweets were strictly banned from the house, which caused the kids to get up to all sorts of

---

2 Examples are the 'low-carb' diets (Atkins, Dukan and Pioppi), which reduce the risk of the body storing energy from food as fat, and the 'Palaeo' diet, which recommends shunning all processed foods and following a natural diet similar to that of our Palaeolithic ancestors. Both diets encourage eating fresh food.
3 Smith was not always such a pescatarian: during his marriage to Henriette Pienaar, he had a liking for underdone meat, 'consuming large quantities of almost completely raw meat from which the blood was still running out' (A-J Tötemeyer, pers. comm., 2017).

mischief buying and hiding sweets in the garden. Even Margaret made secret plans in this regard. When she attended conferences with JLB Smith and Marjorie Courtenay-Latimer, she would ask Marge to buy some chocolates so that she could indulge herself without JLB's knowledge. Marge was horrified that she should be so deceitful but became deceitful herself by buying the chocolate. People got the impression that Margaret was like a butterfly about to emerge from its pupa' (Nancy Tietz, pers. comm., 2017).

Peter Jackson (1996) who, as an undergraduate at Rhodes University from 1946 to 1948 had known Smith, although he was never taught by him, described him as being 'Of brilliant brain and lone-wolf, somewhat valetudinarian nature, he had made the classification of fishes his spare-time hobby'. Smith's hypochondria was, it transpired, not without foundation: it was discovered after he died that he had only one functional kidney. If his medical doctors had known this, they might have better understood the reason for his high blood pressure and may have suggested alternative treatments for his malaise.

Ian Sholto-Douglas recalls (pers. comm., 2016):

'One day Len came back from the doctor, informing his wife that he was seriously ill and needed an operation. Alarmed, she privately went to see the doctor to find out about his condition and if he thought an operation was unavoidable: "Yes, I'm going to operate on him," he replied irritably. "Not a damn thing is wrong with him, but he insists on this operation, so I'm doing it!" Which he did.'

Smith was a willing and popular speaker at local events in Grahamstown. His performance was characterised by humorous anecdotes interspersed with vivid tales of gruelling hardships. After one such talk, about a fish-collecting expedition to 'remote parts', a Mr Eales stated in his vote of thanks:

'Professor Smith spoke for almost two hours with vivid and forceful eloquence. Not only did he hold his audience enthralled and carry them to the distant lands and scenes which he described, but frequent flashes of humour helped to tone down the picture of the sometimes grim conditions he outlined.'

JLB's first questions when he interviewed new staff were revealing of his exacting standards and intolerance of others' habits: do you smoke[4] or use perfume? Due to his health-conscious attitude, he would not consider employing anyone who answered yes to either question, regardless of their qualifications or experience.

In an unpublished memoir on JLB Smith made available by Glyn Hewson (pers. comm., 2017), Glyn remembers JLB's tight control of his staff:

'There was a stir of interest in the early days when, out of the blue, Josephine Chan Henry became a secretary at the Department: young, petite and very efficient. She drove a huge old black Mercury, one of those fifties models with an abundance of chromium teeth in severe need of orthodontic treatment, spilling out below the front bonnet. A friend of mine who was a boarder at Kingswood from Hong Kong, was keen to meet her. We sat and chatted in her office, not unaware of the silence around the rest of the Department where WORK was happening. Sure enough, a commandingly stentorian voice came floating over the top of the partitions from the Professor's domain, "Miss Chan Henry, I asked for the file on Border angling" … Without hesitation: "It's the blue one Professor, third down in the pile on the left hand side of your desk". Then after a few more minutes, "Copy of the letter to the British Museum written the day before yesterday, Miss Chan Henry". "Yes Professor, it's with Mrs Smith at the moment, I gave it to her yesterday …". And then Margaret's voice would also respond from her office, across the top of the adjoining partition, "I've acted on the second paragraph, Professor, the slides will be here tomorrow …". At one point there was [a] rapid sound of sandalled feet along the bare boards and suddenly the Professor's face popped around the doorway. A curt nod to us, another file and he was gone. And we knew it was time to leave!'

A new secretary in the Ichthyology Department in the 1950s once dared to talk to her student boyfriend through the office window. Smith painted the window white so that they couldn't see each other, and she soon left the staff.

---

4   Margaret Smith also detested smoking, especially pipe smoking, and she and Peter Jackson had an ongoing battle in this regard in the new Ichthyology building. His malodorous pipe fumes would permeate the Ichthyology building and she would storm up the stairs and confront him; he, of course, always backed down and henceforth sought succour from his pipe in the garden or on the roof. Although Margaret had largely lost her sense of smell (due to formalin fumes), she still had an uncanny ability to detect cigarette or pipe smoke. She abhorred smoking in the Ichthyology Institute and pursued every miscreant with vigour.

JLB Smith was, however, very kind to his diligent employees. When Jean Pote lost goods at the supermarket, he reimbursed her, and, when she was ill, he delivered health food to her home (Gon, 1996). When Nancy Tietz arrived in Grahamstown to take up a post as provincial museum librarian, JLB welcomed her with a bunch of gladioli from his garden.'

Doris Cave, the first Ichthyology librarian, wrote of Smith after his death:

'I feel I have been very privileged to have worked under the Professor, a kinder, more considerate and generous person it would be difficult to find. For most of that time I have not really thought of him as my employer but rather as a very kind and warm-hearted man to whom I would have gone with any trouble and been sure of ready sympathy and help' (SAIAB archive).

Staff of the original Department of Ichthyology in 1966. From left: Peter Castle, Gladys Arnot, Doris Cave, Jean Pote, Rose Spannenberg, Margaret Smith and JLB Smith, with Marlin.

Hans Fricke (pers. comm., 2017) related a story told to him by Margaret that, many years earlier during a train trip to Cape Town, Smith's false teeth had fallen out of the train window and he had stopped the train in order to retrieve them (this story has not been verified). Jenny Day (pers. comm., 2017) recounts that Professor John Day, then Head of Zoology at the University of Cape Town, once visited JLB Smith in his cottage at Knysna, and 'JLB sat paring his toenails at the kitchen table while they were talking. I think that to John, this entirely summed up JLB.'

Smith's antisocial behaviour was probably the root cause of the animosity that developed between some marine biologists in Cape Town and Smith in Grahamstown; his publicity seeking, the fame he had acquired from the coelacanth, and his 'amateur status' as an ichthyologist were other probable causes. Margaret was never the target of this ire, although she was accused of hero-worshipping JLB and 'probably pandered to him more than was good for either of them' (J Day, pers. comm., 2017).

An earlier example of this friction occurred in the late 1940s when John Day and his team of students were surveying the Knysna Lagoon:

'The most scandalous incident happened at Knysna. Some young men from the village, including the mayor's son, had joined our party and one morning the local policeman came to make a complaint. It appeared that Doc Smith of coelacanth fame had a cottage in Knysna which he had painted a startling blue to keep the mosquitoes away. During the night this had been splashed all over with whitewash and members of our party were suspected. Of course I assured the policemen that we had all been hard at work. We could see that he was still suspicious but he never did find out who the culprits were although most of the people in Knysna could have told him' (Day, 1977).

Smith's lack of social finesse and uncompromising attitudes irritated and even infuriated some people. Mary-Louise Penrith, editor of the *Annals of the South African Museum* for several years, found that he was not a good reviewer as 'any manuscript that criticised, did not agree with or refuted anything he had written' was rejected by him. On one occasion she sent him a manuscript and received back the comment that it needed rewriting in good English as it was 'full of Afrikanerisms', even though the author of that paper did not speak or write Afrikaans.

German researcher Professor Hans Fricke, who had been inspired to study coelacanths by reading *Vergangenheit steigt aus dem Meer*, the German edition of *Old Fourlegs*, was frank when asked about JLB Smith:

'JLB was not my favourite character. In *Old Fourlegs* many hidden racist opinions – in a video clip dynamite fishing – a very unsympathetic behaviour towards a black person – he was egomanic [sic] towards many people. A hypochonder [sic] and not an easy person – as a neighbour he was unpleasant – if he was scientifically brilliant I almost doubt it, for example Miss Latimer's find was not identified by him as a prehistoric fish, it was an expert (?palaeontologist) of the Rhodes University – also why JLB did not go straight away to East London when he was convinced of the importance of the fish but 6 weeks later? I would have gone immediately even in my sleeping dress' (H Fricke, pers. comm., 2017).

(In this excerpt Fricke pulls no punches in his reference to the 'created myth', but he is wrong – see Chapter 8).

JLB's lack of social graces was legendary. Ian Sholto-Douglas (pers. comm., 2016), Margaret's sister Flora's son, first met JLB (whom he knew as 'Len') in 1937. He remarked that Smith 'had aggressive traits, rude, self-centred, selfish. He was arrogant, expected everyone to run around meeting his every need, ordered people around, dominating.' When Ian referred to Margaret as 'Mary', JLB would respond, 'There is no Mary here, her name is Margaret', even though everyone in the family called her 'Mary'.

Smith's politics were pragmatic rather than ideological: he supported politicians who supported his work, irrespective of whether they were liberal or conservative. He disliked Field Marshall Jan Smuts, Prime Minister of South Africa during some of Smith's most productive years, after Smuts spurned his requests for help and was unsupportive of his research, even though he himself was a published scientist. In contrast, he had high regard for the conservative Afrikaner Daniel ('DF') Malan, who, against all odds, provided a military airplane in December 1952 for Smith to fetch the second coelacanth from the Comoros.

Peter Jackson (1996) had this to say:

'Smith was a nationalist, with little concern for other countries. He was a fluent Afrikaans speaker and as he states in his autobiographical book (1956) he found himself resentful of criticism of South Africa. I suspect his antipathy to Field-Marshall Smuts clearly stated to me, to everybody else and in writing (Smith 1956), had almost as much to do with Smuts' internationalism and pro-Britishness as with his refusal to supply him (probably in about 1945) with a military aircraft to take him to Walvis Bay to collect specimens killed by a submarine disturbance. … In discussions on taxonomy he was hostile to the idea of my research staff and myself lodging type specimens of new species overseas, particularly the British Museum of Natural History. "These are African fish and you should keep them in Africa", he told me.'

Maylam (2017), in his recent history of Rhodes University, comments on Smith's politics:

'And his political leanings were towards the National Party. He admired D.F. Malan, while disliking Smuts; he resented outside criticism of South Africa's apartheid policies; and evidence of his own racism can be found in Old Fourlegs. The extent to which a scholar's reputation can be tarnished by politics is a matter of debate.'

JLB Smith expressed racist views in *Old Fourlegs* as well as in *High Tide* and some other popular articles; these statements are not condoned here. For instance, in *Old Fourlegs* he comments:

'The Comoran natives are not distinguished by great energy; indeed, in that respect they fall below the average, already low, and they are not uniform in performance – those on Anjoaun being considered the most progressive and energetic, while those on badly disease-ridden Mohilla [Moheli] are notoriously lethargic and hard to move.'

In *Old Fourlegs* as well as in some of his popular articles in angling and outdoor magazines, JLB projects a patronising attitude of colonial superiority to native people and even to foreign colonials. In a letter dated 6th August 1946 to a Portuguese friend, Commandante Tomas Vitar Duque, Port Captain in Lourenço Marques, he makes a revealing comment,

'I am rather aloof in my life and have few friends in my own race, and it has been queer to find myself feeling for a man of another race [Portuguese!] what I hardly ever expected to feel again. I judge men mainly by whether I could rely on them in what we call in English "A tight corner", any desperate emergency. There are few men I know whom I would sooner have with me than you in such circumstances' (Rhodes University Archive).

In an article about JLB's book *The Sea Fishes of Southern Africa* in *The Rhodian* magazine, Smith (1949) makes the following statement:

'Ever since commencing scientific work on fishes some twenty years ago, I have been increasingly impressed by the widespread interest, almost fanatical interest, shown by a great proportion of people in these finny creatures. Apparently common to most civilised peoples, this interest seems indeed to be most highly developed in the Anglo-Saxons who may justifiably be classed among the most enlightened peoples' (Smith, 1949).

He appeared to be in denial about the socio-economic problems faced by most South Africans living under apartheid. In a letter circulated to colleagues around the world in early June 1965, he claimed that 'Despite the often deliberately falsified reports about South Africa that repeatedly appear in the world press, I have visited no other country in which life generally is more normal, secure and pleasant, for all races.'

JLB was nevertheless revered by the 'Coloured' fisherfolk of Knysna, with whom he readily shared his knowledge of fish and fishing. And in an article published in *Grocott's Daily Mail* on 30th August 1955, he strikes a more moderate tone:

'Racial "bitterness" will soon be confined largely to a naturally diminishing number of older "die-hards" and to the more isolated small towns and villages where one or other racial group predominates. What happened in America [racial integration] is taking place as naturally here, and there is emerging, especially in the cities, a growing South African element, whose outlook from both sides is broader and more racially tolerant, indeed truly international.'[5]

---

5 Many other early writers expressed views that would be regarded as racist by today's standards, including Charles Darwin, Alfred Russel Wallace, Charles Dickens, Rudyard Kipling, Hugh Lofting (in *The Adventures of Dr Dolittle*), Jack London, HC McNeile ('Sapper') and his character, Hugh 'Bulldog' Drummond (the 1920s and 1930s equivalent of James Bond), HP Lovecraft, Ernest Hemingway and even Agatha Christie. Some of their writings reflect the unfortunate attitudes of their times.

There is no doubt that JLB Smith was territorial, both in terms of his academic discipline and the real estate that he owned, as the following two examples illustrate. George Branch, famed marine biologist from the University of Cape Town, recalls an encounter with JLB Smith during an excursion organised by Professor John Day to sample marine life in Knysna Lagoon in 1964:

'He packed off me and one other student to the westward side of the heads to survey the intertidal there. We were engrossed in sampling with the usual bucket, spade and sieves, when JLB emerged, enraged that we should be invading "his" shore. I suspect he thought we were bait-diggers as I know he zealously guarded the shore. I protested with righteous indignation that we had every right to be on the shore and had been sent there by Professor John Day to do sampling. I was unaware of the animosity, and that invoking John Day's name was probably adding fuel to the indignation. JLB used a few choice words indicating we should "go away", and when I failed to respond, he retreated, only to appear with a shotgun. One blast over our heads was enough to persuade us that retreat was better than buckshot, and we rowed back in record speed! I remember John Day being outraged, but he failed to convince us [that] we should return to complete the sampling' (G Branch, pers. comm., 2016).

George Branch relates another story, this time about Frank Talbot, a zoology graduate from the University of Cape Town, who visited JLB Smith in Grahamstown on 7th January 1957:

'In his youth, Frank Talbot was infatuated with the idea of becoming an ichthyologist, and his father packed him off to Grahamstown to talk to JLB to find out what is really involved ... a fairly arduous journey by bus and train at that time. After he arrived, he was kept waiting for ages before finally gaining an audience, and explained his life's desire. JLB glowered over his desk and then pronounced, "My boy, there is only room for one ichthyologist in this country, and that's me!" And that was the end of the interview. Frank told me this story himself while we were in Australia' (G Branch, pers. comm., 2016).[6]

---

6 Fortunately, this rebuff didn't appear to dent Talbot's ambition: after leaving South Africa in the 1960s and turning down opportunities at Yale and Harvard, he was appointed curator and then Director of the Australian Museum in Sydney before going on to appointments at Macquarie University, the California Academy of Sciences and the Smithsonian's National Museum of Natural History.

William Smith summed up his father's eccentricity well:

'He was considered eccentric by many who did not know him for he mostly kept to himself, preferring the long stretches of beach and the wild waves pounding the rocks, to other men's company. But he did have a range of people who got to know him over the years, from the very highest to the very lowest. And friends these people were. People he could count on and who admired him greatly. He was a fine scientist, seeking the truth, pioneering the future in ichthyology, and sparing none, let alone himself' (W Smith, 1996).

A young William Smith with his parents in Grahamstown, early 1950s.

CHAPTER 25

Margaret's metamorphosis
Caterpillar to butterfly

M ANY PEOPLE have commented on the extent to which Margaret Smith's personality, as well as her dress code, sociality, participation in music and singing, and her engagement in social work and conferences, changed dramatically after JLB Smith's death. People who knew her both before and after his death talk of a visible 'blossoming'. She dispensed with her severe bun and cut her hair, and moved from their small, rather awkward house in Gilbert Street, designed by JLB, into a lovely old colonial manor house at 37 Oatlands Road in Grahamstown. She also took to committee life like a fish to water and would often be seen scurrying between meetings; she *loved* meetings and talking, and particularly enjoyed the social aspects of conferences, assiduously collecting the names and details of everyone she met at such events and recording them in a little 'black book'. After JLB Smith died Margaret was also in the habit of knitting during conferences and workshops, often for the benefit of one of her favourite charities, the Red Cross.

Keith Hunt (pers. comm., 2017) highlighted the extreme contrast between their personalities: JLB Smith, he recalled,

'took himself very seriously. Didn't smile much and was very reserved. Margaret was totally devoted to JLB & was really remarkably subservient to him and dressed dowdily. ... What nobody could believe was the change in Margaret after JLB died. She must have gone on a round-the-world tour when she first became Director to see other Institutes & she returned quite flamboyant. It was a delight to see she never lost her positive outlook on life.'

Shirley Bell observed:

'Margaret had almost a sort of reverence for JLB and devoted her life to helping him in his research in every way she could, although she also remained very much her own person since she had such a strong personality. She was such a bright woman herself, but she protected JLB in every way she could and devoted herself to smoothing life for him so that he could get on with his work. She was the perfect wife for him. There was certainly nothing even vaguely subservient about her, though. She had a great sense of what her mission was, just as she had a sense of his mission. They were partners, which JLB never failed to acknowledge. He was so proud of her. He trusted her completely and relied on her. And that was what Margaret most wanted. … When [her sister, Flora] went to live with Margaret, she devoted herself to Margaret's well-being, rather like Margaret had devoted herself to JLB's well-being. It was Margaret's time, she felt, and certainly Margaret deserved Flora's devotion and revelled in it. After his death she made a new life for herself. She had to do this because of who she was. I never saw her as living in his shadow, because he did not see this in the least. For him, their work was their shared endeavour. But once he had gone, she had to re-make her life, and she re-made it in her own terms' (S Bell, pers. comm., 2017).

It was almost as if she had undergone a metamorphosis from a working caterpillar into a vibrantly colourful butterfly that could spread its wings and fly. Peter Jackson (1996) commented:

'There was a total transformation. Gone was the austere, athletic, quiet young woman and in her place was the matronly, loquacious kindly Margaret Smith, so well known. I was reminded of Ecclesiastes iii, 7 "… a time to keep silence, and a time to speak". Clearly, with her husband's inhibitory influence on anything approaching gaiety in her ceasing with his death and his enjoinment to her to seize the torch and carry on with his work, she felt the time to talk had come.'

And talk she did! She loved to reconstruct conversations in the first person, I said 'this', then he said 'that', and I angrily responded like 'this', usually to demonstrate how she had overcome some insuperable obstacle (in the style of JLB) or deflated a pompous male ego. Some of her favourite expressions were 'Over my dead body', 'I was shattered', 'I was livid!', 'I'm appalled', 'You hellion', 'How dare you?', 'Boy, was I cross!', and 'I'll wring his neck'. Later in life she tended to add a touch of hyperbole to her stories, not to deceive, but to force home her point. For instance, in the 1976 SATV documentary, she states that she and JLB walked barefoot from the border of 'Natal' to Algoa Bay, whereas the evidence suggested that they only walked as far as Port St Johns.

Allan Heydorn remembers that he and turtle guru George Hughes once accompanied Margaret on a hike in Gorongosa in northern Mozambique during which her incessant talking became annoying. Their tour guide, the highly respected ecologist Ken Tinley, had cautioned everyone to be silent. 'But Margaret was not to be subdued, to the extent that George and I got quite irritated. So, during one of the excursions on foot, we ducked behind a huge termitarium while she continued talking. When we emerged on the other side, there she was, quite annoyed. She said: "But I was talking to you!" Such was her irrepressible spirit (A Heydorn, pers. comm., 2017).'

Shirley Bell (pers. comm., 2017) commented:

'I think Margaret's change of life-style, almost a metamorphosis, owed much to Flora. Flora was extroverted, bright, outspoken and often deliberately outrageous in her comments. I found her hugely entertaining. I would [sit] at the table in their large kitchen and watch Flora acting out stories about local characters as she went about preparing a meal.'

Flora had moved from Johannesburg to join Margaret in Grahamstown in 1972, and spent 15 happy years with her there until she died shortly before Margaret in 1987.

Samantha Weinberg (1999) commented that Margaret 'was nineteen years younger than her husband, and perhaps to disguise the age gap, he insisted that she wore no make-up, and pinned her dark hair in a severe bun'. Mary-Louise Penrith (pers. comm., 2017) remembers that, not long after JLB's death in 1968 or 1969, 'Margaret was still wearing a bun, no make-up, sandals, bare legs and the faded blue dress, but by the next Museums Conference she appeared with her hair cut short, smart clothes, high heels, and far too much make-up – liberated at last!' She also commented about Margaret, 'you have to be crazy about somebody to have worn the same old blue dress and flat sandals for him for 30 years or so!'

Nancy Tietz (pers. comm., 2017) summed it up well:

'Before JLB Smith died Margaret wore a lab coat at work over a long, mid-calf dress and sandals, with no stockings. She was slim and had long and wavy hair that was usually neatly pinned back in a "French Knot" at the back of her head. She wore no make-up and very little jewellery, except an occasional pearl necklace at formal events. After JLB died she immediately cut her hair and began wearing a little make-up, some jewellery (drop earrings, but mainly fish-themed brooches and necklaces) and bright, flowing, long dresses, which would have been unthinkable in JLB's time. Released from JLB's strict diet (and his strict ban on chocolate), she rapidly put on weight, then lost some, but never regained her slim figure again. ... Despite the huge change in outward appearances, for those who knew her Margaret was the same person with a good sense of humour, an infectious laugh (when JLB wasn't around), interested, enthusiastic, concerned.'

Shortly before Margaret embarked on her 1969 world tour, a dressmaker in Grahamstown, Anna Engels, made six dresses with loud, bright colours for her to wear on the trip. This was further evidence of her 'coming out' after JLB's death, as prior to that she had mainly worn austere 'shirtwaisters', dresses with a tailored bodice and buttons down the front, resembling a shirt, and a one-piece gathered skirt (R Hunt, pers. comm., 2017).

According to Flora's son, Ian Sholto-Douglas (pers. comm., 2016), 'within six weeks of JLB Smith dying Margaret was back in the body of the church, attending services, singing in the choir and teaching in the Sunday School'. In contrast, JLB Smith 'was a proclaimed atheist, at a time when there were few open atheists. His religion was his austere life style and his work.' Ian also stated that their diet had consisted of 'fish, fish, fish and potatoes'.

Hans Fricke's comment (pers. comm., 2017) was, 'Margaret seems to me to be the total opposite of JLB'. Several people have pointed out that, in photographs of Margaret taken before 1968, she is serious, even severe, and hardly ever smiling, whereas she was almost always smiling in photographs taken after that date.

The most obvious explanation for Margaret's rejuvenation after JLB's death is that, in the interests of their work, he had suppressed her natural *joie de vivre*. Suddenly, freed of the burden of his 'greatness', she started living again: eating for enjoyment, dressing colourfully, attending church, wearing jewellery, becoming involved in charities, singing in choirs, and leading an active social life.

Perhaps the most overt sign of Margaret's transformation was her re-engagement with the world of music. According to Denys Davis (1986), an illustrator who worked with the Smiths in the 1940s, JLB Smith 'cut music out of his life as it stirred emotions, and this was wasteful. Practical efficiency was all-important, and every object, activity, idea and standard was closely scrutinised; and all non-essentials were ruthlessly trimmed away'. This must have been hard on Margaret.

Cathy Braans (pers. comm., 2017), Flora's granddaughter, recalls that Margaret

'loved singing and would often burst into song. When I lived in Johannes-burg (where Flora was staying with us) Margaret would arrive singing and Flora would join her – that was the way they greeted each other before giving each other a big hug (still singing!).'

Margaret, with characteristic stoicism, commented to journalist Glynis Horning in 1979:

'My husband couldn't stand the sound of the human voice, so the only time I sang was when we were out fishing on the Knysna River in our little motor boat, and he couldn't hear me above the noise of the outboard engine!'

Of this sacrifice, Shirley Bell commented:

'She [Margaret] had that rich lovely laugh and a very fine singing voice. She had dropped choir singing while JLB was alive, as she said JLB was not enam-oured of the human voice, so singing did not interest him. I can't imagine that he would have actually prevented her from singing. It would probably rather have been that Margaret was so attuned to his needs and so wrapped up in their shared work that she did not seek her own interests beyond fulfill-ing their shared vision. If singing took away from anything JLB wanted, she would have thought nothing of dropping it' (S Bell, pers. comm., 2017).

Those who are critical of Smith for forbidding Margaret to sing during their marriage do not realise that she happily complied with his request. She knew that he associated the female singing voice with traumatic experiences from his childhood, when his violent mother would sing loudly to drown the cries of her children after she had administered beatings.

After JLB Smith's death, there was a marked change in Margaret's professional attitude too: she became assertive, sometimes feisty (some would say bossy) and started to exert her will on the course of ichthyology in Grahamstown. But she was always a kind leader who mastered the art of team building. Her leadership style, laid-back and carefree, was completely different from that of JLB, and she created a big, happy family in the new Ichthyology Institute. She managed people, not through fear or intimidation, but by establishing good and trusting relationships, although some regarded her as a poor judge of character as she was occasionally misled or deceived by charlatans or dilettantes.

Margaret had an informal approach to staff meetings and would readily abandon an important discussion to cuddle the baby of a visitor or talk to children about fishes. But she was also a formidable foe if any government official or academic criticised her management style; to her, happiness and harmony were of paramount importance. Tea was a loud and boisterous affair that often continued well over time, as she recounted hilarious happenings from her early expeditions with JLB or aired her views on people she had met, her stories typically spiced with exaggeration.

According to William Smith:

'Mom was a saint, the only person I know who could get into a lift full of strangers on the ground floor, and by the third floor, she would know their names and family history and they would all be friends. It was like she developed to be a foil for Dad – and she paid a price for it. When she was growing up and at university, she was tremendously career-minded, but when Dad was alive she had to play second fiddle to his greatness. You can't change nappies and be a great scientist: she was very good at nappies. But she was also great, and she got her greatness through people' (reported in Weinberg, 1999).

CHAPTER 26

Triumph

Birth of the JLB Smith Institute of Ichthyology

M ARGARET TOOK the matter of building on JLB Smith's legacy very seriously. It was effectively the *raison d'etre* for everything she said and did after he died, in and out of work hours, and became an all-consuming passion. Her fear was that, with the death of Smith, the university and the CSIR would lose interest in perpetuating the study of ichthyology in the small inland city of Grahamstown and would relocate it to one of the large, coastal cities, such as Cape Town, Durban or Port Elizabeth – a not unrealistic fear. It is widely considered that, had Margaret pre-deceased JLB Smith, the Ichthyology Institute (now the SAIAB) would not have been established in Grahamstown.

Furthermore, the CSIR had reservations about continuing to support the practice and teaching of ichthyology in Grahamstown without an ichthyologist of high standing at the helm, and Rhodes University was not interested in taking sole financial responsibility for the department, the fish collection and the ichthyology library (Gon, 1996). Two alternatives were considered: moving Smith's fish collection and library to the South African Museum (now the Iziko South African Museum) in Cape Town, or moving it to the Oceanographic Research Institute in Durban, both logical suggestions.

Margaret Smith opposed any move from Grahamstown and refused to part with the book and reprint collection, which she now owned (Gon & Skelton, 1997; Gon, 2002). After much lobbying, by the end of 1968 Margaret had not only convinced the authorities that she could step into her late husband's shoes but also that the Ichthyology Institute needed far more space! When she was passionate about a task, she was a formidable foe.

That same year the President of the CSIR, Dr Chris van der Merwe Brink, visited the Department of Ichthyology in Grahamstown and expressed concern about the primitive and unsafe accommodation that housed the priceless collection of fishes (in which the CSIR had invested a huge amount of money). Fortunately, the Vice-Chancellor of Rhodes University, Dr JM Hyslop, whole-heartedly agreed with him and, on 13th December 1968, the CSIR and the university jointly resolved to establish the JLB Smith Institute of Ichthyology in honour of Smith's legacy and to continue teaching and research in ichthy-ology in Grahamstown. The Institute was to be housed in a specially-designed, modern building in Somerset Street. All this happened within a year of JLB Smith's death.

Margaret resigned from her position as Research Assistant which, despite her considerable accomplishments she had held for 21 years (since 1947), and accepted appointment as Director of the new Ichthyology Institute. The Board of Control of the new Institute met for the first time on 14th April 1969 under the chairmanship of Dr JM Hyslop with representation from the CSIR (Dr C van der Merwe Brink, Dr AEF Heydorn and Dr B van D de Jager) and Rhodes University (Mr Justice JD Cloete and Professor BR Allanson).

Carl Hubbs (1968) reported in his obituary on JLB Smith that 'Professor Smith … for many years had made arrangements that his wife, Mrs Margaret Mary Smith, should continue his work'; but the decision to establish the Insti-tute was, in fact, made only after his death and was by no means a foregone conclusion. Nevertheless, in a letter to Marie-Louise Bauchot at the Muséum National d'Histoire Naturelle in Paris dated 17th January 1968, 10 days after JLB had died, Margaret stated:

> 'For 22 years I have worked closely with him on the understanding that I would continue his work after his death. You see I am 19 years younger than he is and have always considered it a very great privilege to have lived with and helped him in his work so I feel I have not lost him entirely in being able to continue along the lines that he laid down.'

Thereafter, Margaret's sole mission in life was to ensure that JLB's initiative would become a permanent and productive component of the Grahamstown and South African scientific landscape, no matter the effort required. She took to the task of supervising the transition from the old Department to the new Institute with renewed vigour. In order to make informed recommendations on the design of the building and its research facilities, she undertook a seven-month world tour from May to November 1969, visiting fish research institutes, public aquaria and museums in Europe, North America (including Hawai'i), Japan, New Caledonia, New Zealand, Australia and Mauritius. She investigated trends in ichthyology research, methods of cataloguing and curating fish specimens, and the design of preparation rooms, collection rooms, libraries and specialised research facilities. With the help of Peter Castle, a visiting Research Fellow in Ichthyology at the time, she submitted a detailed set of specifications for a specialist research institute building to the architects, Vos Lane & Vincent of East London.

Her plan, from the outset, was to design the building around the Collection Room, given that the fish collection and the library were, in her opinion, the Institute's most valuable assets. This opinion is shared by other systematists to whom 'The most important tool of the marine fish systematist is the fish collection' (Gon, 1996, 2002). Margaret stipulated that the collection room should be 100,000 square feet (9,290 square metres) in area[1], the size of the Great Hall at the university, which made the other members of the planning committee sit up and take notice. 'It was a hot February day and everyone was rather sleepy ... but that woke them up!', she later recalled (Richards, 1987).

Work on the new building began in 1973 and was completed in July 1975. The roof-wetting was celebrated on 21st February 1975, when Margaret presented a copy of the *Fishes of the Tsitsikama Coastal National Park* to all those involved in constructing the building. The new building was officially opened by Dr Basil Hersov, President of the South Africa Foundation and Head of the Anglo-Vaal group of companies, on 26th September 1977, the 80th anniversary of the birth of JLB Smith and Margaret's 61st birthday. The end product was a magnificent research facility, which visiting ichthyologist, Dr P Humphry Greenwood, Head of the Freshwater Fish Section at the British Museum (Natural History) at the time, described as 'one of the most outstanding centres of ichthyological excellence in the world, with facilities, collections and access to material that make it a wonderful place for a research worker who is interested in African and Indian Ocean fishes' (reported in Richards, 1987). In his recent history of Rhodes University Paul Maylam (2017) states:

---

1   In fact, Margaret underestimated the size that the collection room needed to be and today the SAIAB has a new two-storey Collection Room building, with a floor area about the same size as the entire original building, and a large preparation room in the main building. The library now occupies most of the space of the original collection room. One of the key success factors of the SAIAB has been the meticulous and professional way in which the fish collection has been developed, preserved, labelled and made available for study.

'Of all the science research institutes established at Rhodes University, including the Leather Research Institute, Institute for Freshwater Studies which became the Institute for Water Research, Tick Research Institute, it was the Ichthyology Institute that earned the most international recognition.'

Drawing by Dave Voorvelt of the new JLB Smith Institute of Ichthyology building.

Margaret was particularly proud of the magnificent carved wooden door that graced the entrance to the new Institute, which has become an architectural landmark in Grahamstown. The door was commissioned by the building's architect, Roy Bridge, at Margaret's request, as she wanted to incorporate art with science in the design of the new building. The door was designed and carved in 1976 by the well-known Eastern Cape sculptor Maureen Quin, based on Margaret's illustrations in *Fishes of the Tsitsikama Coastal National Park*. It measures three by two metres, weighs 680 kilograms and pivots in the centre, and is made from laminated imbuia and metal plate. The door depicts 15 fish species, including sharks, rays, seahorses, butterflyfish, kingfish and various line fishes. Flynn & Du Plessis (2014) remark: 'The disciplined and stylised carvings of the fish-forms link in a subtle way to African carvings. Maureen has experimented with asymmetrical cubist shapes in which forms are framed, giving this work a modern abstracted character. The brushed satin finish of the steel over-frame accentuates this.' Now in her 80s, Maureen Quin is still active in Alexandria where her 'Quin Sculpture Garden and Gallery' is a popular tourist destination.

Initially the Institute had five members of staff – Margaret Smith (Director), Jean Pote (secretary), Rose Spannenberg (clerical assistant), Doris Cave (librarian) and Liz Tarr (artist). The next few years were joyous ones – arranging the fish collection in the enormous new collection room, establishing and expanding the library, making new staff appointments, and increasing collaboration with ichthyologists worldwide.

David Papenfus, a scholar at Kingswood at that time, remembers helping to move the enormous fish collection in 1978 when he was 12 years old:

'The whole fish collection had to be moved to the new building and it also made sense to replace the formalin ... in most of the specimen bottles and tanks. With that in mind Mrs Smith asked a couple of school kids who were on holiday at the time if we wanted to help out and at the same time make a bit of pocket money. It sounded like fun and so a group of us spent three or four weeks helping out.

'For those three or four weeks we fetched and carried thousands of these specimen bottles, jars and tanks: off the old shelves, onto the other side. ... Many of the specimens were ancient and had been popped into their containers years ago and not touched since. What we then had to do was empty them of all their old, brown and stinking preservative and replace it with clean formalin.

'For weeks we waded around in this stuff – sometimes ankle deep. I have no doubt that we were a little high half the time [the main preservative used at that time was ethyl alcohol, not formalin] and we smelled of the stuff for ages afterwards. ... Occasionally an accident would happen and we would drop something. For some reason it always seemed to be a container full of little specimens (as opposed to just one unfortunate sea creature) and we would have to scramble around the floor ... trying to retrieve hundreds of inch-long eels or minute little fish' (Papenfus, 1998).

The new Institute's mandate was to continue research on fishes and, because it incorporated the old Department of Ichthyology, also develop the teaching of ichthyology at the university. During his ichthyology career JLB Smith had done virtually no teaching and had had no postgraduate students. Margaret knew that she could not match her late husband's research output and realised that a commitment to teaching was the next best option to keeping ichthyology at Rhodes University (Gon, 1996). However, like JLB Smith, she had had no training in biology and was not qualified to teach ichthyology. She had learned from her husband about basic fish taxonomy but had little expertise, other than her own field observations, in fish ecology, population biology, behaviour and physiology, or in the more applied fields of fisheries management and aqua-culture. She had also had no exposure to research on fish evolution, genetics and modern methods of classifying fishes, although she was always receptive to new ideas.

Margaret was shrewd enough to surmount this problem: she needed to find a suitably qualified person to lecture in ichthyology. She chose Tom Fraser, a PhD candidate at the Institute of Marine Science at the University of Miami in Florida, USA; he was offered the post of Senior Lecturer in Ichthyology and arrived with his family in Grahamstown in March 1970. MSc and PhD courses in Ichthyology were now offered to students with an Honours degree in Zoology. Paul Skelton, who would later become the third Director of the Ichthyology Institute, was his first postgraduate student.

Margaret, while developing the physical fabric of the Ichthyology Institute, also demonstrated that she was aware of her shortcomings in other fields in which she had less expertise, and willingly accepted advice on how the Institute, and ichthyology in general, could and should be developed in Grahamstown and South Africa. As the Institute's staff complement developed, initially through temporary fellowships and then through staff appointments, she accepted advice from those who were better qualified, and implemented many of

their recommendations. In so doing she expanded the scope of the Institute's research work beyond taxonomy and zoogeography into other fields; and she facilitated development of the teaching of ichthyology and fisheries science, thereby securing the long-term future of the Institute.

Prior to JLB Smith's death, in 1965, the Anglo American Corporation of South Africa offered him the John S Schlesinger Fellowship for one to three years so that he could choose a promising young ichthyologist, preferably from abroad, who could benefit from his knowledge and experience by working with him. Smith chose Dr Peter Castle (1934–1999) from New Zealand, whose main research interest was the

Peter Castle and JLB Smith with their new X-ray machine in 1967.

taxonomy of eels, especially larval forms. He arrived in July 1966 and left in May 1969 after a productive period of research.

An American ichthyologist, Tom Fraser, joined the staff as Senior Lecturer in 1970, and the first postgraduate student (Paul Skelton) was enrolled in 1973. A Freshwater Research Fellow, PBN Jackson, was appointed in 1973 and, when Fraser returned to the USA in 1973, he was replaced by Rick Winterbottom, son of the famous ornithologist Richard Winterbottom, from the University of Cape Town. He attracted many enthusiastic students to ichthyology and was among the first to use rotenone (a chemical compound extracted from the roots of various African and Asian plants that is toxic to fish) and scuba diving for collecting fishes in South Africa. He and his students carried out a great deal of field research in South Africa as well as in Madagascar. Winterbottom moved to the Royal Ontario Museum at the end of 1976 and was replaced by this author (Mike Bruton) in 1978, who had just completed his postdoctoral study year at the British Museum (Natural History) in London. Bruton subsequently became the founding Head of the Department of Ichthyology & Fisheries Science (DIFS) at Rhodes University in 1981 and then the second Director of the JLB Smith Institute of Ichthyology (1982–1994). The subsequent Heads of DIFS were Tom Hecht (1997–1999), Peter Britz (2000–2009) and Warwick Sauer (2010–present).

In 1980 the JLB Smith Institute became a Declared Cultural Institution under the Department of National Education and, in 2001, its future was further secured when it became a National Facility of the National Research Foundation within the Department of Science & Technology. It was renamed the South African Institute for Aquatic Biodiversity (SAIAB) with a broadened long-term mandate: to make collections and study all aquatic organisms in and around South Africa – a challenging but important task. The change of name of the Institute was controversial. It was not an easy decision, and not everyone agreed with it. But the National Research Foundation had a broader vision for the Institute – to include research, and the making and curation of collections, on all aquatic animals, not just fishes, which necessitated the change. Notwithstanding this decision, the Institute is very proud of the Smiths' legacy and continues to honour it through the 'JLB Smith Collections Facility', 'Margaret Smith Library', annual 'Smith Memorial Lecture', 'Smiths' Sea Fishes' book, and other means. Their legacy is therefore still very much part of the Institute's DNA.

Notwithstanding the magnificent achievements of the Smiths and their staff members in building up the fabric of SAIAB, a dark shadow now looms over the future of fish taxonomy in South Africa. Few young South Africans choose taxonomy as a career trajectory (Gon, 2004), which has created a crisis in the museum world. JLB Smith highlighted this threat over 50 years ago when he wrote to the Rhodes University Registrar, W Askew, in a letter dated 6th August 1964: '... despite all one reads today about the importance of marine biology ... there is no guarantee of a position, let alone a well paid one' (Gon, 2004).

Furthermore, the few fish taxonomy posts that do exist have a very slow turnover, and new posts are not being created. Funds for taxonomy are also hard to come by, and promotion opportunities typically take taxonomists out of research and into administration. In 2018 all the active fish taxonomists at SAIAB were retirees who simply continued conducting research. There is not a single traditional taxonomist on the staff, although the sole molecular geneticist is doing excellent work. In contrast, other subdisciplines within ichthyology are thriving, but all of them depend in some way on taxonomy.

None of this, however, detracts from Margaret's achievement in founding the Institute. She faithfully followed the pattern set by JLB Smith, and carried out his plans for the running of the Institute during her tenure as Director. This included succession planning that would ensure the Institute's continued survival and growth. In her single-minded endeavour to continue the good work, she really showed her mettle as well as her wide range of skills, not only in working with fishes and people, but also in fundraising and big-picture strategic planning. She laid much of the groundwork for what was to become the modern JLB Smith Institute of Ichthyology (and later the SAIAB) in Grahamstown, which is testimony to her tremendous success.

CHAPTER 27

Gone fishing

Ichthyology thrives in Grahamstown

DESPITE HER huge administrative load after the establishment of the new Ichthyology Institute, Margaret initiated her own research, publishing and editing programme, with her publication rate increasing substantially after JLB Smith's death in 1968 (Pote, 1997). Between 1969 and 1977 she published JLB Smith's unpublished work on the kingfishes (Carangidae) under her own name (MM Smith, 1970), collated his previous publications in four bound volumes (MM Smith, 1969b, c; 1973a), published further research on kingfishes (MM Smith, 1972, 1973b), described a new species of kob from KwaZulu-Natal (MM Smith, 1977), and collaborated with Tom Fraser on the description of a bizarre flatfish larva that had washed up near East London (Fraser & MM Smith, 1974).

In 1975 she published a handbook, *Sea and Shore Dangers: their Recognition, Avoidance and Treatment*, illustrated by Liz Tarr and Jean Pote, which proved popular among anglers, divers and holidaymakers. Curtis (2015) wrote of this book:

Margaret Smith in 1970 with a model of the coelacanth.

'Read this booklet and you will want to stay as far away from the sea as possible. Although fairly short at 65 pages, each page is dedicated to the endless ways the sea can kill you. By biting, crushing, poisoning, stabbing, spearing, drowning, electrocuting and eating you alive. There is death by rip tides, whirlpools, rogue waves, white sharks, red tides, stone fish, puffer fish, sea snakes, food poisoning, poisoned spines, boat accidents, propeller wounds ... The sea is a world of teeth – big teeth, little teeth, snapping teeth, cutting and slashing teeth, ripping and tearing teeth. Human flesh provides little armour especially to sharks that consider man a bonus delicacy to their usual fish or seal menu.'

Also in 1975, she produced, jointly with Peter Jackson, a catalogue of the *Common and Scientific Names of the Fishes of Southern Africa*. This publication took three years to complete and highlighted the need to produce a new edition of the *Sea Fishes* book. The 'politics' of naming fishes had its humorous side. Some fishes with 'politically incorrect' names had to be redubbed, and others had to have new common names coined. Our marine fishes now include a measles flounder, warthog flounder, giraffe seahorse, lookdown fish, prodigal son, old woman, jumpingbean, gorgeous gussy (which could have been named after Margaret's sister Flora!), harry hotlips, sergeant major, chocolate dip, evil-eyed blaasop and even a puzzled toadfish. We also have an englishman, roman, scotsman, dane, fransmadam, zulu damsel and arab blenny! Our fresh-water fishes include the cornish jack, churchill, ghost sandbasher, thinfaced largemouth, fiery redfin, slimjannie, bulldog, nkupe and nembwe.

Margaret did not neglect field work and organised a series of fish-collecting expeditions to Mozambique and Zululand. During these trips she insisted on sharing even the most arduous tasks and it was not unusual to see her helping to launch the boat or work late into the night on specimen identifications. The aim of the September/October 1973 expedition she led to the Quirimbas islands in northern Mozambique was to help the Portuguese authorities establish a marine reserve[1] there, based on her prior experience in the Tsitsikamma National Park in South Africa. Margaret became increasingly involved in marine reserves there-after, as shown by her voluminous correspondence on this topic in later years

---

1 The Quirimbas Archipelago Marine National Park was established in 2002 and comprises part of the Mozambique mainland coast as well as the islands of Ibo, Matemo, Quilalea, Medjumbe, Quirimba and Vamizi, and the ocean in between.

(Rhodes University Archive) and her authoritative article, 'The importance of establishing marine parks in the Western Indian Ocean', published in 1976.

In October 1973 she joined the famous diver/scientist John ('Jack') Randall from Hawai'i, in Réunion and Mauritius, where they made further fish collections. In June 1977 she led another fish-collecting expedition to northern Zululand with Randall, Wouter Holleman, Mikkel Christensen, Robin Stobbs and Liz Tarr. In April 1979, at the age of 63 years, she led a final expedition to Sodwana Bay in northern Zululand with Gerry Allen from Australia, Jack Randall, Malcolm Smale from the Port Elizabeth Museum, Robin Stobbs and this author. The Ichthyology Institute's new ski boat, *Marlin* (named after JLB's dog), was used for the first time on this expedition but was damaged on the rough roads of northern Zululand and had to be repaired, and the Land Rover hired from Rhodes University broke down so many times that it was eventually returned with a carrot dangling from its bonnet (Gon, 1996).

Jack Randall, who had spent so much time underwater that he had become careless with diving protocols, nearly drowned on this expedition to Sodwana Bay when he forgot to turn on his aqualung's air supply before he plunged into the water; this author had to respond to his wide-eyed gestures and turn it on.[2]

Despite the mishaps, many additional fish specimens and photographs were collected on the Sodwana expedition for the *Sea Fishes* revision, and valuable information was obtained on the fishes of the St Lucia Marine Reserve, which would undergo radical changes over the next few years. The Greater St Lucia Wetland Park would be proclaimed a World Heritage Site in 1999 and renamed the iSimangaliso Wetland Park in November 2007. A colony of living coelacanths was waiting to be discovered there in 2000.

The JLB Smith Institute of Ichthyology thrived under Margaret's directorship. During her tenure the research staff produced 70 scientific papers, 25 books or book chapters and attended 55 conferences. Six major expeditions were organised, including four to foreign countries, and 11 exhibitions were

---

2   Malcom Smale relates another story about Jack when he was collecting over a remote reef with only a boatman to assist him. He came up and asked for the last bottle full of air for his decompression but was told that he had used it up; so he was forced to suck each and every bottle dry as he underwent decompression. His long-term diving buddy Gerry Allen told us around a fire one evening at Sodwana about a dive that they had done together off a remote seamount with no-one to mind the boat. From a depth of about 30 metres they heard a scraping noise and then silence, and realised that their anchor had broken loose. They ascended as quickly as possible but, by the time they reached the surface, the boat had already drifted away to the far horizon. Gerry, a strong swimmer, swam after it for hours, retrieved the boat, and then returned to miraculously rescue Jack in the open ocean after dark!

held on the life and work of JLB Smith. The staff also wrote 57 popular articles and gave 176 public lectures and 95 TV and radio interviews (annual reports of the JLB Smith Institute of Ichthyology).

Margaret's ambition for building on the legacy of JLB Smith knew no bounds. In 1978 she initiated a complete revision of *The Sea Fishes of Southern Africa*, which had previously been written by JLB Smith alone and illustrated by her and other artists. Initially she believed that she could handle the revision herself with a research assistant, but she soon changed her mind. On 12th March 1978, on the recommendation of Jack Randall, Phil Heemstra from the University of Florida was appointed Curator of Marine Fishes to assist Margaret with the *Sea Fishes* revision. Phil proved to be a massive asset to the Ichthyology Institute and 'Smith & Heemstra' became a very productive partnership, co-editing the *Sea Fishes* revision, together publishing scientific papers and chapters in books, and jointly describing three new species of fishes over the next nine years. Although Heemstra carried out the bulk of the new research for the book, Margaret played a vital role by co-ordinating the whole project and inspiring all the collaborators to complete their work on schedule.

Beryl Richards interviewed Phil about his work with Margaret and reported:

Jack Randall of Hawaii
in diving gear in 1963.

'Speaking of Margaret Smith as a co-worker and colleague, Phil Heemstra said she was an easy person to get along with, a lovely person, full of life and enthusiasm for the work. However they did sometimes have "big arguments", because she was a strong-willed person and if she thought she was right about something she would stick to it. In these good natured arguments a favourite threat of hers was to wring his neck … upon reflection Dr. Heemstra said … "If she'd carried this out she'd probably have wrung my neck once a week while we were working together!"' (Richards, 1987).

In view of the specialisation that had taken place in ichthyology (and in science in general), Margaret and Phil realised that they could not produce the book alone and instead enlisted the services of the leading authorities from around the world on each fish family that occurs in the southern African region to write the account of that family. The project eventually involved 77 collaborators from 15 countries and produced an authoritative and comprehensive book that is still widely regarded as the best of its kind in the world. Margaret reviewed the South African fingerfins (MM Smith, 1980), revised the *Halichoeres* wrasses with Jack Randall (Randall & MM Smith, 1982) and described three new fish species with Heemstra (Heemstra & MM Smith, 1980, 1981, 1983). She also wrote or co-authored 41 family accounts in the new book, which was called *Smiths' Sea Fishes*, to recognise the work of both JLB and Margaret.

The new book (MM Smith & Heemstra, 1986) included over 2,200 species, a 57% increase over the 1,400 species covered in the previous edition. It also included substantial taxonomic revisions; for instance, the number of rockcod species increased from 40 to 77, and the deep-sea lantern fishes from 17 to 125 species. The book was beautifully illustrated with paintings by Margaret Smith, Liz Tarr, Dave Voorvelt and other artists, as well as with brilliant photographs taken by Jack Randall.

Margaret also facilitated the development of a research programme on anguillid (freshwater) eels in Grahamstown, which was initiated by Peter Castle and David Forrest in 1973 and continued by PN Hine, Robin Stobbs, Peter Jackson, Martin Davies and others until 1983, as these fish were thought at the time to have aquaculture potential. This research programme led directly to the establishment of the Experimental Fish Farm adjacent to the Ichthyology Institute, which was officially opened by Dr Derek Henderson, Vice-Chancellor of Rhodes University and Chairman of the Board of the Ichthyology Institute, in September 1985 and was managed by Martin Davies until 2016, when it was discontinued.

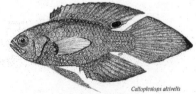

Calloplesiops altivelis

In 1984 Margaret underwent surgery to relieve pain in her knee caused by an old hockey injury sustained in her schooldays, exacerbated by arthritis. She stayed with Mike and Mary-Louise Penrith in Pretoria at the time of the operation and told them:

Comet, *Calloplesiops altivelis*, drawn by Margaret Smith for *The Sea Fishes of Southern Africa* book (1949).

'… it was very painful and that she was totally ashamed of herself, because it was so sore that she had actually sworn at the physiotherapist, a thing that she had never done to anybody in her life before! The physiotherapist reassured her that most of the patients swear at them but it didn't comfort her at all, she felt that she had let herself down badly' (M-L Penrith, pers. comm., 2017).

Unfortunately, the operation did not solve the problem as the pain became worse and she was eventually confined to a wheelchair from June 1986 onwards. This handicap did not soften her resolve to remain actively involved in ichthyology and the Institute. It was a common sight to see Margaret arrive at work in her old blue Ford Cortina, when Edward Matama, the Collection Manager, would rush out, unpack the wheelchair, and help her into it. Nick James, an MSc student in ichthyology in 1985/6, recalls:

'Margaret used to cruise the three floors of the JLBSI building in her wheelchair, going between floors in the lift, but had to yield road space for the much faster skateboard of Michelle Hoebeke, one of the 1985 Honours students who was known to suddenly arrive around a corner at high speed on two wheels!'.

Margaret resorted to taking large doses of cortisone to relieve the pain so that she could continue her work (W Smith, 1996) but the drug impaired her immune system and, in the last two years of her life (1986–1987), she was plagued by illness (Gon, 1996). William Smith believes that the excessive cortisone injections that Margaret took hastened her demise.

Consequently, by 1986, Heemstra had taken over all her work, but she continued to show a keen interest in the progress of the book. Fortunately, she survived to see it published in September 1986.

Ofer Gon and Eric Anderson.

In 1982, Ofer Gon from the Hebrew University of Jerusalem had been appointed to assist Margaret and Phil with the *Sea Fishes* revision. Ofer has also had a distinguished career at the Institute, publishing numerous papers and chapters in books and also co-editing with Phil Heemstra the pioneering compendium *Fishes of the Southern Ocean* (Gon & Heemstra, 1990) on the fishes of the circum-Antarctic Southern Ocean. Ofer was appointed lead researcher, with Phil acting as co-editor, bringing to bear his vast experience in producing *Smiths' Sea Fishes*.

Like the *Sea Fishes* book, *Fishes of the Southern Ocean*[3] was a major, multi-national undertaking that took seven years to complete. Thirty-two ichthyologists from 11 countries contributed 49 family revisions and 272 species accounts, 179 of which were illustrated by Dave Voorvelt,

163 in ink drawings and 16 in colour paintings. It was the first book on Antarctic fishes since JR Norman's (1938) classic, *Coast Fishes, Part III – The Antarctic Zone*, published over 50 years earlier.

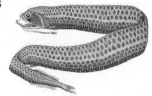

The completion of *Smiths' Sea Fishes* and *Fishes of the Southern Ocean* further enhanced the Institute's international reputation and laid to rest any reservations that the CSIR or the University might

Drawing of a scaly dragonfish, *Stomias gracilis*, by Dave Voorvelt for the *Fishes of the Southern Ocean*.

---

3 In June 1992 the State President, FW de Klerk, presented a deluxe copy of the *Fishes of the Southern Ocean* to Emperor Akihito of Japan during a state visit to South Africa. The book was illustrated with an original painting by Dave Voorvelt that depicted two species of fish that had been described as new to science by the Emperor, an ichthyologist and an expert on gobies.

Alan Whitfield, who developed research on estuarine fishes in the Ichthyology Institute.

have had about the wisdom of retaining the Institute in Grahamstown, or of appointing Margaret as its first Director. The Institute had, in fact, gained in stature during her term at the helm, and augmented its status as a major contributor to international ichthyology. In 1996 Ofer Gon reported that Institute scientists had described 446 fish species and subspecies as new to science, in addition to the 43 new species described by JLB Smith between 1931 and 1945, and that the number of marine fish species known from South Africa had more than doubled over the past 50 years. The Institute had also expanded the geographical range of its work from southern Africa to the Western Indian Ocean and Antarctica.

In the realm of inland waters, Institute staff also completed detailed studies of the fishes of estuaries, rivers, floodplains, lakes, swamps and lagoons throughout southern Africa. In this way the tentacles of the Ichthyology Institute had gradually spread, and the impact of the Smith legacy been felt far and wide.

Donations of major fish collections were made to the Institute (both before and after the JLB Smith Institute of Ichthyology had been established) thanks largely to the collaborative partnerships that the Smiths established. Today it forms South Africa's 'National Collection of Fishes' and, with the Institute's expanded mandate as the South African Institute for Aquatic Biodiversity (SAIAB) since 2001, the collection has been extended to include all aquatic organisms. It is, by far, the largest fish collection in Africa and one of the best in the world.

The rapid growth of the Ichthyology Institute in the 1970s placed a severe strain on the financial resources of Rhodes University, with the annual cost of the Institute representing about 80% of the government's research subsidy to the university. In her 1974/75 annual report Margaret Smith stated:

ICHTHYOLOGY THRIVES IN GRAHAMSTOWN

'My greatest preoccupation ... is lack of sufficient funds to run the Institute. Despite practising every economy I find our present grants are inadequate. Salaries have rocketed, printing, books, and paper, chemicals, office and laboratory ware – everything, in fact, has increased so incredibly in price that it is imperative to find more money for the Institute.'

Despite the Director's best efforts, the Institute went into debt in 1976 and some staff had to be retrenched in 1977 to reduce costs (Gon, 2002). The Institute's Council, and Rhodes University, sprang into action and convinced the government that the expansion of the Institute, the quality of its fish collection, library and research publications, and the international impact of its research, justified its being established as a National Museum. These successful approaches led to its establishment, on 1st April 1980, by the South African government as a Declared Cultural Institution under the Department of National Education (Henderson, 1996), effectively a National Museum. Margaret Smith and Derek Henderson, assisted by this author, were the driving force behind the move, which made the Institute an autonomous body, independent of Rhodes University, yet retaining close and cordial links with it.

In view of this new relationship it became necessary to establish a teaching department of ichthyology within the university. The task was undertaken by this author, then Senior Lecturer in Ichthyology, in collaboration with Margaret Smith. She had always shown a keen interest in the work of the students, often attending and commenting on their seminars. Her kind and generous nature also resulted in her helping many students who found themselves in financial or emotional difficulties.

Peter Jackson (1987, 1996) had this to say:

'... the amount of good she [Margaret] did by stealth was apparent only to those who knew her closely. Nobody with a hard-luck story was turned away ... She helped innumerable people with school fees or books, she lent large sums of money without interest to those needing a down payment on a house. If something was needed and could not otherwise be got she would dip into her pockets, and never say a word.'

According to Nancy Tietz (pers. comm., 2017), Margaret was 'always thoughtful, generous to a fault, encouraging'. Nick James (pers. comm., 2016) remembers her as 'a warm person who was interested in people at all levels of society'.

Ishbel and Ian Sholto-Douglas remember that when they moved to Grahams-town with their five children in 1972, Margaret 'adopted the children as her own and was a very attentive aunt. She adored the kids and liked to talk to them one-on-one to find out about their interest and activities' (I Sholto-Douglas, pers. comm., 2016). In contrast, when Ian and Ishbel had visited the Smiths while JLB was still alive, they were told not to bring the children as JLB did not like kids.

The story of the eccentric Welshman, Martin Davies, who arrived in Grahams-town on 1st February 1976, is an example of Margaret's kindness and generosity. He had initially contacted Margaret from the Tsitsikamma National Park, where he was working on intertidal energetics, and enquired whether he could do some research on fish farming in the Ichthyology library before going on to farm oysters in Kenya. He hitchhiked to Grahamstown with 'no money, no friends and no prospects' (M Davies, pers. comm., 2016). Margaret welcomed him, accommodated him at her house for four months, organised a salary of R200/month, signed surety on his debts, encouraged him to start a fish farm at the Ichthyology Institute, and subsequently arranged for him to be employed on the eel research project. He is still in Grahamstown, 42 years later!

Although Margaret was very supportive of Davies' and others' ventures, and was generous with her own money, she was extremely frugal with the Institute's budget. She tended to spend lavishly on research, buying books for the library, field trips and curation, but cut back on staff salaries and benefits. She was well off at that stage and voluntarily accepted a low salary as Director, and expected others to do likewise. This policy was perpetuated by the equally thrifty chairman of the Institute's Council, Derek Henderson, to Davies' cost (and that of other colleagues).

In 1980 Margaret Smith was appointed, at the age of 64 years, as a one-person commission to investigate the so-called 'Shad Ban' in KwaZulu-Natal; this appointment was an indication of the esteem in which she was held in ichthyo-logical circles at the time. Shad, or elf (*Pomatomus saltatrix*) is an important angling fish in the area. The commission later became the three-person 'Smith Committee of Inquiry' whose brief was to make recommendations to the Administrator regarding restrictions on the capture of shad in the nearshore waters of KwaZulu-Natal. The inquiry became necessary after a long-term research programme conducted by a highly respected ichthyologist, Rudy van der Elst of the Oceanographic Research Institute in Durban, had shown that there had been a decline in the catch-per-unit-effort (CPUE, an indirect measure of fish abundance) and the average size of elf.

The other members of the Committee of Inquiry were Dr Garth Newman, a statistician from the Department of Sea Fisheries in Cape Town, and Professor Phillip van der Watt, Professor of Mathematical Statistics at Rhodes University, with RI Leisegang acting as secretary. Those who gave evidence or made comments during the two-day inquiry included conserva-

Margaret Smith at a fish-tagging prize-giving event in Durban at the time of the 'Shad Ban' inquiry.

tion agency administrators, conservationists, shore and skiboat anglers, divers, commercial and subsistence fishermen, marine biologists, ichthyologists and fisheries scientists.

The inquiry became quite fiery at times and Margaret had to use all her tact and guile to keep the discussions rational and on track. Some extracts from the commission's 450-page, three-volume report, entitled 'Smith Committee of Inquiry into the Restriction on the Taking of Shad (Elf) in the Nearshore Waters of Natal', published in February 1981, provide an insight into Margaret's way of dealing with awkward people and difficult decision-making, and her use of humour to break the ice. The report also provides insights into some of the arcane yet important issues with which ichthyologists are involved. Although Margaret does make some remarks that would be considered today to be 'politically incorrect', her forthright yet empathetic attitude did ensure that everyone had their say and that the discussions were fruitful. These notes also indicate the extent to which Margaret had become involved in fish conservation issues, to a far greater extent than JLB Smith, and they give examples of how she frequently referred to her husband's work after his death.

Her deference to her late husband is clear:

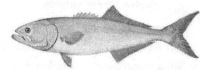

The shad, *Pomatomus saltatrix*, a political fish?

'This is called the Smith Committee of Inquiry, it is in part a tribute to my husband as well, I worked with him for over 30 years as you know, but perhaps what some of you don't know is that his favourite angling fish was the elf or shad, as you call it here, and so I know how to catch them, I know how to hunt them, I know how to cook them, I know how to eat them, and my sympathies are with you people as well as with the fish itself' (pages 1, 2).

After a comment by Mike Bloxham (page 17) that 'the shad ban is political as well', she argued:

'Political Mr Bloxham? Could you explain that? I have never met a political fish before, in fact the fish have managed to combine all the political parties. ... I mean if a politician wants to go fishing, surely that's not a political fish? I mean this is the first time in my experience I have ever heard of political fish, and the shad most certainly doesn't look to me like a Progressive Party or a United Party or anything like that, I mean to be a bit frivolous, but quite honestly I am very interested in this because I cannot understand how the protection of an animal can be political' (page 19). ... if an animal dies it's not political, if it becomes extinct it's not political. What is political, is that the powers that be have not taken the necessary precautions to stop that animal from being killed and becoming extinct ...'

Margaret had this to say in acknowledgement of our growing plunder of the oceans:

'This [is] very pertinent you know, throughout the whole world, because there was a time when the fishes in the sea were limitless, we could do what we liked with the sea, we could dump waste in it; we have suddenly been brought up within the last 20 years, we were brought up short, you can't do that sort of thing' (page 117).

And on the role of scientists:

'Scientists disagree, we fight like mad, just as everybody else does; it's good for us, it makes us tow the line. You know that if you put your foot out of line, someone else is going to tramp on it hard, and that is what keeps us up to scratch' (page 207).

'In fact I remember my husband saying once that a businessman hides his mistakes in the bank balance, but a Scientist publishes his for everyone to see' (page 220).

There were light-hearted times in the midst of what was a serious inquiry. One of the witnesses, Anthony ('Ticky') Forbes, together with Aldo Berruti, found themselves in the same restaurant (an Italian joint in lower West Street) as Margaret Smith, who was dining with her publisher, who happened to be an Italian. Margaret's guest knew that the restaurant owner, also an Italian, was a skilled piano accordionist, and he was also aware of Margaret's singing ability. The result – a memorable and boisterous soirée, with Margaret singing at the top of her voice and the restaurateur accompanying her, much to the delight of the diners!

The Committee's ultimate recommendation that restrictions should be imposed on shad catches, through closed seasons and/or bag limits, would be the first catch restrictions for a popular angling fish in South Africa.

Margaret served on various other committees and boards, including the Transkei Environmental Advisory Board, and a national committee on the advisability of using electric barriers to protect bathers on KwaZulu-Natal beaches from shark attacks.

The high public profile of the Smiths[4] in their later years tended to lend them an air of moral authority in the eyes of the public, which encouraged many public-spirited organisations to seek their help or endorsement on issues such as coastal pollution, the immorality of fishing competitions or the need to conserve Africa's coastline (Gon, 2002).

They happily obliged and this public-spiritedness, on top of their earlier contributions to ichthyology, rendered their input immeasurable.

---

4   Margaret was so well-known that she received letters from local and foreign anglers and ichthyologists that were simply addressed to, 'Prof Margaret Smith, South Africa'! JLB once received a letter addressed to 'Dr Smith, Icthyologist (Coelacanth Discoverer), South Africa'.

CHAPTER 28

Fauna and Flora

Reconnecting in their dotage

THE YEAR 1968 had seen the deaths of both JLB Smith and Margaret's brother-in-law, Robert Sholto-Douglas. In 1972, after retiring as a teacher, Margaret's sister Flora (now a widow) moved to Grahamstown to live with Margaret so that they could reconnect in their dotage. This was a welcome development for Margaret as Flora, who had a happy-go-lucky approach to life and a wicked sense of humour, provided strong support for her during her last years as Director and first years of retirement. In Grahamstown the pair was affectionately known as 'Fauna and Flora'.

Margaret, now secure in her career and with her son successfully fulfilling his own remarkable ambitions elsewhere, could concentrate on developing an active, independent life. Although Margaret had achieved fame as a fish illustrator, Flora was the more artistic of the two and she brought colour and light into Margaret's life and also helped to ease her work load by preparing meals, supervising the household and keeping her entertained.

She encouraged Margaret to become her own person again and was a major factor in her 'coming out'. Whereas JLB and Margaret's house had been austere, with nothing decorative or luxurious, Margaret and Flora's home was richly furnished with curtains and drapes. It was also festooned with memorabilia – Margaret was an avid collector of all things fishy, including fish-decorated cushions, ashtrays, hairbrushes, vases, cutlery, postcards, postage stamps, brooches, necklaces, fabrics and crockery, and developed a network of people who helped her add to her burgeoning collections. In retirement, Margaret

Margaret Smith at the age of 56 years in 1972.

298

also found time to indulge her love of children; nothing made her happier than having a house full of rowdy kids. She tended to treat children as people in their own right, rather than as undeveloped adults.

They both loved music and singing (especially traditional Scottish songs) and Ian Sholto-Douglas (Flora's son) remembers them having a 'white vinyl record of Mary and Flora singing' – 'Mary' being the name by which Margaret's family knew her. Flora, in charge of cooking, was pronounced 'not too good at fish' (Horning, 1979), so that Margaret was relieved of a 'fish, fish, fish' diet. They loved to eat rich chocolate cake and indulged in huge meals. According to Ian, 'the children watched in horror at the amount [Margaret] ate'.

Martin Davies, who ran the fish farm at the Institute, remembers that Flora's meals at Oatlands Road were bland; and that it was pointless spicing them up as Margaret had lost her sense of taste (and smell) due to formalin fumes.[1]

Flora had a special aptitude for puncturing the egos of pompous professors and dignitaries, and she and Margaret enjoyed relating stories, to uproarious laughter, of their latest 'conquest' in this regard. Margaret's favourite ego-popper, always directed at men, was, 'I've forgotten more than he ever knew'.

Margaret had a great sense of humour and loved to relate witty if slightly risqué stories to anyone in earshot. She remarked that watching a man change his underpants was like watching a hermit crab change its shell! Once, as Margaret sat in the front row of a lecture theatre waiting for a visiting academic from Cape Town to start his presentation, she whispered in Afrikaans, slightly too loudly, 'Hy's só lelik, hy's mooi' ('He's so ugly, he's pretty'), which triggered off peals of laughter. Margaret and Flora also enjoyed hosting hysterically funny 'joke parties', where the humour was at times embarrassingly ribald, almost as if Flora was helping her to chip away at what Flora considered to be the academic façade.

---

1 According to Martin, Margaret was not a keen cook, although she prepared excellent pickled fish. In the *Ichthos* seafood cookbook, *Fisherman's Favourites*, edited by Carolynn Bruton and Liz Tarr and launched in June 1992, to which many leading ichthyologists and fisheries scientists contributed their favourite seafood recipes, Margaret's only contribution was a note on how to prepare sand shark for cooking. In contrast, Marjorie Courtenay-Latimer contributed *Crayfish soufflé*, Jean Pote *Shark and Avocado Cocktail*, *Fish Bobotie* and *Bream Sauvière*, Phil Heemstra his *Silwood Snoek*, the Jubbs their *Fish Pudding à la Jubb*. Allan Heydorn's recipes were the simplest and the best: *Perlemoen al la Seaweed* and *Perlemoen Potjie*. This recipe book arose from a tradition in the then JLB Smith Institute of Ichthyology to host a 'Traditional Fish Supper' in September each year when the DIFS students presented seminars on their work.

Nancy Tietz (pers. comm., 2017) remembers Margaret as '… a people person. Huge sense of fun, which only came to the fore after JLB died. To me she always referred to him as "The Professor" never "my husband".'

Jean-Pierre de Kock (pers. comm., 2016), who did odd jobs in the Ichthyology Institute as a teenager in the early 1980s, remembers her:

'[She was a] strong woman not easily deflected from her course or purpose. Generous and caring to a fault. I can remember getting a Coelacanth from Rhodesia/Zimbabwe which was the first received on ice rather than formalin. Phil Heemstra and a couple of others were debating how to get a piece off to taste without her noticing. The first thing she said when she walked through the door was, "Right! Let's taste it!".'

Allan Heydorn (pers. comm., 2017) remarked of Margaret that 'She had the gift of the gab and at times her incessant talking became tiring'. Many a highly motivated scientist, itching to get back to his/her work, got stuck in Margaret's office during one of her lengthy monologues. This author made a habit of meeting with her 15 minutes before closing time, but she was savvy to this tactic and chattered on anyway.

Malcolm Smale (pers. comm., 2017) of the Port Elizabeth Museum said of Margaret, 'Jovial, very interested in people and anything fishy. A great story teller and always friendly and warm.' Shirley Bell described her as a 'robust, energetic and very likeable woman who was nevertheless a formidable foe and a tenacious campaigner' (Bell, 1982).

She always went out of her way to make new friends and delve into the family backgrounds of those she met. Once, after a flight from Cape Town to Johannesburg, Margaret so endeared herself to the other passengers that she was cheered off the plane![2]

In 1976, for Flora's 70th birthday, Margaret took her on a trip to Europe and Alaska, the first time that Flora had ventured beyond southern Africa (except for a trip to New Zealand when she was three). They departed on 14th May 1976, headed for Greece, England, Scotland and then Alaska, where Margaret attended an American Society of Ichthyologists & Herpetologists (ASIH) conference, and then flew back via San Francisco, Miami and Rio de Janiero. Flora

---

2   According to Rénee and Johan Muller, Henriette Pienaar, JLB's first wife, had the same habit; she naively talked to complete strangers on the London Underground when she visited the Mullers in London. JLB appeared to choose wives with personalities opposite to his own!

commented after this trip that Margaret 'has the enjoyment of a child but the capacity of an adult' (I Sholto-Douglas, pers. comm., 2016). Flora also accompanied Margaret to a Southern African Museums Association (SAMA) conference in Durban in May 1977.

Cathy Braans, granddaughter of Flora, had this to say about her grand-mother's relationship with Margaret, her great-aunt:

'[Flora] brought a huge amount of sunshine into [Margaret's] life and [Margaret] was thrilled when Flora followed us from Jhb [Johannesburg] and came to live with [her]. [Margaret] had not always had an easy life and Flora filled that with laughter and a huge amount of mischief! They were always up to something! Aunty Mary never drank [alcohol] but Flora man-aged to convince her that ginger square was non-alcoholic – she drank it for years! My grandmother and her were two very colourful characters, my grandmother's theatrics mixed with Aunt Mary's larger than life personality and volume, meant that there were seldom dull moments, even in the Presbyterian Church. They were incredibly special and spoilt us with their time, knowledge and stories.

'We all remember Aunty Mary's love for planting trees and every one of them had some sort of fish fossil in the hole before it was covered up. She assured us this would make the tree flourish. I remember her laughing uncontrollably when Angus [Margaret's great-nephew and one of Ian and Ishbel Sholto-Douglas' five children] saw the coelacanth lying in the for-malin. Above it was a photograph of the fish. He turned round and said, 'Aunty Mary – that is the same as this fish except this one is having a bath!' ... Through Margaret's influence Angus became very environmentally con-scious, campaigned against the hospital trade in animals and today owns a private game reserve' (I Sholto-Douglas, pers. comm., 2016).

According to those in the know, Margaret did not display a good dress sense in everyday life but she could look very glamorous (after JLB Smith had died) when she made an effort, in bright, flowing dresses or shirtwaisters, with some make-up and extravagant fish jewellery. She tended not to engage in deep scien-tific discussions, especially in the company of Flora, but preferred talking about people and relationships.

Later in life she confessed, 'Sailing around our shores collecting fish specimens I found I got sick of the company of men. If I found a woman who could talk to me about lace-making or show me pictures of her children I was thrilled, though in other circumstances I might have been bored stiff' (Horning, 1979).

Margaret Smith retired as Director of the JLB Smith Institute of Ichthyology on 30th April 1982, aged 65 years, and was made a Professor Emeritus by Rhodes University. She left behind her a vigorous and growing Institute containing the world's largest collection, library and image archive of southern African and western Indian Ocean marine fishes.

When this author succeeded her as Director on 1st May 1982, Margaret took on the role of 'dowager duchess', priding herself in dealing with difficult staff and officials. We worked very well together and she was the perfect ex-Director – always available for discussions but never interfering in my decision-making. She realised that I would take her Institute in new directions, but she was comfortable with that.

As a young married woman Margaret worked for the Child Welfare Society, becoming its honorary treasurer until ichthyology claimed her. After JLB's death she became involved with many civic societies, including the Red Cross, South African Association of University Women, National Council of Women, Soroptimists International, the South Eastern Areas Development Association and the St John's Ambulance Brigade. She was also involved in many scientific societies, including the South African Society for the Advancement of Science, Barologia (the society for underwater sciences) and the Southern African Museums Association (SAMA). Although she attended many meetings of SAMA, she was not an active participant in SAMA committees and gave few presentations, but 'when she got up to speak it was clear and very much to the point. People listened' (N Tietz, pers. comm., 2017).

Margaret making a speech at her retirement banquet in May 1982.

Some argue that Margaret spread herself too thinly with her many civic engagements and was not able to make a major impact on any of them, although she was particularly dedicated to supporting the Red Cross and St John's Ambulance Brigade. She was also assiduous about her involvement with animal welfare through the Trinity Church. Tesza Musto (pers. comm., 2017) remembers her being 'involved with the terrible plight of the donkeys in Grahamstown. She would have harnesses made for them as they were used for carting wood etc.' While she was still Director of the Institute, her office was always cluttered with donkey harnesses, boxes of stamps for the Red Cross, and the other paraphernalia associated with her charity work.

Margaret was also appointed Patroness, Patron Member, Honorary Vice President and Honorary Member of many angling and underwater unions and clubs. In 1977 and 1980 the South African Angling Union awarded her their silver medal, and in 1980 she was granted the merit award of the Public Relations Institute of South Africa (PRISA) for her services to the Eastern Cape. During her directorship of the Ichthyology Institute she also served on the Faculty of Science and on the Senate of Rhodes University from 1968 to 1982.

She was a Trustee of the Albany Museum, Honorary Curator of Fishes for the Eastern Cape Provincial Museums in Port Elizabeth, Grahamstown and East London (as JLB Smith had been) from 1968 to 1987, and also served on the Council of Kingswood College and the Grahamstown School Board. Keith Hunt (pers. comm., 2016) remembers, 'Margaret and I served on the Board of the Albany Museum together and supported each other in debate. I had a lot of time for Mary Smith; she certainly deserved the honours that came her way.'

During her remarkable life she progressed from chemistry demonstrator and research assistant to wife, mother, artist, scientist, editor, administrator and inspirational leader. She co-authored three books, edited three others, and authored or co-authored 35 scientific papers and numerous popular articles, and produced over 2,000 colour and monochrome illus-

The author with Margaret Smith shortly after he had assumed the directorship of the then JLB Smith Institute of Ichthyology in 1982.

trations of the fishes of southern Africa and the Western Indian Ocean. Margaret also established a network of collaborating ichthyologists, which resulted in the Ichthyology Institute in Grahamstown becoming a mecca for researchers in the field. Her infectious enthusiasm for fishes also inspired a generation of artists, anglers, naturalists, aquarists, divers, students and, especially, children in South Africa and abroad.

In the 1980s Margaret's health, once so robust, started to fail her. A bad attack of arthritis resulted in her having one of her knee joints replaced. In 1985, while working on the next edition of the *Sea Fishes* book, she contracted pneumonia, septicaemia and bacterial meningitis, following which she was in a coma for several hours and was not expected to live. However, as Phil Heemstra recalls,

'Her indomitable will and determination to finish the book pulled her through. She just refused to die. And even after she was confined to a wheelchair she continued to be an active presence, driving herself around in an automatic car, lifting herself painfully out of the chair' (Weinberg, 1999).

Shortly after the 1986 edition of *Smiths' Sea Fishes* was completed she contracted leukaemia and was hospitalised in Port Elizabeth. When Hans Fricke and this author visited her in hospital in July 1987, we projected onto the wall facing her bed the first video footage of live coelacanths in their natural habitat in the Comoros taken by Hans and his *Jago* crew. She was absolutely enthralled and tears were streaming down her cheeks by the end of the screening. She told us that seeing the live fish had closed the circle of her life and that she was now ready to die and take the memory to JLB Smith. Despite suffering from depression and considerable pain, she told us that she suddenly felt animated and revitalised. Her grand-niece, Cathy Braans, later confided, 'Her being able to watch a video of a coelacanth in her hospital bed, was for her an incredible privilege' (Braans, pers. comm., 2016). She died six weeks later.

Tesza Musto (pers. comm., 2017), who was a Research Assistant in the Ichthyology Institute in 1986 and 1987, has fond memories of her:

'We were told that Prof Smith wanted to rent out half of her home in Oatlands Road. We jumped at the opportunity. ... What an experience of a lifetime this would be. Imagine sharing a home with such a famous, wonderful, humble and mischievous woman. We lived a happy little family, Prof Smith, her sister Flora Sholto Douglas, their sheepdog Kelmar, our Siamese cat and Jack Russel puppy. From the time Prof came home from the hospital she was in a wheelchair. She was gentle and kind. Her sister, Flora used to tell very naughty jokes and she was the feisty one. From the day we got our Jack Russel, 'Atemi' … Prof was in love. The two of them were partners in crime. He constantly sat on her lap and was wheeled around everywhere with her.

'At a certain stage Prof was given the bad news that she had leukaemia. We used to try and convince her to eat her vegetables but she became obstinate and said, 'Why should I?'. Throughout her illness Prof was very positive and kept her sense of humour. … When Prof was bedridden with the Leukaemia, Jenny her daughter in law came to take care of her. Paul [Tesza's husband], Jenny and I took turns to be with Prof. I used to rush home at lunchtime and after work to give Jenny a break and care for Prof. I used to get Prof books in the form of tapes [from the South African Library for the Blind]. This would keep Prof entertained. … It is incredible how it all worked out. Kelmar died first, then Flora (very suddenly) and then Prof. Prof was always worried about who would look after Flora if she passed away before Flora. In the days before [she] passed away Prof told me that she could see her brother in the room. The day Prof died I had rushed home at lunch time to relieve Jenny. While I was sitting with her I realised she was leaving us. I was torn between staying with her or calling Jenny. I felt Jenny should be with her as she was family. Jenny and I were privileged to be with Prof as she left us.'

Margaret retained her wicked sense of humour to the end. Shortly before her death, after she had contracted leukaemia and put on weight, she joked with Ian Sholto-Douglas (Flora's son), that she was concerned that they would not be able to find a coffin big enough. He responded by saying that they would have to use a round coffin, and she laughed uproariously, saying that they could 'roll her away'! (I Sholto-Douglas, pers. comm., 2016).

Margaret Smith died on a warm spring day on 8th September 1987, 17 days short of her 71st birthday, at her home at 37 Oatlands Road, Grahamstown. Ever the educator, on her death bed she explained to her young greatnephew, Angus Sholto-Douglas, what leukaemia is, and 'even made leukaemia sound interesting' (I Sholto-Douglas, pers. comm., 2016). A memorial service was held on 10th September 1987 in the Rhodes University Chapel with the Reverend Calvin Cooke presiding. Her memorial plaque can be found on the Remembrance Wall of the Trinity Presbyterian Church in Grahamstown.

Shortly after her death, this author wrote,

'We will remember her for her gritty determination, her kindness and generosity, her public-spiritedness and humility, and for the indelible mark which she has left on our community. Her life's work, and that of her late husband, will be remembered through the Institute established in their name. A great scientific partnership has ended, but many will bear the fruits of their creative collaboration.'

CHAPTER 29

Pride and joy
The Smiths' amazing legacy

THE INDIVIDUAL legacies left by JLB and Margaret Smith were impressive in themselves. But, as with other great partnerships, the whole was greater than the sum of its parts: together, they achieved what neither would have succeeded in doing on their own. While their sights were set on the same goal, and many of their contributions supported this shared ambition, their contrasting styles set their legacies apart.

Margaret's role changed during the course of her life. Initially she acted as the faithful factotum, doing whatever JLB Smith asked of her, and more, always in support of the legacy he was building. When he needed an artist, she developed expert skills in illustrating fishes; when he needed a personal assistant, she was close at hand, as she was for all the roles that she played, albeit as an equal partner in their joint endeavours. When JLB died, she took over the reins, bullied the university and the CSIR into establishing an Ichthyology Institute in his name, developed the Institute into a world-class facility, and built on his legacy by co-editing updated editions of the *Sea Fishes* book with Phil Heemstra.

Margaret had a positive impact on virtually everyone she met, except perhaps some of the austere professors on the Rhodes University Senate and Faculty of Science who objected to her knitting during meetings. (She argued that she was quite capable of multi-tasking and that the Red Cross welcomed her jerseys.) She is warmly remembered, both as a friend and a revered mentor – a colleague who supported the trajectories of her peers and nurtured emerging talents, as attested to by many scientists in the field today.

Rudy van der Elst (pers. comm., 2016) remembers that Margaret was 'A fiercely loyal and committed person, fair and warm, quite transparent in her dealings, which made her endearing'. But under her cordial exterior there lay a fiercely competitive spirit. At a national anglers' meeting in Johannesburg in 1981 Rudy presented her with a copy of his newly published book, *A Guide to the Common Sea Fishes of Southern Africa* (Van der Elst, 1981), which exactly met the needs of the angling community. 'She was a bit anguished at first being concerned that I might have clashed with her own work – she soon "adopted" me as a real friend and supported me greatly.'

Lynnath Beckley (pers. comm., 2016) remembers sending Margaret strange fishes that she had collected along the Eastern Cape coast while she was still at school.

'She was a fantastic mentor to me. She was always very helpful and kind and gave me lots of encouragement to study fishes. When I was doing my PhD comparing juvenile fishes in various Eastern Cape coastal habitats, I used to drive up to Grahamstown with samples of small fishes which she used to help me identify. Eventually, one day, out of exasperation with some particularly difficult small specimens, she said, "My girl, these fish are just too small for me to identify – you will have to become a larval fish expert".'[1]

Glenn Merron (pers. comm., 2017), who joined the staff of the Institute from the University of Michigan in 1983 to carry out research on wetland fishes, remembers her as 'one heck of a dynamo! So gracious when I first came over to G'town and RU. Always a very warm memory of her. I didn't deal with her academically, but [she] was a pillar of support for the Oko [Okavango] work.'

Margaret's generosity knew no bounds and played a little-appreciated role in establishing ichthyology in Grahamstown. Wouter Holleman worked for her in a temporary capacity soon after the move into the new building and one of his responsibilities was to purchase equipment for the new laboratories. Years later he learned that she had paid for all of this equipment from her own pocket (W Holleman, pers. comm., 2017). Holleman also commented that she was 'a lot smarter an ichthyologist than she was given credit for'.

At one of her first SAMA conferences, budding ichthyologist-entomologist-pathologist Mary-Louise Penrith was very obviously nervous during a presentation and Margaret 'cornered me afterwards and advised me to take singing

---

1 This is precisely what Lynnath Beckley went on to do, becoming a Professor in Marine Science at Murdoch University, Perth, Western Australia.

lessons as it helped with nervousness and voice projection! I didn't get round to that but I thought it kind, and it probably was very good advice. Fortunately I got over the nervousness with practice' (M-L Penrith, pers. comm., 2017).

Allan Heydorn (pers. comm., 2017) commented:

'In contrast to her husband, who at times seemed introverted and who did not waste words unnecessarily, Margaret was outgoing and always bubbled with enthusiasm. She was a knowledgeable ichthyologist and fiercely loyal to her husband as whose assistant and research partner she had worked for many years. The best expression of her loyalty to JLB Smith was her willingness to take over the Directorship of the JLB Smith Institute after his death. She flung herself into this task with the energy which was typical of her and she represented the institute at many scientific meetings and conferences. This contact promoted good collaboration with other research organisations including, *inter alia*, ORI and SAAMBR.'

Colin Buxton (pers. comm., 2017), who was on the staff of the Department of Ichthyology & Fisheries Science at Rhodes from 1987 to 1995, remembers her as a 'kind, generous and interesting person, always keen to share a story. She had a special love of sparids and loved the fact that I had chosen a career studying sparids.'

Paul Skelton (pers. comm., 2017) opined, 'Strong character, decisive and direct. She was empathetic and very supportive if she believed in you or your cause. Caring and very determined in her mission and tasks.'

Having fought, against the odds, to set up the JLB Smith Institute of Ichthy-ology in Grahamstown, Margaret Smith crowned that achievement by serving as Director of the Institute from 1968 until 1982, when she retired, aged 65 years. She had initiated, nurtured and overseen the growth of a thriving and esteemed Institute, as well as a flourishing teaching department.

ICHTHOS logo, designed by Liz Tarr.

Senior research staff of the then JLB Smith Institute of Ichthyology in the early 1980s: Back: Robin Stobbs. Top row, from left: Mike Bruton, Phil Heemstra, Peter Jackson, Glenn Merron. Middle row: Alan Whitfield, Paul Skelton, Tony Ribbink. Bottom row: Len Compagno, Eric Anderson, Ofer Gon.

On her retirement, she was made a Professor Emeritus by Rhodes University. Generous gifts, donations and congratulations poured in from around the world. A 'Margaret M. Smith Bursary in Ichthyology' was established in recognition of her contributions to African ichthyology, with Glenn Merron being the first recipient. When ICHTHOS, the Society of Friends of the JLB Smith Institute of Ichthyology, was founded in September 1982, Margaret was elected Life President, a role that she fulfilled with aplomb.

In 14 short years she had engineered the transition of the Institute from a classical taxonomical research unit into an institute integrally involved in national and international research programmes on fish biology, systematics, zoogeography, morphology, ecology, behaviour, life-history styles, fisheries management, aquaculture and conservation.

Through her achievements as a scientist, administrator and fish artist, she joined an elite group of woman ichthyologists that includes Edith Grace White (1890–1975), Margaret Hamilton Storey (1900–1960), Ethelwynn Trewavas (1900–1993), Laura Clark Hubbs (1893–1988, who formed a formidable ichthyology team with her husband, Carl), Grace Evelyn Pickford (1902–1986), Marie Poland Fish (1902–1989), Frances Vorhees Hubbs Miller (1919–1987, the eldest child of Laura and Carl Hubbs), Rosemary Lowe-McConnell (1921–2014) (Balon *et al.,* 1994), and many others.

On 25th February 1986 Margaret received *The Order for Meritorious Service Class 1: Gold* from the State President, PW Botha, at Tuynhuis in Cape Town 'for rendering exceptionally meritorious service in the general public interest'.

Two months later, on 11th April 1986, she was awarded the degree of Doctor of Laws (*honoris causa*) by Rhodes University. She was wheelchair-bound at this stage and this author had the honour of wheeling her across the stage to be capped by the Vice-Chancellor, Derek Henderson, and robed by the Registrar, Keith Hunt, who broke all protocol by giving Margaret a big hug to raucous applause from the audience! It was a joyous occasion that contrasted with the dignified solemnity of university graduation ceremonies at that time. Margaret

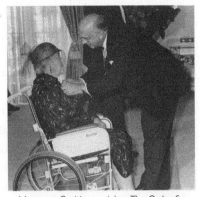

Margaret Smith receiving *The Order for Meritorious Service Class 1: Gold* from the then State President, PW Botha, at Tuynhuis on 25th February 1986.

Smith House, a woman's residence at Rhodes University, was named after her; it is situated on a hill overlooking the university close to Marjorie Courtenay-Latimer Hall. The plaque at the entrance reads:

'An inspiring woman, a role model and world renowned ichthyologist.
Her human touch made the interaction with students her special strength.
She was loved by all.'

JLB Smith was a great intellect who strode the South African and international stage with authority, and commanded considerable respect. He was also a brilliant and much-loved teacher who inspired several generations of students and made a lasting impact on chemistry and ichthyology in Africa and beyond. Despite his frail body, he was a man of incredible energy, drive and enthusiasm who lived several lifetimes in one. He was intolerant of laziness and inefficiency and set very high standards for himself and his colleagues.

He refused many of the honours and awards that he was offered later in life, saying, 'Give it to a younger man who is still climbing and would really appreciate it – it would be wasted on me.' In spite of this, he was honoured in many ways. In addition to being elected a Fellow of the Royal Society of South Africa in 1935 and receiving the Marloth Medal in 1945, he was awarded the

Senior Captain Scott Medal for Biology by the South African Biological Society in 1949 and also elected a Corresponding Foreign Member of the Zoological Society of London.

In 1949, despite never having attended any of their annual conferences, he was elected an Honorary Foreign Member of the American Society of Ichthyologists & Herpetologists, which is limited to 24 members! The latter honour brought considerable material reward to the Ichthyology Institute as it included a free subscription to their prestigious journal, *Copeia*. With his newfound status, Smith was sent not only rare books on fishes but also back copies of *Copeia*, with the result that, for many years, the Institute in Grahamstown had the only full set of *Copeia* in Africa. He was also awarded the Coronation Medal in 1953 and, the same year, became a *Commandeur de l'Etoile de la Grande Comore*. He was also, like Margaret, Patron, President or Honorary Life Member of numerous angling unions, clubs and associations.

In 1993 the 'JLB Smith Memorial Lecture', which has since been renamed the 'Smith Memorial Lecture'[2], was introduced to commemorate the contributions

Len Compagno and his beloved sharks.

---

2   The other 'Smith Memorial' lecturers have included Colin D Buxton (1994), Dave Hensly (1995), Mike Bruton (1996), William Smith (1997), Phil Heemstra (1998), Rudy van der Elst (1999), Alfredo Massinga (2000), Malcolm Smale (2001), Tom Hecht (2002), Tor Naesje (2004), Charles Griffiths (2005), Steven Chown (2006), William Froneman (2007), Brian Marshall (2008), Gene Helfman (2010), Mark Penning (2011), Kevern Cochrane (2012), Kerry Sink (2013), Deena Pillay (2014), Michelle Hamer (2015), Renzo Perissinotto (2016), Judy Mann-Lang (2017) and Mike Bruton (2018). No memorial lectures were held in 2003 and 2009.

of both Smiths. Len Compagno delivered the first lecture, an engrossing and masterful exposé on the feeding and breeding strategies of sharks, rays and chimaeras worldwide, from cookie cutters to megamouths, egg-layers to uterine carnivores.[3]

In January 2000 JLB Smith was posthumously inducted into the International Game Fish Association's (IGFA) 'Fishing Hall of Fame' in recognition of his extensive work in ichthyology and his love of angling. In his presidential address at this event Michael Leech said, 'All the men being inducted this year had a true dedication to conservation, as well as the sport of fishing, which is one of the major missions of the IGFA' (Pullen, 2000). Smith was the first South African to be honoured in this way, joining international worthies such as Izaak Walton, Dame Juliana Berners, Ernest Hemingway, Zane Grey and Lord Baden-Powell.

For better or for worse, publications are the currency that is used to measure a scientist's worth. JLB's publication rate in chemistry was moderate but, as Mike Davies-Coleman (pers. comm., 2017) has pointed out:

> 'JLB Smith was not an outstanding organic chemist if measured in today's terms as far as research outputs go. It was a different era, it was not easy to solve complex organic molecular structures especially in Africa and outputs were mediocre by today's standards. JLB Smith's influence was not his research outputs but his ability to inspire the next generation of young organic chemists who went on to lead South African natural products chemistry into the golden age of organic chemistry when modern analytical techniques eg NMR [nuclear magnetic resonance spectroscopy] became ubiquitous. Doug [Doug Rivett] went on to Cambridge and Princeton from Rhodes and was the only South African organic chemist I know to have published continuously over seven decades (his first paper with JLB in 1942 and his last with me in 2005).'

---

3 Len later followed this up with a scientific paper of extraordinary virtuosity on 'Alternative life-history styles of cartilaginous fishes in time and space' (Compagno, 1990).

But JLB's publication rate in ichthyology was phenomenal (MM Smith, 1969; Pote, 1996). Besides the massive *Sea Fishes* book, as well as *Fishes of the Seychelles* and *Fishes of the Tsitsikama Coastal National Park*, which he co-authored with Margaret, he authored 33 of the 65 *Ichthyological Bulletins* published by Rhodes University between 1956 and 1968, in his 59th to 71st years, as well as numerous other scientific papers. His most productive year was 1957 when, aged 60, he published 18 papers (Pote, 1996). Although most of his publications were on marine fish taxonomy and distribution, he also wrote on fish larvae, growth, the use of formaldehyde as a fish preservative, freshwater fishes (including gobies, barbs and eels), stonefish poisoning, sexual dimorphism, self-inflation by gobies, pugnacity of marlins, swordfish and whale shark behaviour, shark attacks, and the organisation of a library for research in systematics.

By the end of his life JLB Smith had published nine scientific books (three in chemistry and six in ichthyology), 14 scientific papers in chemistry and 213 scientific papers in ichthyology. His books included the monumental *The Sea Fishes of Southern Africa*[4], first published in 1949 and republished in various editions in 1950, 1953, 1961, 1965, 1970 and 1977.

In the first edition of *The Sea Fishes of Southern Africa* (1949) JLB Smith authored every fish family account as well as all the species accounts – an extraordinary achievement. In subsequent multi-authored editions of the book published after his death, such as the 1986 edition (Smith & Heemstra, 1986), he co-authored the Pomatomidae (elf), Sparidae (seabreams) and Mugilidae (mullets). Margaret continued to edit further editions of the *Sea Fishes* book with Phil Heemstra and was a prolific author in her own right of fish family accounts, authoring or co-authoring 43 of these, including those for the sixgill stingrays, coelacanth, ladyfishes, tarpons, coffinfishes, sauries, tadpole fishes, pineapple fishes, seamoths, flagtails, dottybacks, podges, rubberlips, fusiliers, emperors, galjoens, soapies, pomfrets, klipfishes, boxfishes and blaasops. In the 1986 edition of *Sea Fishes* Phil Heemstra authored or co-authored a very substantial 74 fish family accounts, including those for the cowsharks, flyingfishes, opahs, oarfishes, slimeheads, dories, gurnards, rockcods, bigeyes, scatties, moonies, kobs, butterflyfishes, remoras, stargazers, duckbills, soles and ocean sunfishes, six of them with Margaret.

---

4 Completely revised editions were published in 1986, 1995 and 2003. The 1977 edition, published by Valiant Publishers, was titled *Smith's Sea Fishes*, with JLB as the sole author. The completely revised *Smiths' Sea Fishes*, co-edited by Margaret Smith and Phil Heemstra, with 76 authors of the 270 fish family accounts, was published by Macmillan in 1986, long after his death.

The latest editions of *Smiths' Sea Fishes* were published by Southern Book Publishers (1995) and Struik (2003). In 1986 Springer-Verlag in Germany published *Smiths' Sea Fishes* in soft cover (for sale outside of southern Africa only) and also produced an e-book edition in December 2012. In 1989 Margaret Smith (posthumously) and Heemstra were joint winners of the Bill Venter Book Award for the revised edition of *Smiths' Sea Fishes*. This annual award is made to the most outstanding publication by a full-time member of staff of a South African university.

It is interesting to note that, from 1931 to 1947, 21 of JLB Smith's 32 scientific papers (66%) were published in the *Transactions of the Royal Society of South Africa*. Smith was a staunch supporter of the Royal Society and chose to publish his seminal papers on the first and second coelacanths in the Society's publications. He unquestionably lived up to the Society's motto, *Nullius in verba*, 'take nobody's word for it', an expression of the determination of its fellows and members to withstand the domination of authority and to verify all statements by an appeal to facts. Five scientific papers and two books that he wrote in 1967 were published posthumously in 1968 and 1970. Considering that he only became a full-time ichthyologist at the age of 49 years, his productivity was very high.

JLB Smith also wrote a prodigious number of popular and semi-scientific articles in angling, diving and natural history magazines and newspapers: 445 in total, 'for the layman whom he said supported his work indirectly through taxation and so should be told something of the excitement of scientific research' (MM Smith, 1969). He also shared his knowledge of fishes with the public through radio broadcasts in English, Afrikaans and Portuguese, hundreds of informal articles in newspapers and magazines, and popular books in English and Afrikaans (Smith 1956, 1968a and b).

Not least of JLB's diverse accomplishments was his role as a mentor, mainly in chemistry but also in ichthyology, for the next generation of scientists. Bob Crass, who later became a leading freshwater ichthyologist in KwaZulu-Natal, remembers:

'Doc, who gave me the best course of lectures and the best practical instruction of any of those who taught me at Rhodes. Doc, who would always help a student seeking information, no matter how busy he might be. Doc, the indefatigable worker who never lost his dry, down-to-earth sense of humour … but his refusal to become a burden to others was typical of the man' (SAIAB archives).

Michael H Silk, one of his students, wrote after his death:

'Doc was my tutor at Rhodes and led me along the first faltering steps of a scientific career. I shall always remember him as a great man who was strict in disciplining himself and others but who always showed a deep understanding of students and was generous in his praise if it was earned through hard work.'

Dr AS Galloway, a staff member of the university, commented, 'He helped me a great deal when I first began to lecture at Rhodes. He offered me genuine sympathy and encouragement when I was ill and disabled, and his own triumph over ill health was an inspiration to me' (SAIAB archive). Professor CH Price commented after his death, 'There don't seem to be men cast in his mould any more' (SAIAB archive); and a student, Pierre Faure, wrote, 'He certainly demonstrated a fellowship between staff and student that would be difficult to surpass, if not impossible these days. It was a privilege and an honour to have known him and be guided by him.'

In a further tribute in 1968 Evelyn Strickland said, 'As I write I have before me the names of 15 Chief Chemists and Assistant Chief Chemists holding these positions from Phalaborwa, through Rhodesia, to Bancroft upon the Copper Belt. Everyone of these is a Rhodes Graduate and a pupil of Prof. J.L.B. Smith' (SAIAB archives). Dinnie Nell remembers, 'I see him now as I always knew him, lean, virile, fearless and absolutely honest in all his dealings both with men and with scientific facts and theories' (SAIAB archives). LM Dugmore recalls, 'If ever a man made good and effective use of his life "Doc" did. Doc had a tremendous capacity for friendship – a quality I appreciated when we were together at Rhodes and after my marriage' (SAIAB archives).

During his career as an ichthyologist JLB Smith developed from having a 'modest reputation as a descriptive ichthyologist' (Hubbs, 1968) into an internationally respected taxonomist who grappled with complex taxonomic problems at the level of species, genus and family. He was sometimes criticised for being too hasty in describing new fish species, and there is some merit in this argument. He described 392 species of fishes as new to science, 387 as the sole author and five with his wife, Margaret. Of this total, 121 species (31%) have retained the name given to them by Smith, 94 (24%) have been placed in another genus as a result of subsequent taxonomic revisions, and 177 (45%) were subsequently found to have previously been described as new species by other scientists. The proportion of species that JLB Smith described as 'new' that turned out to be junior synonyms of previously described species (45%) is high by any standard. In particular, he was too hasty in assigning the second coelacanth to a new genus and species (*Malania anjouanae*, Smith 1953), even though he pointed out that the fish was damaged during capture and preservation, and was already deformed; it was later synonymised with *Latimeria chalumnae* (MM Smith, 1986).

Several reasons have been advanced for this trend: firstly, that he did not have ready access to the taxonomic literature published in the northern hemisphere; and, secondly, that he was relatively isolated from most active taxonomists. After Keppel Barnard had completed his marine fish work in 1927, JLB was the only marine fish taxonomist active in South Africa until the 1950s. A third reason is that Smith always seemed to be in a race against time due to his failing health. Although he was a meticulous worker, as attested by the 212 species that he described as new and which have remained valid, and his detailed descriptions of many species, both new and known, and especially the first coelacanth, he may have erred on the side of haste in some of his new species descriptions. Because he was one of the first taxonomists to study the fishes of the Western Indian Ocean, he may also have assumed that most of these species were not known to northern hemisphere – or Atlantic or Pacific Ocean – scientists at the time, as there was little appreciation then of the wide distributional ranges of many of these fishes.

Furthermore, much of his research was conducted under adverse conditions with relatively poor library and laboratory facilities, although he did have excellent fish specimen reference collections, which he had largely made himself. Also, he did tend to publish, after 1946, mainly in the in-house journals of his Ichthyology Department, which were not subject to strict peer review. Despite these shortcomings, there is no doubt that he made very significant contributions to African fish taxonomy and zoogeography.

Two of the new fish species that JLB Smith described were freshwater or river/estuarine species, both during his early, 'amateur' days as an ichthyologist. They were the Eastern Cape redfin, *Pseudobarbus senticeps* (Smith, 1936), which Skelton (1988) has since synonymised with *P. afer*, and the river goby[5], *Glossogobius callidus* (Smith, 1937), which is still a valid species.

In an article published in the *Grocott's Daily Mail* on 19th June 1956, JLB wrote, 'It is one of the privileges enjoyed by the research biologist to be able to commemorate in this way [naming new species after people] valuable support of scientific work'. He named a new species of goby, *Trimia naudei*, after the then President of the CSIR, Dr SM Naudé, other new species after Dr Cecil von Bonde (Director of Sea Fisheries), and the Governor-General of Mozambique, and the magenta splitfin, *Nauria addisi* (now *Luzonichthys addisi*), after Sir William Addis, Governor of the Seychelles. He also initially named the second coelacanth after the then Prime Minister, Dr DF Malan.

He was sometimes quite flippant about naming new species. On Vamizi Island in Mozambique in August 1951 he reported, 'Besides many rarities, I found two fishes new to science that morning. One was a beautiful, small creature with a red snout that reminded us of a man who imbibed too freely, so we christened it 'Nosey' – rather irreverently – getting three or four specimens. Later in studying this fish, I found it to be of a new genus as well and christened the fish *Wamizichthys bibulus*, part in reference to Vamizi, where we first found it, and partly from its bibulous appearance' (Smith, 1968b).

JLB Smith named four new fish species after Margaret – *Canthigaster smithae* and *Chlidichthys smithae* from Mauritius, *Trachurus margaretae* from Durban and *Pseudocheilinus margaretae* from Aldabra island. In his description of *P. margaretae* he wrote, 'This exceptionally beautiful creature is named as a small tribute to my wife, whose contribution to all phases of our work is probably greater than my own.' He also named a new species, the kaalpens goby, *Bathygobius william* (now *Monishia william*) from Xora River mouth (where they often spent their winter holidays), after their son, William.

5   The river goby is widespread in rivers and estuaries from the Swartvlei region of the Western Cape to southern Mozambique but the Eastern Cape redfin, which is confined to coastal rivers from Algoa Bay to Mossel Bay, is threatened by alien predators such as bass. Recent research has revealed that *G. callidus* is probably a species complex (Skelton, pers. comm., 2017).

Doug Hoese named the smooth-scale goby, *Hetereleotris margaretae* from Sodwana Bay after Margaret, and William Smith-Vaniz named the halfscaled jawfish, *Opisthognathus margaretae*, after her too, as did George Coulter, when he named a new species of cichlid fish from Lake Tanganyika *Simochromis margaretae*.

Several new species of marine fishes have been named after JLB

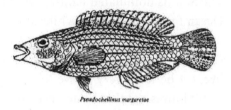

Pseudocheilinus margaretae

"This exceptionally beautiful creature is named as a small tribute to my wife, whose contribution to all phases of our work is probably greater than my own." – J.L.B. Smith, 1955.

Pseudocheilinus margaretae, a new species of wrasse named by JLB Smith after his wife, Margaret, in 1955.

Smith, including the conger eel, *Bathymyrus smithi* from Mozambique, the shortfin pipefish, *Choeroichthys smithi*, from Mozambique, the flounder, *Engyprosopon smithi*, from Durban, the cuskeel, *Ophidion smithi*, from KwaZulu-Natal, and the mini-clingfish, *Pherallodus smithi*, from Durban.

Margaret Smith described 14 new species of fishes, five as the sole author, six with Jack Randall and three with Phil Heemstra; all 14 species are still valid. One of the very significant new fishes that she described with Heemstra was the sixgill stingray, *Hexatrygon bickelli*, a new species, genus, family and suborder of fishes (see above). That would be the equivalent, in the mammal world, of finding the first primate. Phil Heemstra, who assumed JLB Smith's mantle as the leading marine fish taxonomist in South Africa, has described 21 new species both as sole author and with various co-authors, all of which remain valid.

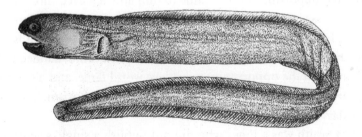

The conger eel, *Bathymyrus smithi*, named after JLB Smith by Peter Castle.

The Smiths dominated ichthyology in South Africa and the Western Indian Ocean for over 50 years. While some expressed dismay at JLB Smith's early death, others were surprised that he had survived for so long. When he married Margaret in 1938, his doctors predicted that he had only five years to live, yet he led a very active life for another 29 years. What is remarkable about him is not that he achieved so much but that he achieved anything at all considering the ill-health that he suffered during the last 53 years of his life. Yet he acquired world fame through his description of the coelacanth, his explorations of remote parts of the oceans of South and East Africa, his single-handed authoring of the first edition of *The Sea Fishes of the Southern Africa*, widely acclaimed at the time as the best book of its kind in the world, and his willingness to share his knowledge with laypeople. He also wrote a scientific bestseller (*Old Fourlegs*), which was translated into nine languages, and played a major role in laying the foundation for the study and teaching of ichthyology in South Africa, which is now permanently entrenched in Grahamstown.

They say that, when a wise person dies, it's as though a library has burnt down. Fortunately, in the Smiths' cases, the library still stands. JLB Smith was a huge intellect with a superb memory and a work ethic to match. He was a brilliant and much-feared, though respected, lecturer in chemistry and a prodigious researcher in ichthyology. He was a man of incredible drive and enthusiasm who took the opportunities that came to him and achieved more than most. Although he was intolerant of inefficiency and laziness, and sometimes abrupt, even rude, he was considerate, kind and generous to close friends and colleagues. The serendipitous discovery of the first coelacanth, handed to him on a plate, gave him the opportunity to achieve world fame, and he grabbed the good fortune with both hands. Never has the Latin aphorism, 'carpe diem' – 'seize the day' – been more apt.

But JLB Smith was a loner who did not publish a single scientific paper, chapter in a book or popular article with anyone other than his wife (and only very rarely with her). In contrast, after his death, the Ichthyology Institute published several multi-author, multi-national books on marine fishes on a collaborative basis with expert ichthyologists from around the world: *Smiths' Sea Fishes, Fishes of the Southern Ocean, Coastal Fishes of Southern Africa* and *Coastal Fishes of the Western Indian Ocean*.

Notwithstanding his 'lone wolf' attitude, and his outstanding personal characteristics and accomplishments, JLB Smith's ultimate success as an ichthyologist was largely due to his partnership with Margaret. Together, they formed one of the great husband-and-wife teams in the history of South African science. Mrs Helen Hyslop, a family friend and wife of the Rhodes University Vice-Chancellor, James Hyslop, wrote after JLB's death:

'Your partnership in scientific research and the fine quality of your relationship each to the other was something which all admired, and in the tribute now paid to Professor Smith you may perhaps find some small degree of comfort, for such a man could not have borne the grief of losing grounds, or becoming a helpless invalid. One has seen this happen to other great men, and has dimly realised their suffering. That suffering is no less for the loved ones who stand by, and I believe that your husband thought deeply of those things.'

Until the end of her days, Margaret was fiercely defensive of JLB Smith's legacy, character and behaviour and tolerated no criticism of him. William Smith summed up their partnership:

'She filled in the gaps. She developed a great love of people and the people loved her. Although totally without artistic training she developed the ability to draw the fish that JLB was working on. He was physically weak (after his experiences in the first world war) so she developed herself physically to fill the gap. He used explosives to get his fish specimens, she used poison. He worked on the surface of the sea, she learned to dive. They both learned the languages of the local population wherever their fish expeditions took them, and they were both in their own way exceptional Ichthyologists' (W Smith, 1996).

William added, revealingly, 'Each had what the other needed, and they were happy together as far as Dad could be happy. I am not sure that people like him can be happy; perhaps that is what makes them great.'

William deserves the final word on Margaret:

'It was Margaret, on the other hand, who supplied the warmth and love and kept everything together. It was her ability, not just as a scientist and artist, but also with people, that made my parents a formidable team. She was dearly loved by everyone: once, when her car was stolen, it was taken to the informal settlement near Grahamstown where it was recognised as belonging to Margaret Smith by the community, who forced the thief to return it. She found it parked the next day in the exact spot that it had been taken from, washed and cleaned!' (W Smith, pers. comm., 2017).

JLB Smith pioneered new fields of research, explored remote areas of Africa that had not been researched before, established new multi-national scientific collaborations, and put South Africa on the world scientific map. He was one of South Africa's greatest scientific sons. He was a flawed genius, and his racism and unconditional patriotic fervour detracted from his brilliance. However, one could argue that some of his flaws – his irascible attitude to those outside his inner circle, his lack of social graces, his excessive haste due to his fear of disability, and his sometimes irrational diets and exercise regimes – probably contributed to his focus and his greatness.

In many ways JLB and Margaret Smith were the archetypal yin-yang couple, a balance between two opposites that were both interdependent and complementary. He had a two-sided personality that swung according to whether or not you were close to him, and a fanatical focus, bordering on terribilità. He was a loner, antisocial, dour and laconic, with just a small group of close friends. Margaret, by contrast, had a range of diverse goals in life. She was the peace-maker, the rational, common-sensical mind in the eye of the storm, unconditionally supportive of JLB no matter how idiosyncratic he was. She was sociable, effervescent and witty, and the centre of a vast interacting network of friends and colleagues. The chemistry between them was unique, and together they formed a formidable and inspiring partnership that changed the course of ichthyology in South Africa, Africa and beyond. We shall never see their like again.

EX LIBRIS

J. L. B. and M. M. SMITH

'Wherever anglers gather his presence will be felt. His name will be spoken by someone in any discussion on fish or fishing. His memorial lies among the solitary fishermen on tidal reefs and his influence will endure amongst those who love the sea.'

Obituary, 1968, to JLB Smith by Reg Griffiths, friend, photographer and angler

Postscript

NINE YEARS after Margaret's death, in 1996, a 50th anniversary volume was published to celebrate the establishment of 'Ichthyology' in Grahamstown. This volume, edited by Paul Skelton and Johann Lutjeharms, featured 27 drawings of fishes on its front and back covers, including three freshwater fishes, representing the range of work produced by Ichthyology Institute artists over the years. Curiously, none of these drawings features the coelacanth, the 'founding fish', which is also illustrated only twice inside the book (in historic photographs), and no account of the coelacanth's discovery is included – a deliberate omission on the part of the editors, given the substantial coverage already enjoyed by this fish.

This could have been taken to suggest that the coelacanth was part of the Institute's past, not its future, but fate had other ideas. In November 2000, some 13 years after Margaret's death, three mixed-gas divers, Pieter Venter, Peter Timm and Etienne le Roux, photographed three live coelacanths at a depth of 104–118 metres in Jesser Canyon off Sodwana Bay in northern Zululand (Venter *et al.*, 2000). In May 2001 they filmed a further three coelacanths there at 108 metres, and another in 2003 at 54 metres, revealing the shallowest colony of coelacanths known. It was a sensation – the best news in South African ichthyology since 1938: coelacanths living off the South African coast, in a protected marine reserve, and at a depth accessible to mixed-gas divers! JLB and Margaret Smith would have been delighted. Today, if you have the right mixed-gas diving qualifications, under certain special conditions, you can dive and see live coelacanths courtesy of Triton Dive Lodge at Sodwana Bay.

In response to the Sodwana Bay discovery, the *African Coelacanth Ecosystem Programme* (ACEP) was launched in 2002 by the South African Department of Science & Technology in collaboration with the SAIAB and other partners, with the goal of launching a new phase of research on the coelacanth and its environment. Coelacanth fever had gripped South Africa again, and 'old four-legs' was back in harness! ACEP continues today in its third phase (ACEP 3) under the supervision of SAIAB's Director, Dr Angus Paterson.

Acronyms

CSIR   Council for Scientific & Industrial Research; established in 1945

DIFS   Department of Ichthyology & Fisheries Science, Rhodes University; established 1981

FAO   Food & Agriculture Organisation of the United Nations; founded in 1945

JLBSI   JLB Smith Institute of Ichthyology; established in 1968

ORI   Oceanographic Research Institute; established in 1951 as a division of SAAMBR; now uShaka Marine World, established in 2004

RUC   Rhodes University College (1904–1952), which became Rhodes University

S2A3   South African Association for the Advancement of Science; founded in 1902

SAAMBR South African Association for Marine Biological Research; established in 1951

SAIAB   South African Institute for Aquatic Biodiversity; established in 2001

References and further reading

Anon. 1953. Sea 'Scapes. *Diocesan College Magazine* March 1953: 56.

Anon. 1968–1987. *Dictionary of South African Biography.* Volumes 1–5. Human Sciences Research Council, Pretoria.

Anon. 1988. Margaret Mary Smith: 26 September 1916–8 September 1987. *South African Journal of Marine Science* 6(1): 1–2.

Anon. 2013. *Building on the South African Coelacanth Legacy.* South African Institute for Aquatic Biodiversity, Grahamstown. 45 pages.

Anthony, J. 1976. *Opération Coelacanthe.* Arthaud, Paris. 200 pages.

Anthony, J. 1980. Évocation des travaux français sur *Latimeria* notamment depuis 1972 (Review of French research on *Latimeria* particularly since 1972). *Proceedings of the Royal Society of London* Series B 208: 349–367.

Anthony, J & Millot, J. 1972. Première capture d'une femelle de coelacanthe en état de maturité sexuelle. *Academie des Sciences, Paris Séries* D 274: 1925–1926.

Atz, JW. 1976. *Latimeria* babies are born, not hatched. *Underwater Naturalist* 9(4): 4–7.

Balon, EK. 1990a. The living coelacanth endangered: a personalized tale. *Tropical Fish Hobbyist* 38 (February): 117–129.

Balon, EK. 1990b. Tracking the coelacanth: a follow-up tale. *Tropical Fish Hobbyist* 38 (March): 122–131.

Balon, EK, Bruton, MN & Fricke, H. 1988. A fiftieth anniversary reflection on the living coelacanth, *Latimeria chalumnae*: some new interpretations of its natural history and conservation status. *Environmental Biology of Fishes* 23: 241–280.

Barnard, KH. 1925. A monograph of the marine fishes of South Africa. Part I. *Annals of the South African Museum* 21(1): 1–418.

Barnard, KH. 1927. A monograph of the marine fishes of South Africa. Part II. *Annals of the South African Museum* 21(2): 419–1065.

Barnard, KH. 1943. Revision of the indigenous freshwater fishes of the SW Cape region. *Annals of the South African Museum* 36(2): 101–262.

Barnard, KH. 1948. Further notes on South African marine fishes. *Annals of the South African Museum* 36: 341–406.

Barnett, P. 1953. *Sea Safari with Professor Smith*. Business Services, Durban. 158 pages.

Batten, A. 2004. Some memories of Marge. *The Coelacanth* 42(1): 48–55.

Bell, S. 1969. *Old Man Coelacanth*. Voortrekkerpers, Johannesburg. 141 pages.

Bell, S. 1987. I remember the professors – a personal tribute to Professors JLB and Margaret Smith. *Skiscene* 11(5): 13–14.

Bemis, WE & Simon, AM. 1997. Coelacanth catches. *Science* 278: 370.

Benno, B, Verheij, E, Stapely, J, Rumisha, C, Ngatunga, B, Abdallah, A & Kalombo, H. 2006. Coelacanth, *Latimeria chalumnae* (Smith, 1939) discoveries and conservation in Tanzania. *South African Journal of Science* 102: 486–490.

Bergh, W, Smith, W, Botha, W & Laing, M. 1992. The place of Natal Command in world science. *South African Military History Journal* 9(1): 1–13.

Bickell, D. 1986. What a wonderful book. *Ichthos* 12: 1.

Boy, G. 2001. Kenya's first coelacanth. *Swara* 24: 24–26.

Brown, AC. 1982. Scientists remember. *South African Journal of Science* 78(2): 52.

Brown, AC. 1989. Professor John H.O. Day – obituary. *Ichthos* 24: 4.

Brown, AC (ed.). 1997. *A History of Scientific Endeavour in South Africa*. Royal Society of South Africa, Cape Town. 516 pages.

Brown, ME, Eve, DJ, Kaye, PT, Rivett, DEA & Watkins, GM. 2004. 100 years of chemistry at Rhodes University. *South African Journal of Science* 100(11+12): 530–538.

Bruton, CJ & Tarr, EM (eds). 1987. *Ichthos Recipe Book*. Ichthos, Grahamstown. 104 pages.

Bruton, CJ & Tarr, EM. 1992. *Fisherman's Favourites. Fish, Seafood and Seaweed Recipes*. Southern Book Publishers, Halfway House. 210 pages.

Bruton, MN. 1982. *The Life and Work of Margaret M. Smith*. J.L.B. Smith Institute of Ichthyology, Grahamstown. 12 pages.

Bruton, MN. 1986a. A passion for fishes. *South African Journal of Science* 82: 622–623.

Bruton, MN. 1986b. Keppel Barnard. *Ichthos* 11: 2.

Bruton, MN. 1988. JLB Smith the sportsman. *Ichthos* 19: 3.

Bruton, MN. 1989a. Margaret Mary Smith (1916–1987). *Cybium* 13(1): 3.

Bruton, MN. 1989b. Fifty years of coelacanths. *South African Journal of Science* 85: 205.

Bruton, MN. 1989c. The living coelacanth fifty years later. *Transactions of the Royal Society of South Africa* 47: 19–28.

Bruton, MN. 1990. Tribute to Captain Goosen. *Ichthos* 25: 6.

Bruton, MN. 1992. The mingled destinies of coelacanths and men. *Ichthos* 33: 4–5.

Bruton, MN. 1994. Lungfishes and Coelacanths. pp. 70–74. In: JR Paxton & WN Eschmeyer (eds) *Encyclopaedia of Animals: Fishes*. University of New South Wales Press, Sydney.

Bruton, MN. 1996. What the Ichthyology Institute means to me. *Ichthos* 49: 26–27.

Bruton, MN. 2015. *When I was a Fish. Tales of an Ichthyologist*. Jacana Media, Cape Town. 310 pages.

Bruton, MN. 2016. *Traditional Fishing Methods of Africa*. Cambridge University Press, Cape Town. 96 pages.

Bruton, MN. 2017. *The Annotated Old Fourlegs. The* Updated *Story of the Coelacanth*. Struik Nature, Cape Town. 336 pages.

Bruton, MN. 2018. *The Amazing Coelacanth*. Struik Nature, Cape Town. 96 pages.

Bruton, MN, Jackson, PBN & Skelton, PH. 1982. *Pocket Guide to the Freshwater Fishes of Southern Africa*. Centaur Publishers, Cape Town. 88 pages.

Bruton, MN & Coutouvidis, SE. 1991. An inventory of all known specimens of the coelacanth *Latimeria chalumnae*, with comments on trends in the catches. *Environmental Biology of Fishes* 32: 371–390.

Bruton, MN, Coutouvidis, SE & Pote, J. 1991. Bibliography of the living coelacanth *Latimeria chalumnae*, with comments on publication trends. *Environmental Biology of Fishes* 32: 403–433.

Bruton, MN & Stobbs, RE. 1991. The ecology and conservation of the coelacanth *Latimeria chalumnae*. *Environmental Biology of Fishes* 32: 313–339.

Bruton, MN, Cabral, AJP & Fricke, H. 1992. First capture of a coelacanth, *Latimeria chalumnae* (Pisces, Latimeriidae) off Mozambique. *South African Journal of Science* 88: 225–227.

Buxton, CS, Bruton, MN, Hughes, GR & Stobbs, RE. 1988. Recommendations on the proclamation of marine conservation legislation and the establishment of marine reserves in the Federal Islamic Republic of the Comoros. *Investigational Report of the JLB Smith Institute of Ichthyology* 28: 38 pages.

Cloutier, R & Forey, PL. 1991. Diversity of extinct and living actinistian fishes (Sarcopterygii). *Environmental Biology of Fishes* 32: 59–74.

Compagno, LJV. 1979. Coelacanth: shark relatives or bony fishes? *Occasional Papers of the California Academy of Science* 134: 45–55.

Conradie, RP (ed.). 1966. *Matieland Feesuitgawe* 10(2). Stellenbosch University, Stellenbosch.

Cory, GE. 1910–1940. *The Rise of South Africa: A History of the Origin of South African Colonisation and of its Development towards the East from the Earliest Times to* 1857. Longmans Green & Co., London. 6 volumes.

Cory, GE. 1922/1923. *Recollections of the past: autobiography*. National Library of South Africa (Cape Town Campus), unpublished manuscript MSB125.

Courtenay-Latimer, M. 1979. My story of the first coelacanth. *Occasional Papers of the California Academy of Science* 134: 6–10.

Courtenay-Latimer, M. 1989. Reminiscences of the discovery of the coelacanth, *Latimeria chalumnae* Smith, based on notes from a diary kept at the time. *Cryptozoology* 8: 1–11.

Currey, RF. 1970. *Rhodes University*. 1904–1970. *A Chronicle*. Rustica Press, Grahamstown. 186 pages.

Curtis, P. 2015. *Fishing wider margins: a history and bibliography of angling in Africa*. Platanna Press, Cape Town. 394 pages.

David, J. 2016. On the origin of the name *Nerine*. *Amaryllids* 2016(2): 8–10.

Davis, DM. 1986. 1946 and all that. *Ichthos* (12): 6.

Day, J. 1997. Marine biology in South Africa. pp. 86–108. In: AC Brown (ed.) *A History of Scientific Endeavour in South Africa*. Royal Society of South Africa, Cape Town.

De Sylva, DP. 1966. Mystery of the 'silver coelacanth'. *Sea Frontiers* 12: 172–175.

De Vos, L & Oyugi, D. 2002. First capture of a coelacanth *Latimeria chalumnae* Smith, 1939 (Pisces: Latimeriidae), off Kenya. *South African Journal of Science* 98: 345–347.

Drury, J. 1942. The remounting and casting of the East London fish. *South African Museums Association Bulletin* 1939–1942(2): 137–138.

Earle, SA. 2006. Coelacanths: inspiring conservation of the Blue Planet. *South African Journal of Science* 102: 416–418.

Erdmann, MV. 1999. An account of the first living coelacanth known to scientists from Indonesian waters. *Environmental Biology of Fishes* 54: 439–443.

Fargher, L. 2004. An ichthyologist goes under. *Ichthos* 72: 8.

Fawcett, PH & Fawcett, B. 1953. *Exploration Fawcett*. Hutchinson, London. 312 pages.

FitzSimons, VFM. 1962. *Snakes of Southern Africa*. Purnell & Sons, Cape Town. 423 pages.

Flynn, J & du Plessis, D (eds). 2014. *Maureen Quin, Master Sculptor: Six Decades of Sculptural Excellence*. Alexandria, South Africa. 245 pages.

Forey, PL. 1980. *Latimeria*: a paradoxical fish. *Proceedings of the Royal Society of London* Series B 208: 369–384.

Forey, PL. 1988. Golden jubilee for the coelacanth *Latimeria chalumnae*. *Nature, London* 336: 727–732.

Forey, PL. 1990. The coelacanth fish, progress and prospects. *Science Progress* 74: 53–67.

Forey, PL. 1991. *Latimeria chalumnae* and its pedigree. *Environmental Biology of Fishes* 32: 75–97.

Forey, PL. 1998. *History of the coelacanth fishes*. Chapman & Hall, London. 419 pages.

Fricke, H. 1988. Coelacanths: the fish that time forgot. *National Geographic* 173: 824–838.

Fricke, H. 1997. Living coelacanths: values, eco-ethics and human responsibility. *Marine Ecology Progress Series* 161: 1–15.

Fricke, H. 2001. Coelacanths: a human responsibility. *Journal of Fish Biology* 59: 332–338.

Fricke, H. 2007. *Die Jagd nach dem Quastenflosser, Der Fisch, der aus der Urzeit Kam.* Verlag CH Beck, Münich. 302 pages.

Fricke, H, Hissmann, K, Schauer, J & Plante, R. 1995. Yet more danger for coelacanths. *Nature, London* 374: 314.

Fricke, H & Plante, R. 2001. Silver coelacanths from Spain are not proofs of a pre-scientific discovery. *Environmental Biology of Fishes* 61: 461–463.

Gardener, J. 1997. *Bishops 150. A History of the Diocesan College, Rondebosch*. Juta, Cape Town. 299 pages.

Gon, O. 1993. A history of ichthyology in South Africa. Part II. John D.F. Gilchrist, the father of South African ichthyology. *Ichthos* 39: 17–18.

Gon, O. 1994. A history of ichthyology in South Africa. Part III. Barnard at the South African Museum. *Ichthos* 41: 13–14.

Gon, O. 1995. A history of ichthyology in South Africa. Part IV. Collections in the Eastern Cape. *Ichthos* 46: 17–19.

Gon, O. 1996a. Fifty years of marine fish systematics at the JLB Smith Institute of Ichthyology. *Transactions of the Royal Society of South Africa* 51: 45–78.

Gon, O. 1996b. In the footsteps of the Smiths on Inhaca Island. *Ichthos* 54: 16–20.

Gon, O. 1998. Captain Planet and Old Fourlegs. *Ichthos* 59: 21.

Gon, O. 2001. Department of Ichthyology at Rhodes University. Setting the record straight. *Ichthos* 65: 10–11.

Gon, O. 2002a. The Hugh le May Ichthyological Research Laboratory. *Ichthos* 68: 6–8.

Gon, O. 2002b. *The History of Marine Fish Systematics in South Africa.* MA thesis, Rhodes University. 215 pages. http://hdl.handle.net/10962/d1007800.

Gon, O & Heemstra, PC (eds). 1990. *Fishes of the Southern Ocean.* JLB Smith Institute of Ichthyology, Grahamstown. 462 pages.

Gon, O & Skelton, PH. 1997. A history of the fish collections of South Africa pp. 133–168. In: TW Pietsch & WD Anderson (eds) *Collection Building in Ichthyology and Herpetology.* American Society of Ichthyology and Herpetology Special Publication No. 3, Allen Press, Lawrence, Kansas.

Greenwell, JR. 1989. Remembering the coelacanth: a 50th anniversary. Interviews with Marjorie Courtenay-Latimer and Hendrik Goosen. *International Society of Cryptozoology Newsletter:* 1–18.

Greenwell, JR. 1990. The lady and the coelacanth: remembering the zoological discovery of the century. *The Explorers Journal* 68: 117–123.

Greenwood, PH. 1968. Professor JLB Smith; obituary. *Nature, London* 217: 690–691.

Heemstra, PC & Smith, MM. 1980. Hexatrygonidae, a new family of stingrays (Myliobatiformes: Batoidea) from South Africa, with comments on the classification of batoid fishes. *Ichthyology Bulletin of the JLB Smith Institute of Ichthyology* 43: 1–17.

Heemstra, PC, Freeman, ALJ, Yan Wong, H, Hensley, DA & Rabesandratana, HD. 1996. First authentic capture of a coelacanth, *Latimeria chalumnae* (Pisces: Latimeriidae), off Madagascar. *South African Journal of Science* 92: 150–151.

Heemstra, PC & Heemstra, E. 2004. *Coastal Fishes of Southern Africa.* NISC/South African Institute for Aquatic Biodiversity, Grahamstown. 488 pages.

Heemstra, PC, Fricke, H, Hissmann, K, Schauer, J, Smale, M & Sink, K. 2006. Interactions of fishes with particular reference to coelacanths in the canyons at Sodwana Bay and the St Lucia Marine Protected Area of South Africa. *South African Journal of Science* 102: 461–465.

Hess, A. 2004. Quastenflosse in Tanzania (first Tanzanian coelacanth discovery). *Habari* June 2004 19(2): 2–4.

Hewson, G. 1999. A remembrance: JLB and Margaret Smith. *Ichthos* 62: 5–7.

Hodgson, AN & Craig, AJFK. 2006. A century of zoology and entomology at Rhodes University, 1905 to 2005. *Transactions of the Royal Society of South Africa* 60(1): 1–18.

Horning, G. 1979. Margaret's reel story. *Natal Mercury* 20.2.1997: (1): 1.

Hubbs, CL. 1968. James Leonard Brierley Smith, 1897–1968, *Copeia* 1968(3): 659–660.

Jackson, PBN. 1987. Margaret Smith the humanitarian: a time to keep. *Ichthos* 17: 17–19.

Jackson, PBN. 1996. Variations on a theme: the three directors of the first fifty years of the JLB Smith Institute of Ichthyology. *Transactions of the Royal Society of South Africa* 51: 33–43.

Jewett, SL. 2004. Marjorie Courtenay-Latimer: more than the coelacanth! *The Coelacanth* 42(1): 17–28.

Kingwill, DG. 1990. *The CSIR: the First 40 Years.* CSIR, Pretoria. 352 pages.

Kirk-Spriggs, AH. 2012. The life, career and major achievements of Brian Roy Stuckenberg (1930–2009). *African Invertebrates* 53(1): 1–34.

Le May, BC. 1949. The Sea Fishes of Southern Africa Book Fund. In: JLB Smith *The Sea Fishes of Southern Africa.* Central News Agency, Cape Town. p. iv.

Locke, H. 1986. My recollections as an artist. *Ichthos* 12: 18–20.

Long, P. 1999. Seeking a life of adventure. *Ichthos* 62: 3–4.

Louw, T. 2012. *The Murray Family Register 1794–2012*. Minit Print, Pretoria. 122 pages.

Malherbe, EH. 1981a. Student pranks in 'sleepy hollow'. *Matieland* 3: 23–26.

Malherbe, EH. 1981b. *Never a Dull Moment*. Howard Timmins, Cape Town. 419 pages.

Maylam, P. 2017. *Rhodes University, 1904–2016: an Intellectual, Political and Cultural History*. Institute for Social and Economic Research, Grahamstown. 383 pages.

McCabe, H & Wright, J. 2000. Tangled tale of a lost, stolen and disputed coelacanth. *Nature, London* 406: 114.

McCosker, JE & Lagios, MD (ed.). 1979. The Biology and Physiology of the Living Coelacanth. *Occasional Papers of the California Academy of Sciences* 134: 1–175.

McIntyre, D. 1950. *The Diocesan College, Rondebosch, South Africa. A Century of 'Bishops'*. Juta, Cape Town. 136 pages.

Millot, J. 1953. Notre coelacanthe. *Revue Madagascar, Tananarive* 1: 18–20.

Millot, J. 1954. Les troisième coelecanthe. *Naturaliste malgache* suppl. 1: 1–26.

Millot, J. 1955. First observations on a living coelacanth. *Nature, London* 175: 362–363.

Minshull, J. 2009. Memories of the past – the Zimbabwe coelacanth. *African Fisherman* 20(3): 8–11.

Murray, C. 1978 (revised 2012). *The Murray Family Register 1794–1977*. Minit Print, Pretoria. 122 pages.

Musick, JA, Bruton, MN & Balon, EK (eds). 1991. *The Biology of* Latimeria *and Evolution of Coelacanths*. Kluwer Academic Publishers, Dordrecht. 446 pages.

Norman, JR. 1939. A living coelacanth from South Africa: a fish believed to have been extinct. *Proceedings of the Linnean Society of London* 151: 142–145.

Nulens, R, Scott, L & Herbin, M. 2011. An updated inventory of all known specimens of the coelacanth, *Latimeria* spp. *Smithiana Special Publication* 3: 1–52.

Papenfus, D. 1998. Going back ... a little bit of reminisce from an old Kingswoodian pupil. *Ichthos* 58: 24.

Poland, M. 2008. *The Boy in You: A Biography of St Andrew's College*, 1855–2005. Fernwood Press, Simonstown. 496 pages.

Pote, J. 1997. Looking back: selected milestones in the life of JLB Smith. *Ichthos* 54: 5–11.

Pote, J. 1996. Historical highlights: the JLB. Smith Institute of Ichthyology and the Department of Ichthyology & Fisheries Science 1946–1996. *Transactions of the Royal Society of South Africa* 51: 5–31.

Pouyaud, L, Wirjoatmodjo, S, Rachmatika, I, Tjakrawidjaja, A, Hadiaty, RK & Hadie, W. 1999. Une nouvelle espèce de coelacanthe. Preuves génétiques et morphologiques. *Comptes rendus de l'Académie des Sciences – Sciences de la vie* 322(3): 261–267.

Pullen, G. 2000. JLB Smith honoured by IGFA. *Ichthos* 64: 15.

Quammen, D. 1994. Everything old will be new. *Aquaticus* 24(2): 4–15.

Ribbink, AJ. 2004. Marjorie Courtenay-Latimer: a tribute. *Ichthos* 72: 13–14.

Ribbink, AJ & Roberts, MJ. 2006. African Coelacanth Ecosystem Programme: an overview of the conference contributions. *South African Journal of Science* 102: 409–415.

Richards, B. 1987. A fascination with fishes – a profile of Margaret Mary Smith. *Scientiae* 4: 26–35.

Rivett, DEA. 1996. JLB Smith, the chemist, as I knew him. *Ichthos* 48: 6–7.

Ryan, A. 1997. Memories of JLB. *Ichthos* 54: 12–14.

Shell, SR. 2017. *Protean Paradox. George Edward Cory (1862–1935). Negotiating Life and South African History.* Graham's Town Series 16, Rhodes University, Grahamstown. 286 pages.

Skaife, SH. 1964 (reprint). *Strange Adventures under the Sea. A Nature Story for Children.* Nasionale Boekhandel, Cape Town. 81 pages.

Skelton, PH. 1988. Rex Jubb – a tribute. *Ichthos* 18: 4–5.

Skelton, PH. 1996. 50 years of ichthyology in Grahamstown. *Ichthos* 49: 12–17.

Skelton, PH & Lutjeharms, JRE (eds). 1996. The JLB Smith Institute of Ichthyology – 50 Years. *Transactions of the Royal Society of South Africa* 51: 1–320.

Smith, CL, Rand, CS, Schaeffer, B & Atz, JW. 1975. *Latimeria,* the living coelacanth, is ovoviviparous. *Science* 190(4219): 1105–1106.

Smith, JLB. 1931. New and little known fishes from the south and east coasts of South Africa. *Records of the Albany Museum* 4(1): 145–160.

Smith, JLB. 1936. New gobioid and cyprinid fishes from South Africa. *Transactions of the Royal Society of South Africa* 24: 47–55.

Smith, JLB. 1939a. A living fish of Mesozoic type. *Nature, London* 143(3620): 455–456.

Smith, JLB. 1939b. The living coelacanthid fish from South Africa. *Nature, London* 143(3627): 748–750.

Smith, JLB. 1939c. A surviving fish of the order Actinistia. *Transactions of the Royal Society of South Africa* 27(1): 47–50.

Smith, JLB. 1939d. A living fossil. *Cape Naturalist* 1(6): 187–194.

Smith, JLB. 1940a. *A Simplified System of Organic Identification.* Nasionale Pers, Cape Town. 48 pages.

Smith, JLB. 1940b. A living coelacanthid fish from South Africa. *Transactions of the Royal Society of South Africa* 28: 1–106.

Smith, JLB. 1940c. A living fossil. *Cape Naturalist* 1: 321–328.

Smith, JLB. 1941. *A System of Qualitative Organic Analysis.* Nasionale Pers, Cape Town. 63 pages.

Smith, JLB. 1949a. *The Sea Fishes of Southern Africa.* Central News Agency, Cape Town. 550 pages.

Smith, JLB. 1949b. 'The Sea Fishes of Southern Africa' was an experiment. *The Rhodian, Summer* 29: 1.

Smith, JLB. 1949c. Fish do feel pain – but nothing more than a toothache in man. *South African Angler* 4(4): 6, 24.

Smith, JLB. 1950a. We hope to produce a major treatise. *South African Angler* 5(1): 7.

Smith, JLB. 1950b. Recent research on the sea fishes of southern Africa. *South African Angler* 5(2): 4.

Smith, JLB. 1951a. Hunting fishes in East African coral. *Ha-Yam* 4(4): 4–8.

Smith, JLB. 1951b. First stage of a job that will take 10 years. *South African Angler* 6(1): 4.

Smith, JLB. 1951c. A case of poisoning by the stonefish, *Synanceja verrucosa. Copeia* 1951(3): 207–210.

Smith, JLB. 1952a. We need information about sharks: anglers can help science. *South African Angler* 6(11): 6, 7, 22.

Smith, JLB. 1952b. 10,000 fishes in 10 days. *South African Angler* 7(5): 13.

Smith, JLB. 1953a. The second coelacanth. *Nature, London* 171: 99–101.

Smith, JLB. 1953b. The second coelacanth. *Copeia* 1953(1): 72.

Smith, JLB. 1953c. The two coelacanths. *South African Museum Association Bulletin* 5(8): 206–210.

Smith, JLB. 1953d. Problems of the coelacanth. *South African Journal of Science* 49(9): 279–281.

Smith, JLB. 1953e. Freshwater eel on Zanzibar. *South African Angler* 7(8): 13, 26.

Smith, JLB. 1953f. Professor Smith tells his own story of the coelacanth. *South African Angler* 7(9): 6, 23.

Smith, JLB. 1953g. A coelacanth in Kenya waters? *South African Angler* 8(4): 8, 19.

Smith, JLB. 1954. Os peixes e a pesca desportiva em Moçambique. *Clube Naval de Lourenço Marques, Julho* 1954: 6, 7, 27.

Smith, JLB. 1955. Live coelacanths. *Nature, London* 176: 473.

Smith, JLB. 1956. *Old Fourlegs. The Story of the Coelacanth*. Longmans Green & Co., London. 260 pages.

Smith, JLB. 1958a. The marine fishes of Inhaca. pp. 113–116. In: W MacNae & M Kalk (eds) *A Natural History of Inhaca Island, Mozambique*. Witwatersrand University Press, Johannesburg.

Smith, JLB. 1958b. Explosives wrest secrets from the sea. *Outlook* 9(2): 4–8.

Smith, JLB. 1961. World-wide demand for 'Sea Fishes'. *Talk of the Times* 1961: 3.

Smith, JLB. 1962. Most interesting discovery since the coelacanth. *Field & Tide* 4(2): 12–13.

Smith, JLB. 1963. The funeral of a stonefish victim in northern Mozambique. *Stywe Lyne-Tight Lines* 4(3): 16–17.

Smith, JLB. 1965. *The Sea Fishes of Southern Africa*. Central News Agency, Cape Town. 550 pages.

Smith, JLB. 1966. The whale shark can be dangerous. *Field & Tide* 8(7): 16–17.

Smith, JLB. 1968a. *Our Fishes*. Voortrekkerpers, Johannesburg. 263 pages (also available in Afrikaans as *Ons Visse*).

Smith, JLB. 1968b. *High Tide*. Books of Africa, Cape Town. 165 pages.

Smith, JLB. 1968c. The lost home of the coelacanths. *Stywe Lyne-Tight Lines* 9(11): 19–23.

Smith, JLB. 1971. Coelacanth. In: *Standard Encyclopaedia of Southern Africa*. 12 volumes, 1970–1976. Nasou, Cape Town.

Smith, JLB. 1977. *Smith's Sea Fishes*. Valiant Press, Sandton. 580 pages.

Smith, JLB & Rivett, DEA. 1932. The essential oil of *Agathosma apiculata* Meyer. *Transactions of the Royal Society of South Africa* 31(2): 111–124.

Smith, JLB & Rindl, M. 1941. *Numerical and Constitutional Exercises in Organic Chemistry*. Metheun, London. 213 pages.

Smith, JLB & Smith, MM. 1966. *Fishes of the Tsitsikama Coastal National Park*. National Parks Board, Pretoria. 161 pages (also available in Afrikaans as *Visse van die Tsitsikama Seekus Nasionale Park*).

Smith, JLB & Smith, MM. 1969. *The Fishes of the Seychelles*. JLB Smith Institute of Ichthyology, Grahamstown. 223 pages.

Smith, MM. 1959. My life under the sea. *Personality*. 12th March 1959. 5 pages.

Smith, MM. 1969. JLB Smith, his life, work, bibliography and list of new species. *Rhodes University Department of Ichthyology Occasional Paper* 16: 185–215.

Smith, MM. 1975. Common and scientific names of the fishes of southern Africa. Part 1. Marine fishes. *Special Publication of the JLB Smith Institute of Ichthyology* 14: 1–178.

Smith, MM. 1976. The importance of establishing marine parks in the Western Indian Ocean. *Travaux et Documents de l'ORSTOM* 47: 361–363.

Smith, MM. 1979. The influence of the coelacanth on African ichthyology. *Occasional Papers of the California Academy of Sciences* 134: 11–16.

Smith, MM. 1977. *Sea and Shore Dangers. Their Recognition, Avoidance and Treatment.* JLB Smith Institute of Ichthyology, Grahamstown. 80 pages.

Smith, MM. 1980. The search for the world's oldest fish. *Oceans* 3(6): 26–36.

Smith, MM. 1987. It all started this way. *Ichthos* 15: 1–2.

Smith, MM & Heemstra, PC (eds). 1986. *Smiths' Sea Fishes*. Macmillan, Johannesburg. 1,047 pages.

Smith, RB. 1994. Some thoughts on the late Prof. J.L.B. Smith as an angler. *Ichthos* 42: 17–18.

Smith, WM. 1996. Reflections. My parents. *Ichthos* 49: 28–29.

Smith, WM. 2017. Foreword. pp. 6–7. In: MN Bruton *The Annotated Old Fourlegs. The* Updated *Story of the Coelacanth*. Struik Nature, Cape Town.

Smith Woodward, A. 1898. *Catalogue of the Fossil Fishes of the British Museum (Natural History)*. Volume II. British Museum (Natural History), London.

Spargo, P. 2008. Smith, James Leonard Brierley. pp. 475–478. In: N Koertge (ed.) *New Dictionary of Scientific Biography*. Thomson Gale, New York.

Stobbs, RE. 1993. The story of an incredible bird and an equally incredible fish: the Dakota and the Coelacanth. *Ichthos* 38: 4–5.

Stobbs, RE. 1996a. The changing face of *Latimeria* – and more mythology. *Ichthos* 50: 3–6.

Stobbs, RE. 1996b. Eric Ernest Hunt – the aquarist. *Ichthos* 48: 3–4.

Stobbs, RE. 1996c. Hiariako – the broken thread. *Ichthos* 49: 17–20.

Stobbs, RE. 1997. Explosives and other destructive fishing practices. *Ichthos* 55: 4–8.

Stobbs, RE. 2002a. Grahamstown and the first 'fish-jacking'. *Ichthos* 69: 8–9.

Stobbs, RE. 2002b. It's a gombessa! … reflections 50 years on. *Ichthos* 70: 1–3.

Stobbs, RE & Bruton, MN. 1991. The fishery of the Comoros, with comments on its possible impact on coelacanth survival. *Environmental Biology of Fishes* 32: 341–359.

Summers, RFH. 1975. *A History of the South African Museum 1825–1975. Compiled from Museum Records*. AA Balkema, Cape Town. 245 pages.

Thomson, KS. 1966. The history of the coelacanth. *Discovery* 2(1): 27–32.

Thomson, KS. 1969. The biology of the lobe-finned fishes. *Biological Reviews* 44: 91–154.

Thomson, KS. 1973. Secrets of the coelacanth. *Natural History, New York* 82: 58–65.

Thomson, KS. 1991. *Living Fossil. The Story of the Coelacanth*. Norton, New York. 252 pages.

Tietz, RM. 2004. Field trips and friendship: a memoir of Marjorie Courtenay-Latimer. *The Coelacanth* 42(1): 37–47.

Van der Elst, R. 1976. Game fish of the east coast of southern Africa. I. The biology of elf, *Pomatomus saltatrix* (Linnaeus), in the coastal waters of Natal. *Investigational Report of the Oceanographic Research Institute* 44: 1–59.

Venter, P, Timm, P, Gunn, G, le Roux, E, Serfontein, C, Smith, P, Bensch, M, Harding, D & Heemstra, PC. 2000. Discovery of a viable population of coelacanths (*Latimeria chalumnae* Smith, 1939) at Sodwana Bay, South Africa. *South African Journal of Science* 96: 567.

Voorvelt, D. 1996. 50 illustrating years. *Ichthos* 49: 25.

Warren, FL. 1977. Organic and biological chemistry in southern Africa. pp. 283–317. In: AC Brown (ed.) *A History of Scientific Endeavour in South Africa.* Royal Society of South Africa, Cape Town.

Watson, BW. 2004. Marjorie Courtenay-Latimer. *The Coelacanth* 42(1): 7–11.

Watson, DMS. 1921. On the coelacanth fish. *Annals and Magazine of Natural History* 8: 320–337.

Weinberg, S. 1999. *A Fish Caught in Time.* Fourth Estate Limited, London. 239 pages.

White, EI. 1939. One of the most amazing events in the realm of natural history in the twentieth century. *London Illustrated News.* 11th March 1939, Supplement.

White, EI. 1953a. The coelacanth fishes. *Discovery, London* 14: 113–117.

White, EI. 1953b. More about the coelacanths. *Discovery, London* 14: 332–335.

Woodward, AS. 1940. The surviving crossopterygian fish, *Latimeria. Nature, London* 146: 53–54.

www.dinofish.com
www.en.wikipedia.org/wiki/Coelacanth
www.ir.nrf.ac.za/handle/10907/232
www.vertebrates.si.edu

Index

Page numbers in **bold** refer to photographs or illustrations.

Smith, JLB: health 4, 7, 9, 10, 26, 49, 56, 58, 109, 223, 224, 225, 247, 255, 262, 317, 320
Smith, JLB: Heavenly Quartet 10, 11, 12
Smith, JLB: house 'Blue House' 36, 63, 98, 185
Smith, JLB: house 'Eastford House' 2
Smith, JLB: house 'Steenbras' 75
Smith, JLB: household 160, 193, 260
Smith, JLB: ichthyologist 20, 32, 37, 39, 49, 65, 77, 80, 83, 107, 230, 254, 315
Smith, JLB: identification keys for fishes 41, 42, 43
Smith, JLB: international reputation 238
Smith, JLB: JLB's Rock 46, 107, 108, 236
Smith, JLB: Karoo 35
Smith, JLB: Knysna 1, 2, 33, 35, 36, 37, 45, 46, 63, 71, 79, 80, 82, 98, 107, 185, 214, 215, 230, 231, 236, 265, 268, 269
Smith, JLB: languages 62
Smith, JLB: lecturer 17, 18, 23, 25, 32, 35, 55, 114, 123, 130, 159
Smith, JLB: lifestyle 47
Smith, JLB: loner 75, 253, 254, 257, 262, 320, 321, 322
Smith, JLB: Margaret Mary Macdonald 55, 56, 58
Smith, JLB: memorable catch 242
Smith, JLB: mentor and advisor 252, 315, 316
Smith, JLB: military training 9
Smith, JLB: MSc degree 14
Smith, JLB: Noupoort 4
Smith, JLB: organic chemist 26, 47, 248, 260, 311, 313
Smith, JLB: organic chemistry 19, 21–28, 44, 48, 54, 113, 313
Smith, JLB: ox-wagon 36, 47
Smith, JLB: personal appearance 123
Smith, JLB: personality 18, 79, 112, 250, 256, 320, 322
Smith, JLB: PhD degree 15
Smith, JLB: photographic memory 18, 65, 79, 255
Smith, JLB: physics 235
Smith, JLB: plants 21, 45, 49, 111
Smith, JLB: politics 3, 266, 267
Smith, JLB: pranks 10, 11, 12, 13, 13, 15, 43
Smith, JLB: Professor of Ichthyology 114
Smith, JLB: publications 37, 38, 40, 41, 48, 49, 111, 141, 153, 215, 227, 228, 234, 238, 239, 240, 313, 314, 315, 318
Smith, JLB: publicity seeking 38, 156, 187, 188, 254, 265
Smith, JLB: racist opinions 266, 267, 268
Smith, JLB: radio talks 82, 184, 215, 230, 234, 235, 236, 239, 315
Smith, JLB: religion 274
Smith, JLB: research 7, 15, 21, 24, 26, 28, 36, 39, 41, 48, 49, 59, 68, 82, 100, 111, 113, 117, 122, 153, 159, 161, 226, 252, 317
Smith, JLB: Rhodes University College 16, 35, 156

Smith, JLB: risk-taker 46, 147
Smith, JLB: rugby 16
Smith, JLB: Rwanda 9
Smith, JLB: *Sea Fishes* book 42, 43, 68, 75, 84, 141, 153–166, 177, 178, 215, 216, 220, 228, 235, 244, 287, 288, 289, 291, 304, 314, 315, 320
Smith, JLB: species described by him 41, 59, 317
Smith, JLB: species named after him 319, **319**
Smith, JLB: sport 10, 27, **27**
Smith, JLB: Stellenbosch 3, 4, 9–14, 15, 30
Smith, JLB: Tanzania 9
Smith, JLB: teaching 23, 25, 48, 59, 111, 311
Smith, JLB: textbooks 48, 111
Smith, JLB: tributes 252, 253, 254, 316
Smith, JLB: unconventional collecting 152
Smith, JLB: Victoria College 3, 9, 10, 14, 15, 30
Smith, JLB: weight formulae for fishes 43
Smith, JLB: work ethic 47, 49, 97, 125, 128, 320
Smith, JLB: writing style 240
Smith, JLB: Wynberg 3, 4, 9
Smith, Joseph 1, 2, 3, 30
Smith, Margaret 53, 100, 104, 119, 122, 130, 131, 136, 140, 182, 186, 199, 215, 227, 245, 264, 270, 285, 295, 298, 302, 303
Smith, Margaret: awards and honours 115, 302, 303, 310, 311, 312, 315
Smith, Margaret: BSc degree 55
Smith, Margaret: career in scientific illustration 41
Smith, Margaret: charity work 302, 303
Smith, Margaret: Chemistry Department 55
Smith, Margaret: childhood 52, **52**, 60
Smith, Margaret: children 294, 299
Smith, Margaret: collecting fishes 151, **151**
Smith, Margaret: commemorating plaque 311
Smith, Margaret: death 305
Smith, Margaret: devotion to JLB 272, 275, 321
Smith, Margaret: diet 261, 299
Smith, Margaret: directorship 259, 271, 278, 281, 284, 287, 292, 294, 302, 309
Smith, Margaret: diving 61, 129, 134, 135, 142
Smith, Margaret: dress code 274, 301
Smith, Margaret: early life 54
Smith, Margaret: fish artist 57, 62, 129, 130, 141, 158, 160, 238, 239, 253, 280, 289, 303, 310
Smith, Margaret: gatherings and conferences 54, 259, 271, 293, 294, 300, 302, 308, 309
Smith, Margaret: Grahamstown 53, 54, 58, 59, 271, 277, 280, 298, 305
Smith, Margaret: health 57, 60, 289, 304, 305
Smith, Margaret: house 'Inverness' 52, 53
Smith, Margaret: household 160, 193, 260, 298, 299
Smith, Margaret: Indwe 52, 53, 60
Smith, Margaret: JLB Smith 55, 56, 56
Smith, Margaret: languages 62
Smith, Margaret: mathematical ability 57
Smith, Margaret: music 53, 55, 275, 297, 299